Education and Democracy

Education and Democracy

The Meaning of Alexander Meiklejohn
1872–1964

Adam R. Nelson

THE UNIVERSITY OF WISCONSIN PRESS

The University of Wisconsin Press
2537 Daniels Street
Madison, Wisconsin 53718

3 Henrietta Street
London WC2E 8LU, England

Library of Congress Cataloging-in-Publication Data

Nelson, Adam R.
Education and democracy : the meaning of Alexander Meiklejohn,
1872–1964 / Adam R. Nelson.
pp.   cm.
Includes bibliographical references and index.
ISBN 0-299-17140-X
1. Meiklejohn, Alexander, 1872–1964.   2. Educators—United
States—Biography.   3. Education, Humanistic—United
States—History—20th century.   I. Title
LB875.M332 N45   2001
370'.92—dc21   00-011979

Publication of this volume was made possible in part by funds provided by the
Evjue Foundation and the generous support of the Anonymous Fund of the
University of Wisconsin–Madison.

For my family:
Mom, Dad, and Matt

Should you ask me what the relation is between liberal education and democracy, the answer would be easy: they are the same thing.

Alexander Meiklejohn
"Education and Democracy," 1923

One of the deepest and most active convictions just now in our . . . society is this: that there is no common basis for men's reasoning; that at the bottom of all reasoning there is irrationality; that every man starts from his own private designs; that, after all, reasoning is rationalizing, and the old dream of a common truth, a common intelligence, a common intellectual inquiry, is gone, and gone forever.

Alexander Meiklejohn
"Higher Education in a Democracy," October 1941

Contents

Contents

Illustrations

Illustrations

Preface: Meiklejohn, Socrates, and the Paradox of Democratic Education

H E IS AT HIS DESK. He is surrounded with his numerous correspondence. He puts down his pen. He seems to want to. He waits for you to speak, intently and anxiously, almost with childlike breathlessness. And you go on. His words, short phrases of his understanding, a nod of his head, a sensitive, sympathetic smile. A kindly air of appreciative intent always on his countenance. He sometimes suggests a word of his outlook, but stops if you manifest the slightest reaction. You enjoy his sincere intentness." As the young men who wrote these words in 1928 well knew, Alexander Meiklejohn was, first and foremost, a teacher. He had an uncommon ability to relate to students, to cultivate close bonds with colleagues, to lead people of all ages to realize their own best selves. To many, he was nothing short of an inspiration. "He can stir a sluggish brain into action and prod an imagination," admirers observed, "and at the same time he can stimulate his associates to adopt similar tactics with nearly as effective results." His penchant for Socratic debate, exhibited repeatedly throughout his long career, cast an almost magical spell over acquaintances, arousing passionate loyalty among friends even while it provoked bitter antagonism among enemies. An expert in logic and casuistry, he could be remarkably persuasive in the classroom; his strong convictions added weight to virtually any argument he made. He was clever, witty, and shrewd, but also quiet, calm, and reserved. According to participants in the famed Experimental College he established at the University of Wisconsin in the late 1920s, Meiklejohn often risked being perceived as a "dangerous person" whose charisma was a threat to under-graduates too "tempted to idealize him." Yet, he carefully avoided the sort of pedagogical demagoguery that led his ancient hero Socrates into trouble in Athens. As a teacher, he was actually quite shy. "His hesitant, at times almost timid air, is a pungent antidote for those who are afflicted with exalted ideas," one eighteen-year-old Experimental College student noted. "His willingness to 'follow the truth wherever it may lead' and the firm conviction that all men should be created with an equal chance to prove their worth in this world seem the signal features in his educational policy." Here, in brief, were the essential qualities of Meiklejohn's life and work. A gifted, zealous, but also somewhat diffident teacher, he was pro-foundly motivated by a belief that all people "should be created with an equal chance to prove their worth in this world."[1] Indeed, he spent more than seventy years investigating the process by which liberal education could actually *create* a more just and equitable democracy.

For Alexander Meiklejohn, the relationship between education and democracy rested on a paradox—a paradox linked directly to the moral and intellectual leadership provided by teachers like himself. Nowhere was this paradoxical role of educators illustrated more clearly than it was in Plato's *Republic,* a text Meiklejohn assigned as the culminating work for freshmen in his Experimental College. At the end of book III of *The Republic,* Socrates informs his interlocutor, Glaucon, that liberal educa-tion must somehow "create" the self-governing citizens who constitute a democratic state. Yet, in a subtle twist, Socrates adds that the youth of a republic must never discover that they *learned* the ways of virtue and democracy from wise old "philosopher-kings." Rather, he says, the youth must believe that they achieved their understanding entirely on their own—freely, autonomously, and independent of any "external" teaching. They must believe that they *taught themselves* everything they know and, thus, that their knowledge is intrinsic, universal, and pure. As Socrates eloquently explains, "[T]hey are to be told that their youth was a dream and that the education and training which they received from us were only appearances. In reality, during all that time, they were being formed and fed in the womb of the earth. When they were completed, the earth, their mother, sent them up; and so, their country being their mother and also their nurse, they are bound to advise her for good and to defend her against attacks."[2] According to Socrates, even if citizens must ultimately learn from others how to be democratic, they are better off ignorant of their education, lest they begin to doubt the integrity, originality, or au-thenticity of their commitment to virtuous *self*-government. Only if the process of learning is hidden from the youth will they have the confidence to teach the ways of democracy to their own children and, thus, from generation to generation, to defend that ideal against attacks.

Like Socrates, Meiklejohn cared deeply about the link between liberal education and democracy in an ideal republican state. He believed that education must *precede* democracy and, further, that citizens must ultimately teach themselves—or at least imagine that they could teach themselves—how to construct a good and just society. He was convinced that each succeeding generation had to re-create democracy practically from scratch, to summon it, as it were, from the very "womb of the earth." And yet, like Socrates, he recognized that the only way to realize such an ideal was to *learn how* from wise and generous teachers—educators who subtly concealed their own prior role as philosopher-kings in order to cultivate a sense of freedom in their students. To teach democracy, Meiklejohn believed, was to present the process of education as an appearance, a vague reflection of the process of living itself, to make it seem as if education were simply part and parcel of each student's autonomous existence—even if, as Jean-Jacques Rousseau so clearly demonstrated in his classic *Emile*, it was not. To learn how to be democratic was to imagine being fully human, both individually and collectively, as an *independently* attainable ideal, even if that ideal proved a fiction or a myth. So Socrates thought. So Rousseau thought. And so, too, Meiklejohn thought in his most idealistic moments of philosophical reflection. Taking his cue from the ancient idealism of Plato and, more, from the late eighteenth-century idealism of Immanuel Kant, Meiklejohn believed that liberal education, properly conceived, could actually *create* an ideal democratic society, and he devoted his entire life to that goal. As dean of Brown University, president of Amherst College, director of the Experimental College at the University of Wisconsin, founder of the San Francisco School of Social Studies, adviser to St. John's College in Annapolis, delegate to UNESCO, and prominent interpreter of the First Amendment, Alexander Meiklejohn made a profound and meaningful contribution to the theory and practice of democratic education in the United States.

To understand the meaning of Alexander Meiklejohn is to understand the tremendous cultural, political, and intellectual significance of idealism in late nineteenth- and twentieth-century America. Idealism was not just the philosophical antithesis of pragmatism, though it certainly was that, too. For Meiklejohn, idealism was the ethical core of liberalism, the moral center of social reform, the very heart of the democratic project as a revolutionary human goal. Coming of age in the increasingly diverse, secular, and chaotic industrial society of the 1880s and 1890s, Meiklejohn saw in idealism a way to reconcile competing claims of personal freedom and public order, individual liberty and institutional authority that dominated his historical milieu. As a bulwark against the rising tide of "agnostic" science and "amoral" technology, idealism offered a sense of certainty and stability in a rapidly changing world. Yet, in the first half of the twentieth century, Meiklejohn and his idealist friends fought a losing battle, especially in the field of education. Immersed in a thoroughly pragmatic age, Meiklejohn stood in direct opposition to his more famous contemporary, John Dewey, whose best-known work, *Democracy and Education*—published in 1916 when Dewey was fifty-seven and Meiklejohn was forty-four—spread the gospel of "practical," "instrumental," and "progressive" schooling far and wide. Both Meiklejohn and Dewey characterized themselves as liberals and even socialists throughout their long lives, but the two men differed dramatically in their approaches to democratic education. The most crucial difference between Meiklejohn and Dewey lay in their divergent ways of explaining the educational *origins* of democracy—the ways in which education *created* democracy through the authoritative processes of teaching. Here, of course, was the basic dilemma that Socrates tried to solve by first highlighting and then hiding the kinds of teaching given by philosopher-kings. Dewey had good reasons for trying to avoid Socrates' surreptitious approach to teaching—not least his desire to avoid the seemingly "state-centered" implications of Platonic schooling. Yet, in Meiklejohn's view, Dewey's incessant calls for individualized and child-centered instruction elided the question of just how democracy was created or, in other words, how the authority inherent in teaching could ever be democratic in the first place. Asserting that Dewey simply "took democracy for granted," Meiklejohn believed he had found the Achilles' heel of pragmatist-progressivist educational theory. Education *always* entailed authority, he argued. The crucial question was, what kind?

The title of this biography, *Education and Democracy*, reflects the subtle yet significant distinctions between the educational theories of John Dewey and Alexander Meiklejohn. Where Dewey, in 1916, put democracy before education, believing that education could not be liberal unless it were wholly democratic from the outset, Meiklejohn put education before democracy, insisting that democracy could never even *exist* unless it were taught authoritatively by citizen-philosophers. "We haven't even tried democracy yet," Meiklejohn lamented in 1923 at the nadir of his educational career, "but we cannot say we shall fail until we have tried, until we have tried by means of education."[3] Like Dewey, Meiklejohn believed ardently in the greatness of democracy as the most virtuous form of government humanity could possibly devise. He did not, however, believe that democracy was inborn in human nature, nor did he think, as Dewey often suggested, that democracy was somehow intrinsic to the objective methods of modern science. Rather, he believed that humanity must *learn* how to be democratic through critical intelligence and ethical understanding, which could develop only through the guidance of a liberal education. The question was, how? How could educators teach people to be free? Meiklejohn's answer to this question was both complex and controversial. Following the late eighteenth-century rational idealism of Kant, he insisted that the only way to teach freedom was to assume that human beings would submit themselves *voluntarily* to the transcendental authority of pure reason. Essential to Meiklejohn's educational and political philosophy was his conviction that democracy rested on the basic reasonability of humankind and, moreover, on the moral authority of reason as an organizing principle for all human relationships. Without rationality as an authoritative ideal, Meiklejohn simply could not conceive of liberal education as a creative force for the development of democracy.

In recent years, philosophers and historians of education, eager to address the pedagogical and curricular implications of postmodernism, have revisited pragmatism, seeking its wisdom on a wide variety of issues, including the nature of knowledge and intelligence, the cultural construction of identity and language, the implications of power and authority in the classroom, and the very possibility of "progressive" social reform. In the process, they have rediscovered the paradox inherent in the phrase *teaching freedom.* How, they ask, is it possible to teach people to be free without compromising their subjective autonomy or their cultural integrity in the process? As a multilayered examination of Meiklejohn's significance in the history of American education, this biography places him squarely in the middle of these debates. Stressing the critical imperatives of reason and the collective possibilities of democracy, Meiklejohn's Neo-Kantian idealism yielded a provocative solution to the paradox of democratic education. In words directed unmistakably against Dewey, but reminiscent of Josiah Royce, Meiklejohn asserted that "the problem of social reconstruction is based on the faith that we can find truth and that there are ways of doing things which can be found. Let the college stand for that faith."[4] Admittedly, from a twenty-first-century perspective, such a solution to the paradox of democratic education seems problematic. Having abandoned the quest for an intellectual synthesis based on eternal principles or the concept of a legitimate cultural authority based on transcendental reason, many find it easy to scoff at Meiklejohn's work. And yet, this biography suggests the need to study Meiklejohn not only critically but also sympathetically. Like Socrates before him, Meiklejohn was right to note that education, almost by its very nature, cannot be purely democratic, and he was sensitive to the poignancy of this problem. "If I cry out against the agnosticism of our people," he confessed in 1912, "it is not as one who has escaped from it, nor as one who would point the way back to the older synthesis, but simply as one who believes that the time has come for a reconstruction, for a new synthesis."[5]

One final note. Had Meiklejohn had his way, this biography would not have been written.[6] When he embarked upon the task of organizing his personal papers at the age of ninety, he asked his second wife, Helen, to discourage any such undertaking. His reluctance to have a biography reflected his vain desire to hide the less flattering—and, in some cases, even shameful—aspects of his life, as well as his distrust of historical writing in general.[7] As he wrote to a close friend in 1961, "[T]he appeal to historical fact or opinion, whether recorded in the past in question or by some later historian, always makes me uneasy. It is, of necessity, one man's view or one party's view which, in either case, is not accepted by other men or other parties. So the historical narrative can never be authoritative *for us,* nor free us from the necessity of making up our own minds."[8] In many important ways, Meiklejohn was right. Every biography is, of course, one person's view of its subject, and this biography is no exception. Its goal is not to give a complete chronicle of Meiklejohn's life but to give him an opportunity to speak for himself. Wherever possible, it allows both the tone and the meaning of Meiklejohn's ideas to come through in his own words—in books, articles, essays, journals, and, most of all, letters to family and friends. If it errs, it errs on the side of allowing Meiklejohn to say too much. At various times throughout his life, Meiklejohn exposed serious discrepancies between his philosophical ideals and his personal behavior. Usually, these discrepancies revealed the inevitable failings of a self-proclaimed idealist. In a few cases, however, they proved more difficult to explain. This biography does not attempt to rationalize Meiklejohn's mistakes; rather, it allows him to express, and to contradict, himself. In this way, it presents us—as Meiklejohn the Socratic teacher surely would have wanted—with the necessity of making up our own minds.

Acknowledgments

BIOGRAPHIES TELL AS MUCH about the *relationships* their subjects cultivated as they tell about their individual subjects themselves. Alexander Meiklejohn had many friends and many enemies, each of whom influenced his activities and his beliefs in different ways, both great and small. My job as a biographer has been to discover, describe, and ultimately interpret the relative importance of Meiklejohn's many relationships. As a writer, researcher, and scholar, I, too, have relied on relationships—with friends, relatives, and even total strangers—to aid me in my work. I take this opportunity to acknowledge a few of those relationships here.

First and foremost, I must thank John L. Thomas, my graduate adviser, for his constant support and encouragement. Every doctoral student should have a mentor as kind and considerate as he has been to me. Second, I am indebted to James Patterson, whose extremely close readings and incisive criticisms made my manuscript more concise, more clearly written, and more cogently argued than it might otherwise have been. Third, I thank Tom James, who generously agreed to serve on my dissertation committee after a single semester-long tutorial and then remained on my committee after moving to New York University. Fourth, I wish to thank Carl Kaestle, who joined my committee after he came to Brown during my final year of graduate school and gave me time to finish my thesis when I should have been doing research for him. To these professors and others who remain unnamed, I owe a profound debt of gratitude.

The writing of this book would certainly not have been possible without the aid of several outstanding archivists. At the Brown University Archives, I benefited from the unfailingly friendly assistance of Martha Mitchell, Gayle Lynch, and Ray Butti. At the Amherst College Library, I enjoyed the good-humored help of Daria D'Arienzo, Carol Trabulsi, Donna Skibel, Janet Poirrier, Barbara Trippel Simmons, and Peter Weiss. At the University of Wisconsin Archives, I was assisted by both Bernard Schermetzler and Frank Cook. At the archives of the State Historical Society of Wisconsin, I benefited from the efficient and professional service of Gerry Strey, Dee Grimsrud, and many other staff members. Finally, at the Meiklejohn Civil Liberties Institute in Berkeley, I appreciated the time and openness of Ann Fagan Ginger. For providing the gracious surroundings in which I composed most of my dissertation, I owe special thanks to the staff of the John Nicholas Brown Center for the Study of American Civilization, particularly Joyce Botelho, Jane Hennedy, and Denise Bastien.

Since the bulk of the research for this book was done far away from my home, I must thank those who provided food and shelter during my extended trips. In South Hadley, Massachusetts, I stayed for an entire week with Susie Castellanos. In Oregon, Wisconsin, on three separate occasions, I enjoyed the easy-going hospitality of Lori, Arlan, and Kietra Kay, as well as their many pets. In Lake Geneva, Wisconsin, I had the pleasure of five weeks over the course of two years with my cousins, Aaron and Nathan, and my uncle, Mark Schafer. In Berkeley, California, I stayed for two summer months with the extraordinary Parsley family, including Janet, Allen, Nathan, Tom, Ruth, and Mickey. Chapters 7, 8, 9, and 10 might not have been as detailed and chapters 3 and 4 might not have been written without the nourishment I received from Janet's unparalleled cookies and conversation.

I have received a great deal of helpful feedback from readers solicited by the University of Wisconsin Press, including Paul Boyer, Charles Anderson, Michael Hinden, Rodney Smolla, Robert Booth Fowler, and E. David Cronon. I have also received feedback from alumni of the Experimental College, which Alexander Meiklejohn created at the University of Wisconsin in the late 1920s. Comments came chiefly from Robert Frase, Leslie Orear, E. R. Lerner, and R. Freeman Butts. Roland Guyotte of the University of Minnesota–Morris read chapters 5 and 6 as well as the afterword in their unabridged dissertation form and offered comments that were later forwarded to me. I also received three very helpful letters from Meiklejohn's son Donald, who offered suggestions that helped to focus my analysis of his father's life and work.

Drafts of this book improved immensely as a result of the comments and criticisms I received from friends. Peter Baldwin, Chrissy Cortina, Julie DesJardins, Nathaniel Frank, L. E. Hartmann, Laura Prieto, and Ed Rafferty all contributed to the process of revising my text and reconsidering my ideas. Members of the Rhode Island Biography Group, Joan Richards, Eileen Warburton, and our ever-gracious host, Jane Lancaster, helped with the difficulties of transforming a dissertation into a book. Other friends gave immeasurable support. I thank in particular Shilpa Raval, Ted Bromund, and Laura Souders, who top a list much longer than I have room to print.

The editors at the University of Wisconsin Press have been invaluable in making this a better book. Steve Salemson, the son of an Experimental College alumnus, accepted the manuscript and guided it into the capable hands of Robin Whitaker, who edited my work with efficiency and precision. I owe a tremendous debt to the editorial staff, including Juliet Skuldt, who saw the book through production, but I take full responsibility for any and all mistakes that may remain in the text.

Last, but certainly not least, I want to thank my family—my parents and my brother, Matt. From them I received countless suggestions and bits of advice—in letters, calls, and e-mail messages from Pakistan—each lovingly bestowed. I cannot express how grateful I am for the care, concern, and support my family has given during the process of completing this project, which I dedicate, above all, to them.

PROVIDENCE

1872–1911

1

"A Voyage across the Atlantic" and "Kant's Ethics"
1872–1899

IN THE SPRING OF 1869, James and Elizabeth Meiklejohn moved with their seven sons from Glasgow, Scotland, to Rochdale, England. Ever since his childhood in the early 1840s, James Meiklejohn had worked as a color designer in the textile mills surrounding Glasgow, Barrhead, and Paisley, but the possibility of higher wages and better working conditions eventually lured him and his large family south. The town of Rochdale, located ten miles north of Manchester in the rolling hills of Lancashire, was famous for its manufacture of high-quality flannels, broadcloths, and other cotton fabrics. It was even more famous for its large and well-established workers' cooperative, which Meiklejohn and his wife hoped to join. Rooted in the producerist ideals of Robert Owen as well as the Shakers, the Chartists, and other utopian socialist communities of the mid-nineteenth century, the Rochdale Society of Equitable Pioneers attracted the Meiklejohns with its motto: All who contribute to the realization of wealth ought to participate in its distribution. According to its charter of 1844, the cooperative's chief purpose was to provide for the "pecuniary benefit and improvement of the social and domestic conditions of its members," and so it did.[1] Collecting one pound per year from each member, the cooperative was able to open a wholesale store, build modest homes for workers and their families, and hire those who were temporarily unemployed. It also provided educational services, including teachers, lectures, and a free library, for children. When the thirty-five-

3

year-old Meiklejohn arrived in Rochdale with his family in 1869, he took an enthusiastic interest in the cooperative's work. He and Elizabeth held meetings in their home, served on social and charitable committees, recruited new members, and genuinely embraced its ideals of economic equality and mutual aid.[2] It was in Rochdale, on February 3, 1872, that James and Elizabeth's eighth son, Alexander, was born.

From a very early age, young "Alec" took pride in his family's Scottish working-class heritage. "I was the youngest of eight sons in a Scottish, Presbyterian, working-class family," he later recalled. "My earliest allegiance was to the Scottish culture. . . . My second loyalty came from my father's occupation." Indeed, Meiklejohn grew up surrounded by the members of the Rochdale cooperative. As a boy, he found friends among the children of the millhands and played cricket and soccer outside the factories.[3] Many days, he followed his father to the dye house in the morning and home again in the evening. As they walked, he listened to stories about the ideals of social and economic cooperation. He heard how "human society is a body consisting of many members, the real interests of which are identical." He learned that "true workmen should be fellow-workers." He discovered that "a principle of justice, not of selfishness, must govern [human] exchange." And, above all, he understood that the best government was always democratic. Indeed, in both structure and spirit, the Rochdale cooperative was deeply democratic. Each household had one vote, regardless of the number of shares it owned, and a general assembly of members settled all internal disputes.[4] Emphasizing the equal value of different opinions and beliefs, the cooperative shunned sectarian orthodoxy and insisted on nondenominational toleration for all religious affiliations.[5] As George Jacob Holyoake, a labor activist who published the first history of the cooperative in 1882, noted, "[T]he moral miracle performed by our cooperatives of Rochdale [is] that they . . . had the good sense to differ without disagreeing, to dissent from each other without separating, to hate at times, and yet always to hold together."[6] Though Meiklejohn was much too young to realize it at the time, such sentiments laid a foundation for his own moral and political education. As he noted many times throughout his life, "[T]he textile workers were my people."[7]

In addition to a wide network of friends and factory acquaintances, the Rochdale cooperative supplied James and Elizabeth Meiklejohn with a regular forum for political debate. Often, the cooperative's members assembled at the Meiklejohn home to discuss labor relations and the possibilities for social reform. They expressed strong support for Britain's Liberal prime minister William Gladstone, who ardently endorsed the workers' cooperative movement and criticized the dominant capitalist ideology of laissez faire. They praised Gladstone's views on moral economy, which associated poverty with virtue and wealth with vice, and they admired the theories of such "new liberal" intellectuals as Thomas Hill Green, who assigned ethical importance to economic equality. They commended the ideas of John Ruskin and William Morris, who sought to preserve a producerist aesthetic in the arts and crafts, and they enthusiastically debated the heroic folklore of Scotland, especially its bloody struggle for independence from England. They often quoted the robust poetry of Robert Burns, whose late eighteenth-century vernacular verse appealed to their sense of democratic solidarity, and they gathered regularly to share family occasions, including birthdays, weddings, and funerals, which reinforced members' sense of class connection. For the Meiklejohns, the Rochdale Society of Equitable Pioneers symbolized not only a social and economic aid society but also a moral, political, and intellectual *community*. As its charter stated, the cooperative constituted a "self-supporting home-colony of united interests," and, though these values might have escaped the conscious attention of four-year-old Alec, he spent much of his adult life trying to reconstruct the voluntary ethical communitarianism that pervaded his early childhood in Rochdale.[8]

As a young boy growing up in a mill town, Alexander Meiklejohn experienced the love and caring of a large and close-knit family. One of his fondest memories was that of standing by his mother's side, "turning the socks" and helping her with load after load of laundry. "He adored his parents and was on warmest terms with his brothers," a friend recalled.[9] Certainly, with so many older brothers, he had no shortage of playmates. He could always find someone with whom to try new games, explore city streets, roam the countryside, or simply make mischief at home. His seven brothers—Andrew, Henry, James, John, Matthew, Maxwell, and William—teased him mercilessly, not only for being the youngest, but also for being the only member of the family born outside Scotland. As Meiklejohn bemusedly recalled, his siblings constantly needled him for being a "foreigner," an "alien," and a "Johnny Bull."[10] And yet, despite such taunting, his childhood was happy, joyful, and secure. From his mother, whose Presbyterian faith filled their small home, he learned the Golden Rule: "Love thy neighbor as thyself." From his father, whose generosity belied his modest means, he learned a deep sympathy for the poor. From both parents, he learned to see the world from the perspective of the working classes. "From his family environment," one friend noted, Meiklejohn learned "an inner peace, free from disguised fears, hostilities, and frustrations."[11]

For more than a decade, the Meiklejohns lived quite contentedly in Rochdale. In 1880, however, James Meiklejohn considered moving his family again, this time from England to the United States. Ever since the American Civil War, when a sharp drop in cotton imports caused British mills to buckle, thousands of workers had emigrated overseas. Dozens of enterprising Scots had started new mills abroad or bought factories from American families weakened by the war. Typical was the J. & P. Coats Company of Paisley, Scotland, which, in 1877, took possession of the Conant Thread Company in Pawtucket, Rhode Island. Like other Scottish textile companies with recently acquired branches on the opposite side of the Atlantic, the Coats Company recruited large numbers of Scottish workers, especially skilled dye masters and color technicians, to teach their American counterparts the latest manufacturing methods.[12] The Coats Company advertised for employees in Scottish newspapers and posted fliers in workers' neighborhoods, including the Meiklejohns' district of Newbold in Rochdale. In an effort to persuade millhands to leave their current jobs, Coats offered to subsidize their ocean passage and promised to help them find affordable housing near the company's new mill in Pawtucket. Given such powerful incentives, James Meiklejohn faced a difficult choice. On the one hand, he hated to leave Rochdale and the camaraderie of the workers' cooperative. On the other hand, he wanted to provide the best possible life for his large family. After careful consideration, he and Elizabeth decided to leave England for America, if not necessarily for the Coats mill, then for another mill like it.

In the spring of 1880, all ten Meiklejohns boarded the giant *Britannic* steamer of the White Star Line and sailed for New York. Little Alexander was only eight years old at time. Like any inquisitive boy, he stowed his belongings, including his most prized possession, his cricket bat, and went off to explore the ship. "When a person gets fairly started," he later wrote in a characteristically precocious school essay, "he begins to look for his berth, and he is lucky if he gets there without bruises. Trunks, boxes, bags, and bundles of every size, shape, and kind seem to be lying just where they ought not to be, and everyone you speak to is either a German, an Italian, or at least someone who speaks a different language from your own." To young Alec's delight, there were several lively musicians on board, including a Dutch violinist and an Italian concertina player. After a brief stop in Queenstown, Ireland, for additional passengers and mail, the *Britannic* began its "real ocean voyage" over what quickly became some very rough seas. "That night," Meiklejohn recorded, "the winds began to blow, the waves to toss, and the ship to rock. It was only with the greatest difficulty that I managed to stay in my berth, and the way in which the boxes and bundles tried to run across the deck, regardless of knocking anyone down, was alarming in the extreme." Finally, after a few close encounters with icebergs off the coast of Newfoundland, Meiklejohn spotted Manhattan. "It was a beautiful morning and the view of Governor's Isle was very grand to one who had not seen land for ten days or more. After breakfast, we sailed to the quay belonging to the White Star Line, where we left the vessel."

Safely docked in New York, Meiklejohn disembarked and followed his parents to Castle Garden, where they exchanged their British pounds for American dollars and waited for their baggage to pass inspection.[13] The next day, the whole family set out for Appanoag, Rhode Island, where they stayed for four years before finally settling fifteen miles farther north in Pawtucket. Unfortunately, neither Meiklejohn nor his relatives left any record of their years in Appanoag, and it was not until the family moved to Pawtucket that traces of Meiklejohn's childhood began to reappear. Pawtucket in the 1880s was unmistakably a textile town. With a skyline dominated by steeples and smokestacks, its labyrinth of narrow brick streets ran along both sides of the Blackstone River, which flowed over the picturesque Pawtucket Falls at the center of town. In 1884, the name "James Meiklejohn, color mixer" appeared for the first time among the twenty-three thousand inhabitants listed in the *Pawtucket–Central Falls Directory*.[14] It was in that year that Meiklejohn's father found a job, not at the Coats mill, but at the Dunnell Manufacturing Company, also known as Dunnell Print Works, on Dunnell's Lane in Pawtucket.[15] Ever since its establishment in the mid-1830s, the Dunnell Print Works had been one of Pawtucket's largest textile factories. Following its incorporation in 1853, it had expanded rapidly to include not only spinning and bleaching but also calico printing and dye work.[16] In 1884, when the Meiklejohn family settled in Pawtucket, the Dunnell Manufacturing Company had just completed a new structure for the finishing of "fancy" bleached goods and the printing of twelve-color patterned pieces. Part of the new structure was a state-of-the-art dyehouse, which eventually employed at least four Meiklejohns.

It was not long before the Meiklejohns became involved in both the industrial *and* the commercial aspects of Pawtucket's growing economy. One year after "James Meiklejohn, color mixer" appeared in the town directory, the name "John Meiklejohn, retailer" appeared alongside it. In

Alexander Meiklejohn at the age of ten in Appanoag, Rhode Island, 1882 (Brown University Archives)

1885, James's brother John left England and joined the Meiklejohns in Pawtucket. With capital saved from James's work in the mills, the two brothers opened a business partnership selling "pianos, organs, sheet music, musical instruments, and fancy goods."[17] Both Meiklejohn families lived at 76 Summit Street in Pawtucket, and the new Meiklejohn Music Company was located at 184 Main Street just a few blocks away. Over the next several years, the number of Meiklejohns listed in the *Pawtucket–Central Falls Directory* multiplied as the family moved from 76 Summit to 12 Prospect, to 8 Prospect, to 72 Prospect, and, finally, to 118 Prospect, where they remained for many decades. Slowly by surely, the Meiklejohns began to acquire a measure of social and economic stability in Pawtucket. A survey of leading manufacturers and merchants in Rhode Island, published in 1886, noted that the Meiklejohn Music Company was already flourishing just a year after it opened. "The store is large and commodious, being twenty by fifty feet in size," the survey stated. "The firm are agents in Pawtucket for the sale of the celebrated Mason and Hamlin pianos and organs and for the Wilcox and White organs and have on hand at all times a line of samples of these desirable instruments. They also keep a stock of musical merchandise, including sheet music."[18] By 1898, James and John Meiklejohn had expanded their business to include the sale of bicycles as well as the management of the Pawtucket City Auditorium next door, which hosted a wide array of concerts and other community activities.[19] With John running the business and James working in the mill, the Meiklejohn family, like many other Scottish immigrants in Pawtucket, gradually climbed into Rhode Island's middle class.

To be Scottish in Pawtucket was not unusual in the 1880s. Indeed, when the Meiklejohns arrived in Rhode Island, they entered a large and well-established Scottish immigrant community.[20] Between 1880 and 1890, more than 800,000 immigrants left Scotland and England for the United States, and most of them settled in the Northeast.[21] Like other immigrant groups, Scottish immigrants in Pawtucket tended to congregate in residential enclaves, to pursue similar occupations, and to gather together for various social engagements. For Scottish immigrants throughout New England, the center of work was often the textile mill, the center of religious life was typically the Presbyterian or, if necessary, the Congregational Church, and the center of social interaction was almost always the "clan."[22] In 1889, the *Pawtucket–Central Falls Directory* announced the first meeting of the Clan Fraser, part of the National Order of Scottish Clans.[23] The Meiklejohns were among the first to join Pawtucket's Clan Fraser, which functioned for them as a substitute for the workers' cooperative they had left behind in Rochdale. The clan, like the cooperative, created an atmosphere of solidarity and mutual aid among the city's Scots. A friend of the Meiklejohns recalled the special ethnic bond he felt as a participant in the annual Pawtucket Scots Day Parade. "It was one of the proudest moments of my life," he informed Meiklejohn many years later, "when I marched down through Main Street at the head of the clan with your father on one side and Walter Scott of New York on the other. After the parade, we went down to Crescent Park and had a real old-fashioned clam bake."[24] Young Alec appreciated the sense of community he witnessed in Pawtucket's Clan Fraser. He also valued the religious community of the Pawtucket Congregational Church, where he and his parents attended weekly services and heard the stirring sermons of the Reverend Alexander MacGregor, a Scottish American minister who attracted more than three hundred parishioners to worship every Sunday.[25]

Besides associating with their clan and church communities, the Meiklejohn family was full of avid and accomplished cricket players. When the Pawtucket Bowling and Cricket Club met for the first time in May of 1886, James Coats (Peter Coats's brother) served as its president, and John Meiklejohn volunteered as secretary.[26] Alexander himself was a excellent cricketer, whose abilities contributed to victories for the Dunnell mill amateur team as well as for the Pawtucket high school club team.[27] Years later, the *Providence Journal-Bulletin* described Meiklejohn's expert and proven bowling technique: "With an easy delivery, he bowled at medium pace and relied on pitch, change of pace, and variation in the flight of the ball to get wickets—and usually he garnered quite a crop of them. Against average batsmen, he was most extremely successful, being straight and deadly to hesitation and indecision."[28] Indeed, young Meiklejohn was a superb athlete. By the time he entered high school, he had reached his full height of about five feet seven inches. His strong, sinewy frame and shrewd, sharp eyes made him a star sportsman. He was lithe and agile, a fast runner, and a versatile team player. He learned games quickly, and he never let his diminutive size inhibit his physical activity. His thin neck, narrow jaw, prominent cheekbones, and high forehead made him look more gentle and delicate than he actually was. As a schoolboy, he spent many hours on the playing fields, and when he was not on the field, he was usually thinking about sports. He even devoted his school essays to the subject. He gave due consideration to boxing, wrestling, rowing, swimming, curling, bowling, and croquet, but returned time and again to his favorite, cricket.

As his love of cricket showed, Meiklejohn was not ashamed to be the child of immigrants. In fact, in a high school composition titled "Foreign Immigration," he openly wondered why native-born Americans failed to appreciate their foreign-born neighbors.[29] "In reading American newspapers, in listening to American orators, and, in fact, in considering American opinion," he observed, "it is strange to notice how many of the greatest evils of this country are traced to the immigration of foreigners." At a time when fears of excessive immigration were rapidly rising, Meiklejohn felt a strong need to defend himself and his family against negative stereotypes. In the minds of most Americans, he noted, "drink is used almost exclusively by immigrants, anarchy is wholly supported by them, crime is committed, labor is made cheaper, and almost everything which is bad is attributed to these great hindrances to American advancement." For some reason, Meiklejohn noticed, native-born Americans rarely considered the positive qualities of foreigners. Since jingoists were "too selfish to give the immigrants credit" for the advantages they brought, he wrote, "we," the newcomers, "must try to do it for them." In Meiklejohn's view, the United States owed its greatness chiefly to the contributions of immigrants. "It cannot be denied that the immigrants have brought many vices into this country and that they commit a great portion of the crime," he admitted, "but it is hardly fair for the Americans to be ungrateful to those who have built up their country for them and have placed them in the high position which they now hold." Citing the industriousness of the Scottish millworkers he knew in Pawtucket, Meiklejohn advised native-born Americans to commend immigrants for all their hard work.[30] Only then could the country overcome its xenophobia and forge a truly unified national culture.

As recent immigrants striving to fit into Pawtucket's middle class, the Meiklejohns did not live a luxurious life. Indeed, had it not been for the additional income generated by profits from the family business (assessed at a thousand dollars in property, all taxed under John Meiklejohn's name) and the supplementary wages earned by his working sons, James Meiklejohn might not have been able to support his large family nearly as well as he did. As it was, he could afford to give only one of his eight sons a complete education, and Alexander, being the youngest, benefited immensely from his older brothers' labor. Heeding an old Scottish tradition to designate the youngest son a scholar, Meiklejohn attended school full time. After a year at the Grove Street Elementary School in 1884, he entered Pawtucket Public High School and followed the "classical," or college preparatory, course. His curriculum consisted of grammar, penmanship, arithmetic, algebra, Latin, Greek, drawing, and music in the first two

11

years and added geometry, physics, chemistry, astronomy, French, and ancient history in the later two. He read Homer, Cicero, Virgil, Ovid, and Thucydides as well as Jefferson, Franklin, Hawthorne, Longfellow, and Emerson. In the field of British literature, he encountered Chaucer, Milton, Byron, and Shakespeare along with Macaulay, Dickens, and Wordsworth. This rigorous literary curriculum was intended to prepare bright students for college, and Meiklejohn set his sights on that goal. According to the high school course announcement for 1888, Pawtucket's classical course was "sufficient to admit a pupil to Harvard, Yale, or Brown University," and nearby Brown had a policy of admitting any qualified Pawtucket boy automatically "on certificate," a standard practice in the late nineteenth century.[31]

With ambitions for college, Meiklejohn excelled in his schoolwork. He demonstrated a special gift for clear and concise writing, which he displayed in essays on timely social and political topics. For example, after the narrowly contested presidential election of 1888, which put Benjamin Harrison ahead of incumbent Grover Cleveland and brought the labor question to a head, Meiklejohn composed a short paper expressing his contempt for parading and other "wasteful" displays of political emotion. "Parading, although not wrong or morally injurious, is to my mind one of the most silly and nonsensical things that a political enthusiast can do," he wrote. "The men buy uniforms, spend hours in drilling, pay large sums of money for car-fare, and waste their strength and tire their legs in trudging through the streets with a kind of uncertain idea in their tired brains that, if they only keep it up long enough, they will be sure to elect their candidate." But parades were just one aspect of the political pageantry that characterized late nineteenth-century campaigns, which also included conventions, rallies, and countless candidate speeches. Of all these activities, Meiklejohn argued, speechmaking was "by far the most sensible and instructive," because it brought diverse citizens together into "one immense debating society" and enabled them to consider the important social questions of the day. As Meiklejohn saw it, campaign speeches allowed "the most intelligent and gifted men of the country [to] act as the leading debaters [and thus] to instruct the mass of the people." Expressing an idea that stayed with him throughout his life, Meiklejohn asserted that political speechmaking constituted a profoundly *educational* activity, an ideal opportunity for citizens to discuss matters of significant public concern. As Meiklejohn put it, political speeches were "an elevating and educating exercise which it would be well for more of our Pawtucket High School boys to attend."[32]

12

In 1889, Meiklejohn graduated first in his high school class. His commencement oration addressed another timely topic, prohibition, which had made its way onto Pawtucket's law books only two years before. In many ways, Meiklejohn's valedictory speech hinted at the development of a nascent political philosophy, a germinating sense of what democratic self-government might entail. His support for prohibition exhibited not only the moral self-confidence that characterized the anti-alcohol movement and its predominantly Anglo-Saxon, middle-class adherents but also the belief that municipal governments should protect the general social welfare, even if it meant infringing on certain individual liberties. "The declaration that the government has no right to limit the choice of individuals in the matter of drinking, though it may sound very brave and defiant coming from the mouth of some demagogue with big nose and little eyes, is indeed supremely ridiculous," Meiklejohn declared in suspiciously ethnophobic language. "No man, however red his nose, will deny that law is made to protect the citizens from harm, and no man can deny that the dealer by selling and the drinker by drinking inflict untold misery, suffering, and woe upon their poor unfortunate relatives and children."[33] Though Meiklejohn would revisit and revise this position many times throughout his life, it nevertheless expressed his early political philosophy, especially his interest in the relationship between personal liberty and public order in a democratic society. In Meiklejohn's half-formed high school opinion, democracy bore a fundamental responsibility to defend the public good over and against the supposedly private right to drink, even if such protection entailed the use of coercive authority. Democracies, in other words, had a basic duty to protect their citizens from harm.

In the months following his high school graduation, three important events occurred in the life of seventeen-year-old Alexander Meiklejohn. First was the death of his older brother Henry. A textile colorist like his father, Henry, who went by the nickname "Harry," died on July 6, 1889, at the age of twenty-four. The cause of death, not uncommon in the last decades of the nineteenth century, was acute phthisis, a progressive consumptive disease that very often took the form of pulmonary tuberculosis.[34] The second event, following close on the heels of the first, was a fire that destroyed virtually all the buildings of the Dunnell Print Works. Blazes of this sort happened all too frequently in Pawtucket's unregulated textile mills, where high temperatures from huge boilers and extreme exhaustion from long hours often combined with disastrous results.[35] The third event, much happier than the previous two, was Meiklejohn's matriculation at Brown. At first, Meiklejohn's mother had wanted him to study theology at Yale, but the proximity of Brown made it a more attractive option. In order to cover the $150 annual tuition, the Meiklejohn family pooled its resources, with Alexander's six remaining brothers paying a significant proportion of the bill. For his part, Meiklejohn agreed to live at home during his sophomore year and to walk or bicycle three miles each day to class. On occasion, he was able to ride to campus on a cable car or, if he missed the trolley, on a horse-drawn cart. Beginning in his sophomore year, he benefited from Brown's Whipple Scholarship, which paid fifty dollars a year toward his tuition and thus lightened the financial burden somewhat. Despite the cost, which amounted to more than nine months' wages for Meiklejohn's father, the opportunity to go to Brown was not to be missed. Indeed, it was an opportunity that changed Meiklejohn's life.

In 1889, Brown was still a small New England college. Sitting atop a steep, tree-covered hill just east of downtown Providence, the university consisted of only eight buildings, sixteen professors, six instructors, two librarians, a registrar, and fewer than three hundred undergraduates. Meiklejohn's class, for example, had only sixty-one members, more than half of whom came from high schools in Rhode Island. Henry Robinson Palmer, a member of Brown's class of 1890, noted that the school was small enough for students to know the first, middle, and last names of every classmate. The intimate size facilitated close relationships between students and faculty, but it also fostered cliques, particularly among rival fraternities. "Small as it was," Palmer remembered, the all-male college "was sharply divided by secret society lines. A fraternity man was under suspicion among his own society brothers if he kept company with the members of another fraternity." In the fall of 1891, at the beginning of his junior year, Meiklejohn pledged Theta Delta Chi, a house known for the academic achievements of its members. "There was a strong family feeling among the members of a society," Palmer noted. "The chapter hall was home in a sense that no other place on the campus was, and the upperclassmen exercised a powerful and wholesome influence on the younger men." For Meiklejohn, the fraternity provided a comfortable home away from home. It also provided an outlet for his athletic interests. Sports played a significant, perhaps even predominant, role in late nineteenth-century undergraduate life. First baseball, then football, and eventually a whole range of other intercollegiate athletics, including tennis, crew, and track, commanded the attention of virtually every American college male.[36] As an undergraduate, Meiklejohn avoided football but continued to enjoy cricket, soccer, and "ice polo," a game played frequently on Ham-

Alexander Meiklejohn, sixth from right, and members of the Theta Delta Chi fraternity at Brown University, ca. 1891 (Brown University Archives)

mond's Pond in Pawtucket.[37] At Brown, he quickly became the epitome of a student-athlete.

Meiklejohn enjoyed the company of his fraternity brothers and cricket teammates, but no one influenced him more profoundly than Brown's new president, Elisha Benjamin Andrews. Born in Hinsdale, New Hampshire, in 1844, Andrews had fought in the Civil War and lost an eye in the siege of Petersburg in 1864. The son of a Baptist minister, he had graduated from Baptist-affiliated Brown in 1870 and, like other aspiring academics and future college presidents of the mid-nineteenth century, had spent time studying philosophy and political economy in Germany. After a year's call to ministry in Beverly, Massachusetts, and a four-year term as president of Denison University in Ohio, he had returned to his alma mater as a professor of history and economics. In 1889, after a year at Cornell, he accepted a nomination to become Brown's eighth president. Only forty-five years old at the time of his inauguration, E. "Benny" Andrews brought strong convictions and tremendous charisma to the task of university administration.[38] During his ten-year presidency, he doubled the size of the faculty and student body and quadrupled the university's course offerings, with additions primarily in the natural and applied sciences. Professor of English Walter Bronson later identified the causes of Brown's rapid expansion under Andrews. "Growth in wealth and population," Bronson explained in his *History of Brown University,* "made it natural that more and more youth should seek a college education." Furthermore, "the multiplication and improvement of high schools put the means for preparing for college within the reach of an increasing number." Regarding the augmentation of the science curriculum, Bronson pointed out that "the intellectual life of America was rising to a higher plane, chiefly under the stimulus of modern science; the scientific spirit was permeating every department of thought and arousing multitudes to a new realization of the value of trained intellect in confronting the problems of life on all its levels."[39]

Bronson was right to stress the stimulus of modern science as the most important factor influencing Brown's growth in the late nineteenth century. Riding the high tide of American industrial prosperity and technological discovery in the 1880s, Brown, along with countless other research universities at the time, experienced a sort of scientific renaissance at the end of the nineteenth century. President Andrews's establishment of new programs in mechanical engineering as well as political and social science was not surprising given the proliferation of technological breakthroughs at the time. Only a few years earlier, Thomas Edison had perfected the incandescent light bulb, and the magic of electricity spread quickly across the nation. Before long, electric streetcars had completely transformed urban and suburban transportation, even between Providence and Pawtucket. As Bronson astutely noted, "the scientific spirit was permeating every department" when President Andrews took the helm in 1889. It would have been no less accurate to say that the scientific spirit was transforming the very structure of American social thought. The years between 1889 and 1893, which Meiklejohn spent as an undergraduate, coincided exactly with Brown's transition from a required "classical" system to an open "elective" system of teaching. No other aspect of Meiklejohn's college experience had a more lasting impact on his later educational philosophy than the university's science-heavy elective curriculum.

When Meiklejohn enrolled as a freshman at Brown in 1889, *all* of his classes were prescribed, including two semesters of Greek (Homer, Thucydides, Herodotus, and Euripides), two semesters of Latin (Livy, Cicero, and Horace), two semesters of French (Racine, Fénelon, and Corneille), and two semesters of mathematics (basic algebra, solid and spherical geometry, and trigonometry). His sophomore and junior years involved required English, elocution, history, and German, but, in stark contrast with his freshman year, everything else was elective, including his classes in Greek, Latin, French, and mathematics, plus botany, chemistry, physics, engineering, mechanics, and surveying. By the time Meiklejohn graduated from Brown in 1893, his senior year was *entirely* elective, with literally ninety-nine different courses from which to choose.[40] As Meiklejohn later noted, "the elective transition was on and there seemed to be no guiding ideas" in the undergraduate course.[41] First adopted at Harvard under President Charles William Eliot in 1869, the elective system gave students total freedom in the choice of courses in the belief that the unfettered search for knowledge would lead eventually to a coherent understanding of the whole. Such a complete absence of structure, however, did not benefit every student equally. Meiklejohn, for one, felt lost in a sea of unrelated studies. As he later interpreted it, Brown's curriculum seemed trapped "between two worlds." The first was a world of philological training and mental discipline, a world of character building and cultural refinement. The other was a realm of narrow specialization and scientific research, a world of technical expertise and preprofessional preparation. The first looked back to the moral authority of mid-nineteenth-century Victorianism. The second pushed forward to the intellectual aimlessness of twentieth-century modernism. Even if young Meiklejohn could scarcely guess at the dramatic effect this transition would have on American education in the future, he sensed, even as an undergraduate, that the cultural stability and moral certainty of the classical curriculum were quickly slipping away.[42]

Slowly but surely, Meiklejohn found his bearings and discovered that "there were personal contacts of very great power" at Brown—stimulating professors whose integrity and wisdom could guide students like himself through the apparent "anarchy" of the elective system. Besides the influence of historian John Franklin Jameson, Meiklejohn greatly admired the energetic young teachers in the Department of Philosophy.[43] In the early 1890s, Brown's philosophy department consisted of two professors: Edmund Burke Delabarre, who had just received his doctorate from the University of Freiburg in Germany and who served as an instructor in the newly emerging field of psychology, and President Andrews himself, who had also studied in Germany and who, like most college presidents in the nineteenth century, doubled as professor of moral philosophy. In 1892, Brown's philosophy department added James Seth, a thirty-two-year-old Scotsman from Edinburgh who became professor of ethics and metaphysics.[44] Andrews, Delabarre, and Seth provided the model for Meiklejohn's own eventual success as a teacher. All agreed that the chief purpose of undergraduate education was *not* to accumulate discrete scientific facts but rather to cultivate intellectual values. "In my conviction," Andrews asserted in his presidential report for 1890, "the power to think clearly, reason logically, analyze keenly, and generalize truthfully—in a word, to be master of one's self intellectually—is an attainment infinitely superior in worth to any possible bulk of unassorted mental stores."[45]

Meiklejohn took as many philosophy classes as he could with Andrews, focusing especially on the study of ethics and epistemology as a way to sort out the "confusion" of his undergraduate course. As a senior, he enrolled in both "Advanced Theoretical Ethics" and "Mental Philosophy," which covered logic, psychology, and metaphysics. The purpose of these courses, Andrews explained in his annual report to the trustees, was "to ground the student in the nature and validity of human knowledge and to demonstrate the ultimate and substantial character of mind and the futility of any and every form of general skepticism."[46] The purpose, in other words, was to build a foundation for ethical understanding in an increasingly scientific world. Under Andrews's guidance, Meiklejohn and his fellow students encountered the great minds of Western philosophy, including Plato, Aristotle, Anselm, Aquinas, Hobbes, Hume, Rousseau, Mill, Bentham, Bradley, Bosanquet, Sidgwick, and Green. One philosopher, however, stood out from the rest, and that was Immanuel Kant. "Kant was the greatest thinker humanity has yet produced," Andrews liked to say, and in the 1890s he was not alone in his enthusiasm.[47] After 1881, the centennial anniversary of Kant's famous *Critique of Pure Reason,* and then after 1888, the centenary of his *Critique of Practical Reason,* the philosophy of Kant received increasing attention from scholars and lay people alike. Universities hosted lecture series on Kant, publishers produced centennial editions of his treatises, and academics met to discuss his influence in the history of Western thought. When Meiklejohn matriculated at Brown in 1889, Kant stood very much in the foreground of American philosophy. Even if the full significance of Kant's philosophy did not become apparent to him for many years, its initial impact came when he was an undergraduate and embarked on a thorough examination of idealism as a way to build a system of ethical standards for modern life.

"KANT'S ETHICS"

Why was Kant so important for Meiklejohn? The short answer was that Kant refuted the skepticism of Hume and offered a secular system of moral understanding in a scientific world. The slightly longer answer was

18

Alexander Meiklejohn as a senior at Brown University, 1893 (Brown University Archives)

that Kant offered a highly sophisticated epistemological response to British empiricism and its seventeenth-century predecessor, Baconian science. In its most basic form, empiricism held that all human knowledge originates in personal experience as opposed to divine inspiration. Rooted in the assumption that understanding comes from direct observations and sense perceptions, empiricism searched for truth through the use of scientific experiments and the discovery of reproducible results. Conceiving of

19

the universe as a giant machine that operates according to consistent mathematical and physical laws, empiricism laid a foundation for the rise of the modern scientific method. Yet, for all its confidence in raw experience as the source of human knowledge, empiricism maintained a strict duality between subjects and objects, between mind and matter, between ideas on the one hand and reality on the other. This duality became the main focus of Scottish philosopher David Hume, who carried empiricism to its most extreme conclusion in skepticism. Arguing that human beings could neither know nor prove the existence of anything external to consciousness itself, Hume rejected the medieval characterization of God as the "First Cause" of all human experience and, instead, advocated religious agnosticism and moral relativism. For Hume, such abstract notions as truth, beauty, goodness, justice, and virtue had no real meaning outside the individual human mind.[48] It was here that Kant disagreed. Unlike Hume, who asserted that all knowledge derives from individual—and thus radically differentiated—experience, Kant argued that the meaning of experience derives from transcendental—and thus perfectly unified—reason. According to Kant, reason *creates* meaning out of experience. As Meiklejohn put it in one undergraduate essay, "Hume asked, 'Why do I relate the impression of "sound" as effect to the impression of "speaker" as cause?' Kant replied, 'Because the meaning of that impression is entirely my own and that meaning is based on a rational unity; hence, for me, the relation of causality is necessary; it is the presupposition of experience.' "[49] It was Hume's radical skepticism and moral relativism that Kantian idealism endeavored to refute.

Trained as a physicist in Germany in the mid-eighteenth century, Kant had a deep respect for science and the scientific method. He wondered, though, about the division between scientific theories and the reality those theories sought to describe. To what extent, he asked, could human beings actually understand the nonhuman world? To what extent was empirical knowledge even possible? In the late eighteenth century, these questions drew Kant away from physics toward the study of philosophy. In the *Critique of Pure Reason,* published in 1781, Kant posed the basic epistemological question, How do human beings know? His answer to this query changed the direction of Enlightenment thought. Unlike Hume and the empiricists, who argued that human beings know the world only through experience and sense perception, Kant asserted that human beings know through the mental processes of thought itself. In other words, knowledge derived not from external stimuli but rather from the internal *organization* of external stimuli. This process of internal organization

Kant called pure reason. Pure reason, he asserted, conformed to certain unchanging principles, such as the physical and geometrical principles of space and time. In order for an idea to be reasonable, it had to be reasonable in every space and every time. Reason, therefore, constituted a universal, or a priori, structure for all human ideas. The significance of these assertions could hardly be overstated. Quite simply, they suggested that pure reason (or "apperception") transcended the individual mind and, therefore, was accessible to every human being in exactly the same form. For Kant—and also for Meiklejohn—pure reason, as an ideal representation of reality gathered from experience, replaced God as the First Cause of human knowledge. As Meiklejohn put it in another class essay, "[B]eyond a question, Kant demonstrated the synthetic unity of apperception; he has given to our knowledge a rational necessity; he has proven the impossibility, in our experience, of a cause without an effect or an effect without a cause."[50] Pure reason, in other words, was a secular substitute for divine inspiration in a scientific world.

With his rationalist argument for the transcendental unity of apperception, Kant began to dismantle the skepticism of Hume. He did not, however, dismantle the dualism that had brought Hume to skepticism in the first place.[51] He still upheld the dichotomy between ideas on the one hand and reality on the other. Kant's idealist epistemology insisted that human beings could know only what reason represented in consciousness, and that ideas, while they might appear to describe reality, were not reality itself. This distinction between appearance and reality, between ideas and the world, meant that a true and complete apprehension of the universe qua universe lay permanently beyond the realm of pure reason. As Meiklejohn learned from his reading of F. H. Bradley's influential book, *Appearance and Reality,* published in 1893 during his final semester at Brown, human beings could have a valid idea of the universe, but the idea and the universe were not identical objects in space and time. In the same way, a true and complete apprehension of God (or morality or immortality or the nature of the human soul) lay beyond the realm of empirical observation. As Meiklejohn wrote in his class notebook for James Seth's course "The History of Philosophy from Leibniz to Kant," "we cannot get totality, but reason urges us to seek it."[52] This conclusion had crucial implications for Meiklejohn's emergent moral theory. It implied that pure reason lacked not only a pure intuition of the divine essence but also a sure route to a direct apprehension of universal ethical values. If consciousness and reality occupied fundamentally different realms, then how could human beings really know God? How could individual thinkers share a common understanding of truth? How could different people accept a common moral code? For Meiklejohn, these were the crucial questions of modern ethics. Unfortunately, Kant's *Critique of Pure Reason* stopped short of giving answers.

In order to rescue a knowledge of universal moral values from the realm of philosophical abstraction, Kant supplemented his theory of pure reason with a theory of practical reason. In his *Critique of Practical Reason,* published seven years after the *Critique of Pure Reason,* Kant located the source of transcendental moral understanding in the quality of reasonableness itself. Morality, Kant argued, meant nothing more or less than conformity to "practical" human nature, which was, by definition, reasonable. Emphasizing his claim that the idea of pure reason implied the existence of a universal, a priori order in the universe, Kant argued that a reasonable life was a life lived according to universal moral laws, the basic essence of which he called the categorical imperative. The categorical imperative required every human being to behave as if every other human being were reasonable and, therefore, obedient to the same universal moral code. In other words, the categorical imperative reiterated the Golden Rule to "love thy neighbor as thyself" but translated it into secular rationalist terms. So, in the end, Kant grounded morality in the natural realm of practical reason rather than in a supernatural realm of divine inspiration. He was careful to stress, however, that practical reason was *not* infallible. It was not divine. It did not have the power to create moral laws—a power reserved for God alone. Practical reason did, however, have the capacity to postulate ethical principles and, thus, to rescue humanity from moral doubt and spiritual despair. "This was not an afterthought for Kant," Meiklejohn explained, noting the link between practical reason and moral conviction. "It was the real culmination of the work [*The Critique of Practical Reason*]."[53] In Meiklejohn's view, Kant's greatest contribution to modern philosophy was his reconstruction of a universal ethical standard accessible to every individual by the transcendental power of practical reason.

Because of his faith in a universal moral structure, Kant became known as the founder of "transcendental idealism." In the early nineteenth century, a trail of other German philosophers, most notably Fichte, Schelling, Schleiermacher, and Hegel, extended Kant's work into new areas and developed a distinctly "post-Kantian" idealist philosophy. Contending that Kant's critiques remained unfinished, the post-Kantians searched for ways to resolve the lingering duality between pure and practical reason. They did so, in short, by identifying the subjective apprehension of reality with the objective structure of reality itself. In other words, they conflated ideas and the world, mind and matter, self and other, rendering them identical in both form and substance. The effect of this conflation was to see consciousness and reality as different representations of one Absolute Spirit or Transcendental Will. Eventually, this distortion of Kant's philosophy led to the mystical romantic belief, especially in Hegel, that human beings could somehow apprehend divine essence itself—a notion Kant himself never espoused. By the middle of the nineteenth century, both Kantian and post-Kantian idealism receded behind other emerging philosophies, particularly the scientific positivism of August Comte and the evolutionary hypotheses of Charles Darwin, both of which turned back to the empiricist model. In the late nineteenth century, Darwinism clashed with Neo-Hegelian idealism to produce a new and distinctly American philosophical movement known as pragmatism. The founders of pragmatism, including Charles Sanders Peirce, William James, and John Dewey, all acknowledged their debt to Immanuel Kant. It was no wonder, then, that Kant became the centerpiece of Meiklejohn's philosophical studies at Brown.

Toward the end of his junior year, Meiklejohn made his first extended attempt to grasp Kant's significance in the history of Enlightenment thought. His essay titled "A Defense of Empirical Knowledge" listed the philosophers he had encountered in his classes thus far, including Descartes, Malebranche, Spinoza, and Leibniz, along with Locke, Rousseau, Berkeley, and Hume. Towering far above these others, however, was Immanuel Kant. For Meiklejohn, Kant represented the Great Synthesizer who solved the riddles of empiricism and gave the key to intellectual unity and transcendental understanding in the modern world. The most important aspect of Kant's idealism, Meiklejohn wrote, was its assertion of the unifying—and, thus, the meaning-creating—power of reason. "The first element in empirical knowledge is that matter of sensation, given by an external world," he argued. "This sensation is, as such, unformed, unrelated, and unmeaning; it becomes intelligible only as it is formed by the relating activity of the mind." "Thus," he continued, "mind is dealing with a matter to which it itself has given all the meaning, and it is relating that matter in forms and categories, of which each implies the other, and which all are but expressions of the central unity." Rejecting the strict empiricist dichotomy between subject and object, between ideas and reality, Meiklejohn insisted on a more direct idealist relationship between knowledge and the world it knows. "If knowledge has not an object known," he noted, "then the nature of knowledge can never be learned, for it can

23

never be an object of study. Such a skepticism, like all others, cuts away the ground upon which it stands."[54] According to Meiklejohn, pure reason possessed the ultimate epistemological power—the power to apprehend itself as both a subject *and* an object in the world, to recognize itself as both the source *and* the product of its own apperception, *all at the same time.* Pure reason, in other words, perceived the unity of all reality in the transcendental unity of itself. When taken to its extreme in Hegel, pure reason constituted an epistemological substitute for God.

For Meiklejohn, Kantian idealism functioned as a secular replacement for the outmoded Presbyterian and Congregationalist beliefs of his youth. Indeed, the search for an "ethical synthesis" of rational and religious ideals became the central concern of his philosophical studies as an undergraduate. In his junior year, perhaps to test the strength of modern rationalism, Meiklejohn took himself back to the pre-empiricist world of medieval theology. Exploring the thirteenth- and fourteenth-century writings of Thomas Aquinas, John Duns Scotus, and William of Ockham, he wrote a short but significant essay on scholastic philosophy. The essay, titled "Nominalism and Realism," examined the dialectic relation between soul and substance, between essence and existence, between universals and individuals in the late Middle Ages. Meiklejohn noticed that the scholastics, when faced with such questions as How can human beings know God? or How is God present in the sacraments? drew a basic distinction between humanity on the one hand and divinity on the other, between individuals and universals, between reason and faith. Nominalists such as Ockham argued that humanity could never achieve a *direct* knowledge of God, asserting instead that human understanding was limited to mere *signs* of God's existence in the world. The bread and wine of the Eucharist, for example, were only symbols of Christ's body and blood; until these earthly substances were sanctified by God, they could be only *potential* purveyors of divine forgiveness and grace. Realists, on the other hand, argued that human beings could indeed achieve a direct knowledge of God through faith. Aquinas, for instance, asserted that human beings, through revelation, could truly know God as the universal essence of all Being. For Aquinas, the bread and the wine were essentially, substantially, and *actually* the body and blood of Christ. Whereas nominalists contended that universals were merely *actus intelligendi,* or subjective concepts, realists held that universals had real, objective, and substantial existence in the world.[55]

In the end, Meiklejohn sided with the nominalists and agreed that "the universal" was a "mere subjective concept." This conclusion did not, however, imply that human beings must remain forever ignorant of universals. Instead, it implied that *reason,* rather than faith, must be the source of universal knowledge. The distinction between reason and faith was crucial for Meiklejohn, because it suggested that reason, and, in turn, reality, was not only knowable but knowable as a metaphysical unity for all people in all places and all times. "Reality, though we view it as dynamic," Meiklejohn wrote, "must be, in Essence, a One Unchangeable Unity. It must never be other than it is. It must be not only a Numerical, but also a Substantial Unity, that is, a Unity in which Difference is lost in an All-Inclusive Principle."[56] The notion that reality must be a unity in which difference is lost in an all-inclusive principle had a deep and abiding effect on the development of Meiklejohn's own idealist philosophy. It not only highlighted the importance of intellectual coherence in any philosophical system but also maintained the possibility of achieving a shared consciousness of universal moral laws through the transcendental structure of reason. In Meiklejohn's view, the pursuit of transcendental consciousness was vital to overcoming the disintegrating forces of modern skepticism and doubt.

In December of 1892, Meiklejohn wrote his final essay for Professor Andrews's course, "Advanced Theoretical Ethics."[57] The paper, titled simply "Plato," synthesized much of what he had learned about idealism, about ethics, and about the study of philosophy in general. The purpose of philosophy, he argued, was to overcome skepticism and give meaning to life in the form of universal moral principles. Comparing Plato's teacher, Socrates, to his great hero, Kant, Meiklejohn noted that both philosophers, despite their historical distance, had addressed the same basic question, Can human beings agree about the nature of truth? Whenever people disagree on the nature of truth, Meiklejohn explained, "the question naturally arises, how is it that all these fellows who claim to know the truth cannot agree among themselves; does it not seem as if there were no truth to know, or at least as if it lay beyond the power of the human mind to grasp?" Whereas Socrates had addressed the Sophists on this question, Kant addressed Hume. Both philosophers, however, clung to ethics as the core of the philosophical project. "We must ever regard it as a most significant fact that the two men to whom has fallen the lot of raising our moral and intellectual ideals from the ruins of skepticism were men for whom the universe exists primarily and essentially as an ethical and moral order," Meiklejohn concluded.[58] "In both cases, skeptical empiricism was overthrown by a more careful psychology and a deeper epistemology than its own. Men were brought to recognize that the human consciousness is

25

not a string of disconnected states but that, throughout the whole, there runs a constant element which gives it unity and renders it a valid knowledge of truth. This element, for Socrates as well as for Kant, is the framing of general ideas, the relating of particular impressions, the construction of concepts." Even if humanity could not apprehend universal reality as such, the transcendental structure of pure reason gave hope that human consciousness was nonetheless unified on a cosmic scale. Reason, therefore, not faith, was the foundation of universal consciousness and the cornerstone of true virtue.

Through his undergraduate studies in philosophy, Meiklejohn forged the channels of his own intellectual and ethical idealism. While still in its embryonic form, it nevertheless revealed the basic tenets of his life-long philosophical convictions. First and foremost, he identified humanity as fundamentally rational: all human beings possessed an equal capacity for practical reason. Second, he characterized humanity as essentially unified: all human beings conformed to the universal structure of pure reason. Third, he portrayed humanity as ultimately moral: all human beings knew an identical categorical imperative in reason. Fourth, he defined humanity as essentially spiritual: all human beings participated in the same transcendental reality called reason. And finally, he cast humanity as fundamentally progressive: all human beings had the power to improve themselves and their world by becoming more reasonable. "Man has dignity which must be respected," Meiklejohn wrote in a short essay titled "Kant's Ethics." "Hence, he must seek his own perfection. He must not lie or commit any other sin, for these are implicitly or explicitly denials of his dignity as a rational being."[59] Although Meiklejohn sometimes betrayed his own beliefs and ignored his own philosophical convictions, he nevertheless insisted that the freedom of moral choices rested on the categorical imperative to be reasonable at all times and all places. As he grew into adulthood, he strove to embody this ideal of reasonable behavior in an otherwise unreasonable world, even when it seemed to others that his efforts to be reasonable defied reason itself.

In May of 1893, Meiklejohn graduated as the valedictorian of his senior class at Brown. His commencement oration, delivered "under the elms" on the campus green, returned to the themes of reason, faith, and idealism that had intrigued him throughout college but explored these concepts in a more literary context. His topic was a scene from Goethe's *Faust*.[60] Depicting a quiet conversation between Faust and his young admirer, Margarete, the scene Meiklejohn chose to interpret raised the issue of the universality of religious belief. "In the scene before us," Meiklejohn told his audience, "the lovers, seated in a garden at evening, are discussing the problems of religion. Margarete, with the simple devotion of love, cannot endure the thought that one so dear to her should wander from the Church, in which are centered all her joys and hopes." Implicitly comparing the tragic hero to himself, Meiklejohn continued with an explanation of Faust's decision to leave organized religion behind. "For you who believe," he said, "such faith as this may well suffice; in ritual and praise the Christian finds revealed the presence of the Eternal Power. And yet this cannot be the only way of knowing God, for what of those who never have heard the story of your faith or, having heard, cannot believe?" What of those unacquainted with the organized church, or, worse, unsympathetic to church doctrine? What hope could such nonbelievers have for emotional comfort or spiritual redemption? "Does the Eternal Power provide for you and leave the man of independent thought without a spark of hope?" Meiklejohn asked. "If your faith be true, then why do not all hearts accept its joy?" Pausing briefly for dramatic effect, Meiklejohn answered his own question and brought Faust's religious conflict to a close. "The Christian creed does tell us of God's love, but so does every form of faith reveal to its own worshippers the eternal truths. . . . The Christian faith is true, but it is not and cannot be the Truth."[61] With this statement, Meiklejohn ended his undergraduate years at Brown, confident in the universality of human intelligence and secure in his belief that reason, not faith, could rescue humanity from modern skepticism and despair.

After graduating, Meiklejohn did not immediately leave Brown. As he told his roommate, Frederick Pierpont Ladd, years later, President Andrews encouraged him to continue his studies in philosophy with Professor Seth. "When the good old days were ending and the time of our departing was at hand, not knowing what else to do, I naturally went to 'Benny,' " Meiklejohn explained to Ladd. "He looked me over, heard my tale, and said, 'Well, Meiklejohn, you're a Scotsman; so far as I can see, you're not very strong on whiskey, so I guess you must be long on philosophy. You'd better stay here a while and study with this man Seth. He's as good as they make 'em, Meiklejohn. You won't regret it."[62] And so, for two additional years, Meiklejohn remained in Providence to pursue a master's degree in philosophy at Brown. As a graduate student, he shifted his scholarly focus from idealism back to empiricism—or, more specifically, to the subject of natural or scientific evolution, which had become the most hotly debated philosophical topic of the time. Even as an undergraduate, Meiklejohn had been fascinated by the evolutionary theories of Charles

27

Darwin, Herbert Spencer, and William Graham Sumner, but their influence on his intellectual development was profoundly negative. As a student of ethics, rather than psychology or economics or political science, he doubted that evolution had any meaningful application to human civilization. Indeed, in an essay titled "The Value of the Evolutionary Method, as Applied to Ethics," he asserted that Darwinian concepts such as species differentiation, natural selection, and the survival of the fittest had no ethical significance whatsoever. The theory of evolution, he proclaimed, "has not a word to say as to the validity of any moral principle."[63]

Meiklejohn furthered his critique of evolution and empirical science in an essay titled "The Significance of the Scientific Movement of the Nineteenth Century." "Science deals with the world of appearance, the world of sensuous fact," he argued in terms outlined in F. H. Bradley's work, *Appearance and Reality*, in 1893. "If we wish for truth concerning the things of the Spirit, then we must go beyond science, seeking yet another realm of knowledge." As reasonable, and therefore moral, creatures, human beings affirmed "a deeper, truer knowledge of reality which, revealing the world as spiritual, shall give to the human life that worth and value which we desire."[64] According to Meiklejohn, the logic of animal competition simply did not apply to human beings, for whom the violent struggle for existence was not only wasteful and destructive but also unreasonable and, therefore, in Kantian terms, immoral. In January of 1894, Meiklejohn joined Brown's newly formed Philosophical Club for an informal debate on the ethical meaning of evolution. The debate positioned Herbert Spencer on one side against Thomas Huxley on the other. Meiklejohn spoke for Huxley. "Spencer tried to show that the ethical life of man is dependent upon evolution," he explained, "but Huxley disagreed with this. . . . In Huxley's treatment, living according to *reason* was the accepted doctrine. Huxley maintained that the individual should aid his fellows."[65] In Meiklejohn's view, Darwinism overlooked the necessity of individual moral responsibility—the categorical imperative—in a modern, secular, industrial world; therefore, it was invalid as a social, political, or economic doctrine. Like Lester Frank Ward, a prominent evolutionary theorist who later joined the faculty at Brown, Meiklejohn believed that the true aim of philosophy, or "sociology" in Ward's case, was to understand the connections between mind and matter and, ultimately, to demonstrate the power of reason *over* nature. The essence of humanity was its capacity for rational, and thus ethical, behavior.

As a graduate student, Meiklejohn did not devote himself full time to his philosophical studies. He reserved plenty of time for sports, including tennis, soccer, squash, lacrosse, and ice polo. In the summers of 1893 and 1894, for example, he served as captain of the Pawtucket Cricket Club, in which capacity he distinguished himself as "the greatest bowler who ever stepped up to a wicket in Providence."[66] Unfortunately, cricket and philosophy did not mix. After two years of championship play, Professor Seth advised Meiklejohn to devote less energy to sports and more to studying. "Jimmie finally decided that the sportive atmosphere of Providence and Pawtucket was more favorable to cricket and football than to metaphysics," Meiklejohn explained in a letter to his old roommate Ladd, "so, after gently reproaching me, he sent me to Cornell."[67] In September of 1895, having completed his master's degree in philosophy at Brown, Meiklejohn left the familiar surroundings of Providence and traveled to the recently opened Sage School of Philosophy at Cornell, where James Seth had just been hired as the Sage Professor of Moral Philosophy. Despite a heavy workload, Meiklejohn still made time for recreation, especially ice polo.[68] In 1897, he joined several other ice polo players in a series of exhibition matches in Canada and, as it turned out, played a large role in introducing the new game of hockey to American intercollegiate athletics. "The Canadian trip had its inception at Niagara Falls," he later recalled, "when Canadian and United States tennis players had some days together there in a tournament." When the tennis players discussed their favorite winter sports, they discovered that they played somewhat different games on ice. "Out of that talk," Meiklejohn noted, "came the invitation for an intercollegiate team to go to four Canadian cities (Montreal, Ottawa, Kingston, and Toronto) and play both games." The Canadians won all four games of hockey and two of the four games of ice polo, and, Meiklejohn admitted, "it was pretty generally agreed among us that the Canadian game was better than ours."[69] A year later, in 1898, Brown faced off against Harvard in the first intercollegiate hockey game in the United States, and the Bears—led by Meiklejohn—beat the Crimson six goals to none.

Somehow, in between tennis matches and hockey games, Meiklejohn managed to pass his qualifying exams at Cornell and finish a 153-page hand-written dissertation titled "Kant's Theory of Substance."[70] After graduating with his Ph.D., he started to look for a teaching job, and President Andrews once again came to his aid.[71] "When the time came that I was out in the world once more, again old Benny took me in and gave me a chance to teach Logic and Metaphysics," Meiklejohn wrote to Ladd.[72] In the fall of 1897, he accepted a position as assistant professor in the philosophy department at Brown. He taught several courses, including "Logic," "An Introduction to Philosophy," "Scientific Methods," "Discussions in Casu-

Alexander Meiklejohn, in spectacles in front, and members of the Brown University ice polo team, 1894 (Brown University Archives)

istry," and, no doubt his favorite, "Kantian and Post-Kantian Philoso-phy."[73] In this last course, Meiklejohn devoted an entire term to the first hundred pages of the *Critique of Pure Reason,* including the difficult "De-duction of the Categories," which he considered the heart of Kant's work. As Arthur Upham Pope, an undergraduate who took every one of Meikle-john's courses, later remembered, students in this grueling course spent weeks grinding through Kant's treatise but "were rewarded when the ex-citing conclusion, which [Meiklejohn] made them earn, finally emerged, formulated with his contagious exultation and deep feeling: 'mind builds the world.'" It was "a simple phrase," Pope acknowledged, "but how deep!"[74] As a young professor, Meiklejohn quickly distinguished himself as one of the best instructors on campus. He avoided lectures, preferring instead to engage his students in Socratic debate. "He loved to stimulate the minds of young men," another student later recalled, "and our course in 'Logic' with him at Maxcy Hall was an unforgettable experience. He would stand before us—slender, smiling, his hands in his pockets or tug-ging at his lapels—and he would deal with us according to the pattern which Plato of Athens describes. Like Socrates, Dr. Meiklejohn was an in-tellectual 'gadfly.'"[75]

When he taught, Meiklejohn focused on the lessons he had learned in his own education at Brown, foremost among them the need for a secular system of ethical values in a skeptical scientific world. As one student explained, Meiklejohn's course in logic, taken by hundreds of undergraduates and known as Rag-Chewing 19, was "essentially a search for a definition of truth as the ultimate term of the intellectual life and the touchstone of all thinking. The underlying purpose is to show the inadequacy of the scientific interpretation of the world and to indicate the more fundamental insights of philosophy and religion." To many, it appeared that Meiklejohn was "a religious man to the core," whose teaching found "its climax and final purpose in laying the groundwork of well-reasoned religion." And, in some sense, such observations were true.[76] Meiklejohn did believe in the need for authoritative moral guidelines to teach people how to live compatibly together, and he insisted on the transcendental quality of true virtue. Yet, he found the origins of morality in reason, *not* in religious faith per se. He was a student of ethics, not theology. Indeed, his minister, the Reverend Frank Goodwin, admired him not so much for his apparently religious convictions as for his warm and friendly personality. "Affable in manner, he at once gives you the impression of sincerity, intelligence, and strength," Goodwin recalled. "When you address him, you feel that he is so fair and courteous a listener, so impartial and open-minded, that propositions which spring from folly, self-interest, or prejudice falter on your lips. His clear, frank eyes penetrate without piercing. You are aware that you are in the presence of a man of kind and friendly spirit, who has no ready professional artillery to level against those who do not agree with him, but who, in his sanity and manly strength, desires to have others see the truth as he sees it."[77]

Goodwin's comments captured one of Meiklejohn's central character traits. As he settled into his first teaching position, Meiklejohn did indeed desire to have others see the truth his way, and he expended a great deal of energy to ensure that they would. Always eager to hear a different point of view, he was equally eager to prove the rightness of his own. He was catholic in his openness to new ideas but critical in his evaluations of their merit. Like Socrates, he believed his chief responsibility as a teacher was to foster students' capacity for rational deliberation, to *teach* them to be intellectually "free." In his view, reason did not evolve out of nowhere in the minds of young students. Rather, it developed in response to examples of reasonable behavior and reasonable discourse in the world. In Kantian terms, reason followed its own example, which meant that it apprehended itself as both a subject and an object in the world. As Meiklejohn later

31

wrote, a "student's attitude toward scholarship is simply an expression of his estimate of the men who represent scholarship in the world of his acquaintance."[78] And Meiklejohn strove tirelessly to embody this ideal. As a young professor at Brown, he continually tested the implications of his Kantian idealist philosophy in his own teaching and, increasingly, sought to apply his academic training to the broader problems of American higher education at large.

2

"College Education and the Moral Ideal"

1900–1911

A S AN ASSISTANT PROFESSOR and handsome bachelor in his late twenties, Meiklejohn was all that an up-and-coming academic professional could be at the turn of the century. Well educated and gainfully employed, he earned a salary that was almost as high as his six brothers' annual wages combined. Certainly, he had come a long way from his working-class childhood in Pawtucket, but he had not forgotten his roots. After graduate school, he moved back into his parents' house and contributed the bulk of his income to his family while commuting to his office at Brown. Though he apparently splurged on a short trip to Italy in 1899, he soon returned to his hometown and joined the local school board, winning by a substantial majority a seat formerly held by his father.[1] And yet, by 1900, his personal and professional horizons began to stretch beyond the boundaries of Rhode Island. In the fall of 1901, he became a charter member of the American Philosophical Association, one of several new professional societies then bringing academics and nonacademics together for the sake of scholarly collaboration. Like the American Historical Association, the American Economic Association, and the American Psychological Association, each of which emerged in the last decades of the nineteenth century, the American Philosophical Association created opportunities for academic cooperation on a national, or at least a regional, scale. Although the membership of the new association was still small, young Meiklejohn took full advantage of the personal and professional network it provided.

In 1901, together with his colleague Walter Goodnow Everett, Meiklejohn attended the inaugural meeting of the American Philosophical Association in New York. James E. Creighton, a philosopher from Brown who had recently joined the Sage School of Philosophy at Cornell, presided.[2] Others in attendance included William James and John Dewey, the two greatest luminaries in the field of American philosophy at the time. Meiklejohn remembered his first encounter with the eminent Dewey at an association conference in 1902. "I still remember with gratitude and affection his kindness to me when I much needed it," Meiklejohn recalled. "I had just read my first paper at a meeting of the then newly-formed American Philosophical Association, and was wandering about with all of a tyro's lack of assurance that the paper was worth giving. At that point, John Dewey put his hand on my shoulder and invited me, with a few others, to his room. I fear he hadn't much to say in appreciation of the paper, but he did give me the sense that I was not disowned, that I was one of the crowd. His gentleness and friendliness at that time gave me one of my most treasured memories."[3] By the turn of the century, Meiklejohn had taken his first tentative steps into a widening group of educational and philosophical associates. Although he was still quite young, he grew increasingly familiar with the leading figures in American philosophy, a small cadre whose work he assiduously read and—at least in the case of pragmatists such as James and Dewey—often criticized.

In the summer of 1901, just as Meiklejohn was beginning to participate in the activities of this broader community of scholars, his career took an unexpected turn. On a visit to the vacation home of Brown's new president, W. H. P. Faunce, who had replaced E. Benjamin Andrews in 1899, Meiklejohn received an invitation to serve his alma mater as dean. The position, created less than two years before, became available when the first dean fell ill, and Faunce thought Meiklejohn the perfect candidate for the job. But Meiklejohn did not immediately accept Faunce's offer, which implied a shift in focus from teaching to administration. At the turn of the century, deans were still relatively rare in American higher education. Where they existed, they worked mainly as disciplinarians and deputies when presidents were away, or, in the case of affiliated women's colleges like Harvard's Radcliffe or Brown's Pembroke, they supervised the work of all female students. Given that Meiklejohn's teaching career was only three years old, he took several weeks to weigh his decision. He did not want to cut back on his classes, nor did he want to lose contact with the wider community of scholars. As he wrote to his old friend Ladd, "[M]y deepest interest has been and will continue to be . . . the problems

34

and principles of philosophy," but, at the same time, he was eager for the chance to apply his philosophical training to broader institutional policies.[4] Perhaps it was the substantial salary increase that led him, in the fall of 1901, at the age of twenty-nine, to accept the title of dean of men at Brown.[5] Whatever clinched his decision, it was well received. In a front-page story, the *Providence Journal-Bulletin* predicted great success for the newly appointed dean. "He seems to feel a lively interest in all student enterprises," the paper reported, "and is probably one of the most influential members of the faculty with that body."[6] Indeed, as Meiklejohn's success in the dean's office quickly proved, he had an extraordinary talent for dealing with undergraduates. The fact that he was only a few years older than most Brown students probably contributed much to his popularity.

A few months after Meiklejohn's promotion, the *Providence Journal-Bulletin* had even more exciting news to report: the dean was engaged to be married. On June 14, 1902, following a long-distance courtship of at least three years, Meiklejohn married Nannine Annaletta La Villa at her family's home in Orange, New Jersey.[7] Nannine, the daughter of a wealthy Italian father and an English mother, Paolo and Adelaide La Villa, met Meiklejohn at Cornell, where she had studied art, literature, and music as an undergraduate.[8] It was Nannine who had inspired Meiklejohn to visit Europe in 1899. As Meiklejohn later told the story, "[T]here was a girl in the academic department at Cornell when I was there, with whom, if I remember rightly, I studied on several occasions the beautiful country which surrounds the university. Strangely enough, we met again in Florence in 1899, and there made a systematic study of the treasures of the Old World city."[9] After graduating from Cornell, Nannine had taken a job as an elementary school teacher at the Balliol School in Utica, New York. She adored children and wrote children's books as a hobby.[10] In the summer of 1902, after their wedding, Meiklejohn and his bride moved into a small house on Waterman Street in Providence.[11] In 1907, they celebrated the birth of their first son, Kenneth, who soon shared the house with two younger brothers, Donald, who arrived in 1909, and Gordon, who came in 1911. The children were as happy, active, and precocious as their father had been as a boy growing up in Rochdale. In between philosophy classes and administrative duties, Meiklejohn taught his sons to play sports, particularly hockey. "My interest in hockey was so keen," he later recalled, "that, as soon as my three boys could stand on their feet securely, I got them on skates and tried to teach them the game. Perhaps I had better luck there than in teaching philosophy."[12] Meiklejohn kept extremely busy with his various

Alexander Meiklejohn as dean of Brown University, ca. 1902 (Brown University Archives)

responsibilities at Brown, but he enjoyed nothing more than spending time with his family.

As dean, Meiklejohn continued to teach his famous course in logic, which received rave reviews from students. The most engaging aspect of Meiklejohn's teaching was his ability to make philosophy seem relevant to the lives of undergraduates. Whether he was teaching Socrates or Kant, he inspired his students to think, and think hard, about the moral and intellectual implications of everyday behavior. As one student remarked, he was able to translate the "remote abstractions of Aristotelian logic" into meaningful debates on "vital personal and contemporary college and public questions," including such critical issues as baseball, fraternities, drinking, and girls.[13] With his rimless spectacles perched high on his narrow nose, his starched collar buttoned tightly around his thin neck, and his impeccable cravats tucked neatly inside pressed suits, Meiklejohn may not have looked the part of a modish professor. But, if he did not at first win his students' admiration in class, he certainly won their respect on the cricket field, the hockey rink, or the tennis court. Just as he used philosophy to teach the moral significance of contemporary issues, so, too, he used sports to sharpen his students' moral sensibilities and ethical sense of fair play. For Meiklejohn, physical and intellectual contests were very much alike in their dependence on a basic respect for the rules of the game. Both required mutual agreement to set the terms and boundaries of human conflict, and both revealed the need for shared standards in the construction and preservation of a self-governing community. For Meiklejohn, both sports and philosophy functioned as substitutes for real battles that might otherwise divide, or even destroy, a democratic college community, which was precisely the sort of community he endeavored to create at Brown.

As dean, Meiklejohn had diverse administrative duties, but one preceded all others: admissions and financial aid.[14] No other activity had a more direct impact on the creation of a democratic community at Brown.[15] Between 1870 and 1900, the number of college students in the United States nearly quadrupled, rising from 62,000 to 232,000.[16] In the last decade of the nineteenth century, enrollments jumped more than 90 percent.[17] This rapid increase, attributable to a growth in population, a rise in general affluence, and a steady professionalization of the work force, had a dramatic effect on college admissions. As the number of applicants grew, institutions began to devise ways to limit the number of students they admitted. In 1900, Nicholas Murray Butler, president of Columbia University, along with several other college and university administrators, estab-

Alexander Meiklejohn with his cricket bat, ca. 1911 (Brown University Archives)

lished the College Entrance Examination Board, which wrote, distributed, and scored national standardized university entrance exams. According to the members of the college board, standardized entrance exams were designed to ensure the "intellectual homogeneity," and thus the efficiency and productivity, of the learning environment.[18] As dean at Brown, Meiklejohn supported standardized exams and endorsed the need for intellectual homogeneity in the student body. "The one advantage of the teacher over every other speaker in the world," he wrote while dean, "is that he can count on the intellectual homogeneity of his audience."[19] But Meiklejohn did not equate intellectual homogeneity with intellectual conformity. In his view, the great danger of standardized exams was their tendency to stress arbitrary information and particular facts over more general mental habits and a genuine desire to learn. Intellectual homogeneity did not necessarily mean the mastery of certain academic subjects; it simply meant that all students should aspire to the highest levels of intellectual achievement.

For Meiklejohn, intellectual motivation was the *only* legitimate criterion for assessing a student's fitness for college. Neither race nor religion nor economic status was relevant to the admissions process. As dean, he carefully and consistently distinguished between students whose intellectual and personal shortcomings were "due to their own stupidity or neglect" and students whose weaknesses were due "not to their own fault but to some external hindrance or disadvantage, as, for example, coming from a school which is poorly equipped or which does not conform to the demands of our system of admission, or from study in an evening school." When it came to college admissions, he advised greater severity for the former group and greater leniency for the latter. "I should like to see admission refused to a boy who has had opportunity to obtain his credits in school and has failed to do so even in a single subject," he asserted. "On the other hand, we can well afford to give a chance to a man who really wants an education and is willing to fight for it."[20] Recalling his own working-class background, Meiklejohn adamantly defended the need to admit poor students to Brown. At a time when tuition cost $150, and living expenses, including gas heat and servants' wages, ranged from $130 to $300 annually, the typical student spent about $325 a year to attend Brown. While the wealthiest families in Rhode Island still sent their sons to Harvard or Yale, working families more often sent their academically talented sons to Brown. As Meiklejohn later recalled, "many students were from working-class backgrounds," and he liked it that way.[21]

Nearly half of Brown's undergraduates received financial aid, which Meiklejohn, as dean, disbursed.[22] Usually, student aid took the form of university scholarships, which covered either full or partial tuition.[23] Between 1900 and 1910, approximately half of each class received such aid.[24] Many students also held campus jobs as laboratory assistants, chapel monitors, office aides, choir members, library proctors, or gymnasium attendants.[25] As dean, Meiklejohn received dozens of letters from students needing financial aid. "Having a strong desire to take up a scientific course at college, but not having the means with which to do so," one typical letter began, "I would like to know whether I could obtain sufficient assistance, by way of scholarships, work, or postponement of payment of tuition. . . . As to ability for earning money, I am an experienced stenographer and typewriter, understand bookkeeping, and am thoroughly familiar with general office work. I might also make some money by singing."[26] Often, secondary schools requested scholarships for promising students. A

39

headmaster from suburban Philadelphia informed Meiklejohn that his school had 321 separate scholarships—mostly from Swarthmore, Haverford, Bryn Mawr, and the University of Pennsylvania—at its disposal.[27] A principal from Washington, D.C., however, found himself in a different position. Such scholarships were not available to his students because all of them were black. "To none of the scholarships granted are the children of the colored high school eligible," he explained. "As principal of the colored school I feel that the possibility of acquiring a scholarship in college would be an inspiration to many a worthy lad who already has aspirations in that direction but possibly sees no open doors."[28] Meiklejohn assured this principal that black students were indeed eligible for scholarships at Brown.

Especially in times of economic hardship, a significant number of Brown students worked outside the university in order to cover their expenses. One student described his exhausting work schedule in a note to Meiklejohn. "I worked as a ticket collector on the Colonial Line which docked at the Point Street Bridge," he explained. "The hours were 6:00 to 8:15 a.m., and I had to get up at 5:00 every morning in order to arrive at the dock at 5:50 a.m. I had to go down seven days a week. I received $3.50 a week and breakfasts for this work. On my return from the boat, I stopped at a house on Congdon Street where I tended furnace. I would get to school just in time for chapel and sometimes would have to hustle real hard to make it and would sometimes miss your Logic class, too. I waited on table at noon and at night, and at 8:15 p.m. I assisted a nurse put an old invalid to bed and also attended her furnace. For this I received $2.50 a week. I also attended a large furnace at the fraternity house where I lived, and this had to be looked at perhaps six times a day. At 9:15 p.m. I felt tired enough to retire, as I generally did, for if I were to sit down and try to concentrate my attention on my books, I invariably dozed and fell asleep. So, under these circumstances you can readily see that I didn't have much time for real serious study or for doing much work in the library."[29] Meiklejohn, who was familiar with such struggles, tried to provide the means for poor students to attend Brown, even if they did not always succeed. Some of his students withdrew from college at their parents' request. Others quit to seek more remunerative employment opportunities. Still others never even considered attending college, finding it irrelevant to their professional pursuits. Yet, when it came to selective admissions and financial aid, Meiklejohn recognized that the very possibility of a democratic college community was at stake.

Meiklejohn's duties as dean extended beyond the realm of admissions, financial aid, and curriculum organization to the realm of student conduct. After admissions, discipline had the most direct impact on the creation of a self-governing democracy at Brown. Indeed, disciplinary actions took more of Meiklejohn's time than any other responsibility. One example of his work as disciplinarian was his memorable intervention to stop the daily postchapel scuffle between freshman and sophomores. The melee usually started when a gauntlet of sophomores formed to terrorize freshmen as they exited Sayles Hall. "As time went on," one student recalled, "the custom became more boisterous until finally it included holding the great oaken doors against the freshmen and led to a daily free-for-all fight on the chapel steps." Brown's older faculty smiled indulgently on these antics, but Meiklejohn was determined to end the raucous tradition once and for all. "As the straining and shouting sophomores pressed madly against the doors," an alumnus later recounted, "there came a sudden lull in the opposing pressure from within. Suspecting a trick the sophomores waited and then fell back. The high doors opened and a small wiry figure, bespectacled and scholarly with blazing eyes and set jaw, appeared on the top step. The Dean! Not a word was said. No word was necessary, for, as if by magic, the storming hordes melted away in all directions."[30] Meiklejohn did not relish his role as disciplinarian, but he was capable of stern control, especially in cases of public rowdiness.[31] The *Providence Journal-Bulletin* related one such incident in 1902, when students drenched a group of local boys as they collected coins thrown out of dormitory windows. "Their eagerness for the pennies and the complimentary cheers from spectators continued to amuse them until Dean Meiklejohn appeared on the scene and requested the students to desist. The lads with dripping garments retreated when they realized that an official was among them, but they had scarcely reached the gate when more water accidentally fell from the windows. Quick as a flash the Dean darted into the building and up to the rooms from which the water came. The remainder of the entertainment was private, and perhaps the end is not yet."[32]

As such stories indicated, students at the turn of the century searched constantly for novel ways to display their adolescent enthusiasms among their peers. In 1907, one undergraduate wrote Meiklejohn to suggest an alternative to the freshman-sophomore "scrap," which had a reputation for being a yearly bloody brawl. The proposal called instead for a "bowl-rush," an activity recently made popular at the University of Pennsylvania. As the student explained, a large wooden bowl, about two feet in diameter, would be placed in the center of a field with freshmen and sophomores stationed at either end. At a given signal, the two classes would rush together for possession of the bowl, and the class with the most hands on the bowl would win. Best of all, the student noted, "the fighting may take place where there is little danger of damaging property, and, if it is not desirable to have the townspeople as spectators, it may take place in an enclosed field."[33] Often, student rowdiness resulted in serious damage to both person and property. Bonfires, especially, destroyed chairs, doors, carts, tables, boxes, beds, bureaus, brooms, bookcases, coat racks, stepladders, and countless other wooden objects stolen from college buildings. In 1908, a bonfire on the night of the interclass basketball game caused damage amounting to $20.32. This figure was small, however, compared with the $132.70 in damage caused by a fire on a similar occasion a year earlier.[34] As dean, Meiklejohn did not allow such behavior to go unpunished. If the offenses were not severe enough to warrant suspensions or expulsions, he at least demanded written apologies from those who broke the rules. "In behalf of the Class of 1914," submitted one penitent student, "we wish to offer our apologies to you and to those members of the faculty whose classes were disturbed by the disorderly actions of the class on Wednesday, March 7th, and we wish to assure you that a like disorder will not occur in the future."[35] Discipline, like philosophy and sports, gave Meiklejohn an opportunity to teach the virtues of morality, order, and self-control.

As dean, Meiklejohn earned a solid reputation for fairness in his dealings with students. In his president's report of 1905, President Faunce praised "the devoted labors of Dean Meiklejohn, who, by his rare insight into student attitude and opinion, his close sympathy with student needs, and his unflinching resolve to hold students to the highest ideals, has achieved results which are of lasting value."[36] Faunce was not alone in his appreciation of Meiklejohn's work as dean. "Of all the cases of discipline that have occurred during Dean Meiklejohn's long service," commented a member of Brown's class of 1910, "not one student has been punished on merely circumstantial evidence and against his own protest. You can realize that the dean is no ordinary Justice-of-the-Police-Court." Furthermore, the student noted, "the one or two boys whom I have known and who were suspended by the dean's order are (and were at the time of suspension) among those most eager to acknowledge the brilliancy of his logical powers, the vigorous justice of his decisions, but, most of all, the warm and sympathetic understanding and encouragement of his thoroughly likable character."[37] Charles Evans Hughes, Jr., son of the future secretary of state, agreed. "He takes a warm a personal interest in the students at Brown," Hughes wrote. "He assumes toward them—and demands from them—an attitude of perfect frankness on all matters, and their feeling that he understands them causes them to meet him half way."[38] As dean, Meiklejohn demanded obedience to the rules of the college, but tried, as he put it, to reason with those who strayed from the path of virtue. He always listened to students' side of the story and, when punishment was necessary, never risked the appearance of arbitrary or despotic power. The ideal form of discipline, in his mind, was *self*-government, even if students had to *learn* the ways of democracy before they could practice them on their own.

Nothing tested Meiklejohn's faith in student self-government more than intercollegiate athletics. It was not difficult to trace rambunctious student behavior back to the playing fields, where lawlessness and violence reigned. Football, in particular, provided ample opportunities for fighting and brutality. One perceptive mother, inquiring about the source of her son's failing grades, wrote to the dean for an explanation. "What is the cause?" she cried to Meiklejohn. "Is he not applying himself, or is he not capable, or is it the Murdering Football that is the cause of it?"[39] Many parents were quick to blame football for the disintegration of ethical standards among undergraduates, and the onus was not misplaced. A typical turn-of-the-century headline in the *Brown Daily Herald* read "Brown 6; Manhattan 5; in a Game Marred by Unsportsmanlike Conduct." Describing the savage contest, the paper told readers that "there was no limit to the scrapping." Manhattan's goal "seemed to be to play as dirty a game as was possible. Slugging, kicking, kneeing, and every trick known in football to injure players seemed to be at their command."[40] In 1903, Brown's football manager noted the futility of matches against the not-so-saintly College of the Holy Cross. "The game gives Brown no standing," he declared. "It is not even a practice game, it is more like a free fight as far as respect of rules is concerned. I have seen the past three or four games and the 1901 game was the worst of all. The wrangling and delays were disgusting to both spectators and players."[41] More than any other student activity, intercollegiate athletics challenged the personal virtue and moral integrity so central to Meiklejohn's ideal of a democratic college community.

Corruption ran rampant in intercollegiate athletics at the turn of the century. So strong was the desire to win that coaches took extraordinary steps to recruit talented athletes from strong secondary school teams. In 1904, R. W. Swetland, the headmaster of the Peddie School in New Jersey, informed Meiklejohn that, "only last week, our best football player was kidnapped by the University of Pennsylvania coach." Swetland went on to declare that "the same boy had been offered at Princeton a summer's board and tutoring, together with all expenses the following year at college, if he would come there next year. One can imagine what the U. of P. man must have offered!"[42] Similarly, M. H. Buckham, president of the University of Vermont, told Meiklejohn that he was "currently dealing with a case of forged entrance papers to secure membership for a star football player."[43] By the winter of the following year, Archibald Freeman, the director of athletics at Phillips Academy in Andover, Massachusetts, urged Meiklejohn to exercise his moral authority over his athletes. "The greatest evil of the situation of recent years," Freeman complained, "has been the impossibility of enforcing rules, and consequently lowering the moral sense of the college boys, who are willing to evade a rule if they can do so without discovery. I believe that the athletic feeling is altogether too intense, and there is too great a desire to win."[44] Meiklejohn agreed with Freeman and vociferously opposed the corruption of college sports, especially the aggressive recruitment tactics used to attract talented athletes. Athletic recruitment, he protested, was "an evil harmful alike to the schoolboy and to the college man," not least because it undermined the basic spirit of amateurism in undergraduate sports.[45]

In Meiklejohn's view, the corruption of amateur athletics was especially obvious in the case of "summer ball." *Summer ball* referred, quite simply, to the practice of playing baseball during the summer for pay. In the late nineteenth and early twentieth centuries, seaside resorts and other businesses sponsored professional and semiprofessional baseball teams and arranged for them to play exhibition games throughout the summer for advertising purposes. The players, outfitted with matching uniforms and supplied with room and board, earned extra money to apply toward their university tuition. A number of Brown students played summer ball. In August of 1903, for instance, an executive with the Caledonian Insurance Company on Cape Cod wrote to Meiklejohn asking if he could employ Brown's best pitcher and best batter on his summer team.[46] A few days earlier, the *Boston Globe* had listed dozens of students from universities all over New England who played summer ball in semiprofessional leagues and then returned to their college teams with skills greatly sharpened.[47] From coast to coast, hundreds of college students supported themselves and paid their educational expenses by playing summer ball. When these students donned their college colors in the fall, however, they faced a barrage of accusations for being professional players on amateur university teams. Summer ball, critics cried, promoted the professionalization—and, even more regrettably, the commercialization—of intercollegiate athletics.

In January of 1904, the conflict between professionalism and amateurism in college sports erupted in controversy. The previous season, Brown's baseball team, which included several summer ball players, won the New England baseball championship. But, when Brown's opponents discovered that the undefeated team had ignored the university's own rule debarring professionals from its athletic teams, they declared the championship invalid. Brown, in turn, insisted that its athletes had not done anything that other schools' athletes had not done also. Unwilling to relinquish its hard-won victory, Brown opted simply to repeal its rule against summer ball. "Practically every Brown man from the president down to the youngest undergraduate has, after years of experiment and careful consideration, come to the conclusion that the rule is impracticable," Brown's athletic committee stated. "Its enforcement is a farce and results merely in hypocrisy and deception, thereby inculcating a low standard of morality in the student body."[48] Within days of the committee's decision, newspapers across the nation printed editorials criticizing Brown for letting professionals masquerade as amateurs.[49] Meiklejohn, as dean, received scores of letters from alumni who were embarrassed by the university's action. "The implication of the story," one alumnus complained, "is that the Brown faculty does not dare to enforce its own rules against the prominent athlete. Of course nothing could bring the college authorities into greater contempt among thinking men, and among the students themselves in the long run."[50] Another alumnus wrote all the way from Honolulu to express his anger and dismay. "I sincerely hope that some measure will be taken to prevent the suicidal policy determined on by the committee and that a team will be turned into the field this spring, every member of which is a bona fide amateur, undefiled by any taint of professionalism. For, most certainly, last season's victory was the hollowest and most disgraceful imaginable."[51] Clearly, the professionalization of university athletics had struck a nerve with alumni, many of whom thought Brown should provide a refuge from the commercialism that was becoming increasingly pervasive in American life.

The editors of the *Brown Alumni Monthly* similarly denounced athletic commercialization as a most regrettable state of affairs. "Intercollegiate games are advertised on every blank wall and on every street car," they noted, adding contemptuously that "an admission fee is charged at the gate *and* at the grandstand." Observing that Yale's Athletic Association netted more than fifty thousand dollars in profits in 1903, they pointed an accusatory finger back at Brown. "It was considered, a year ago, that the Brown football season had been successful hardly more because the eleven had won many of its games than because the enterprising manager had closed the year with a large financial surplus." Practically bursting with moral outrage, the editors declared, "COLLEGE ATHLETICISM IS BECOMING TOO MUCH OF A BUSINESS!"[52] And Meiklejohn agreed. As dean, he sat on Brown's athletic committee but did not support its decision to revoke the amateur rule. Shortly after the committee released its statement regarding the impracticability of the amateur code, he resigned his seat in protest.[53] In his mind, the *practicability* of the amateur ideal was the very crux of the issue. Even if a majority of athletes broke the antiprofessional rule, he maintained, it was still a virtuous rule, and as such, it was deserving of the university's heartiest support. As Meiklejohn's fellow dissenter, Professor John E. Hill, put it, "[H]owever far beyond our reach an ideal may be, constant striving cannot possibly work for evil. The spirit of amateurism must ever remain the guiding star in the college athletic firmament."[54] If the university could not stand up for its own ideals simply because they seemed impracticable, then the university had nothing of value to teach its students.

In 1905, the nationwide controversy surrounding intercollegiate athletics climaxed with the game-related deaths of 18 players and the serious injuries of more than 150 others. That winter, Meiklejohn addressed the subject of corrupt athletics in an article for *Harper's Weekly* magazine. Pointing to the evasion of athletic rules as a source of grave moral concern, he asserted that, "if games are to be played, then there must obviously be some agreement between the competitors as to the conditions of the contest. It is a lamentable fact that these agreements are not kept with loyalty nor even with honesty." Student athletes not only lied about their professional status but also broke the rules of the game. Too often, Meiklejohn observed, "players are taught by their coaches to win, and they are encouraged and directed to win by unfair means if fair means fail. The war is made *real war,* and the generous rivalry of a friendly contest is lost from sight in the spirit which tries to 'rattle the pitcher,' to 'put a good man out of the game,' to 'block a runner' or to 'drown the signals' by well-timed cheering. Such tactics are mean and ungenerous. In their pettiness, they are often more distressing than deliberate unfairness and deceit."[55] In Meiklejohn's view, cheating undermined the democratic spirit of undergraduate games. More specifically, such blatant disregard for the rules jeopardized the very idea of a self-governing college community. Inasmuch as democracy depended on a voluntary acceptance of common standards of virtue and behavior, Meiklejohn expected students to obey the rules of fair play. In his view, the playing field was a metaphor for the good society, a training ground where shared moral values and a unified effort promised to hold the entire system together.

Cheating, however, was merely the tip of the iceberg. As Meiklejohn saw it, the most pernicious evil of all was the tendency of intercollegiate athletics to commercialize the university. "In these recent years," he proclaimed, intercollegiate athletics "has been exalted to a place in the general university policy—it has become a *method of advertising*. Winning teams pay, we are told; they attract students, and with more students come better athletes, and so the fame and welfare of alma mater are assured. In this scheme of athletics, the aim must be not clean manly sport, but victories. This is the evil which is most fundamental, most subtle, most dangerous of all." Not just a source of physical exercise or intercollegiate rivalry, Meiklejohn argued, athletics had become a source of profit. Universities had begun to value athletes over scholars, to pursue immediate financial gains over long-term educational objectives, to cater to practicability and popular appeal over the ethical virtue of the amateur code. The only possible solution to this problem, he surmised, was to take control of athletics away from corrupt coaches and college administrators and give it back to the students. "The undergraduates should be given control of their own games," he boldly argued. "It should be recognized that, if this cannot be done, the justification for the existence of the games is gone." If students could not agree among themselves to obey the rules—indeed, if students could not agree among themselves what the rules should be—then the democratic spirit of the entire college was dead. A student-run athletic board, he argued, would "give for the first time a definite scheme of intercollegiate cooperation; it would render evasion impossible by placing control in the hand of those who know the facts; it would appeal to a student's sense of loyalty to a voluntary agreement."[56] Only student self-government could overcome the corruption and commercialization of intercollegiate sports.

Meiklejohn could demonstrate his disgust with commercialized athletics by resigning his committee seat and publishing his views, but he still had to resolve the matter administratively among the undergraduates at Brown, and it was here that his talent as a teacher truly showed. Rather than declaring an edict in opposition to summer ball, he took a more idealistic, and far more democratic, approach: he called a college meeting. To prove his commitment to the principles of self-government, he shed his role as dean and attended the meeting as if he were just another student. When he arrived, he faced a clamorous and hostile majority. He spoke softly, calmly, and carefully, trying to convince the students that the baseball team should uphold the amateur rule and return its championship trophy. He built his case on the solitary principle of high honor, arguing that a rule, once established, should not be broken, neglected, or rescinded at the very moment when its revocation would give Brown an advantage. In the future, he acknowledged, the amateur rule could be changed by a democratic vote. For the time being, however, it had to stay. "As a result of this and other meetings," the *Boston Transcript* reported, "college opinion was reversed and the rule was enforced and, as a graduate writes of the period of the conflict, 'I had my first lesson in standing by a principle.'" Over time, Meiklejohn's college gatherings, which resembled New England town meetings in their openness to deliberation and their commitment to settling disagreements by consensus, became legendary among Brown's undergraduates. "Issue after issue has been settled in this fashion," the *Transcript* said.[57] While some viewed Meiklejohn's college meetings as an occasion for personal coercive authority, most realized that they provided a forum for collective moral suasion in the college community, a technique otherwise known as democratic education.

For a full year, Brown students voluntarily enforced the principle of amateur athletics, even after the repeal of the university's official rule. Then, in the fall of 1906, Meiklejohn carried student self-government to its logical conclusion by turning control of intercollegiate athletics completely over to the students. Almost immediately, they reversed their policy and elected to allow summer ball. Meiklejohn was shocked and disappointed by their decision, but he honored the democratic vote that had produced it. In his dean's report the following year, he reviewed the baseball controversy and highlighted the most recent—and in his view, unfortunate—turn of events. "There is undoubtedly room for question as to the wisdom of the student rule which allows the men to play baseball during the summer with the minor professional teams," he wrote. "On this latter point, we stand almost alone among our competitors. But the students in great majority believe heartily in the principle, and they are confident that students of other institutions are of the same mind. The principle is one for which the students have fought and suffered, and it is thus worthwhile—not only for its own sake, but also for the college world in general—that it should have a thorough trial."[58] Meiklejohn disagreed with his students' action, but he was determined to let it take its course. In 1908, he noted that Amherst, Wesleyan, and Williams had followed Brown's lead in accepting professional athletes, while Dartmouth

(Brown's archrival) had voted to keep the amateur code.[59] Concluding his dean's report of 1908, he quipped that "no one need complain that life is tame and lacking in entertainment while he has opportunity to watch this phase of the athletic situation with all its tragedies and oddities."[60]

For Meiklejohn, the controversy over summer ball had provided a unique opportunity to test his theory of democratic education. It gave him a chance to see whether liberal education could in fact *teach* students how to organize a self-governing community of their own. Although he was reluctant to admit it, his experiment with summer ball had produced mixed results. As soon as he had given the students the freedom to make their own choice, they had made what he considered to be a bad decision. Rather than upholding the amateur tradition, with its commitment to self-government in the form of unpaid players, unpaid coaches, and no material incentives to win, the students had opted for a professional code, with its focus on financial gains, rule breaking, and victory at any cost. In Meiklejohn's view, the students had made a democratic choice that served primarily to undermine the democratic spirit of intercollegiate sports. They had voted democratically to repudiate the democratic integrity of the college. It was a deeply sobering outcome for Meiklejohn's first experiment in the practice of democratic education, but it was an outcome he would experience time and again, not only in the context of higher education, but also in the context of American society at large. How could institutions of education create democracy if their students—indeed, their students *and* their faculty—were not innately inclined toward virtuous self-government and enforcing the rules of the game? How could education *teach* people to be free without undermining their freedom or autonomy in the process?

In the spring of 1908, Meiklejohn outlined his theory of democratic education in an important article for the progressive teachers' journal *Education*. The article, "College Education and the Moral Ideal," summarized much of what he had learned over the course of his first six years as dean. Perhaps more important, it revealed the ethical assumptions so clearly evident in his handling of summer ball. For Meiklejohn, the key to democratic self-government was voluntary adherence to "reasonable" standards of collective moral behavior. "It is assumed," he wrote, "that every human being has laid upon him the task of making a life and, further, that this may be done well or ill, nobly or ignobly, finely or coarsely, happily or unhappily, successfully or unsuccessfully." For Meiklejohn, living well meant living according to the ethical imperatives of reason, and he explicitly invoked Kant to clarify the meaning of this conviction. In the

Critique of Practical Reason, Meiklejohn explained, Kant gave two principles to guide a moral life. First was the principle of consistency, which demanded that human beings never contradict themselves in their moral choices. Second was the principle of generosity, which commanded that human beings always share whatever was good in the world. For Kant, these two principles were universal for all humanity. "If Kant be right concerning these forms," Meiklejohn asserted, "then they are not of his time, his race, or his people; they are the forms of human experience." The challenge was to cultivate these universal ethical principles among all people in a democratic community, even if each individual in the community was different. "While the forms of human living are universal," Meiklejohn acknowledged, "the content of each human life is and must be different from those of its fellows."[61] The challenge, therefore, was to teach the essential principles of ethical behavior without belying the fact of individual human diversity. But how?

How could institutions of democratic education teach diverse individuals the essential principles of an ethical life? "Is it not hopeless," Meiklejohn asked, "to attempt any common task of education, to strive after any common mode of living which is better than all others?" This was an extremely complex question—one that would continue to perplex Meiklejohn for more than thirty years. "I think it must be frankly admitted," he wrote in 1908, "that no such uniform education is possible. All that we can do for any man is to develop the interests and powers that are already latent within him." At first glance, it seemed that Meiklejohn's statement relinquished the possibility of universal ethical principles in a single unified curriculum. Yet, on closer examination, it became clear that his conception of interests already latent within a student was extraordinarily broad. In his view, every student possessed an innate interest in "the great impersonal universal things of human existence."[62] The challenge was to direct these latent interests toward the task of positive social change. At a time when most progressive educators stressed the need for social *service,* Meiklejohn emphasized the importance of active social *reform.* "If Kant is right," he concluded, "then the function of the college is not to do what it is told, but to study deeply into the art of living, to see what is needed in human experience, and to send men out instructed and inspired by the possession of the best things of which our human nature is capable." The purpose of liberal education, in other words, was to guide the interests and powers latent within each student toward the goal of progressive social change. "If the time shall ever come when our colleges must follow the world's directions as to its methods rather than lead the world to better things, if it shall come about that instead of teaching the world the college is instructed by it, if it shall come to pass that the college teacher is not big enough and strong enough to set up his own spiritual visions and by means of these to condemn that which is mean and unworthy, then the college will have ceased to do its work."[63] Here, in a nutshell, was Meiklejohn's vision of the ideal liberal college, an institution dedicated to moral instruction by democratic means.

By the time Meiklejohn published his article "College Education and the Moral Ideal" in 1908, the controversy over summer ball had given way to a different, but no less difficult, disciplinary concern at Brown, namely, the conduct of student-owned and student-run fraternities. The main problem with fraternities, Meiklejohn felt, was their tendency to isolate their members from the rest of the student body and thus to undermine the unity of the college as a whole. As a result, they exercised a profoundly disintegrating and undemocratic influence on the undergraduate community.[64] In 1909, after conducting a survey of twelve other colleges, Meiklejohn declared that fraternities at Brown must conform to the same social policies as applied to dormitories. "If gambling and drinking are prohibited on the campus," he wrote, "then they should [also] be kept out of the fraternity house; if persons not members of the college should be excluded from residence in the dormitories, then they should not stay in the fraternity houses; if sanitary regulations and the supervision of an accredited physician are essential in the one case, then they are equally essential in the other."[65] If fraternities disrupted the peace and tranquillity of the college as a whole, then the university had a right, even a responsibility, to interfere in their activities. While Meiklejohn regretted such intrusion in private student affairs, he nevertheless thought it justifiable in order to protect the democratic integrity of the college in general.[66] As he wrote in his dean's report of 1910, "[S]o far as interference with the private and social life of the students is necessary, as it certainly is in some cases, it should be regarded not as a thing good in itself, but as a necessary evil, that is, as a substitute for something worse."[67] When the private activities of individual students impinged on the public well-being of the college as a whole, then the rights of the rebellious students gave way to the right of the college to assert its own overarching moral authority.

Meiklejohn's criticism of fraternities was not limited to the housing issue. It extended also to fraternities' consistently inferior academic performance.[68] In the spring of 1910, he compiled a detailed report on the relative academic standings of students belonging to fraternities. In the process, he devised a primitive method for calculating grade-point averages. By translating the grades of H (honors), C (credit), P (pass), and F (fail) into the corresponding numbers of 3, 2, 1, and 0, Meiklejohn was able to compare grades numerically for the first time.[69] According to his numbers, eleven out of nineteen fraternities fell below the scholastic average at Brown.[70] Not surprisingly, the alumni of the fraternities protested Meiklejohn's study. The *Providence Journal-Bulletin* printed a long and contentious article headlined "Dean Meiklejohn's Findings Disputed: Alumni Combat Indictment Brought against Fraternities." The newspaper quoted one disgruntled Psi Upsilon pledge who attributed the fraternities' low rankings to recent increases in membership.[71] Meiklejohn, however, doubted the correlation between increased membership and decreased grade-point averages. Instead, he blamed the fraternities' poor performance on a distinctly anti-intellectual sentiment among their members. "The most serious defect of our American college life," he wrote, was "the lack of a genuine primary interest in things intellectual."[72] Far too many students lacked any genuine enthusiasm for academic work. "The man who tries my patience is not the one who has interests which distract him from his studies," Meiklejohn complained, perhaps recalling his own involvement with sports, "but the one who has no interests at all."[73] Such deficiencies in intellectual motivation—or volitional inadequacy, as Meiklejohn called it—put the very possibility of a self-governing community at risk.

Meiklejohn's criticism of fraternities, like his criticism of summer ball, did not endear him to Brown's older alumni. He received many angry letters denouncing his approach to fraternity life. Some considered him an intellectual snob. Others accused him of coddling only the smartest students on campus. Still others thought his moral standards were simply too high.[74] Few, however, disputed his fairness as an administrator. "His ability to discuss all questions with impersonal candor and rigorous thoroughness while keeping personal relations cordial and sympathetic is one of his best gifts," noted Professor Walter Everett. "Opposed to all hasty and impulsive action, insistent upon hearing all sides of a question, and inclined to delay a decision as long as possible in order that all the evidence may be at hand, he is perfectly fearless in carrying out a policy when his decision has finally been reached. Once convinced that he is right, he is able to pursue a course of action in the face of opposition and in total disregard of the cost to himself." And, in some cases, the personal costs of administrative action were high. Public criticism was a constant feature of Meiklejohn's tenure as dean. Some students thought him too strict in his use of authority, while others praised his strong sense of moral conviction. "In long years of disciplinary work, during which he has found himself in many trying situations," Professor Everett wrote, "I have never known him to draw back or hesitate because his personal fortunes might suffer loss or disaster. Like most strong men who are bent upon accomplishing something in which they profoundly believe, he is not anxious about his personal reputation or careful to justify his conduct."[75] Once convinced he was right, Meiklejohn did not back away from his goals.

In his ranking of fraternities, Meiklejohn acknowledged that some groups would inevitably rise to the top while others fell to the bottom. He insisted, however, that every fraternity should aspire to be the best so that all might cluster at the high end of the grading scale. Throughout his teaching career, Meiklejohn disagreed strongly with anyone who suggested that democracy and excellence were incompatible educational goals. He believed that every student should strive for perfection in all things, and it was for this reason that he took such an active interest in the Cammarian Club, Brown's honorary society for seniors. Each year, the Cammarians selected their successors from the brightest and most prominent students in the junior class. Meiklejohn often complimented the Cammarian Club for its fine work and academic achievements, but he questioned its distinctly undemocratic method of selecting new members. "There has always been and must continue to be serious question as to whether the essentially aristocratic organization of this club is compatible with its predominance in such a democratic community as that of our undergraduates," he noted in his dean's report of 1907. "Party cliques among the students or distrust of its elections will destroy its position by raising the democratic outcry against a self-perpetuating aristocracy."[76] Feeling the pressure of Meiklejohn's moral criticism, the Cammarian Club eventually voted to modify its election procedures. In his dean's report of 1910, Meiklejohn observed with satisfaction that future Cammarians would be elected not by exclusive vote of the seniors but rather by a general vote of the three lower classes. "The change is made," he proudly announced, "not so much in the hope of better selection of members, but with the desire to secure a stronger hold upon the democratic college community."[77]

By the end of the first decade of the century, Meiklejohn was increasingly well known in American higher education. In 1908, he received his first invitation to leave Brown—an invitation from Cornell to serve as dean of its recently established School of Education. Professor James Creighton, who knew Meiklejohn from meetings of the American Philosophical Association and taught in Cornell's Sage School of Philosophy, suggested Meiklejohn's name for the job. "There is certainly a big opportunity here for a man to do something for the cause of education,"

Creighton wrote to Meiklejohn. "If you could get interested in that kind of work, I am sure you could do it effectively. There would be a good deal of administrative and organizational work as well as teaching." Creighton told Cornell's trustees that Meiklejohn was an ideal candidate for the position—a man with "a practical temperament" who liked "to carry ideas into practice," a man with "good sense, tact, lots of good feeling, enthusiasm, and administrative experience."[78] Yet, despite the attraction of returning to the spectacular Finger Lakes region of upstate New York, Meiklejohn graciously declined Cornell's offer. "It would be hard to find a better place for such work as this than the one suggested in your note," he replied to Creighton, "but, on the other hand, it seems pretty evident both to me and to my friends that I am not best adapted for the task, at least in this form. My general interests seem pretty definitely fixed now as, first, the study and teaching of philosophy to persons who want it and, second, the dealing with individuals as one finds them in the student life."[79] All in all, Meiklejohn was quite content to stay at Brown.

President Faunce, for one, was delighted to have Meiklejohn stay. "Meiklejohn has been strongly urged to accept another deanship at Cornell," he told Brown's trustees, "but he declined before speaking with me about it, cherishing no higher ambition than to give his life to the service of his alma mater."[80] While Meiklejohn may have told Faunce that he had no higher ambition than to give his life to the service of his alma mater, he had other reasons for wanting to stay in Providence as well. Just two months before the offer came from Cornell, his mother had become seriously ill. Despite being active well into her seventies, spending many hours playing with her grandchildren, Elizabeth Meiklejohn had begun to deteriorate. She occasionally felt short of breath, and her stamina had noticeably decreased. She grew weaker and weaker, and, from time to time, experienced sharp pains in her chest. Finally, on March 24, 1908, just a few days before her seventy-seventh birthday, she quietly succumbed to congestive heart disease and died at home in Pawtucket.[81] Her funeral at the Pawtucket Congregational Church brought together her extended family as well as dozens of friends from the Clan Fraser and the Dunnell mill. After his mother's death, Meiklejohn spent more time caring for his aging father, who took great pride in his youngest son's professional and personal achievements. "His pride in you was good to see, and it was not wholly because of the distinguished position which you have earned," wrote a family friend. "It was, even more, perhaps, the satisfaction that your success had not lessened, but rather increased, your thoughtful care for him. It was, of course, a great pleasure to be so cared for, but, to him, it evidently meant that you developed the character which, above all things, he would desire for you."[82]

Meiklejohn's family responsibilities, combined with his duties as dean, kept him extremely busy, but not too busy to consider his career ambitions. In 1911, just as his fraternity reforms were attracting attention in colleges and universities throughout New England, the trustees at Amherst College asked if Meiklejohn might be willing to serve as that school's next president. Amherst had already considered such candidates as Alfred Stearns, headmaster at Phillips Academy; Rush Rhees, president of the University of Rochester; Frederick Woodbridge, professor of philosophy at Columbia; and Dwight Morrow, a partner at J. P. Morgan in New York. Finally, though, John Franklin Jameson, a former Brown history professor who ran the Department of Historical Research at the Carnegie Institute in Washington, submitted Meiklejohn's name.[83] Despite Meiklejohn's youth—he was only thirty-nine at the time of his nomination—Amherst's trustees took an active interest in him. In the spring of 1912, they solicited letters from dozens of Brown alumni in an effort to assess his qualifications for the presidency. "I believe Dean Meiklejohn to be admirably fitted for a college presidency," Charles Evans Hughes, Jr., told the trustees. "He would bring to that position the highest intellectual and moral ideals."[84] Another Brown graduate echoed Hughes. "Perhaps I can best make myself clear," he remarked, "by noting that I recently heard a fraternity man characterize him as the 'squarest man living' . . . and that a classmate of mine wrote beneath a newspaper picture of the dean, which he kept over his desk: 'Even Hand!'"[85] Amherst's trustees were interested in Meiklejohn's handling of student affairs, but they were also interested in his religious views. Since Meiklejohn stood to be the school's first nonclergy president, they were pleased to learn that, in at least one student's view, "his work both as a teacher and as a college officer and his influence as a man make clearly and positively for the upbuilding of character that is fundamentally religious."[86] After hearing such high praise for the young dean from Providence, Amherst's trustees offered Meiklejohn the job.[87]

When President Faunce heard about Amherst's offer, he begged his dean to stay. Indeed, Faunce was so worried about Meiklejohn's departure that he sent an urgent telegram at 2:00 A.M. from a hotel in Nashville, Tennessee. "Am too profoundly moved for words," he pleaded. "Please decide nothing till I return Sunday STOP Cannot bear to face the breaking of our relation STOP All that Brown can do for you personally and financially shall be done if you will stay STOP."[88] But Faunce was too late. Meiklejohn had already accepted Amherst's offer. The chance to lead his own college, to construct a democratic community according to his own ideals, was simply too attractive to pass up. Less than a week later, Meiklejohn received a letter from John D. Rockefeller, Jr., a graduate of Brown's class of 1897 who had been negotiating two separate salary increases to keep Meiklejohn at his alma mater. "I am not surprised at the decision which you have reached," Rockefeller wrote, "for, as I said to you frankly, the Amherst offer holds out many attractions which neither proposition which I made carry with them. I should have been glad to have been more closely associated with you, if that had seemed best, but assure you that my good wishes will attend you should you go to Amherst, and I will very heartily congratulate Amherst."[89] A few weeks later, Rockefeller wrote again. "Your going will be a serious blow to Brown," he conceded, "but the best wishes of all your friends follow you as you undertake the important task to which you have been called."[90]

President Faunce eventually accepted Meiklejohn's decision and expressed his heartfelt appreciation for Meiklejohn's years of service to Brown. "For eleven years, he and I have worked at the same task in adjoining rooms," Faunce wrote. "Many times a day, I have heard his quiet knock on the door between us, and he has walked through that door—never once without a cheery smile, a word of hope, and a grip of reality that made life better worth living. He is a man incapable of selfishness, absolutely loyal to a friend or a truth. He is at his best when the sky grows dark and obstacles abound."[91] In contrast with Faunce's melancholy mood, others were more excited about Meiklejohn's move to Massachusetts. Mary E. Woolley, a fellow Rhode Islander and Brown graduate who was president of Amherst's neighbor, Mount Holyoke College, sent congratulations from South Hadley. "There are so many reasons for my pleasure that you are to be president of Amherst College that I hardly know which one to emphasize first!" Woolley exclaimed. "I am glad for Amherst, glad that we are to welcome you to this part of New England, glad that you were an 'academic contemporary' at Brown, and last but not least glad that you are a Pawtucket boy!"[92] Pawtucket congratulations also came from Meiklejohn's father, who was deeply gratified by his son's success. "My Dear Son," the elder Meiklejohn wrote in a rugged, but legible, script. "Fondest Congratulations from your loving father and dear departed mother. Had your mother been spared to see her youngest boy so highly honored, it would have been a source of great joy and comfort to her warm affectionate heart. May God bless you, and keep you, and guide you through life, is the sincere prayer of a devoted father and a loving departed mother."[93] No other letter meant as much to Meiklejohn as this heart-felt benediction from his father.

On May 29, 1912, his last day at Brown, Meiklejohn stood before the assembled students and faculty to deliver his farewell address as dean. As he stepped forward to speak, the students rose en masse and cheered. Visibly affected by the loud applause, he waited a moment for the clapping to stop. When he regained his composure, he offered the undergraduates two pieces of parting advice. "I want to talk a few minutes about this college and what Brown stands for," he said. "It means two things and always has: fair play and think." Too often, he lamented, Brown students had forgotten these principles. When it came to the controversy over summer ball, they had forgotten the importance of fair play. When it came to the battle over fraternity grades, they had forgotten the importance of academic excellence. In both cases, they had forgotten the central purpose of the liberal college: to cultivate the moral sensibilities and intellectual ideals so often absent from the modern world at large. "What makes my heart sore," Meiklejohn declared, "is to see fellows year after year walk along with their eyes shut to the wonderful opportunities of college—to understand the big things of life, to see himself as he is, and to have a chance to think of these things before he goes to work. When I see you men doing foolish things with your fun and jollity, I can laugh and enjoy it with you, but when a man goes through college *merely* for these things, truly it makes my heart sick." Too often, Meiklejohn remarked, the students at Brown had lost sight of the larger purpose of their education. Too often, they had failed to grasp the moral meaning of a democratic college community. It was his job, one last time, to teach them what they needed to learn. "We both have had in mind the welfare of the college," he concluded. "We've often disagreed. You have sometimes deserved a black eye, and I have tried to give it to you. You are boys and have to learn to think, but if you love the college, don't be afraid to think and to think hard."[94] With these admonishing words, Meiklejohn departed for Amherst.

AMHERST

1912–1924

3

"The College as Critic"

1912–1919

O N OCTOBER 16, 1912, Amherst celebrated Meiklejohn's inauguration as the eighth president of the college. "The day,"
wrote the editors of the *Amherst Graduates' Quarterly,* "was
ideal for the inaugural procession—the sky bright with sun, the trees glorious with color, and the air mild and balmy, with just enough tang of autumn coolness to make it bracing." A procession of college and university
representatives, brilliantly bedecked in full academic regalia, marched en-
ergetically through the streets of Amherst before sweeping onto the tree-
covered campus lawn, where tents and chairs were waiting and musicians
from the Amherst College Orchestra and Chorus performed an arrangement of Schubert's "Die Allmacht" as well as selections from Gounod's *St.
Cecilia Mass.*[1] Meiklejohn, robed in black with a tasseled mortarboard
atop his head, exuded a confidence and conviviality befitting the festive
occasion. "Never were cap and gown worn with more life and grace," recalled one underclassman.[2] His quick step and ready smile reminded everyone in attendance that, at forty, he was one of the youngest college presidents in America. Not tall, of slender build, "and lithe instead of
powerful," ran one published account, Amherst's new leader was an enthusiastic educator "just in discipline, capable of commanding loyal obedience, and both profound and stimulating in his philosophic teaching."[3]
As Meiklejohn led his inaugural procession from the Amherst town commons down onto the campus green, storekeepers, housewives, and school-
children all craned to see the dashing new president. Expectations ran exceedingly high as the long parade of delegates, faculty, students, trustees,
and guests moved from the main yard toward Johnson Chapel, where
Meiklejohn prepared to deliver his inaugural address.

The academic parade at Amherst College during the inauguration of Alexander Meiklejohn, 1912 (Amherst College Archives and Special Collections)

When Meiklejohn arrived at Amherst, he had a rather mixed reputation as an orator. His voice was high, reedy, and thin (one student called it shrill), and he tended to speak quietly, even tentatively, in public. "[W]hen he spoke, at the start of any public occasion, one felt a slight uncertainty in his delivery," one listener recalled. "But, once well launched on his subject, his voice and manner strengthened appreciably, and he became a very convincing speaker."[4] Certainly, he was convincing the day he delivered his inaugural address. For many who heard it, Meiklejohn's speech marked what could only be called an intellectual and educational epiphany. Scott Buchanan, a student who later became one of Meiklejohn's closest friends and a prominent educator in his own right, remembered the exciting address in vivid detail. Johnson Chapel, he recalled, "became for me that morning, a freshman sitting in the balcony, a place of vision. Part of the vision was indeed visual, a human spirit clothed in academic costume," but even more striking than Meiklejohn's sartorial splendor was the vision conveyed by his words. "Not everybody present understood what was said, certainly not every freshman," Buchanan noted. "But everybody knew that something cardinal and consequential had been said, something that one might spend the rest of one's life trying to understand. Even the speaker might need that much time."[5] Buchanan's recollections were more accurate than he probably realized.

Meiklejohn did indeed say something cardinal and consequential in his inaugural address, and he did indeed spend most of his adult life trying to unravel the myriad social and educational implications of his message. His theme that day, the cultural and intellectual responsibilities of a liberal college in a democratic society, sounded the keynote for the rest of his educational career.

Speaking from a white-washed pulpit perched high above the pews, Meiklejohn opened with characteristic shyness. "[T]o be liberal," he said in a slight Scottish accent, "a college must be essentially intellectual. It is a place . . . in which a boy, forgetting all things else, may set forth on the enterprise of learning."[6] To most listeners, Meiklejohn's first sentences seemed simple and straightforward, but behind their apparent simplicity lay a complex and far more controversial meaning. By casting the liberal college as an essentially intellectual place, he set himself apart from the predominant educational views of his day. He distinguished himself most specifically from the pragmatist educational theories of John Dewey. Unlike Dewey, who insisted that school and society should be closely connected, Meiklejohn suggested that, in a higher educational context, the college should be a place fundamentally set *apart* from the mainstream, an intellectual haven where ideas, and not just practical, vocational, or professional skills, could develop. Invoking the spirit of Ralph Waldo Emerson's famous essay "The American Scholar," he asserted that a truly liberal college must be an intellectual sanctuary, an institution dialectically opposed to the problems and pitfalls of everyday life, a place where ideas and ideals could flourish. The liberal college, he declared, must be a refuge for cultural *criticism*.[7]

Easing into his address, Meiklejohn's voice grew steadily stronger. Far too many schools, he argued, had abandoned their intellectual focus. They were preparing students not for life but merely for jobs, and, as a result, they were quickly losing their sense of educational purpose. The proper aim of a liberal college, Meiklejohn asserted, was not the short-term achievement of professional expertise but the long-term attainment of intellectual excellence. "The issue is not between practical and intellectual aims," he asserted, "but between the immediate and the remote aim, between the hasty and the measured procedure, between the demand for results at once and the willingness to wait for the best results." According to Meiklejohn, the purpose of the liberal college was not to prepare students for gainful employment—that was something trade schools and research universities could do—but rather to foster a capacity for critical intelligence and social reform. "The intellectual road to success is longer

63

and more roundabout than any other," Meiklejohn admitted, "but they who are strong and willing for the climbing are brought to higher levels of achievement than they could possibly have attained had they gone straight forward in the pathway of quick returns. If this were not true, the liberal college could have no proper place in our life at all."[8] The purpose of the liberal college, in other words, was to be the "intellectual leader" of its community.

Meiklejohn traced the intellectual disintegration of the liberal college back to the elective system and its origins in the mid-nineteenth century. The elective system, or, as Meiklejohn called it, "the belief that all knowledge is so good that all parts of knowledge are equally good," had, in his opinion, betrayed the critical intellectual purposes of modern liberal education. "Ask many of our scholars and teachers what subjects a boy should study in order that he may gain insight for human living," he lamented, "and they will say 'It makes no difference in what department of knowledge he studies; let him go into Sanskrit or bacteriology, into mathematics or history.' " With no underlying principles to guide students in their educational choices, the elective system had stripped the undergraduate curriculum of its intellectual purpose, allowing it to become infected by a pervasive moral relativism. "This [relativistic] point of view, running through all the varieties of the elective system, seems to me hopelessly at variance with any sound educational doctrine," Meiklejohn charged. "It represents the scholar of the day at his worst both as a thinker and as a teacher. Insofar as it dominates a group of college teachers, it seems to render them unfit to determine and administer a college curriculum. It is an announcement that they have no guiding principles in their educational practice, no principles of selection in their arrangement of studies, no genuine grasp on the relations between knowledge and life. It is the concerted statement of a group of men each of whom is lost within the limits of his own special studies, and who as a group seem not to realize the organized relationships between them nor the common task which should bind them together."[9] For Meiklejohn, who believed that a curriculum should discriminate between subjects in order to discern what was truly worth knowing, the fundamental aimlessness of the elective system was anathema to liberal learning.

"[I]t seems to me," Meiklejohn proclaimed at the peak of his address, "that our willingness to allow students to wander about in the college curriculum is one of the most characteristic expressions of a certain intellectual agnosticism, a kind of intellectual bankruptcy, into which, in spite of all our wealth of information, the spirit of the time has fallen." Compar-

ing the intellectual climate of Progressive America to that of Enlightenment Europe, Meiklejohn noted that the rapid proliferation of new
knowledge in the late seventeenth and eighteenth centuries, like the explo-
sion of scientific discovery at the turn of the twentieth, had not resulted in
any new intellectual *synthesis* to guide the process of education. "Knowledge," he explained "had not grown; it had simply been enlarged; and the
two masses of content, the old and the new, stood facing each other with
no common ground of understanding." Thus arose the great philosophical endeavor of the eighteenth-century—the endeavor, as Meiklejohn put
it, "to re-establish the unity of knowledge, to discover the relations between these apparently hostile bodies of judgments, to know the world
again, but with all the added richness of the new insights and the new information." Surveying the state of turn-of-the-century social thought,
Meiklejohn adopted the persona of Kant and expressed what it was like to
be an idealist philosopher "trapped between two worlds" in 1912. On the
one hand was the Darwinian world of empiricism and scientific fact; on
the other was the Victorian world of spiritualism and religious belief. The
challenge for a truly progressive educator was to navigate between these
two worlds and, possibly, to forge a middle path that might bring them together. The challenge, in other words, was to create a "new synthesis" for
the twentieth century. "If I cry out against the agnosticism of our people,"
Meiklejohn declared, "it is not as one who has escaped from it, nor as one
who would point the way back to the older synthesis, but simply as one
who believes that the time has come for a reconstruction, for a new synthesis."[10] Recognizing the difficulty, perhaps even the impossibility, of
constructing a new intellectual synthesis for the twentieth century, Meiklejohn nevertheless deemed the attempt imperative for the modern liberal
college.

Meiklejohn was not the first to call for intellectual reconstruction in
the modern liberal college.[11] Woodrow Wilson had made similar statements at Princeton, and Abbott Lawrence Lowell had worked steadily to
revise the elective system at Harvard. Yet, even in the context of these
emerging changes, Meiklejohn's return to intellectualism in higher education struck a new chord in 1912. In the days and weeks following his inauguration, he received scores of letters from friends and colleagues nationwide. One letter came from his old mentor, Elisha Benjamin Andrews,
who was now chancellor of the University of Nebraska in Lincoln. "Your
inaugural struck an immensely important note in emphasizing the importance of strictly mental education," Andrews congratulated. "You must
press that campaign further, you must carry the war into the enemy's

Alexander Meiklejohn as president of Amherst College, 1912, in academic robes and mortarboard (Amherst College Archives and Special Collections)

camps, for these 'ultra' fellows who urge vocational training as if education ought to begin and end with that are enemies of the real education."[12] Recognizing that Meiklejohn had chosen the road less traveled, Andrews warned the young president to be brave in his defense of intellectualism. Given the ever-increasing popularity of "professional" studies for undergraduates, he cautioned that the reclamation of mental training in the liberal college would be an uphill battle. "You certainly are taking a chance, and I believe you know it," wrote Alexander Abbott, one of Meiklejohn's admirers from Brown. "[T]hat's one of your failings, I think—believing that you know what you are doing and why."[13] Indeed, Meiklejohn *was* taking a risk with his plans for intellectual rejuvenation at Amherst, and he did indeed know why he was doing it. As he wrote to James Seth at Cornell after taking office, "[A]ll I really hope to do here is to try to work out philosophical principles in the administration of the college."[14]

Meiklejohn brought unbounded enthusiasm to his new job as Amherst's president. As one student noted, he "swept into Amherst like a breath of fresh air. He was young, he was alert; he walked, played, and talked with vigor and assurance. Erect and smiling, he conversed with everyone."[15] With a genial personality and an unfailingly buoyant spirit, he had an unguarded demeanor and a youthful vitality that appealed to Amherst's five hundred undergraduates. Not long after his arrival on campus, he introduced the idea of a student council to help him with all aspects of college governance. "I doubt if I can run the college successfully unless I have the help of the students," he announced.[16] A few weeks later, he organized a group of eight students to advise him on every facet of campus policy, from fraternities to athletics to the dining service. He was intensely interested in student feedback and eventually launched an alumni program to solicit comments from recent and not-so-recent graduates. In the spring of 1913, he distributed a lengthy questionnaire asking current students to suggest improvements in the undergraduate curriculum. One sophomore recommended simply that the registrar schedule "as few courses as possible at two o'clock—that sleepy, digestive, after-dinner hour," while another wrote that he would "have liked the inter-relationships of [his] various studies brought out more plainly." A more contemplative senior indicated that the "total lack of any force to bring into harmony the studies pursued made the elaborate schedule ineffective and indefinite," and suggested that Meiklejohn make a more "organized attempt to correlate the studies."[17] Meiklejohn appreciated such input, not only because it demonstrated students' desire to improve the academic organization of the college, but also because it revealed their support for significant curricular reform. It was obvious that Amherst students were not wholly satisfied with the education they were getting, and Meiklejohn took their complaints as an unambiguous cue for change.

When Meiklejohn arrived at Amherst in 1912, the college deserved its reputation as a staunchly traditional school. Founded in 1821 as a school

Alexander Meiklejohn as president of Amherst College, ca. 1912 (Amherst College Archives and Special Collections)

for Congregational ministers, it emphasized the development of piety and respectability among its upper-class and upper-middle-class students. Like other private denominational men's colleges in rural New England, it concentrated on character and refinement far more than it pursued rigorous intellectual development. As one turn-of-the-century Boston journalist put it, Old Amherst was really "an agreeable, leisurely, semi-educational country club where by doing a modicum of work you could spend four pleasant years and come away with a college degree."[18] Indeed, Meiklejohn's presidential forebears had done little to disrupt this image. His immediate predecessor, an elderly theologian named George Harris, had spent virtually his entire administration sequestered in the president's house, carefully avoiding institutional change. "In two years," one student commented, "I don't think I ever met him personally or was made aware of his presence on campus outside church or chapel."[19] Amherst's faculty were much like the president. Almost without exception, these aging gentlemen were outmoded in their research and conservative in their approach to teaching. One particularly candid alumnus gave his criticism of the Old Guard in a long letter to Meiklejohn, identifying each geriatric professor in turn. Professor Levi Henry Elwell in Greek, he wrote, had been "a dead load on the College all the time that he has been there, and I think that some method ought to be found of disposing of him." Professor Robert Percy Carpenter in physical education and hygiene faced "an almost unanimous opinion that he is a thoroughly undesirable man for Amherst College." And, in the case of Professor Edwin Augustus Grosvenor in history, the alumnus could find "no charitable way of sizing up a man of this kind, unless one is prepared to say that he is demented."[20] Another student expressed a similar opinion in less guarded language, concluding that "some of the older men of the faculty were just dodoes."[21]

In sharp contrast with these older professors, Meiklejohn received rave reviews from students. "He was one of the finest teachers I have ever known," said Seelye Bixler, who went on to become president of Colby College in Maine. "No one who took his sophomore course in 'Logic' can forget its thrills."[22] The contrast between Meiklejohn and the older faculty became particularly obvious each morning during chapel when Meiklejohn delivered a daily homily. Over the course of his presidency, Meiklejohn experimented with various chapel texts, ranging from Aristotle and Epictetus to articles from the *Nation* or the *New Republic*. Rarely did he read from the Bible—a decision that severely rankled Amherst's Old Guard. As one student wrote many years later, "I well recall our Greek

Alexander Meiklejohn at his desk in the president's office at Amherst College, ca. 1913 (Amherst College Archives and Special Collections)

professor who attended chapel in the faculty seats [and glared at] the president [whenever] he started reading anything other than the Bible. . . . [On such occasions], this Greek professor would ostentatiously take up the hymn book and read it."[23] Meiklejohn's progressive sermons delighted Amherst's students but annoyed the faculty, who could not understand why their president was so reticent on the subject of Christianity. "If you must be reticent," one professor pleaded, "at least tell us that you are reticent upon the subject of religion and religious culture, not because there is nothing behind your silence, but . . . because there is *so much* behind it!"[24] But Meiklejohn did not heed this advice. He continued to preach on nonbiblical texts, and he continued to aggravate the faculty.

Meiklejohn's use of nonbiblical texts in chapel was part of a larger attempt to inject new life into the intellectual atmosphere of Amherst. As he had asserted in his inaugural address, the way to create a new intellectual synthesis in the twentieth century was not through a catechism but rather through a *curriculum*. Gradually, as he became more comfortable and confident in his role as a college president, he began to search for new ways to organize the undergraduate course of study at Amherst. His search for a new intellectual synthesis within a more unified curriculum would take years to complete—indeed, as Scott Buchanan had predicted, it would take a lifetime—but it was a search Meiklejohn first commenced in the second year of his presidency. "I crave some general outline of what is going on in the college which will give some coherence to the whole matter," he wrote to Professor L. A. Crocker at Oregon's newly established Reed College in the summer of 1913, "but it seems to me that nothing short of human experience in the large will ever accomplish it."[25] Yet, despite his hesitations, Meiklejohn began to see a way to bring intellectual unity and moral coherence to the undergraduate program at Amherst. In January of 1914, just five months after writing to Crocker, he announced a plan to develop a new core curriculum for all undergraduates. The goal of the new curriculum, he declared, would be "(1) to put an end to the mere 'smattering' of elective courses" and "(2) to unite all the students in the general task of getting a unified knowledge of human life and experience." Building on ideas he had outlined in his inaugural address, he explained that the new curriculum would be based on a series of eight required classes in philosophy and the social sciences. "[T]he required content is intended to be representative of the system of human knowledge as a whole," he asserted. "[I]t attempts to select the significant intellectual inquiries and to so relate them as to keep the unity of the whole while establishing acquaintance with the parts. The task is not an easy one and there is wide room for differences of opinion. But to do it in some way is better than not to do it at all."[26] Here, in brief, was Meiklejohn's first step toward a new intellectual and educational synthesis in undergraduate education for the twentieth century.

Shortly after outlining his plan for a new core curriculum at Amherst, Meiklejohn announced a record-breaking gift of $100,000 to establish the George Daniel Olds Professorship in Social and Economic Institutions. The anonymous donation, given in honor of Amherst's beloved dean, represented the largest single contribution in the college's history and a ringing endorsement for Meiklejohn's curricular plans.[27] A few weeks later, he released "A Tentative Definition of a Course of Study in Social and Economic Institutions," which quickly became the centerpiece of his new undergraduate program. Conceived as a series of eight classes, Social and Economic Institutions spanned all four years of the undergraduate program. Under Meiklejohn's plan, every freshman would take two required classes, "An Introduction to Social and Economic Problems" and "A General Introduction to the Humanities," while sophomores would enroll in "The Development of Modern Industrialism" and "The Social Order." Juniors would then take "Social Classes" and "Financial Institutions," while seniors took a two-semester capstone course titled "The Social Program."[28] Paying significant attention to "money, credit, banking, and accounting; the mechanisms of trade, foreign and domestic; corporation finance; the financing of the state; valuation of public utilities; and the business cycle," Social and Economic Institutions used social scientific methods to illuminate the major moral and philosphical issues of modern industrial society. It stressed "conservation of human resources; trade unionism; the state in relation to welfare; and schemes of social reform, including socialism." The overarching goal was to help students develop a general perspective on twentieth-century American civilization as a synthetic whole. Its emphasis was on intellectual rather than professional or vocational training, on ethics rather than economics per se.

Not surprisingly, Meiklejohn's vision of a completely restructured undergraduate curriculum was more than Amherst's older professors were ready to accept, and they made substantial revisions to his plan. By the time Social and Economic Institutions was implemented in the autumn of 1915, it had shifted from a four-year comprehensive program to a more modest two-part elective survey for freshmen. Meiklejohn, however, did not lose heart. He simply squeezed his original objectives into a smaller frame. As he explained to Amherst's trustees before launching the new program in 1915, "[W]e wish, if possible, to make students at the very beginning of the college course aware of the moral, social, and economic scheme—the society—of which they are members." "Such a course," Meiklejohn explained, "should not encourage the boys to believe that they have all at once found solutions of the problems by which their elder brothers are sorely perplexed; nor should it cast them down into the skepticism which regards all problems as insoluble. Its functions are, rather, a sane, searching, revealing of the facts of the human situation and a showing of the intellectual method by which these situations may be understood."[29] The specific focus of the course was less important than its more general emphasis on contemporary human problems and timeless moral dilemmas. The aim was to cultivate students' intellectual curiosity as well as their ethical sensibilities, and Meiklejohn found widespread support for his plan. "If it works," wrote President William DeWitt Hyde, of Bowdoin College in Maine, "we shall all probably be trying something of the kind."[30]

Having outlined his new synthesis for undergraduate education of Amherst, Meiklejohn searched hurriedly for someone to teach it. Even with the advantage of a large endowment, he had trouble finding a professor resourceful yet flexible enough to oversee such an unusual and wide-ranging curriculum. Indeed, as Meiklejohn confessed to a colleague, Social and Economic Institutions was "a course which might be taught very badly and become deservedly ridiculous or, on the other hand, be made the foundation of a genuine liberal education." The ideal candidate, he imagined, would combine broad understanding with inspired teaching in a way that motivated students to learn. "We want a man who can suggest to the freshmen the problems with which they ought to concern themselves during the remainder of the college course," he explained, and none of Amherst's older professors seemed up to the task.[31] After a year of soliciting nominations from all over the country—a search that included such diverse figures as Walter Rauschenbusch, the Social Gospel preacher, and Edward A. Ross, the sociologist—Meiklejohn finally chose Walton H. Hamilton, a thirty-two-year-old economist from the University of Chicago. Responding to Meiklejohn's offer in the spring of 1915, Hamilton expressed great enthusiasm for the job: "[T]he possibility of working under a college president whose conception of the functions of his office runs in intellectual rather than clerical terms and who clearly realizes that an educational institution cannot deal with its raw material in the mechanically standardized way of an industrial corporation [makes] tremendous appeal to me."[32] Hamilton arrived at Amherst in the summer of 1915 and offered the first session of Social and Economic Institutions that fall. Although the curriculum started as an elective for freshmen, it eventually became required for all new students. Within a few years, it was considered by at least one professor to be "the most famous college course in America."[33]

As it happened, Hamilton was just one of several new professors Meiklejohn brought to Amherst. Not long after his arrival in 1912, he listed in a letter to the faculty what he considered to be the two most important needs of the college. First was "some modification of the curriculum." Second was "the strengthening and vitalizing of the teaching force." At the bottom of the page, he typed in capital letters, "OUR TEACHING FORCE SHALL BE SECOND TO NONE IN THE COUNTRY."[34] In the summer of 1913, Meiklejohn shared his outlook for the faculty with Professor George Bosworth Churchill in the English department. "It seems to me," he suggested, "that very soon now we must take up the question of getting in one or two very strong men. The trustees have promised to support me in the attempt to make the full professorship attract the very best scholars and teachers in the country. I know that that cannot be accomplished all at once, but it must be adopted as a working principle."[35] Churchill agreed.[36] In the spring of 1915, Meiklejohn tried to woo John Erskine, an up-and-coming literary scholar, away from his post at Columbia. His effort failed, however, because Erskine hated Churchill. In a confidential letter to Meiklejohn, Erskine explained that "any reform in Professor Churchill's attitude might just as well begin before you get the additional instructors. In fact, I think it will have to, for the situation in the Department is pretty well known throughout the country, and I believe I am not singular in my reluctance to make part of my life-work the rejuvenation of Professor Churchill."[37] Meiklejohn responded that he was "somewhat startled" by Erskine's suggestion that Amherst was perceived as a place to which "men of standing" might not want to come. "If such men will not come, and if we, on the other hand, will not take men of any other type," he thought, then "the problem certainly seems to develop in terrifying fashion."[38] Not long after Erskine refused Amherst's offer, Meiklejohn solicited Yale professor Chauncey Brewster Tinker for the job, but Tinker objected to Churchill even more strongly than Erskine. Declining Meiklejohn's proposal, Tinker wrote to Amherst professor Samuel Henry Cobb pitying the president's plight. "I end the negotiations, as I began them, with [the] suspicion that I am dealing with an idealist (God prosper him!) who is confronted by a nasty practical dilemma which will not yield to his theories. The situation demands not high ideals but a high hand."[39] Clearly, the problem with Churchill was too insidious to ignore for long.

Finally, in the spring of 1916, Meiklejohn announced the appointments of Stark Young from the University of Texas and George Windsor from the University of Illinois.[40] The following year, he had even better news to report: Robert Frost, who had recently returned from a three-year stay in England, was considering joining Amherst's faculty as a writer-in-residence. Unfortunately, Frost did not care for Young and hesitated before signing a teaching contract. As Frost later told the story, "I flew off the handle because I suspected a certain poet [Young] got me to read my poetry at his college in order to get me to find him a publisher for his poetry. . . . And here he comes with an invitation to give two half-courses at his college from January on for $2,000. I'm humiliated."[41] Despite his difficulty finding compatible English professors, Meiklejohn managed to entice several other notable teachers to the hilly woodlands of the Connecticut River valley. Among them were Walter Agard in classics, Laurance Saunders in history, and Albert Parker Fitch, who resigned as president of the prestigious Andover Theological Seminary to teach the history of religion at Amherst. Meiklejohn also recruited a promising young philosopher named Clarence Ayres. Like Meiklejohn, Ayres was an idealist who lamented the rise of "valueless" pragmatism in American social thought. His year-long course, "Contemporary Philosophy," investigated idealism in the fall, pragmatism in the winter, and realism in the spring. At one point, Meiklejohn suggested a variation on Ayres's course with pragmatism in the fall and idealism in the spring, but Ayres rejected that approach, saying, "I do not like this so well. I am afraid I should be forced into defending pragmatism."[42] Before long, Meiklejohn had surrounded himself with a remarkably dynamic and philosophically compatible group of young professors.

By the spring of 1916, Meiklejohn had transformed the faculty at Amherst, and the intellectual atmosphere on campus had profoundly changed. "Before Meiklejohn," one alumnus observed, "we sat on the porch at Psi Upsilon, put our feet up on the rail, drank, and talked about fraternities, dates, and sports. When Meiklejohn had been around a while," he compared, "we sat on the Psi U porch, drank, and talked about frats, dates, sports, Epictetus, labor unions, and the problems of the liberal college. What a change!"[43] Another student remembered a similar shift, saying that "almost overnight, incredible as it may seem, the lectures had to be apologized for and justified, the laboratories and the textbooks had to be defended, and likewise the administration and the student government; the usual bull-sessions about religion, women, and politics continued but took on the style of comic dialectic. Much of the behavior of the faculty and students became ironic in the original sense, provocative of questions."[44] A member of Amherst's class of 1913 described the difference between his own years at Amherst and the years that immediately followed. "As I returned to Amherst in the first few years after my graduation," he recalled, "I was aware of increased interest in course-content on the part of the . . . undergraduate students. There were more discussions in Fraternity House about ideas and fewer 'bull-sessions' than in my day."[45] Even the *Amherst Graduates' Quarterly* commented that Meiklejohn's first year in office had been one of "unusual alacrity and heartiness for scholarly and cultural interests. Discussion and ventilation of weighty questions have been rife in the fraternities and at boarding tables. Clubs, seminars and reading circles have flourished."[46] All of a sudden, recalled one student who arrived at Amherst in the fall of 1913, "there was less of the 'social whirl' or 'country club' atmosphere and more real genuine interest in what college should be all about. This was not a solemn, over-serious attitude—rather, it was fun to learn."[47] Within a few years, Meiklejohn had injected new life into an old and, until recently, stagnating institution.

Meiklejohn took great pride in Amherst's progress. Yet, the achievements of his first four years had not come without sadness. For most of his first two years in the president's office, his father had been seriously ill. At the age of eighty-one, James Meiklejohn's health was slowly deteriorating. He suffered from arthritis and fatigue as well as frequent headaches. He had long since retired from his factory job at the Dunnell Print Works, and he saw most of his sons on a regular basis, but he rarely had a chance to visit his youngest son in Amherst. In January of 1914, shortly after Meiklejohn announced his plan for the new curriculum Social and Economic Institutions, he had rushed to be at his father's bedside in Pawtucket. But his father's health continued to wane. A year later, two days before Meiklejohn's forty-third birthday, in 1915, his father died at home of a cerebral hemorrhage. Meiklejohn, along with his six surviving brothers, was devastated. His relationship with his father had always been extremely close. "I note with deep regret the announcement of the death of your dear venerable father," consoled a friend. "I shall always think of him as a sterling man, modest and manly, true in every fiber of his being, with the self respect and the respect for others so characteristic of the noble Scot, with a nature burning with a quiet and steady intensity for the humanities as they appear in the awe and fire of God's presence. He was truly a Christian gentleman, and I shall always remember him as a strong and lively soul."[48] Meiklejohn mourned the loss of his father but lacked any strong religious faith to comfort him in his time of bereavement. Shortly after his father's funeral, he indicated his way of coping with grief when he counseled an Amherst student whose mother had recently died of cancer. "Meiklejohn gave me more help than anyone else simply by saying honestly that he didn't know any comfort but that I had his sympathy," the student remembered. "It was evident that the possibility of life after death seemed very faint [to him]."[49]

The following year, however, Meiklejohn and his family had renewed cause to celebrate. In December of 1916, just as Meiklejohn's new faculty hires were beginning to settle into their posts, his wife, Nannine, delivered their fourth child, this time a daughter named Annaletta, after her mother's middle name. A few days before Christmas in 1916, the Meiklejohns received a warm winter greeting from John Erskine, who delighted at the news of their baby daughter. "Mrs. Erskine joins me in congratulations of the heartiest sort," Erskine wrote. "The young lady finds a brave escort of brothers waiting to look after her, and no doubt she will appreciate the environment of Scotch chivalry and romance into which she is born."[50] Indeed, as the only girl in an active family with three little boys, Anna learned at an early age how to manage the attentions of her brothers. At the time of her birth, Kenneth was nine years old, Donald was seven, and Gordon was five. One undergraduate recalled his hilarious experiences as a babysitter playing with three nearly identical boys all under the age of ten. "They blindfolded me and had me staggering all over the house on a rainy day, trying to catch them and name them," he laughed. "They were all about the same size and I could barely tell one from the other without [the] blindfold. It was a jolly game from their standpoint but one that I could never win."[51] Despite Meiklejohn's busy administrative schedule, he maintained a casual atmosphere at home. When elderly Professor Otto Glaser's rheumatoid arthritis kept him from walking, for example, Meiklejohn put him in his sons' toy wagon and hauled him up to his house. "One evening," a visitor recalled, "I happened to the President's House to find Otto Glaser, Stone Professor of Biology, trussed up invalid-wise on a sofa playing pinochle or something with Mr. Meiklejohn's little boys."[52] Even when his presidential duties seemed overwhelming, Meiklejohn enjoyed nothing more than spending time with his family.

Major curricular reforms and faculty changes, combined with the death of his elderly father and the birth of his baby daughter, kept Meiklejohn more or less distracted from larger world events between 1914 and 1916. Yet it was precisely this time when national and international circumstances were becoming increasingly tense. In June of 1914, the assassination of Archduke Franz Ferdinand by a Bosnian Serb nationalist in

Kenneth, Gordon, and Donald Meiklejohn with their dog on the steps in front of the president's house at Amherst College, 1913 (Amherst College Archives and Special Collections)

Sarajevo tipped the delicate balance of power in Europe and pushed Austria-Hungary and its ally Germany headlong into war with Russia, Britain, and France. Shortly thereafter, Germany invaded Belgium and mobilized its armed forces in the Alsace-Lorraine region near Luxembourg. Horrific tales of looting, raping, and killing began to appear in the press. On May 7, 1915, Americans reacted with anger when a German U-boat sank the British luxury steamer *Lusitania* off the coast of Ireland, drowning 1,198 people, including 128 Americans. Meiklejohn, however, neglected to pay much attention to these wartime reports. Looking back on this period later in life, he marveled at his obliviousness. He recalled the commencement address he delivered at Vassar College in 1915, noting incredulously that it "was written while the First World War was going on, into which we were to plunge two years later, and I didn't even mention it!"[53] By June of 1915, however, the specter of war had begun to seep across the Atlantic. Patriotic Americans, pointing to the fate of occupied Belgium, founded military-preparedness organizations to bolster the nation's defense. The National Security League, the American Defense Society, the League to Enforce Peace, and the American Rights Committee all started preparing the United States for battle. In August of 1915, camps were established to train civilians near Plattsburgh, New York, and by the fall of 1915, Meiklejohn could no longer ignore the spreading spirit of war. Indeed, the war's cataclysmic effect on Amherst and, more generally, on Meiklejohn's lofty educational ideals, made it one of the most traumatic and transformative events of his entire life.

In September of 1915, Governor Channing H. Cox invited Meiklejohn to participate in the Massachusetts State Military Commission, a citizens' committee formed to consider the prospect of military preparedness. Meiklejohn replied that he was "not in active sympathy with the movement" but consented to attend a few meetings after the governor expressed a desire for dissenting opinions on the panel.[54] Four months later, Meiklejohn received a letter from First Lieutenant Edward L. Dyer, a graduate of Amherst's class of 1909, asking his opinion on the preparedness movement. "Would it not be practicable," Dyer asked, "for you, within your sphere as an educator, with the prestige of your name and position, to insist on universal military education and to initiate a course of military training at the college?"[55] Meiklejohn responded that he would make no such appeal. "I . . . regret to find myself in considerable disagreement with the point of view which you present," he replied. "I have felt that there is great danger of the movement for preparedness going too far and so have been inclined to hinder rather than help it, so far as my influence has counted at all."[56] Even after President Woodrow Wilson came around, rather slowly, to the idea of preparedness, Meiklejohn still remained staunchly opposed. As he explained in a note to a friend, Amherst had "not established military training in the college, and I think it very improbable that we shall do so. It is, of course, true that the preparedness forces are doing much more in a public way than are their opponents, but my impression is that, in the Eastern colleges at least, the sentiment among the students is quite as strong against preparedness as for it."[57] Meiklejohn had spent the past four years trying to make Amherst an institution dedicated to the critical contemplation of contemporary social problems, and he did not want to surrender the progress he had made. Yet, in the increasingly hostile political climate of 1915 and early 1916, his isolationist position became more and more difficult to maintain.

In June of 1916, Congress passed the National Defense Act, which authorized a five-year expansion of the army and called for the establishment of the Reserve Officer Training Corps (ROTC) at colleges and universities nationwide. Augustus Bennett, a member of Amherst's class of 1918 who had participated in the military training course at Plattsburgh, volunteered as Amherst's first president of ROTC, in which capacity he found himself "frequently in conflict with President Meiklejohn, who was not in sympathy with the war effort so far as it affected college students. . . ."[58] A month later, in July of 1916, Meiklejohn outlined his objections to preparedness training on campus in an article for *School and Society*, a professional educator's journal. In "A Schoolmaster's View of Compulsory Military Training," he examined why certain curricular subjects should be required while others were only elective.[59] "Under what conditions," he asked, "may a given subject be made compulsory?" As Meiklejohn saw it, a course could be required only if it contributed something essential to the curriculum that no other course could offer. Such was the case with his required Social and Economic Institutions courses at Amherst, which aimed at a synthetic overview of contemporary human civilization as a whole. Military training, by contrast, was too specialized and vocational to be required in the undergraduate curriculum; it simply did not teach anything that other subjects could not teach better. "Is it not possible," Meiklejohn queried, "to demand obedience in the classroom in English, to insist upon precision and order in mathematics, to require subordination of the individual to a common purpose in any classroom? . . . The plain truth is that there is not one of the virtues under discussion which cannot by proper teaching be as well developed in connection with the teaching of other subjects as under the guise of military training."[60]

According to Meiklejohn, rifle drills, tactical maneuvers, strategy lessons, cryptographic studies, and modern ordnance simply had no place in a liberal college—least of all as requirements.

Meiklejohn's opposition to military preparedness stemmed not only from his defense of intellectualism in the liberal college but also from his opposition to the fiercely nationalistic rhetoric that so often accompanied the preparedness movement. As the war intensified abroad, public leaders extolled the virtues of 100 percent Americanism and expressed their desire to "heat up the melting pot" to forge a stronger and more unified nation. Meiklejohn endorsed the goal of national unity and even linked the principles of democracy to America's Anglo-Saxon heritage, but he doubted that a virulent American nationalism was the best way to achieve a shared national purpose. "Ever since William James began to search for the Moral Equivalent of War," he wrote in his article for *School and Society,* "we have been seeking some activity which would fuse us together as a people just as the peoples of Europe are now becoming living flames of fury and zeal. It is my impression that most of these proposals for the integration of our national life are at this point begging the question: 'How shall we achieve the unity of a European nation; by what machinery shall it be done?' " Meiklejohn sympathized with the search for national unity, but he questioned the appropriateness of the melting-pot metaphor. "I do not believe that by any great miracle this people is to be integrated, is to be fused into a single will," he wrote. "A war might do it, but we hope that we shall not have a war. Lacking that, we must win our unity not by some miracle of will, but by growing understanding of each other." According to Meiklejohn, compulsory *moral* education, not compulsory military education, was the nation's best hope for peace. The task of social unification belonged to *students,* not to soldiers. "It seems to me," he argued, "that our hope lies not so much in the growth of a *will* as in the development of a *mind* . . . ."[61]

True to his Kantian idealist roots, Meiklejohn believed that rational deliberation was the only effective way to solve enduring human conflicts. Violence, in his opinion, lay beyond the pale of reason. Although it would take many years and at least two more wars (one hot and one cold) to clarify Meiklejohn's views on this subject, the period leading up to World War I revealed the depth of his faith in a reasonable world. Following Kant, he was convinced that the existence of a reasonable society was always *potential* and that human beings had to *choose* to make such a society a reality. If no one ever chose—or wanted or desired—to create a reasonable human community, then no such community could exist, but the *potential* for such a community was ever present. In the event of war—which, by definition, was unreasonable—the combatants, if they sought to end their fighting, would need to seek examples of reasonable behavior not only *amidst* but also *beyond* the violence that created their conflict in the first place. The challenge was to seek examples of reason in the wider realm of human experience, to translate the universal forms of moral behavior into the actual operation of particular social institutions. For Meiklejohn, this idea gave a transcendental purpose to the liberal college, the function of which was to stand apart from social conflict as a refuge for peace in a violent world. As he put it, "[T]he function of the teacher [is] to stand before his pupils and the community as the intellectual leader of his time. If he is not able to take this leadership, he is not worthy of his calling."[62] Thus, if the United States should choose to enter Europe's war, then Amherst—along with every other liberal college in the country—would need to set itself apart from the fray as a beacon of reason and virtue. Lasting peace could come only from examples of reason in the world.

Speaking in Johnson Chapel in February of 1917, Meiklejohn insisted that Amherst should remain separate from the actual fighting—a critical observer seeking truth *beyond* the war. "As it is the business of the college to weigh and consider conflicting opinions and give each its proper place," he said, "our only allegiance is to the truth. We are neither pacifists nor militarists, Congregationalists nor Baptists. We are students." [63] As fighting raged overseas, Meiklejohn tried to remove the college from the conflict, to set it apart as a haven for truth, intelligence, and virtue. But in so doing, he put the college in a precarious spot. How could Amherst stand apart from the war but still teach students how to end it? How could a liberal college be passionate in its opposition to warfare but dispassionate in its allegiance to truth? These questions cut to the heart of Meiklejohn's vision of a liberal college. A college set apart from its culture was not, in his mind, a college necessarily *at odds* with its culture. Rather, a college set apart was a college set in critical tension with its culture and responsible for representing its culture's highest moral and ethical ideals. The critical American college needed to defend the country's highest intellectual ideals—the ideal of rational and democratic debate foremost among them—and thus to *guide* the nation, and indeed the world, toward peace. Meiklejohn was not alone in his desire to separate the college from the fervor of military combat. "In these days when the militarists are so stridently vocal," one alumnus wrote, "I feel constrained to express to you my sincere gratitude that my Alma Mater has not given evidence of the bellicose hysteria that so many of our colleges and universities have indulged in. . . . It appears to me that in holding aloof from all the agitation for war, with its attendant waste, humiliation, and degradation, both your administration and the students of Amherst have reflected great credit upon a college that conceives its mission to be 'making a mind for the nation' instead of yielding to its impulses."[64]

Yet, less than a week after Meiklejohn received this letter, disaster struck. On April 6, 1917, the *Amherst Student* ran a two-inch headline: "War Extra! Amherst Rises to Meet Nation's Need; Campus to Be Partially Transformed into Training Camp; Course in Military Instruction to Start Monday; President Meiklejohn Makes Inspiring Address." Standing in the same high pulpit from which he had delivered his inaugural address, Meiklejohn tried to calm the excited students below. After reading a copy of Wilson's declaration of war, he described the role the college would play in the fight. "The members of this college know how I have hated the threat of the coming of this war," he said, "how I have shunned every act, every word which might seem to invite it. But it is here." Now that the long-feared event was finally upon them, Meiklejohn urged his students to remember the need for rational criticism in a crumbling world. "As students," he said, "we have two loyalties, the abstract loyalty to principles, to Truth, Goodness, Freedom, Beauty, Youth, and Gladness, and also the concrete loyalties to the institutions of which we are members, to the family, the church, the school, the state, the humankind. And as students we hold ourselves forever free to criticize and to understand the institutions in terms of the principles. That right we will never relinquish. But this does not mean that we have lost our loyalty to the institutions. It means that we are trying to serve them by making them intelligent." On this note, Meiklejohn told his students to obey the laws of the United States, to go to war when called, to fight with conviction and confidence, but also to think— and think hard—about the war and its meaning. He advised them to stay in school as long as possible, to take advantage of the privileges they had as students, to criticize, to condemn, to praise, to pity, to express their anger and their loyalty, to announce their passion and their idealism, to bear witness to Wilson's plea for a defense of what was right in the world. "It is hard to face all the problems of this day," he told the undergraduates, "but I tell you that you have the biggest chance that youngsters ever had. The making of a new world is in the hands of your generation. You must discover and support the ideals and purposes on which it shall be founded."[65] The liberal college, he inveighed, must build a new world, much better and more reasonable than the old.

But Amherst's students did not listen. Starting in 1917, thousands of American undergraduates rushed excitedly to enlist, eager to experience the heroic thrill of battle and prove their manhood in a foreign land. Much to Meiklejohn's disappointment, they rejected rational criticism in favor of irrational conflict. The *Amherst Student* reported the war experiences of one enthusiastic "doughboy," Charles Burton Ames of the class of 1916, who spent six months in the American Ambulance Field Service along the western front. Ames returned to Amherst just a week after the United States had entered the war and gave his personal impressions of the fighting. He noted especially the ways in which technological innovations had transformed the military operations, making them gruesomely efficient. He described the relative merits of rifles versus machine guns, the bowl-shaped helmets donned for protection against enemy shells fired from tanks, the gas masks worn to neutralize the effects of deadly chlorine bombs, and the technique for throwing grenades. He tantalized his fellows with terrifying tales of trench attack. "The first step is to send out aircraft scouts," he told a group of students hanging on his every word. "The aviators draw plans and take photographs of opposing trenches. This enables them to make accurate maps of the immediate territory which is to be the objective of the attack." Then, after receiving surveillance, the soldiers worked "to widen their own trenches to facilitate the handling of the wounded. Wire cutters are sent out in the night to cut down the great mass of barbed wire in 'no man's land.' . . . In the actual attack, it is quite necessary that the men obey the signals implicitly. The whole line also must go together and at the same speed. Otherwise, they would be in danger of being mowed down by their own guns."[66] Before the war ended, unprecedented slaughter in the blood-soaked hills of Verdun, Ypres, Somme, and other sites had killed or wounded nearly twenty-five million men—and Meiklejohn was helpless to stop it.

For many would-be soldiers at Amherst, the war seemed an ideal opportunity to test their physical strength and prove their capacity for bravery and valor. Just as athletics had given boys a chance to become men, so, too, war gave them new opportunities to display their manliness and courage. The best way for young soldiers to demonstrate their capacity for heroism, it seemed, was to survive a life-threatening danger. "While in Paris during the German retreat from Chateau Thierry, we had our first experience of shell fire," one student boasted in a letter to Meiklejohn. "All that day their souvenirs fell within a radius of 500 yards of our building, and one made warfare seem real when it landed 200 feet away. One of the shells dug a hole six feet deep, three feet in diameter, killed three soldiers and the horse that they were driving, tore the side out of a lamp-post, destroyed the side of a nearby restaurant, and tore chips from buildings 100 feet from the ground." Just three lines later, however, the same soldier made warfare seem a lot less real: "For one franc, ten centimes," he noted, "you could purchase ice cream and cake."[67] Indeed, for many of Amherst's student-soldiers, World War I resembled a romantic adventure. "I look forward to many new adventures, and I'm having them daily," young Everett Glass wrote. "This whole life is novel. I should hardly choose it if under normal conditions, but at the moment I would not be out of it." Despite Glass's experience, relatively few Amherst students actually *fought* in the war. As educated—not to mention white and wealthy—volunteers, they received commissions as officers with administrative duties. Rather than digging trenches, driving tanks, or dropping bombs, they typed memos, trained other soldiers, and translated messages from German and French. Indeed, while his bunkmates worried about the possibility of imminent submarine attack, young Glass lay quietly below the deck of his destroyer reading British literature. "I recalled that Shelley was drowned with Keats in his pocket," he mused to Meiklejohn, "but such immortality was spared me."[68]

Meiklejohn tried to sympathize with students like Glass, but it was not easy. Throughout the war, he enjoined his students to transcend the conflict, even if they could not ignore it, and to embody the moral virtues for which war had been waged. "Would it not be a sorry thing," he asked in chapel the day after Wilson's war declaration, "if they should win their conflict only to find we had no better way of living to put in place of that which they had destroyed?" Remembering their compatriots curled up in foxholes and surrounded by artillery fire, Meiklejohn told his students not to feel disconnected from their friends overseas. Instead, they should devote themselves to the study of peace, justice, and truth with more diligence than ever, so that this "war for democracy" would in fact be the "war to end all wars." "Let no man think that right and wholesome and beautiful living lies ready at his hand," he asserted. "Life must be made; it must be wrought by labor of our hands and spirits. And if we would destroy the mode of life that other men have made, we must be ready to make a better life for men to live." The liberal college, he insisted, was a place in which better lives could be made, virtues practiced, and ideals imagined. "Men come to college to study human life because they know that by the studying they can make life more nearly what it ought to be," he declared. "They see how crude and stupid much of living is, how starved and poor, how lacking in taste; and on the other hand, they catch the vision of what it sometimes is and what it may become. And so they set themselves the task of understanding it to make it better."[69]

Meiklejohn urged Amherst's students to stay in school and study the ideals of peace, and in some cases, he actively inhibited those who tried to enlist.[70] When young Eric Marks opted to enter the U.S. Navy against Meiklejohn's wishes, Meiklejohn tried to bar him from graduating. As Marks later explained, "Prexy, fearing that a group of us had rushed to enlist without due consideration, called my father and asked his help in heading us off." The elder Marks warned that withholding diplomas would undoubtedly be misinterpreted outside the college—indeed, at a time when growing numbers of Americans were shedding their neutrality, any attempt to impede military volunteers seemed distinctly unpatriotic, even seditious—but Meiklejohn did it anyway. He refused to help students become soldiers. At the height of the war, Secretary of State Robert Lansing, an Amherst alumnus, openly rebuked Meiklejohn for opposing voluntary enlistment in the armed forces, but he persisted.[71] His response to Eric Marks's enlistment showed how strongly he felt about the issue: "I was called in and told that my college career had ended the day I left Amherst," Marks recalled. "I could attend classes as a 'visitor' [but] I would receive my diploma based on my average at that time without the 'privilege' of taking final exams!" In Meiklejohn's view, Marks's decision to enter the navy had severed his connection with the liberal college. He had chosen to study war instead of peace, to pursue unreasonable realities instead of reasonable ideals. He had thus fallen short of the critical intelligence Meiklejohn expected of his students. Having failed to learn this basic lesson, Marks had no chance of passing Meiklejohn's "final exams," at least not in any figurative or symbolic sense.[72]

But student enlistments were not Meiklejohn's only concern in 1917. In the fall of that year, the U.S. War Department demanded his help in rooting out "subversive and seditious activities" on the home front. As a college president, he was asked to report the political beliefs of his faculty to the National Security League, a nongovernmental agency seeking to preserve domestic loyalty. Meiklejohn was appalled by this request and indicated his anger in a letter to Harvard's president Abbott Lawrence Lowell. "It would seem to me outrageous," he protested, "that a private organization of this sort should feel at liberty to call our colleges and universities to account and to presume the right to direct what they shall do. Please tell me whether or not I am too military in spirit."[73] In fact, Lowell *did* consider Meiklejohn a bit too military in spirit and, while opposing the National Security League in principle, still acquiesced in its probe.

Meiklejohn, however, felt no compunction to submit his loyalty, or that of his faculty, to the scrutiny of an independent watchdog club. He staunchly defended civil liberties at Amherst, even when leaders at other colleges and universities were not so successful. The most publicized breach of academic freedom had occurred at Columbia, where trustees fired James Cattell, a distinguished psychologist, and Henry Dana, a prominent professor of literature, for their antiwar views. Historian Charles Beard, who taught at Columbia with Cattell and Dana, resigned in protest (despite his own prowar views), stating that, "if we have to suppress everything we don't like to hear, then this country is resting on a pretty wobbly basis." Meiklejohn was utterly incensed by what he considered to be an obvious attack on academic freedom, and he expressed his outrage in a letter to Albert Parker Fitch: "I am so much excited by the Cattell-Dana-Beard episode at Columbia that I am ready to hit at anything or anybody I happen to see in my way," he fumed.[74] When a group of professors asserted that Columbia's trustees had overstepped their authority, Meiklejohn wrote to Beard and his friend John Erskine that he was "delighted to know that your men are discussing the question of whether or not college presidents and trustees are anachronisms. It seems almost too much to hope that men might come to that conclusion."[75] Beard thanked Meiklejohn for his support but advised him to keep his criticism of university trustees to himself, at least until the war ended. "You must be a thorn in the flesh of your guildsmen," Beard wrote. "The goblins will get you if you don't watch out."[76]

It was sage advice, but Meiklejohn did not keep quiet. His feelings on the subject of academic freedom ran so high that he requested a special meeting with Woodrow Wilson at the White House to discuss the issue. "I am writing to ask whether or not you could see me for a few minutes if I should come to Washington," he wrote to Wilson on the same day that he mailed his irate letter to Fitch. "Just what the liberal colleges should think and do at present I find it very hard to tell. I am sure we must not be driven into a cowardly and dishonest silence, but, on the other hand, we must work with the institutions of the government and not against them."[77] Despite the measured tone of this letter, Meiklejohn tried to express his strong opinion that the freedom of public deliberation must never be abridged, least of all in time of war and especially not in institutions of higher education. If the United States was truly fighting a war for democracy, then attempts to silence dissent could not be tolerated. As Meiklejohn had tried to convey to his students at Amherst, the only way to win a "just peace" was to uphold the ideals for which America fought, the greatest being the freedom of critical democratic debate. Unfortunately, the federal government, including Woodrow Wilson, was not in a mood to listen. A week after sending his initial letter, Meiklejohn, perhaps embarrassed by his own audacity, withdrew his petition for a personal interview in the Oval Office. "It seems certain that the President will not wish to write me concerning the issue I have in mind, viz., that of the suppression of public discussion, especially within the colleges," he wrote to the president's secretary. "May I ask you therefore to give no further attention to my request?"[78] Given Wilson's poor record with civil liberties during the war, Meiklejohn was probably wise to forgo what was likely to have been a frustrating and ultimately fruitless meeting.

The fact that so many liberals had acquiesced in the war effort infuriated Meiklejohn, but he was not alone in his anger. Randolph Bourne, a well-known cultural critic and former student of John Dewey in the philosophy department at Columbia, lashed out at the apparent moral bankruptcy of government officials who subordinated values to technique in an effort to win the war. In an essay titled "Twilight of Idols," published in *Seven Arts* magazine in October of 1917, Bourne issued a scathing critique of pragmatic bureaucrats who had "learned all too literally the instrumental attitude toward life." Rather than defending high moral principles, the war's "technicians" knew only the administrative procedures and managerial methods of modern social science. "Their education has not given them a coherent system of large ideas or a feeling for democratic goals," Bourne lamented. "They have, in short, no clear philosophy of life. . . . They are vague as to what kind of a society they want or what kind of a society America needs." Despite his own personal sympathy for pragmatism, Bourne argued that Dewey and his followers had systematically subordinated values to technique, and the resulting ethical holiday had been disastrous for American social thought. "To those of us who have taken Dewey's philosophy almost as our American religion, it never even occurred to us that values could be subordinated to technique. We were instrumentalists, but we had our private utopias so clearly before our minds that the means fell always into its place as contributory. And Dewey, of course, always meant his philosophy, when taken as a philosophy of life, to start with values. But there was always that unhappy ambiguity in his doctrine as to just how values were created, and it became easier and easier to assume that just any growth was justified and almost any activity valuable so long as it achieved ends." According to Bourne, the ethical implications of Dewey's pragmatist philosophy had been calamitous. "It is now becoming plain," he concluded, "that, unless you start with the vividest kind of poetic vision, your instrumentalism is likely to land you just where it has landed this younger intelligentsia which is so happily and busily engaged in the national enterprise of war."[79]

In September of 1917, a month before "Twilight of Idols" appeared, Meiklejohn presaged Bourne's message in an article for the *Harvard Graduates' Magazine*. Writing under the title "Fiat Justitia: The College as Critic," he identified what he considered to be a fundamental obstacle to the creation of moral and ethical values in the modern liberal college. "[I]t seems clear, terribly clear, to me that teachers in the colleges are not commanding and dominating the spirits of their boys because they have no purpose which has a proper claim to domination," he wrote. Despite their ever-increasing proficiency in physics, chemistry, economics, and engineering, modern-day professors lacked an ability to make these scientific subjects *meaningful* to their students. They lacked an ability to transform empirical facts into a synthetic understanding of the world. "Can they bring all this knowledge into order, reducing it to principles, making out of it a knowing of the world in which men live and of the human life itself? Can they interpret what we know and make it all significant?"[80] To these questions, Meiklejohn answered a resounding "No!" The proper aim of the liberal college, he insisted, was not technical proficiency or specialized expertise but "the finding of principles that run through many separate things and bind them together, making them one." The purpose, in other words, was a general understanding of the whole. "Learning interprets," Meiklejohn declared. "[I]t takes the fragments of our life, our knowledge, and makes of them a unity, a whole. Each bit, left by itself, is clear but meaningless. Learning interprets them, gives them significance one for another, makes out of them a scheme of life, a system of knowledge which one can understand and use."[81] The ability to interpret, to assign value to the mere facts of human existence, was rapidly disappearing from the liberal college, just as the ability to think critically, coherently, and comprehensively was vanishing from a culture caught in the throes of war.

Meiklejohn readily admitted that the search for meaning, for unity, for totality in liberal education was a profoundly difficult, perhaps even an impossible, quest. He acknowledged that no mortal could ever know all things in their infinite relations. "I know what men will say against this thing I urge," he wrote in his article for the *Harvard Graduates' Magazine*. "How can a man know more than one field well? If one cannot, then what is the value of making judgments in a realm one has not mastered, of trying to understand the things one does not know?" Meiklejohn recognized the apparent absurdity of his lofty and idealistic demands, but he saw no alternative. "Are men to be, so far as they study at all, simply a group of experts, each master in his field?" he asked. "And what of those who do not specialize in any branch of knowledge? Are they to have no intellectual life at all?" According to Meiklejohn, democracy depended on the existence of liberally educated citizens—citizens who could grasp the interrelationships between diverse bodies of knowledge and the ethical significance of them all. "Just as a protest," he declared, "I would define a liberally educated man as one who tries to understand the whole of knowledge as well as one man can. I know full well that every special judgment he makes will be inadequate. I know the experts will have him on the hip, each expert at one point. But, yet, for human living as a whole, for living as men should live, I'll match a liberally educated man against a field of experts and have no fear that any of them will beat him."[82] Without the possibility of liberal education, without a well-developed capacity to interpret the world in its entirety, without an ability to step *beyond* special interests in pursuit of critical understanding of the whole, wars would continue forever. As Randolph Bourne wrote in his attack on pragmatism a month later, "[I]f your ideal is to be adjustment to your situation, in radiant cooperation with reality, then your success is likely to be just that and no more. You never transcend anything."[83]

At the end of his article, Meiklejohn acknowledged the objections of his opponents, the specialists who would say, "I cannot do this task; it is too great." To them he replied with the full force of his idealism. "Whether you can or not, you must," he wrote. "You may not shun the task. To you as critic and interpreter, all men must come. To you the church, the state, the home, the school, rich man and poor, the builder-up, the breaker-down, each one must bring his thoughts, his hopes and fears, his doubts and creeds, his strivings and opinions, and you must show him what they are in terms of their relations to others which his fellows bring. You must be sane as other men are not; you must have knowledge which others cannot gain; you must be fearless and honest as others, tied by interest, may seldom be; you are the student set apart to view the whole, to try to understand, a free untrammeled human spirit seeking the truth for guidance of mankind." To be a teacher was to be the intellectual leader of the community, to stand for the secular ideals of virtue and reason even in the midst of overwhelming social and political conflict. To be a teacher, in other words, was to be a martyr for the truth. Meiklejohn recognized the enormous chasm that lay between the pursuit and the attainment of truth, between the quest for totality and the actual achievement of transcendental understanding. "You will not," he admitted to his fellow teachers, "do it well; your heart will break with disappointment and despair; and yet you will keep on for the very joy of it, because in doing this you make a college, and that is what, as a teacher, you are to do."[84] This tragic hero, this quixotic figure striving eternally after ideals in an increasingly agnostic age, was Meiklejohn himself reliving the Faustian fascination of his youth.

Certainly, "The College as Critic" advanced lofty and idealistic goals—too lofty, in fact, to survive the social and educational dislocations accompanying total war. In July of 1917, just two months before Meiklejohn published his article in the *Harvard Graduate's Magazine,* Congress had passed the Selective Service Act, which enrolled nearly ten million Americans between the ages of twenty-one and thirty (later extended to the ages between eighteen and forty-five). Six months later, in February of 1918, more than 140,000 undergraduates from 516 colleges and universities became "student-soldiers" in the newly created Student Army Training Corps (SATC). The effects of the SATC on American higher education were profound. Overrun by military officers and their uniformed regiments, virtually every college and university in the country, including Amherst, incorporated a series of government-sponsored War Issues courses into its curriculum. The stated purpose of these courses was to make students "feel that they are discharging a national duty to a great cause in a war brought on without cause by an enemy who must be crushed in order to secure the peace of the world in the future."[85] War Issues classes included navigation, sanitation, surveying, modern ordnance, map reading, wireless operation, and French and German conversation.[86] The SATC daily schedule began with reveille and assembly at 6:00 A.M., continued at 7:00 with drills and sick call, and ended at 11:00 P.M. with tattoos and taps. Meals became mess calls, and seminars became school calls.[87] Before long, War Issues had completely displaced Social and Economic Institutions as the core of Amherst's undergraduate program, and Meiklejohn was utterly distraught. His vision of a critical college set apart from the perils of a partisan society, free from unthinking obedience to external authority, detached, quite simply, from the spirit of militarism, had been blind-sided by war.

By the time of Amherst's commencement ceremonies in June of 1918, all but 6 of Amherst's 125 seniors had gone off to war, and Meiklejohn was finally forced to acknowledge that his ideal of a critical college set apart from the conflict had been destroyed. "I wish you could have seen, a few weeks ago, 150 college presidents being told what they should do," he told the few students still remaining on campus. "For two days we sat—meek, old, spectacled, thin-faced things—asking for directions from

Members of the Student Army Training Corps (SATC) marching at Amherst College, 1917 (Amherst College Archives and Special Collections)

young army officers, and we received them. And let me tell you this of which I am proud—we took our medicine, took it without a murmur. We saw our colleges torn to pieces and were told to put them [back] together in another pattern. And without a word we set ourselves to doing it."[88] Technically, Meiklejohn could have prevented the expansion of military training on campus, but such an autocratic decision undoubtedly would have offended the overwhelmingly prowar sentiments among his students, faculty, and trustees. Yet, as he described the decimation of his liberal college ideal, his pain was almost palpable. Why had the college been so weak? Why had it collapsed so easily? Why had it been so vulnerable? "What is the principle?" he asked, trying to find some justification for his dismantled liberal college. "It is, I am sure we are all agreed, the principle of democracy. We are determined that people shall have a chance to be themselves. We will not submit that any man, that any group of men, that any nation, that any group of nations, shall be repressed and dominated by external power. Each shall be free to choose what it shall be within that social group in which it finds itself." Trying to ignore the imposition of government control at Amherst, Meiklejohn attempted to defend the democratic purposes of the war in general. "I ask you, men of Amherst, do

The Amherst Ambulance Unit presenting its flags to Alexander Meiklejohn, 1918 (Amherst College Archives and Special Collections)

you accept the principle that men shall have a chance to be themselves? Do you accept it for the days to follow the war as well as for the time of conflict? If you do, then whatever may come, we will send you with clean hands and pure hearts to the field of battle. . . ." In Meiklejohn's view, even if the college could not stand entirely apart from the war, it could at least represent the moral ideals for which the war had been waged. To join the war solely for the sake of ending it was to see *beyond* the violence and thus to adopt a moral rather than a pragmatic approach to conflict. Only in this way, Meiklejohn believed, could reason and virtue ultimately triumph over the irrational strife of world war.[89]

In October of 1918, Meiklejohn sent a brief letter of encouragement to President Wilson, stating his support for the armistice that was then finally under negotiation. "I feel that I must send you an expression of my delight and gratification," he wrote, his conciliatory tone suggesting a desire to forgive Wilson's blunders with respect to academic freedom. "It is especially what you have done for the young men, such as we have in the colleges, that is thrusting itself upon me. You gave them a great cause when you led us into war; you kept before them high and masterful ideals regarding friend and foe in your conduct of our national policy; and, as the end of the struggle comes, you are defining for them the tasks which are to command the imaginations and the wills of this coming generation." Given his many disappointments during the war, Meiklejohn must have struggled to write these words. Yet, at the same time, he remained tremendously idealistic about the future. "In my opinion," he wrote, "these young fellows who are coming on are much better men than their fathers were."[90] Meiklejohn's timing could not have been better. Two weeks later, the armistice was signed, and the war was over. Almost immediately, the allied victors erupted in elation. "Everyone here went wild," one Amherst student wrote to Meiklejohn from his post in Paris. "A sudden *éclat* of Allied banners and bands—marching, counter-marching, cheering, singing, dancing. The *Place de la Republique* is a seething mass of people—old veterans parading with flags and putting wreaths on statues. Shops closed, bars open. A three days' *après*."[91] Another student was more contemplative about the end of the war. "It is hard to believe but wonderful to realize that all this is over, that the last shell has flown, that this sacrifice of life has ceased," the weary doughboy reflected. "I have played only a small part in it—only a few months—but I saw enough to feel the hell of it all and to feel this wonderful touch of peace."[92]

Shortly after the armistice became official, Woodrow Wilson headed for France, where he proposed the Fourteen Points for peace in the postwar era, including the League of Nations to arbitrate international conflicts. When he returned to the United States, he embarked on a national tour to promote the league, but the tour did not go well. As he traveled through the western states, the sixty-three-year-old president became increasingly exhausted and ill. Passing through Colorado, he collapsed in the middle of a speech. A few days later, back in Washington, he suffered a severe stroke that paralyzed his left side. When Meiklejohn learned of Wilson's failing health, he wrote a gentle letter of support. "May I send a few words of friendly interest and of deep concern?" he asked. "I am writing to beg you not to use your strength just now, but to conserve it for the building up again of your health. I can imagine something of your state of mind. May I therefore tell you that many of us who have been watching you believe that no one else could have accomplished what you have done and that very, very few would even have attempted it. You must not now make impossible demands upon yourself. I am sure that the cause for which you are fighting is moving steadily on and will win. You must save yourself to share the joy of it as well as to play your part in carrying it all forward. Please forgive my advising and counseling. It springs from real friendship for you and eager concern for the interests in your charge."[93] Meiklejohn's note was a generous gesture of compassion, a sincere expression of support from a man deeply concerned about the future of democracy in international, as well as in domestic, affairs.

In subsequent months, Meiklejohn reflected on the causes and the consequences of the war. Such a bloody catastrophe might have been avoided, he thought, if the American public had been more liberally educated. "We knew enough to justify our going into the war," he wrote, "yet we did not know the map of Europe; we did not know the history of France, Germany, England, or even America. We did not know the play of all the economic forces running through the lives of men. We did not know the moral interests, the racial codes, the local prejudices. . . . We entered the war with hearts of steel and minds of feathers. We came out of it triumphant but confused, with scattering wits." Now, after the war, most Americans were no more liberally educated than they had been in the beginning. "We blunder on in stupid arrogance, not knowing the world in which we live, not knowing which way we wish to go, not knowing how best to overcome the obstacles that block our path. We just go on keeping our eyes wide open—in the dark." What the United States needed above all was a more enlightened public opinion, a more liberally educated citizenry that only the colleges could generate. "I wonder if our colleges can cure us of this arrogance," Meiklejohn asked, echoing his earlier article "The College as Critic." "They will be hated if they do. And yet, the colleges must do this work. They are the teachers and critics of our intellectual life. It is their task to see that our people think aright about essential problems."[94]

Indeed, Meiklejohn's conviction on this point only deepened in the coming years. He firmly believed that the liberal college should be an institution set apart from society, an institution seeking truth to reconcile—and ultimately to overcome—the moral, political, and ideological differences that led to violent conflict. "The problem of social reconstruction is based on the faith that we can find truth and that there are ways of doing things which can be found," he wrote in the *Amherst Student* in the spring of 1920. "Let the college stand for that faith. People who are at war cannot trust each other; therefore, let the college, as a disinterested party, represent the judge in the controversy. First [and foremost], the college should be withdrawn from the world of affairs in order to remain entirely unbiased. It should think of the essentials of faith, truth, justice, and fairness. It should keep the quality of a judge, an unpledged man concerned only with principles and not committed to any party."[95] Despite the cataclysm of world war, Meiklejohn's hope for a new synthesis in liberal education had not waned. Still clinging to the central principles of his inaugural address in 1912, he continued to search for the critical intelligence that gave purpose to the liberal college in an increasingly, and perhaps irretrievably, fragmented world. Clearly, his work at Amherst was not yet done.

4

"To Whom Are We Responsible?"

1920–1924

I N JANUARY OF 1920, Meiklejohn traveled to Boston to address the
members of the Harvard Liberal Club. His speech reiterated many of
the themes he had introduced eight years earlier in his inaugural address at Amherst, particularly his idea that a truly liberal college should set
itself apart from mainstream society as a haven for cultural, intellectual, and
moral criticism. Several prominent liberals heard Meiklejohn's presentation,
including William Lloyd Garrison, Jr., the noted labor activist and elderly
son of the nineteenth-century abolitionist. "You perhaps do not realize the
relief it is to hear a college president pitch his thoughts in a philosophical
and idealistic key," Garrison wrote a few days after the Harvard meeting.
"However the heathens may rage, it ought to be good fun, just as an experiment, to develop an atmosphere of Emersonian aloofness in some small college and have it a place where students, between football matches, could
presume to commune with nature and the eternal verities." Meiklejohn,
who much admired the Emersonian scholarly ideal, appreciated Garrison's
support. Even more, he appreciated the rest of Garrison's letter, which outlined a plan for radical political and economic reform in the postwar period.
According to Garrison, the only way to prevent the demise of American
democracy after the war was to socialize the economy. "Either the recapture
of this continent must be accomplished . . . by some rational and legal
process," Garrison asserted, "or else we shall inevitably be faced with the
increasingly dangerous threat of industrial direct action, which opens the
way to the destructive turmoil of class war."[1] And Meiklejohn agreed.

Garrison's warnings about the threat of industrial direct action and the destructive turmoil of class war typified the radical rhetoric of the time. Shortly after the armistice in 1918, America's economy had plunged into recession. Rapid demobilization left prices high, and many young veterans lacked jobs. Wages failed to keep pace with inflation, and workers, hoping to protect wartime earnings, went on strike. By the sweltering summer of 1919, more than four million American workers were embroiled in some three thousand different walkouts across the country. [2] And, as Meiklejohn was well aware, college students often played a key role in breaking these strikes. Undergraduates left school for days or even weeks at a time to take jobs as machine operators when regular sources of labor rebelled. At one point, Governor Cox of Massachusetts asked Meiklejohn if Amherst students would be prepared to aid the state as scabs in the event of a general railroad strike. "I am sure that if such an emergency should arise the students could be of the greatest assistance," Cox wrote.[3] Meiklejohn, however, discouraged his students from participating in strikebreaking. Just as he had discouraged student enlistments—and had initially declined the governor's invitation to participate in preparedness discussions in 1915—so now he refused to endorse strikebreaking. "It seems to me very clear that the college is not justified in taking official action in response to your request," he wrote to the superintendent of the Connecticut River Division of the Boston and Maine Railroad, who had asked for student-strikebreakers from Amherst.[4] True to his conviction that liberal colleges should remain detached from direct involvement in political affairs, Meiklejohn urged his students to abstain from strikebreaking unless officially ordered to do so.

Meiklejohn's opposition to student strikebreaking was controversial and widely interpreted as communistic. In the summer of 1919, at the height of the Red Scare, strikes and various other forms of "radical" protest were openly blamed on foreign revolutionary ideologies. With Russia's Bolshevik revolution as a recent backdrop, antilabor forces linked any kind of industrial conflict to criminal syndicalism and anarchism. In June of 1919, after a bomb exploded near the home of Attorney General A. Mitchell Palmer in Washington, D.C., federal authorities unleashed a series of raids against individuals and groups suspected of subversive activities. A few months later, Justice Oliver Wendell Holmes, Jr., and the U.S. Supreme Court limited the freedom of political speech in the landmark case of *Schenck v. the United States,* which involved an antidraft circular distributed by a leading socialist activist. Such "Red-baiting" was not limited to government agencies. Business groups such as the

National Association of Manufacturers found anti-Communist rhetoric an effective method for suppressing unionization. On the other end of the political spectrum but also contributing to the cultural paranoia of the Red Scare were several student organizations such as the National Student Forum, which openly supported both the American Communist Party and the Industrial Workers of the World and sponsored such leftist speakers as William Z. Foster, Norman Hapgood, and Elizabeth Gurley Flynn. The National Student Forum recruited a small, but vocal, following at Amherst, where Meiklejohn made room for its cause. Meiklejohn did not explicitly endorse student radicalism, but he did not try to stop it, either. Indeed, in many ways, the Red Scare provided a focal point for classroom debates in Amherst's recently revitalized Social and Economic Institutions courses. It seemed increasingly obvious that the country's most pressing social problems involved wage disputes and economic disparities. For Meiklejohn, these issues fit perfectly with the goals of his core curriculum.

In the summer of 1919, just as the Red Scare reached its peak, Meiklejohn left Amherst to travel for five weeks in Europe. He left not to escape domestic social problems but to see what role the liberal college could play in solving them. Traveling chiefly to Great Britain, he and Nannine visited James Seth, his old mentor from Brown, at the University of Edinburgh, and cheered Kent in a crushing defeat of Middlesex in cricket. They devoted most of their time, however, to London and Oxford, where they went to study the recently initiated "university tutorial class" movement. "The purpose of this movement," Meiklejohn explained upon his return to Amherst in the fall, was "to give genuine liberal, non-technical instruction of college grade to men and women of the working classes." With teachers from the universities and students from the nearby factories and mills, the first university tutorial classes had taken place in Meiklejohn's hometown of Rochdale.[5] Almost immediately Meiklejohn thought of importing a similar plan for workers' education to Amherst. In the spring of 1920, he received a letter from John Gaus, an Amherst alumnus who was studying political science at Balliol College, Oxford, suggesting the development of a social settlement for local workers modeled on the program at Toynbee Hall. "Why not unite this tradition of social service with the need for liberal and cultural interpretation of life for those many men and women now shut off from such an interpretation?" Gaus wondered. "Why not extend our educational work, our settlement work, by establishing a summer session of possibly only a few days or two or three weeks, at first open to the workers of Massachusetts, to be given to conferences and lectures?"[6] Meiklejohn agreed enthusiastically with Gaus's idea and quickly drafted a plan for workers' education in Amherst. In June of 1920, he invited Gaus to come to Amherst and work with Walton Hamilton as a teaching assistant for Social and Economic Institutions. "There is the possibility," Meiklejohn hinted at the end of his letter, "that there may be work for you in connection with our proposed classes for working men."[7] And so there was.

A few months later, with financial support from the recently established Commonwealth Fund of New York, Meiklejohn, Hamilton, and Gaus opened a new school for workers from the nearby industrial towns of Holyoke and Springfield, Massachusetts.[8] The classes, which took place in St. Jerome's Temperance Society Hall in Amherst, drew students primarily from the Holyoke Central Labor Union, a textile workers' affiliate of the American Federation of Labor. According to Meiklejohn's promotional material, the weekly workers' classes were "designed to be of use to adults who wish to gain a more complete knowledge of the institutions under which they live. They are open to all men and women in Holyoke and its vicinity who are willing to commit themselves to regular attendance and serious study."[9] For a two-dollar fee, workers had access to a series of twenty-five small-group discussions, each lasting two hours and led by a member of the Amherst faculty. The meetings began in the middle of October and continued through April.[10] According to the *Amherst Student*, attendance "increased slowly but steadily throughout the course, beginning with about twenty and gaining to thirty or more, at some meetings being nearly fifty."[11] The discussion topics were listed in course announcements as "Current Economic Problems," "Industrial and Social History," "The Making of Public Opinion," and "Programs of Radical Social Reorganization."[12] Texts included Henry George's *Progress and Poverty,* Bertrand Russell's *Proposed Roads to Freedom,* Karl Marx's *Communist Manifesto,* Vladimir Lenin's *State and Revolution,* Peter Kropotkin's *Fields, Factories, and Workshops,* and Charles Beard's *Short History of the American Labor Movement.*[13]

Before long, workers' education programs had emerged at several other Massachusetts colleges, including Wellesley and Williams. In 1921, A. J. Muste opened his famed Brookwood Labor School in Katonah, New York. Two years later, Commonwealth College established adult training classes in Mena, Arkansas. By 1923, there were more than sixty such schools in various locations around the country. Just as Meiklejohn had hoped, the workers' classes at Amherst did not shy away from radical interpretations of social and economic problems. For example, the timely topics covered by Professors Paul Douglas of Amherst and William Orton of nearby Smith College were announced as "The Risks of the Worker," "Protective Legislation," "Union Policies," and "Proposals for Social Reconstruction (including Socialism, Anarchism, Syndicalism, Guild Socialism, the Single Tax, and Bolshevism)."[14] Besides teaching workers' classes, Amherst professors also found various other ways to aid labor's cause. Professor Cobb spent two days a week adjusting wage disputes in Rochester, New York. Professor Fitch regularly incorporated labor problems into his chapel sermons.[15] Professor Hamilton routinely aroused suspicion from older faculty who accused him of being a Bolshevik. And Meiklejohn himself openly welcomed these activities. "Personally," he wrote to a friend at the University of Chicago, "I am not very much troubled by the radical quality of a man. A man may be as radical as he likes provided [that] he, at the same time, gives the impression of being fundamentally sane in his method of thinking."[16] As far as he knew, Meiklejohn employed no Communists on his faculty, though he freely admitted that he would be happy to have them "so long as they were good teachers."[17] When it came to a critical intellectual evaluation of labor and economic problems, Meiklejohn was not so concerned about setting the college apart from society. In fact, he actively encouraged political involvement among Amherst's students and younger faculty.

Despite the proliferation of workers' schools in the early 1920s, relations between higher education and labor were weaker than relations between higher education and business in this period. After the election of President Harding in 1920, schools jumped at the opportunity to develop new programs in business administration and the industrial arts. Antioch College in Yellow Springs, Ohio, epitomized the decade's growing emphasis on work-study. In 1919, Arthur E. Morgan, a self-made millionaire, engineer, and social reformer with a penchant for education, had taken control of the virtually insolvent Antioch. He swiftly initiated a "co-op" program whereby students spent half their time working off-campus in a variety of businesses throughout the state. Thanks to an ambitious national advertising campaign, Morgan's experiment was a fast success, and students flocked to Antioch from both coasts. Meiklejohn was aware of Morgan's work but maintained that a liberal college was no place for business training. He agreed much more with Thorstein Veblen's acerbic critique in *The Higher Learning in America: A Memorandum on the Conduct of Universities by Businessmen,* published in 1918. Describing the "permeation of the university's everyday activity by the principles of competitive business," Veblen noted the growing power of applied science in the undergraduate curriculum. Too often, he argued, American colleges placed their emphasis on job preparation and professional training, abandoning moral and intellectual purposes for purely material ends.[18] A truly liberal education, he argued, had no identifiable pecuniary value. Its purpose was not to promote the acquisition of wealth but rather to facilitate the cultivation of intelligence. Not long after Veblen published *The Higher Learning in America,* Meiklejohn invited him to speak at Amherst.[19]

Meiklejohn's opposition to professional training—combined with his support for workers' education, his stand against strikebreaking, and his praise of Thorstein Veblen—did not endear him to Amherst's trustees, many of whom operated large and extremely profitable corporations of their own. By the fall of 1920, when workers' classes were filled to capacity in Holyoke and Springfield, several trustees began to wonder if Meiklejohn's social and economic liberalism really kept the best interests of the college in mind. Indeed, his apparent enthusiasm for radical professors and his constant criticism of conservative causes seemed biased at best and duplicitous at worst. Whatever doubts the trustees might have had about Meiklejohn's political proclivities seemed confirmed when he refused to participate in an important three-million-dollar capital campaign to mark the college's centennial anniversary. As soon as Meiklejohn learned of the campaign, he announced his intention to take a year-long sabbatical in Italy. Explaining his need for a vacation to a friend in Rome, he noted that his wife, Nannine, wanted to visit her relatives in Florence. "Mrs. Meiklejohn is thoroughly acquainted with the language and the country, her father having been Italian. Our servants are Italian, and we shall bring one of them with us to care for our little girl. Our three boys we shall take to England and put them in school in September, afterwards returning to Italy for our year's holiday."[20] Yet, with a major fundraising effort just about to begin, Meiklejohn's timing could not have been worse. In the summer of 1920, the economy was just beginning to recover from its extended postwar recession, and a trip to Europe—Meiklejohn's second in two years—seemed expensive, not to say irresponsible. Meiklejohn, however, seemed oblivious to these concerns. Citing his acceptance of the presidency only on the condition that he, like his predecessors, not be required to solicit financial gifts, he set sail for Florence, leaving Amherst in an uproar.[21]

Ever since his arrival in 1912, Meiklejohn and Nannine had spent money with little regard for Amherst's financial limitations. Indeed, he repeatedly overspent his salary and asked many times for supplemental allowances. His predecessor, President Harris, had enjoyed a salary of $6,000 a year, but Meiklejohn came to Amherst with a salary of $7,500 plus the presidential mansion and several servants. In the years 1914, 1915, 1916, and 1917, he requested additional allowances of $2,500, $4,000, $5,600, and $5,000, respectively, from individual trustees. In 1918, he persuaded Amherst's trustees to raise his salary to $10,000 plus a residential maintenance budget of $2,000 plus an entertainment and travel account of $2,500.[22] On top of this $14,500, he asked for an additional $5,300 to meet expenses already incurred. In 1919, after his first trip to England, he required $2,475.94 more.[23] Given his own working-class childhood, it was difficult for many to guess the cause of such financial irresponsibility. A few trustees discreetly criticized the expensive tastes of Mrs. Meiklejohn, who came from an affluent background and operated the president's house at a cost of more than fifteen thousand dollars a year.[24] Before long, however, the Meiklejohns' spending habits bordered on the scandalous. When it came time to board the luxurious *Priscelliana* for his trip to Italy in 1920, Meiklejohn requested still more advance money from the trustees. According to one account, the trustees "discussed it and seemed to be in a balky mood when the best known trustee smoothed things over for the time being by giving Meiklejohn $20,000 out of his own capacious pocket."[25] Dwight Morrow, a trustee and partner with J. P. Morgan and Company in New York, saved Meiklejohn the embarrassment of an even bigger debt, but his troubles with money were far from over.

In the fall of 1920, when the trustees asked Meiklejohn to write a brief message to spearhead their centennial fund drive, he cabled back from England with a pithy response: "Go ye, Jasons, shear the alumni, and bring the golden fleece back to campus!"[26] Insofar as Amherst carried a budgetary deficit—which eventually totaled more than $300,000 but grew at a decreasing rate—throughout Meiklejohn's presidency, the trustees failed to appreciate his wry attempt at fundraising humor.[27] According to Stanley King, a trustee who later became Amherst's president, Meiklejohn's inability to control his spending caused considerable confusion. "President Meiklejohn was not a man with expensive habits," King wrote. "He did not smoke; he did not drink. He did not dress expensively. He had a wife and three [sic] children. True, the cost of living was increasing, but it was increasing for professors, associate professors, and instructors as well." At a time when most professors at Amherst earned about three thousand dollars a year, Meiklejohn downplayed the financial disparity between his income and that of his faculty. As King wrote, "[H]e seemed to see no incongruity in being president of a college and a teacher of ethics and at the same time making commitments for goods from the merchants of the town for which he knew he could not pay."[28] Indeed,

Alexander Meiklejohn, fifth from right, with members of the Amherst College Board of Trustees at the Centennial Celebration luncheon, 1921. Chairman of the board George A. Plimpton, third from left; trustee Dwight W. Morrow, second from right; dean of college George D. Olds, third from right (Amherst College Archives and Special Collections)

when the town butcher went bankrupt in 1921, his largest asset was a four-year claim against Meiklejohn. Eventually, the milkman refused to deliver to the president's house.[29] Unable to control his household spending, Meiklejohn accumulated substantial debts with many Amherst store-keepers—a topic of serious concern, not only among his creditors, but also among his trustees.

104

In the little village of Amherst, which in the early 1920s had only about five thousand residents, many of whom still traveled by buggy, Meiklejohn's profligate habits became the subject of intense local gossip. A student whose family lived near campus commented on the president's reputation. "Being a town boy," he wrote, "I received first-hand reports on the Meiklejohn controversy from talk around town. . . . The first vindictive town gossip I heard about him was that he did not pay his bills. It seemed that Mrs. Meiklejohn, said to have been an Italian countess, which I . . . always assumed she was, was extravagant." On at least one occasion, the student recalled, a fancy dinner at the Meiklejohns' "had a molded ice cream centerpiece simulating an Italian castle."[30] For years, complaints about the Meiklejohns abounded among Amherst residents. "President Meiklejohn and his family took no part in the social life of Amherst," another student noted. "He did not send his children to the public schools. He looked on the town as a thing apart. He had little to do with the churches."[31] Others recalled that Meiklejohn abstained from voting in local elections. Still others rumored that he had a red-headed mistress.[32] At the center of all the gossip was Meiklejohn's wife, Nannine. Whereas the former first lady, Mrs. Harris, had been loved by almost everyone, Nannine was, in one student's memory, "hard to get acquainted with, of Italian background, I believe, and had her social problems with the gown and financial problems with the town."[33] She made the cardinal mistake of entertaining the wives of younger professors more often than the wives of their older associates—an unforgivable breech of campus etiquette—and she did not improve her image when she refused to join the Amherst Ladies Aid.[34]

Of all the people who disliked the Meiklejohns, none despised them more than Professor George Bosworth Churchill. Churchill served as a state senator and chairman of the Amherst Republican Committee. For twenty years, he sat as moderator at Amherst town meetings, where, according to one admiring student, "He was magnificent, and exerted, I am sure, a certain decorousness to the town's government that was most salutary."[35] Shortly after Meiklejohn's first trip to Europe, Churchill discovered that he was "running up big debts in every store he traded at."[36] Since Churchill knew almost every Amherst citizen by name, he "saw to it that the news spread, and persuaded his friends in town to stop credit to Meiklejohn and demand payment." But he did not stop there. "He arranged for the grocer's boy to come up to the president's mansion with a cartful of goods, and to demand cash before delivery in a loud voice of Mrs. Meiklejohn before a purposefully assembled crowd."[37] No one doubted that

George Bosworth Churchill, professor of English at Amherst College, ca. 1923 (Amherst College Archives and Special Collections)

Churchill was Meiklejohn's nemesis in the town of Amherst.[38] Described as "an austere and crusty gentleman of the old school," Churchill was, according to one professor, "adamantly convinced that Meiklejohn was a dangerous radical who couldn't be trusted, and who had to be stopped before Amherst was seriously damaged."[39]

Over time, the hostility between Churchill and Meiklejohn infected the entire faculty. By the spring of 1921, it had split the professors into two warring camps, a younger pro-Meiklejohn contingent and an older pro-Churchill group. As one student noted, "The feud even spread to the households so that wives in the two factions would not speak. The whole town was split apart."[40] Not only did all relations between the two groups break off, another student noted, "but even, in certain cases, I was told, the children of the two groups were forbidden to play together!"[41] At first, Meiklejohn tried not to let the conflicts between himself and Churchill get in the way of his reforms. He took them whimsically and, when asked about his enemies on the faculty, responded, "Enemies? I have no enemies except the inability to comprehend."[42] In his more serious moments, Meiklejohn told critics that the only way to resolve their disagreements was to state their positions frankly and then to "fight it out" until a sort of consensus emerged. "As I understand a discussion," Meiklejohn said in 1915, "it is some sort of game or a fight in which the people who take part are supposed to get at each other."[43] However, when neither combatant was willing to compromise, stalemates tended to result. Such was the situation between Meiklejohn and Churchill in the early 1920s—a stubborn contest of wills. Always certain of the rectitude of his own ideas, Meiklejohn considered it his intellectual duty to teach opponents like Churchill the errors of their ways.[44]

In contrast with his popular methods of dealing with student conflicts at Brown, Meiklejohn was far less than democratic in his approach to faculty conflicts at Amherst. As early as 1917, he persuaded Amherst's trustees to pass a rule requiring all older professors to retire at the age of sixty-five regardless of tenure; yet, two years later, when one of his supporters reached retirement age, he repealed the rule, calling it "repulsive to the faculty."[45] In 1919, when several professors began to organize against his reforms, Meiklejohn instituted a gag rule requiring the faculty to pass all official communication through the president's office.[46] Not surprisingly, the older faculty were outraged by these rules. Accusations of administrative autocracy flew back and forth between the pro- and anti-Meiklejohn camps. "In time," one alumnus recalled, Meiklejohn grew "very critical of most of the members of the older faculty, and he took no pains to conceal his personal dislike of certain members. . . ."[47] The result was that older members grew alarmed and began to fear they would be cast out, and such fears were not entirely unjustified. Not long after his inauguration, Meiklejohn began to dismiss professors he deemed subpar. Between 1913 and 1921, nearly half the faculty left, some through retirement or death, but others through forced resignation.[48] "I can imagine no one worse as an administrator," one shocked alumnus commented. "Various areas on the faculty needed stiffening up, but the stiffening process could have been done in a much more diplomatic fashion, without the unnecessary stirring up of trouble and of rancor."[49] Meiklejohn had no legal responsibility to seek faculty approval for his dismissals, but he appeared to many as an administrative despot with no regard for the principles of institutional democracy.[50] Shortly after Meiklejohn's departure for Europe in 1920, Robert Frost resigned. "When I came away," he groused about his last day with his students, "I left them with a protective wash against Meiklejaundice."[51]

When Meiklejohn returned from Europe in February of 1921, he found his faculty bitterly divided. Indeed, the older professors had started to hold "hate sessions" featuring "something like a burning-in-effigy ceremony" to protest Meiklejohn's administration.[52] Faculty meetings quickly degenerated into ferocious debates over the president's ability to lead. One meeting in particular proved to be a watershed in Meiklejohn's relation with his faculty. In the middle of the meeting, Professor Churchill stood up and, according to an eyewitness, made several "outrageously snide remarks" about the president. After Churchill's tantrum, another professor tried to correct some of his more obvious misstatements. The next day, Meiklejohn wrote a letter to the second professor to thank him for his support. Meiklejohn's letter ended, however, with an "absolutely unrestrainable tirade of curses against Churchill." The professor who received the letter went to Meiklejohn and said, "Come now, you can't write things like this; here, take your letter and destroy it," at which point Meiklejohn denied ever writing it. The professor, who had defended Meiklejohn's honesty and integrity in front of the entire faculty, was incredulous. Meiklejohn looked at the letter again and claimed that it did not bear his signature. Indeed, his secretary had signed it for him, but the words obviously belonged to Meiklejohn. In an attempt to prove his innocence, Meiklejohn summoned his secretary and asked her "in a terrible voice" whether she had written the letter. Looking distressed and fearful for her job, she muttered that she had. Finally, disgusted, the professor "threw up his arms and walked sadly away."[53] Such episodes cast a dark shadow on Meiklejohn's character. Backed into a defensive position by those with whom he disagreed, he allowed the less admirable side of his disposition to show. Without speculating on the psychological reasons for his behavior, it seemed clear that he harbored a deep-seated need to protect himself from disapproval, even to the point where his own duplicity returned to harm him.

As the strain of his relationship with the faculty increased, Meikle-

john's self-control often gave way. He lashed out at critics and made con-
descending remarks to students. "We thought of him as cold, introverted,
and an intellectual snob," one undergraduate recalled.[54] "He was a very
reserved man," another commented, "and a person difficult to know.
Many considered him cold and impersonal."[55] "To my thinking," a third
student added, "he was a cold individual[;] although I have recollection
that he tried to be friendly, he lacked warmth. His incisiveness in speech
was his handicap because it gave me the idea that he could not tolerate individuals of lower intellectual ability. I think he would have made a good
warden for a prison."[56] Meiklejohn's reputation as a persuasive speaker
eventually came back to haunt him. "He was a menace to Amherst," one
angry alumnus charged, "because he captured the minds of young and in-
experienced boys and gave them a false sense of values and wrong
ideas."[57] Evidently, what had inspired some students intimidated others.
Meiklejohn's gift for logical argument struck some undergraduates as an
expertly honed ability to deceive. "[R]emember the fellow who said that
he had seventeen reasons for not playing poker—the first was that he had
no money?" one alumnus asked. Well, "Meiklejohn could make the other
sixteen reasons so air tight that his listeners would forget all about that
first reason. At first I thought he was wonderful but gradually I sized him
up and found him an almost total fraud."[58] As another student noted,
Meiklejohn faced a "marked difference of opinion as to his skill and tact
as an administrator, and even as to whether he always spoke [the] truth or
could, if occasion suited, be a two-faced liar of deepest dye."[59] For one
who had argued as an undergraduate that intentional falsification of any
kind constituted implicit denial of the dignity of rational humanity, such
caustic accusations cut deep.

Until the spring of 1922, Amherst's trustees had remained largely unaware of the growing animosity between Meiklejohn and his faculty. At
their meeting on March 13, 1922, however, they lost their innocence. As
one trustee later recalled, "[I]t was the most disheartening meeting I have
ever attended." The crisis came when Meiklejohn recommended the appointment of Walter Agard as an associate professor of Greek. The
trustees liked Agard and wanted to hire him, but, before they voted on the
matter, they asked Meiklejohn if he had received the faculty's approval for
the appointment. Meiklejohn replied that he had. But, when Dwight Morrow repeated the question, Meiklejohn retracted his initial statement and
confessed that he had not, in fact, ever sought the faculty's opinion. Meiklejohn had lied to his trustees. Stanley King, another trustee, described the
extraordinary events that followed. "[I]t was clear to all of us that some-

thing unusual was involved and that the president was failing in candor in his answers to the questions," King reported. "The atmosphere grew tense as the president replied that the faculty had no right to express an opinion on his recommendation." At this point, Chief Justice Earl Rugg of the Massachusetts Supreme Court addressed Meiklejohn directly, telling him that failure to give clear and complete answers to the trustees' questions constituted a serious breach of his legal obligations as president. Rugg then asked if the faculty had put its rejection of Agard in writing. Meiklejohn responded that they had and meekly took a faculty memo from his coat pocket. He handed the memo to Morrow but took it back before the trustees could read it. After the meeting adjourned, Meiklejohn pulled King aside and told him that he felt like the victim of a plot, that a small group of professors was out to get him, that they were being totally unfair in their methods, and that they had no right to approve or disapprove his choice of new faculty. As King later recalled, "[H]e told me that if the board would give him autocratic power at the college for ten years, he would make it a good college. That was the nub. He could not work with his board; he could not work with his faculty; his answer was the delegation to him of autocratic power." King was shocked by Meiklejohn's words. "That evening at the hotel," he later noted, "I told Dwight Morrow that, in my judgment, the situation was now hopeless."[60]

In August 1922, as if to forestall the storm, Meiklejohn sailed again for Europe—his third trip in four years. While he was away, Amherst's alumni began to organize a movement to depose him. "I feel that we are facing a crisis," wrote the secretary of Amherst's Alumni Council, which, ironically, Meiklejohn had helped to found. "Something has been lacking in cooperation between the president and the faculty. This absence of harmony has been growing more and more evident, until now a large percentage of the full professors, men whom we learned to revere when in college, are so discouraged that their hearts are not in their work, and some have even told me that, if a change is not made soon, they will have to go elsewhere."[61] The main source of alumni opposition was the Amherst Alumni Club of St. Louis, which spread rumors that Meiklejohn was undermining the school's religious foundations. The alumni in St. Louis conspired with the alumni in Chicago to bring Meiklejohn down. "The latest," Clarence Ayres wrote to Meiklejohn, "is that they are going to send up a carload of delegates to the Chicago meeting with a view to making trouble for your supporters. . . . sending people to talk things over in open meetings does not bother me so much as drunken whisperings across café tables about the president's 'irreligion.'" Such meetings,

Ayres wrote, could work the alumni into "a fine alcoholic frenzy."[62] The Amherst Alumni Club of Boston expressed similar hostility, although its objections pertained more to sports than to religion. "I don't care how good a teacher this Meiklejohn is," one alumnus bellowed. "If he can't give the college winning teams, he is no man for me." According to Boston's alumni, Meiklejohn was simply "too liberal" to represent the best interests of Amherst College.[63]

Whether Meiklejohn was too liberal or too conservative for Amherst was open to debate. On issues of economic and educational reform, he tended to gravitate toward the liberal end of the political spectrum. On issues of institutional management, however, he drifted toward the conservative or even dictatorial end. In the complex ideological climate of the early 1920s, when the Red Scare combined with the Jazz Age to form a confusing cultural mix, Meiklejohn often found himself on the "wrong" side of the ideological fence. At a time when most Americans favored the hands-off fiscal policy and "return to normalcy" of the Harding administration, Meiklejohn cast his lot with the workers, the socialists, and other left-leaning groups. Yet, at a time when growing segments of the middle class embraced mass consumerism, he lamented the lack of intellectualism in American life. Throughout the 1920s, he bemoaned the rise of commercial radio, the spread of pulp fiction, the proliferation of glitzy advertising, and the growth of the motion-picture industry. Revisiting his childhood prohibitionism, he especially decried the lawlessness of bootleggers and gangsters who violated the Eighteenth Amendment.[64] To him, it seemed that American society in the Age of Excess was coming apart much faster than anyone, especially educators, could put it back together. He clung to the idea of a liberal college set apart from the crassness and ignorance of the postwar "booboisie"—a group in which he placed most of Amherst's alumni and trustees—but his own blend of radicalism and moralism seemed anachronistic in his rapidly changing cultural milieu. How could a self-described liberal recover a sense of the reformist optimism that had sustained him in an earlier, more progressive, age? How could he recover his old vision of a democratic college community committed to moral and intellectual excellence? How could he convey to the faculty at Amherst, as he had tried to convey to the students at Brown, his vision of liberal education as a critical cultural ideal?

In the spring of 1922, shortly after his disastrous meeting with Amherst's trustees, Meiklejohn had addressed the recently inducted members of Phi Beta Kappa at Harvard. Recalling the glories of the Cammarian Club at Brown, he chose to speak on the subject of democracy and excellence in the liberal college.[65] "I like to go to Europe," he announced, "because one finds there these excellent things and because there I get the sense of the human spirit soaring into its best—the sense of what men feel in religion—just adequately expressed. The human spirit goes up there. That's all there is to life, the choice between the high and the excellent and the low and the vulgar."[66] In Meiklejohn's view, liberal colleges had a responsibility to teach students, and the rest of society, how to recognize excellence in the world.[67] To educate was to initiate citizens into a wider community of shared cultural ideals. Yet, herein lay the dilemma of democratic education. How could education distribute excellence to a majority of citizens without somehow degrading it in the process? How could education teach democracy's highest ideals if no one wanted to learn? "Human experience shows that if you take excellent things and give them to the crowd, the crowd degrades them," Meiklejohn told Harvard's Phi Beta Kappans. "If you take music and give it to the crowd, it becomes jazz. If you take art and give it to the crowd, you have the movies. If you take language and give it to the crowd, you have slang. Apparently, down they all go when you give them to the crowd." How, then, could democracy cultivate excellence without causing the dilution of virtue? "I don't say excellence can be made universal," Meiklejohn conceded, "but I am enough of a democrat to believe we have started on a venture of seeing whether a whole people and eventually a whole world can embark on some common enterprise of excellence." The time had come to see if America, having survived the horror and stupidity of war, could finally be educated for the kind of virtuous self-government that would distinguish a truly democratic society. "Will democracy work as a principle of government?" Meiklejohn asked Harvard's best and brightest. "There are those who contend that it cannot be done, and perhaps it cannot, but there is glory in trying to bring it about through education."[68]

Meiklejohn's decision to deliver a speech titled "Democracy and Excellence" at Harvard in 1922 was no accident. In the spring of that year, in response to unprecedented demand for admission, Harvard's president Abbott Lawrence Lowell had decided to limit the number of Jews selected for each incoming class. Meiklejohn, for one, was outraged. "Whenever I hear that certain people shall be excluded from excellence, I think it is not right," he said. "When I hear that colleges are closing their doors on certain students, I believe it is not right."[69] In Meiklejohn's view, anyone who expressed an interest in intellectual excellence should have access to a college education. "It is of course true that there should be selection among young people of those who are best fitted for college training," he acknowledged, "but it is not clear just how that selection is to be made. I, for one, should not be willing that the workman's son or the tailor's son or the son of the foreigner should, as such, be excluded."[70] Reiterating arguments he had made more than two decades earlier at Brown, Meiklejohn insisted that the only factors relevant to admission decisions were an eagerness and an ability to learn. The same standards that applied to white, Anglo-Saxon, Protestant students applied to Jewish, Catholic, and other minority students as well. Indeed, at a time when Harvard and other schools segregated black students in separate dormitories, Meiklejohn welcomed them on equal terms to Amherst. "If they do not come," he declared, "then we must go out and bring them in."[71] Between 1912 and 1923, at least seventeen black students enrolled at Amherst, a situation Meiklejohn considered "unusually fortunate" for the school.[72]

But Meiklejohn's vision of a more liberal democratic college community did not necessarily appeal to Amherst's more conservative faculty, alumni, and trustees. In fact, many white Americans strongly resented the educational progress and cultural achievements of black Americans in the 1920s. The Ku Klux Klan gained a nationwide following after 1922, when Imperial Wizard Hiram W. Evans hired professional publicists to increase his organization's membership. Using pseudoscientific information to spread eugenic theories about the inherent inferiority of nonwhites, the KKK preached hatred not only for blacks but also for immigrants, Catholics, and Jews. Its slogan "Native, White, Protestant Supremacy" attracted two million xenophobes by 1923, including a few Amherst alumni. As one alumnus wrote to Meiklejohn in June of 1922, "[I]t is not 'unusually fortunate' for Amherst that she has every year three or four Negro students in each class. It is unfortunate for her. . . . However, I can see fast enough that Amherst is going your way." "P.S.," the alumnus added, "eugenics are coming."[73] Undeterred by such hateful comments, Meiklejohn took a strong stand against racism in the college community. He insisted, for example, that black students should feel free to join Amherst's athletic teams even if their participation meant that other schools would refuse to compete on campus. Once, a few weeks before a football game at Princeton, Meiklejohn received a letter from Princeton's head coach indicating that he was "not sure we can protect Drew [a black student] if he plays in [the] football game down here." Meiklejohn shot back a reply, stating that, "if you can't give protection to the [entire] Amherst College football team—of which he is a member—then there will be no game. We will cancel at once."[74]

Meiklejohn's liberal perspective on racism, like his liberal perspective on radicalism, did not endear him to the older and more conservative members of the Amherst community. Indeed, his support for black student enrollments and his speeches against Harvard's anti-Semitic admission policies had infuriated a number of Boston alumni. But he did not back down. As W. H. P. Faunce had once remarked at Brown, Meiklejohn was "at his best when the sky grows dark and obstacles abound."[75] And by the spring of 1923, the sky was dark indeed. News of imminent conflict among Meiklejohn, his faculty, his alumni, and his trustees had spread far and wide. It was well known throughout New England that Amherst was teetering on the brink of "civil war." Finally, on June 14, 1923, the situation exploded. Just when the campus was preparing for its annual commencement festivities, the faculty voted twenty-four to eleven to demand Meiklejohn's resignation. It was the shot that started the war. Thanks to a persistent young reporter from the *Springfield Daily Republican,* the story of Meiklejohn's endangered presidency made headlines nationwide.[76] The day after the faculty vote, June 15, 1923, the town of Amherst was swarming with journalists. Hearing of Meiklejohn's trouble, supporters began to organize in his defense. Telegrams flooded into the college. Fifteen universities cabled their support. Letters favoring Meiklejohn arrived from all over the world. On June 16, the *New York Times* reported that undergraduate sentiment had been expressed strongly in favor of Meiklejohn. "Some of the seniors have gone so far as to declare that they will refuse to accept their diplomas at the Commencement on Wednesday if they find the president is going to be forced out, and some members of the junior class have asserted they will not return to Amherst next year unless Dr. Meiklejohn remains."[77] By June 17, the battle had begun.

As caravans of alumni pulled into Amherst for their reunion activities, a rumor surfaced that the trustees might fire Professor Churchill instead of Meiklejohn if the president's supporters were strong enough.[78] By the next morning, groups of older alumni were marching around the campus with banners labeled "Resign! Resign!" while younger alumni countered with placards labeled "Prexy for the next hundred years!" In the meantime, Churchill arranged for several friends to carry a flag with the slogan, "We paid his debts. We sent him to Europe. I'll say we're a liberal college!"[79] Caught in the midst of such a humiliating controversy, Meiklejohn showed remarkable grace under pressure. On the opening day of the commencement celebration, he addressed the alumni from the steps of Johnson Chapel and welcomed them back to the campus. "Everyone was aware of the impending crisis and wondered how Prexy would handle the situation," one spectator recalled. "He walked briskly out of the big doors and stood on the top step looking tired but alert. His eyes sparkled and a wan smile spread across his face." Meiklejohn reminded the alumni that the purpose of a reunion was to renew old friendships and recapture the ideals of the liberal college. He urged the alumni to leave the matter of his presidency up to the trustees and implied that, come what may, he would accept their decision. According to one alumnus, Meiklejohn's brief talk "showed no bitterness, but was tolerant and, in a way, impersonal. Had he desired to, he could have swept his followers into a frenzy and thereby split the alumni body into two angry camps. As it was, everyone admired his spirit and left to go his own way."[80]

Meiklejohn had hoped that the matter could be settled by the trustees, and so it was. On the night of June 18, as the campus prepared for the baccalaureate service the next day, a committee of trustees met Meiklejohn in the Philosophy Room on the library's top floor. It was an uncomfortable meeting. According to Stanley King, "[T]he evening was so hot that, although all the windows were open, the room was like an oven, and we all took off our coats to be as comfortable as possible." The time and place of the meeting were well known, and every entrance to the library was watched by groups of newspapermen and younger alumni. Meiklejohn opened the negotiations. He stated that, after consulting with a lawyer, he had decided to fight the campaign against him. He attacked the faculty for its childish behavior, and he criticized the trustees for spreading rumors about his finances. When the committee denied any such act, Meiklejohn asked them to destroy all reports detailing his salary overdrafts. The meeting dragged on for several hours. Bitter accusations—concerning workers' education, black students, faculty relations, fundraising, and curricular reform—flew freely between Meiklejohn and the members of the committee. "The rest of the building was dark," King recalled, "so the watchers knew just where the meeting was taking place, though they could not see the actors. Unknown to us, one of our fellow trustees sat on a neighboring hillside with his powerful binoculars watching intently the faces and the lips of each of us in the room and drawing his own picture of what was taking place." Finally, after more than four hours of sweaty argument, the committee requested Meiklejohn's resignation. According to King, the meeting did not end on a cordial note. Meiklejohn refused to concede defeat, declaring angrily that he would never forgive the trustees for their decision against him. Nevertheless, his presidency at Amherst was over.[81]

The protest, however, was not. When the baccalaureate service began the next morning, the senior class president stood and, "with magnificent timing—ten seconds earlier and he would not have been heard, ten seconds later and he would have been rude to the clergy—announced ringingly that the Class of 1923 had unanimously elected Meiklejohn an honorary member."[82] A deafening ovation ensued.[83] Embarrassed, but also emboldened by the applause, Meiklejohn stepped up to the pulpit to deliver his baccalaureate sermon. He chose for his text the parable of the Pharisees. The Pharisees, he explained, were the practical people of ancient Jerusalem. They were the doers, punctilious in their observation of Jewish law and single-minded in their dedication to making the world a more comfortable place to live. Jesus had preached to the Pharisees, chastising them for their earthly concerns and encouraging them to look beyond their trivial concerns for higher and more excellent things. As Jesus said, "My kingdom is not of this world." Meiklejohn compared the Pharisees to Amherst's trustees, claiming that they had focused on trivialities and thus failed to understand the true purpose of the liberal college as an institution of cultural *criticism*. "We have asked, 'In what sense is our world Christian?' And Jesus seems to answer, 'In no sense at all.' Christianity is not a theory by which the world lives. It is a criticism of this world and its theories; it is a condemnation both of civilization and of the men who make it."[84] Revisiting the idea of a critical college, which he had developed during the war, Meiklejohn cast himself in the role of the Messiah and reiterated his vision of a college set apart for the pursuit of truth. A truly liberal college, he asserted, was "not of this world" but somehow *above* it. And yet, to Meiklejohn's detractors, this idea of a critical college sent down from heaven to save the world was pure sacrilege. "Amherst is no place for him and his Bolshevik, impracticable visions," declared one editorial in the *Brooklyn Standard Union*. "Nor can it be said that the retiring president's farewell baccalaureate, far more dramatic than convincing, helped his case very much. The attempt to stage Jerusalem in the Amherst hills must at best have been but a theatrical gesture. Publicly calling the trustees and alumni 'Pharisees' and 'mere common-sense men' looks in rather questionable taste, and, while the role of the second person of the Deity was not definitely cast, there could be but one inference for whom it was reserved."[85]

The next day at Amherst's commencement ceremony the students were far less controlled than Meiklejohn had been at the baccalaureate service. Several students audibly hissed Professor Churchill as he climbed the podium stairs, and many booed the trustees as they took their seats on the stage. The seating arrangement on the main platform was rather awkward, with Meiklejohn sitting between chairman of the board George

Plimpton and vice president of the United States Calvin Coolidge, an Amherst alumnus and trustee. According to an article in the *New York World*, "[T]he contrast between the views of the two men made the situation difficult." Throughout the ceremony, Coolidge, who supported the trustees' decision to dismiss Meiklejohn, "glared straight ahead, his cigar long since dead," and, after the presentation of degrees, he "hastily turned about and slipped off the dais."[86] Yet, it was the presentation of degrees that provided the most piquant opportunity for protest. As the *Providence Journal-Bulletin* reported, several students, including the president of Phi Beta Kappa and the vice president of the senior class, refused to accept their diplomas. To accept their degrees, they declared, "would be an act of disloyalty to Amherst, the liberal college."[87] Meiklejohn, in an effort to calm the tension created by his students' show of support, stood after the first defiant student left the stage and said, "If there should be any more of you who plan to refuse your diploma, PLEASE do not come forward—just stay in your seat."[88] Remaining in their seats, however, only heightened the drama of their disobedience. By the end of the ceremony, a total of thirteen students, nearly 10 percent of the senior class, had refused to accept their degrees.

The climactic conclusion of the week's events came at the alumni luncheon the following day. Graduates and guests all crammed into the college gymnasium, where Meiklejohn prepared to deliver his final presidential address. Standing on a small stage beneath the flying-rings, pulley-weights, and ropes, he spoke extemporaneously on the significance of his departure. "I came here eleven years ago with very high purpose and with great encouragement," he began. "I was told by trustees to try to change the place as well as to keep it going, and I have tried to do it." Peering out at the assembled crowd, with older alumni seated on one side of the field house and younger graduates seated on the other, Meiklejohn spoke candidly about the antagonisms that had developed between himself and certain older members of the faculty. He confessed that he had tried, albeit perhaps unsuccessfully, to create a more stimulating and dynamic intellectual atmosphere in the college. He admitted that he had tried to update the curriculum, even though many of the faculty had resisted. He would not, he said, apologize for these reforms, nor would he apologize for the controversial ways in which he pursued them. "The thing I was commissioned to do when I came here," he asserted, "was to try to change the faculty for the better in terms of personnel, in terms of teaching method, in terms of course of study. May I say, it is going to be a very hard thing to improve our faculty. The faculty find it exceedingly difficult to improve

117

themselves, and they find it exceedingly objectionable to have anyone else do it to them."[89] And yet, despite his contempt for Amherst's Old Guard, Meiklejohn maintained that, in an ideal college, the faculty, rather than business-minded trustees, should control all academic affairs. "I believe the college should be controlled by its faculty," he declared. Therefore, when a majority of professors expressed their lack of confidence in his leadership, he knew he had to leave.[90]

While Meiklejohn spoke, the tension in the gymnasium was electric. As one listener recalled, it would have been possible to draw a line down the middle of the room between those for and those against the president. "On one side were the elders, unmoved and stolid. On the other were the youngsters, leaning forward, leaping from their seats to shout and cheer as bolts fell. By turns the place would burst into thunders of applause, then as suddenly hush to a stillness in which you could hear your own breathing."[91] Finally, Meiklejohn brought his speech to a stirring close. "The point," he proclaimed, "is that I am a minority man. I am always wanting change. Now, from that point of view, will you let me say that I am amazed that the thing has lasted as long as it has. I expect to be in the minority, but institutions must inevitably be in the hands of majorities." Inasmuch as the majority of the faculty at Amherst had rejected his leadership, he knew he must go, even if Amherst as a liberal college might suffer in his absence. "I am a believer in democracy," he noted, "but my query is whether institutions of learning should be in the hands of majorities." With these words, Meiklejohn reiterated the vision of a liberal democratic college he had outlined eleven years earlier at his inauguration. "I believe in setting learning apart from life and keeping it there that it may be pure and true and clean and free," he announced. "I say the greatest danger to the American college today is that it will be drawn into the common life and will take the standards of our common life as its own, rejoicing in being like other men rather than in the necessary difference which every scholar has with every other man who is not a scholar. Being in the minority, men of Amherst, may I say that I am going because you think I ought not to be here. I go somewhere else. I don't know where, but I am going in the same way." Swearing that he would never abandon his quest for intellectual excellence in the liberal college, even if the majority drifted toward mediocrity, Meiklejohn pledged to continue his educational crusade. "I differ from most of you on most of the issues of life," he said, "and I am going to keep it up."[92] With that, he stepped off the stage.

Immediately, the audience erupted in chaos. "The whole gathering seemed to go off its head," one eyewitness recalled. "Some people cheered.

Some pounded the tables. Some sat perfectly still with tears streaming down their faces."[93] After Meiklejohn's speech, eight professors tendered their resignations, including Clarence Ayres, Walter Agard, Laurance Saunders, and John Gaus. Albert Parker Fitch commented upon leaving that Meiklejohn's presidency had raised Amherst to new heights.[94] "As your presidency conferred national significance upon Amherst, your leaving becomes a matter of national concern," echoed Felix Frankfurter, a Harvard law professor who later became a Supreme Court justice and one of Meiklejohn's closest friends. "Those of us who have come in contact during recent years with the graduates of Amherst have known of your work at Amherst by its fruits. And thus we have come to know that something very significant was happening [there]. . . . I, therefore, feel terribly sad about the termination of your work at Amherst because it means certainly the temporary arrest of forces that are most precious and indispensable to the wise unfolding of our national life."[95] Zechariah Chafee, Jr., another Harvard law professor who had been a student in Meiklejohn's classes at Brown, expressed kindred views. "The news of your resignation comes as a real blow to many of us in Cambridge," Chafee wrote. "You raised the American college to a new plane. Your students were the liveliest crowd of undergraduates I have talked to, much more so than those at Brown or Harvard, and this I attribute largely to you." In Chafee's view, Meiklejohn had fought the same fight that Woodrow Wilson had fought at Princeton. "If you have lost," he concluded, "you have lost in noble companionship."[96]

Parallels between Meiklejohn and Wilson were oft noted. As one editorial remarked, "Dr. Alexander Meiklejohn seems to possess many of those temperamental qualities and strange contradictions that created such pronounced differences between Dr. Woodrow Wilson and the trustees of Princeton. The similarity between these educators goes beyond their natural brilliancy of mind and their abundant aptitude for coining phrases that tickle the eardrums without carrying conviction to the understanding. Both know how to talk enthusiastically about the virtues of democracy while delighting to exemplify autocracy in their personal handling of affairs. Both exalt the majority while siding with the minority. Both are tactful and gracious so long as other men's minds run along with theirs. The possibility that opposing opinion may be wrong does not enter into their calculations. From an insecure premise, both can argue adroitly to illogical conclusions that are dressed up to appear logical. Each has the courage of convictions that are not always well placed."[97] Indeed, both Meiklejohn and Wilson were idealists who occasionally allowed the enthusiasm of their vision to impede the integrity of their leadership. Both failed to distinguish between moral assurance and moral arrogance, and, when pressed, both let self-confidence slip into stubbornness. The idea that Meiklejohn, like Wilson, had tended to exalt the majority while siding with the minority was key to understanding the failure of his presidency. Rather than using the persuasiveness and patience he had developed to such great effect at Brown, he foisted curricular reforms on a resistant faculty and paid no heed to internal dissent at Amherst. He expected unconditional financial support from his trustees and made no effort to hide his antipathy for opponents he considered unreasonable. In his single-minded effort to make Amherst a more liberal and democratic institution, he ran roughshod over principles of toleration, representation, and consent.

Walter Lippmann registered a similar interpretation of Meiklejohn's dismissal in a lengthy editorial for the *New York World*. "The important point," Lippmann wrote, was that "Meiklejohn was building a new faculty, and this meant the shelving and the diminution of the old faculty." The problem was not that Meiklejohn hired dynamic young professors but rather that he mismanaged relations with the old. Making matters worse was his lack of any real attempt to ingratiate himself into the town of Amherst. "He is not a glad-hander nor, in the college sense, a jolly good fellow," Lippmann noted. "He is personally austere, kindly humble, and difficult. He is religious, but not churchly. He is a patriot, but not, by Calvin Coolidge standards, a 100-percenter. He did not go to town meeting. He neglected to vote." In the end, Lippmann judged, Meiklejohn had been overly idealistic and aloof, a man ahead of his time. "He was lots of Woodrow Wilson and none of Lloyd George. He could inspire, but he could not manage. He did magnificently with students and failed lamentably with grown-ups." According to Lippmann, Meiklejohn's dismissal was tragic but inevitable. "Amherst has lost a fine educator and a great spiritual leader of youth because he was an unsuccessful leader of men," he wrote. "Meiklejohn's Amherst was a machine that simply would not work. But, inefficient as it was, it produced as remarkable a student body as I have ever encountered. Hopeless as it was, it made Amherst one of the most distinguished small colleges in America."[98] Lippmann, more than any other commentator, was right. Meiklejohn had pursued his vision to its breaking point—the point at which moral and intellectual idealism yielded to personal authoritarianism. His dual commitments to excellence and accessibility in higher education made him a respected professor—as well as an effective teacher of the ethical principles required of a democratic college community—but these very commitments also alienated him from anyone who disagreed with his point of view, including most of his faculty, alumni, and trustees. Even if Meiklejohn believed in democracy in an abstract sense, he was destined to be a minority man at Amherst. He could not teach democracy if the majority refused to learn.

In September of 1923, Meiklejohn published his own version of the Amherst debacle in an article for *Century* magazine. His title, "To Whom Are We Responsible?" conveyed the crux of his position. Defining *we* as the "community of scholars" broadly conceived, he devoted half of his article to a list of groups to whom the college was *not* responsible, including trustees, alumni, donors, and parents, as well as the church, the public, and the state. According to Meiklejohn, a liberal college had two basic responsibilities. First was its responsibility to the community of scholars at large. "There is a fellowship of learning in which all alike are enrolled, an enterprise of learning in which all are engaged," he argued. "And, in this enterprise, each worker is responsible to his fellow workers." Acknowledging the lack of fellowship that characterized the community of scholars at Amherst, Meiklejohn identified a second, higher, and indeed *prior* responsibility, a responsibility to the truth. "As against the truth which scholars have," he wrote, "there is the truth for which they strive, which never is achieved. It is in terms of this truth that final judgment must be given." Asking himself if this truth was something "other than ourselves," something entirely, even ontologically, apart from the world of everyday existence and thought, Meiklejohn replied that it was. "The beauty which men have not seen but yearn to see, the goodness which no man can reach but which mankind must ever strive to gain, the end toward which he makes his way—these final ends elude our grasp. Yet, they are in some sense real; they are outside ourselves; and, being real and being what they are, they are our masters." Harkening back to his Kantian idealist roots, Meiklejohn asserted that the real purpose of liberal education, the ultimate goal of cultural criticism, was to look *beyond* the way things are, *beyond* the immediate concerns of a particular time and place, to imagine the way things ought to be. "I think," he concluded, "that 'thinking' means that, somehow, in the very nature of the world itself, there is a meaning which we seek, a meaning which is there whether we find it or not."[99] Clearly, Meiklejohn's idealism had survived his dismissal from Amherst. Indeed, it may even have been strengthened by the struggle.

In the end, Meiklejohn carried a mixed legacy away from Amherst. Some, such as his friend Arthur Upham Pope, believed he had emerged almost completely unscathed. "Despite some special frustrations and anxieties," Pope wrote, "Meiklejohn weathered the Amherst defeat without agitation. Like Socrates, he felt no ill will. No hostility on the part of those in power could do any real harm to an honorable man."[100] Others, however, saw the situation much differently. "As I look back on his tenure at Amherst," one alumnus judged, "I can see that this young intellectual leader was perhaps too impatient and, maybe, too intolerant. He surrounded himself with men of his type; he did not succeed in winning over to his camp those who were in senior positions and lacked the drive which characterized Meiklejohn himself."[101] Stanley King said it best when he concluded that Meiklejohn "wanted autocratic power over the faculty and was unwilling to accept the slower and more painful democratic process of persuasion." As King later explained, Meiklejohn betrayed a "curious contradiction" in his approach to administration. "He enjoyed intellectual differences of opinion; he enjoyed dialectic for its own sake; and he constantly cultivated it. He seemed to enjoy the process of dialectic more than he cared for the conclusion arrived at. But faculty opposition to his policies came to be considered disloyalty to the president, and this he could not forgive."[102] In the end, assessing Meiklejohn's presidency at Amherst meant choosing from an array of conflicting perspectives. Certainly, as an administrator, he had failed. He did not foster collegial or trusting relations with his faculty, nor did he win support from his alumni. Most troubling of all, he did not demonstrate a capacity for straightforward honesty—or for prudent financial management—to his trustees. Yet, as a symbol of liberal educational reform and an advocate of intellectual idealism, he undoubtedly succeeded. He instituted a new structure for undergraduate education at Amherst and updated the curriculum. He clearly distinguished intellectual from vocational aims and, despite occasional comments to the contrary, articulated a vision of the critical college as an institution set apart from mainstream political and economic affairs. Ultimately, the question was whether *any* institution could rise to the high standard of Meiklejohn's idealistic educational dreams.

The day after his dismissal, Meiklejohn received a letter from Alvin Johnson, director of the New School for Social Research in midtown Manhattan. "Your place in American education is fixed," Johnson wrote, "and the college cannot drop back into the somnolence of the sunny nineties, however much it tries." Describing his own innovations at the recently established New School, Johnson invited Meiklejohn to join in administering his experiment. "I think that, with adequate organization and energy, such an institution could be made practically self-supporting, free from donors, trustees, alumni, Death and the Devil," Johnson wrote. "Does the idea seem too fantastic for consideration? Then dismiss it. But if it seems real, and if you think you might be interested in helping to float so specu-lative a venture, then let me have a chance to talk to you about it."[103] A similar appeal came from Philip Burnet, president of the Continental Life Insurance Company, who wrote the same day as Johnson. "Why not think of an entirely new educational institution," Burnet queried, "to be gov-erned largely or wholly by the faculty and supported by those thinking people who vaguely call themselves 'liberals,' where the plant investment will be reduced to the minimum and the funds expended chiefly in in-struction—an institution with the avowed purpose of liberating people by teaching them to think, and how to think, and not of adapting them to things as they are, but rather of sending out a band of free spirits bent on keeping alive the flame of spiritual aspiration through the dark age of com-mercial exploitation which is following on the heels of the break-up of the Christian tradition?"[104] Meiklejohn took these letters to heart and began to search for new ways to implement his educational ideals.

Just two days after Amherst's stormy commencement, the *New York World* was already speculating about Meiklejohn's likely future endeav-ors. "His plans are as vague as is possible to imagine," the paper reported. "His most intimate friends say part of his hesitation is due to a lack of ready money. He was not known as a thrifty man. With his salary of $12,000 continued for the next year, he will have the opportunity to look around and make a decision free of the pressure of material aspects. It is expected he may attempt to summarize his theories in book form."[105] A few weeks later, Meiklejohn received a contract from the Century Pub-lishing Company for three books: *Education and Democracy*, *Democracy and Excellence*, and *Is the World Christian?*[106] Before he had time to start these books, however, Frank Davison, managing editor of *The Forum* magazine, contacted him to request an article on "the ideal university." "Here is an opportunity for a wild flight of imagination," Davison wrote. "You could paint as utopian a picture as you choose and end with the question, 'Who will come forward and "back" such an institution?' "[107] Meiklejohn thanked Davison for his offer but signed all his work over to Glenn Frank, editor of *Century*, who asked for exclusive rights to his writ-ings.[108] "I should like to have *Century* be the medium through which, dur-ing the next year or two, your basic philosophy reaches the American public," Frank wrote in July of 1923.[109] Meiklejohn concurred and, in subsequent weeks, arranged for the Century Company to publish a col-lection of Amherst speeches under the title *Freedom and the College*.[110]

In September of 1923, Meiklejohn left Amherst and moved to Man-hattan. He enrolled his three sons at the prestigious Taft School in Watertown, Connecticut, and brought his seven-year-old daughter, Annaletta, to live with him and Nannine in a roomy apartment at 247 West Fourth Street in Greenwich Village. "I am delighted to hear that your boys are to be at the Taft School and that you, yourself, are to have for the present a headquarters in New York," W. H. P. Faunce wrote from Brown. "Immediately after you resigned, I had interviews with President Lowell of Harvard and President Burton of Chicago urging each of them to make a place for you in their Philosophical Departments. Burton seemed impressed by my statement, and I hope something may develop in Chicago, where they sadly need an antidote to Professor Dewey's influence."[111] Meiklejohn thanked Faunce for his help but declined to teach philosophy at either Harvard or Chicago. He similarly refused overtures to serve as president at Reed, Knox, and the University of Oklahoma.[112] Instead, he decided to embark on a brief foray into public speaking. In the fall of 1923, he delivered two addresses to very large audiences in New York. The first lecture was titled "Democracy and Excellence"; the second, "A College of Tomorrow." Taken together, these unpublished talks outlined his developing plans for a next step in American higher education.

On October 21, 1923, three thousand people flocked to Carnegie Hall to hear Meiklejohn's speech "Democracy and Excellence." It was a speech he had delivered many times in various forms over the past year and a half—first to Phi Beta Kappa initiates at Harvard and then to graduating students at Mount Holyoke and Brown. "Oh, I wish we could face the facts in America and see where we are," Meiklejohn began in a jeremiad style that seemed to suit him in the period after his dismissal from Amherst. "We haven't even begun to think about education that will liberate all men and give all the opportunity to be excellent."[113] Calling America a dull mob and a gawky boy led by a bunch of "third-rate minds," Meiklejohn asserted the need to teach citizens how to be excellent, how to be democratic, and how to use their freedom wisely. "How futile it is to give men political opportunities and possessions unless they know how to use them," he asserted. "To give men the vote—what is it worth unless there is understanding of what is going on?" The "college of tomorrow," he argued, would teach Americans how to be free. Describing his proposed institution as "an ultra-modern college of liberal culture in which the faculty and student body shall have complete control," he predicted "a new day in pedagogy" when teachers and pupils would study Great Books together in a common learning endeavor.[114] "Tomorrow," he announced, "students and faculty will do the same thing and all students will do the same thing. I do not mean that all will pursue the same courses

or work even in the same fields, but that all will work with the same purpose and with a common dominating interest."[115] Here, in the form of a
brief thumbnail sketch, Meiklejohn outlined his vision of the future in
American higher education. The only way to teach democracy, he insisted,
was to create a college in which every member of the group voluntarily
subscribed to a unified mission of educational excellence. "Who knows if
we can unite democracy and excellence in the next five hundred or thousand years," he concluded. "I don't, and I don't care. It's a game, a great,
splendid game, and it's well worth the trying."[116]

Meiklejohn's plan for a new college attracted considerable attention in
New York, not only among educators, but also among publicists and potential donors. Abraham Flexner of the General Education Board listened
"with very keen interest" to reports of Meiklejohn's plan. "It is wisely put
forth as an 'experiment,'" Flexner wrote, "which means, I take it, that,
having diagnosed the situation, you are casting about in your mind for
ways of dealing with it." Much as Flexner felt intrigued by Meiklejohn's
plan, however, he confessed that he had difficulty seeing how to put it into
institutional action. He compared Meiklejohn's college of tomorrow to
John Dewey's defunct "laboratory school" in Chicago. "Dewey's philosophy of elementary education was very stimulating," Flexner wrote, "but
Dewey could himself never get it made into a school."[117] Meiklejohn,
however, had every intention of getting his plan made into a school. Over
the summer of 1924, he solicited financier Bernard Baruch, a major con-
tributor to the City College of New York, about the possibility of funding
his new college.[118] When Baruch failed to respond, he contacted Glenn
Frank at *Century.* Frank quickly gathered a committee of prominent New
Yorkers—Alvin Johnson of the New School for Social Research, Mark
Sullivan of *Collier's* and the *New York Evening Post,* and Herbert Croly
of the *New Republic*—to discuss ways of raising three million dollars to
start a "Meiklejohn College" in the city.[119] Croly asked Dorothy Straight,
an heiress to the Whitney family fortune, publisher of the *New Republic,*
and a major benefactor of the New School, to donate two thousand dollars to start the process of planning the new college.[120] Croly and Straight
encouraged Meiklejohn to publish his ideas in the *New Republic,* but
Meiklejohn promised his ideas to Frank at *Century,* with his first article
slated to appear in January of 1925.

When it came to the Meiklejohn College idea, not everyone shared the
enthusiasm of Frank, Croly, Johnson, Sullivan, and Straight. As the *New
York Herald* editorialized, "[I]t is possible that he would work in amity
with professors of his own choosing [but only] if they obeyed his direc-

tions and permitted him to be a virtual autocrat."[121] Indeed, no one was more suspicious of Meiklejohn's plan to start a new college than W. H. P. Faunce, who questioned whether Meiklejohn had a tenable theory of democratic education, or even whether he truly wanted one. "You want college presidents abolished, yet no other college president in New England has been so autocratic as yourself," Faunce wrote in a sternly worded letter. "You want the faculty supreme, yet when you find they are supreme at Amherst you do not approve the situation. . . . You passionately affirm democracy, yet just as strongly affirm aristocracy in your recent Carnegie Hall address, so that one professor said to me: 'My mind went round in dizzy circles while I read that address.' " It was a deeply revealing letter from one of Meiklejohn's closest mentors. Faunce, like so many of Meiklejohn's friends and acquaintances in the months after his dismissal, wondered if he had perhaps lost his personal and intellectual bearings. "Am I imperiling our friendship when I write so frankly of my bewilderment?" Faunce asked. "I recognize in you a mind far superior to my own. I believe you have before you still the greatest work of your life, while my small service will soon be over. Just because I so admire and love you, I dare to write of the curious sense of unreality which plunges me into darkness when I try to follow you. I flounder and grope and then fall back on the hypothesis—am I right?—that you do not wish to arrive, but only to travel; that you want to prevent us from reaching conclusions and simply keep on playing a 'game.' Is this fascinating game, in which nobody can win, all that life has to offer?"[122] Faunce was not alone in his perplexity. Meiklejohn's idealism seemed to require a positive statement of educational aims and a practical program for moral reconstruction in a fallen world. Yet, as his Carnegie Hall address had shown, he often stopped short of such a statement, referring to liberal education and cultural criticism almost dismissively as a great, splendid game. When all was said and done, it seemed to Faunce that Meiklejohn settled for a limp "adversarial" stance fundamentally detached from the possibility of practical social reform.

Meiklejohn, however, did not see himself that way, and he responded enthusiastically to Faunce. " 'Imperiling our friendship'?" he gasped. "I never liked you so much. And that is fairly strong for a dumb Scotchman. Thanks! And thanks again!" Meiklejohn expressed his gratitude for Faunce's honest letter and tried sincerely to address its points. "I have not been autocratic," he replied. "I have believed terribly hard, but I have not tried to force my will on others. . . . When the trustees opposed me, I laughed. When the faculty, by the most devious and underground ways, was recorded as being a majority against me, I stepped out without a question, even though I did not believe that their real judgment was given and was sure someday they would regret it." When it came to the clash between democracy and excellence in the liberal college, Meiklejohn noted his ardent affirmation of both. In his view, the attempt to make life excellent instead of mediocre was the abiding purpose of the liberal college—or, for that matter, of any educational institution. To teach was always to try to make life better than it might otherwise be. To learn was to look beyond the world as it was in order to embrace true virtue, or at least the validity of education as a truly progressive process. As he wrote for *Century,* education was the ongoing quest for "the goodness which no man can reach, but which mankind must ever strive to gain." And yet, if the majority refused to learn, then there was little any educator could do. "In a fundamental sense," Meiklejohn wrote to Faunce, "I do not expect 'to arrive.' You know as well as I that we cannot do that in the sense of solving our problems, finishing our tasks, realizing our purposes. On the other hand, with every moment, we do arrive at what that moment is, and I think you know how eager and determined I am that 'moments' shall be made, as they pass, significant, beautiful, and worthwhile. I do not agree that no one wins in the game. We all win if we play well. But that does not mean that the game is ended and we may proudly strut about enjoying the glory of what has been done."[123]

For Meiklejohn, education was a dialectical process of critical intellectual development, an endless and ongoing attempt to see beyond the social status quo, to grasp essential meanings, and, ultimately, to offer alternatives to the way things were. "I do believe it part of my business to attack the easy solutions, the dictums with which people settle down at ease while others are struggling in despair," Meiklejohn wrote to Faunce. "But I don't play with ideas only for fun. I want fun, and I get it in ideas, but what I really want is the truth about this living world of ours which needs it so sorely. I want to know what we should do and be." For Meiklejohn, the life of a teacher was a life of eternal longing, a life of yearning for ultimate and meaningful *ideals.* As such, a teacher's life was always profoundly tragic, because ideals, even as they pointed toward universals, inevitably operated in a world of particulars. As an idealist, Meiklejohn firmly believed in humanity's ability to think beyond the particularities of everyday existence and, thereby, to imagine alternatives for social reform. Yet, at the same time, he recognized the need for every alternative to take temporal institutional form and, in that process, to sacrifice the transcendence it originally aimed to embody. Thus, seeking excellence through liberal education did not necessarily mean achieving it. Ending his letter to Faunce, Meiklejohn asked for sympathy and support. "I write for fun and in sober earnest," he concluded. "Don't think me a trickster. I find life trying and perplexing. I find it coming at you both ways and I will laugh in its teeth and try to do what can be done with it as long as I have a chance. Please teach me wisdom. I need it pretty badly—and so do you. Perhaps one gets it by giving it."[124] The Amherst debacle had tested Meiklejohn's faith in the viability of progressive educational reform, but it did not deter him from trying again. Indeed, his departure from Amherst was only the beginning.

The excitement surrounding Meiklejohn's plans for a new college was invigorating, but it was also bittersweet. Amidst all the flurry of preparations with Croly, Frank, and Straight, his wife, Nannine, was slowly dying of cancer. Her condition had been deteriorating for several years, and frequent trips to Italy had done little to alleviate her pain. Meiklejohn and Nannine had spent the fall of 1924 in Florence, where Nannine had convalesced in the company of her family, but by the winter of that year, her situation had gotten much worse. In December, she entered the Bon Secours Hospital in Paris, from which she was later transferred to Union Memorial Hospital in Baltimore. Finally, in January, she underwent an operation to remove a large tumor. Doctors discovered a malignancy and recommended that she be moved to the Johns Hopkins University Hospital nearby. Meiklejohn, commuting from New York, visited Nannine as often as possible. In his absence, he asked George Boas, a longtime friend and colleague from Brown who had since taken a position in the philosophy department at Johns Hopkins, to stop in and comfort her from time to time. On one particular occasion, Boas listened as Nannine broke down in tears, lamenting her failing health and her memories of Amherst. "I am responsible for the whole Amherst debacle," she cried in a fit of delirium.[125] A few days later, on February 13, 1925, Meiklejohn visited Nannine at her bedside. That night, she died.[126] Lacking nearby relatives to soothe his grief, Meiklejohn turned to his friends for support. Responding to a card from John Gaus, he wrote that he would always remember Nannine "in terms of her delight in life and her courage. They were, in her, amazing qualities. It is good to know that you will keep the memory of them. Thank you for that."[127] "May I, too, without intrusion, bow my head," submitted Felix Frankfurter. "When grief dominates, it decimates. A friend's thought of you, in common with many such thoughts, is at best irrelevant. And yet it will not be decried. Strength to you."[128]

In the summer of 1925, Meiklejohn canceled all his speaking contracts and returned, once again, to Europe. There, mourning Nannine's death, he took time to draft an essay on the purpose of philosophy and the need for a modern "metaphysics of meaning." "Am I a part of the physical world?" he wondered, "or am I something quite different from it and alien to it? Is a man a soul, a self, a mind, or is he a collection of atoms or cells or tissues and organs?" On one hand, it seemed clear that human beings were part of the physical world, that they were, in his words, "created by the same processes and erased by the same forces." On the other hand, it seemed equally clear that human beings were more than their physical bodies, more than their corporeal selves. The task of philosophy, Meiklejohn argued, was to draw meaningful connections between the physical and the intellectual, the material and the spiritual, the scientific and the religious realms of human existence. The challenge, in other words, was to regain the transcendental hope of idealism. "Idealism is simply the retort to materialism," he asserted. "It suggests that the world which the sciences know as a great mechanism of material forces shall be construed as the play of meanings and values. . . . If this could be done, the conscious self, the person, would no longer be left an isolated and disconnected fragment. He would be at home in a world essentially akin to himself." Insofar as human reason implied a valid representation of the external world in consciousness, philosophy had the task of assigning value to that representation, or at least the task of postulating values in an otherwise valueless world. Even after the calamity at Amherst and the death of Nannine, which marked the nadir of Meiklejohn's life to date, he continued to see himself as a philosopher, a critic, a visionary, and a prophet. His next task would be to create a college where philosophy and philosophers could flourish.[129]

MADISON

1925–1932

5

"A New College with a New Idea"

1925–1928

IN JANUARY OF 1925, Meiklejohn's long-awaited article, "A New College: Notes on a Next Step in Higher Education," appeared in *Century* magazine. "What can be said," he asked, "in favor of the establishment of a New College? I find a desire for it, a belief in it, from one side of the country to the other. It is active in the minds of many of the best teachers and many of the best students in our colleges."[1] Indeed, by the mid-1920s, the spirit of reform was alive and well in American higher education. Dozens of experiments had already begun, and dozens more were on the drawing board. Bennington College in Vermont and Sarah Lawrence in New York were pioneering new forms of artistic education for women, while Deep Springs College in California started a rugged new work-study program for a small community of men. Reed in Oregon and Swarthmore in Pennsylvania introduced honors programs with more rigorous and unified courses of study for undergraduates. Rollins College in Florida initiated a striking new "conference plan" of individualized instruction, while Black Mountain in North Carolina sponsored innovative arts and humanities programs for adults. The Claremont Colleges in California (including Pomona, Pitzer, Scripps, Harvey Mudd, Claremont McKenna, and the Claremont Graduate School) and the all-black Atlanta Consortium in Georgia (Spelman, Morehouse, Morris Brown, Clark Atlanta, and the Atlanta University) created educational cooperatives with separate schools contributing to a larger institutional whole.[2] By the time

133

Meiklejohn's plan for a new college appeared in *Century* in 1925, the idea of educational experimentation garnered considerable support in colleges and universities nationwide. "The liberal education of American youth is today a task so fascinating in its quality and of such tremendous importance in its consequences," he declared, "that life in a community attempting it cannot fail to be thrilling and worthwhile."[3]

Stressing the experimental nature of his new college proposal, Meiklejohn described its two principal goals. First, in an attempt to overcome the failures and inadequacies of the elective system, it would aim to develop a more unified curriculum for the first two undergraduate years. Second, in an attempt to create a more cohesive and cooperative learning community, it would aim to develop closer instructional relationships between teachers and students. As he sketched out the details of his college, Meiklejohn explained that its course of study would be entirely prescribed and its method of instruction would be primarily tutorial. Above all, the new college would be small, with no more than thirty-five teachers and three hundred students. "It seems to me the first essential," he asserted, "that the attempt be made to form and place a faculty that will become a coherent, self-determining body, definitely committed to a well-formulated purpose and directing all its efforts, individual and corporate, to the realization of that purpose. It is for the sake of this coherence that we chiefly need smallness." In keeping with the goals of unity and coherence, Meiklejohn's new college would not divide its program into discrete or disconnected disciplines. Rather, it would attempt to study human civilization as an organic and living *whole*. "We would have the freshman attempt acquaintance with an ancient civilization as a whole, and the sophomore with a modern one in the same way," Meiklejohn explained, "and our principle is fairly clear. The college is trying to get the student to make for himself an understanding of himself and the society in which he is living. We wish him to know this not simply in some of its aspects, but as a total human undertaking."[4] Acknowledging that the choice of civilizations to study would, on some level, be arbitrary, Meiklejohn suggested a two-year curriculum based on ancient Athens in the first year and modern America in the second.

Halfway through his article, Meiklejohn described the tutorial relationship he envisioned for teachers and students in his new college. "Each member of the faculty could take five or six students under his guidance. . . . He could hold conferences with them, criticize their reports of work, discuss their difficulties, suggest lines to follow, and challenge and direct their thinking." In an ideal sense, teachers and students would

134

be coequal partners in the learning process. Students would collaborate with "a guide and fellow rather than an instructor," Meiklejohn explained. "The whole community would thus be seen and felt to be bound together by common interests and a common purpose." Ultimately, this unique "college of tomorrow" would stimulate students to take responsibility for their own learning. "We wish that the pupil be treated as one who intends, and who is expected, to learn for himself rather than as one who is to be supplied with knowledge by us out of the stores of our information." The students, in other words, would choose *independently* to participate in the work of liberal education. They would join *voluntarily* in the creation of a self-governing community. Herein lay the basic idea of Meiklejohn's new college. In every respect, it was an experiment in democracy, a test of the link between education and self-government. It was an opportunity to see if students, given the free and unfettered chance, would choose to make a democratic college community entirely of their own volition. "Unless he will do this for himself," Meiklejohn argued, "no one can do anything for him."[5] The new college tested every aspect of Meiklejohn's educational idealism, from his epistemological assumptions about the transcendental unity of pure and practical reason to his moral assumptions about the place of excellence in an increasingly mediocre society. Most of all, it challenged his belief—first developed in the context of the baseball controversy at Brown and later crushed in the turmoil of his dismissal from Amherst—that liberal education could somehow create democracy as a unified and virtuous human community.

At the end of his article, Meiklejohn listed details of his new college that still remained unsettled: Where would it be located? What would it need in the way of libraries, labs, and other physical equipment? What would be its tuition and what its provision of scholarships? What would be its entrance requirements? What extracurricular activities, athletic or otherwise, would it establish or encourage? What would be the living arrangements of students, faculty, and staff? What would be the daily routine of study and teaching? And, perhaps most important of all, how much freedom would its students actually have? Answers to all of these questions would come in due time. For the present, Meiklejohn simply wanted to reiterate the idea, already present in the minds of many educators around the country, that a new college was needed. And others agreed. A few weeks after the publication of his article, Meiklejohn received a letter from Herbert Croly, who worried that Meiklejohn's plan for a new college already ran the risk of overexposure, especially in the liberal intellectual circles of New York. "All here are somewhat bothered about the statements that have recently been appearing in the papers to the effect that Mr. Wilson's friends are proposing to start a 'Woodrow Wilson College,' the plan for which seems to be borrowed very considerably from the indications you have given of the kind of college that you wish to found."[6] Croly's fears, however, were unnecessary. Within a matter of months, Meiklejohn had an opportunity to make his new college a reality. In May of 1925, Glenn Frank resigned his post at *Century* to accept a position as president of the University of Wisconsin. Shortly thereafter, he invited Meiklejohn to open his new college in Madison.[7]

With Glenn Frank at the University of Wisconsin, plans for the new college progressed rapidly—and secretly. "I want no beating of drums until company is ready to march," Frank wrote to Meiklejohn in December of 1925. "Trust me on this."[8] Meiklejohn agreed to keep quiet about the new college, but he was eager to know what his salary arrangements at the University of Wisconsin might be. For more than a year, he had been living on lecture and writing fees, and, while a temporary teaching job with Walter Agard at St. John's College in Annapolis had tided him for awhile, his latest trip to Europe after Nannine's death had seriously depleted his savings.[9] Professor E. B. McGilvary, chair of Wisconsin's Department of Philosophy, asked Meiklejohn if he would accept a salary of six thousand dollars a year, which would equal McGilvary's own, but before Meiklejohn could respond he received an urgent telegram from Frank. "I have almost completed arrangements for creation of three distinguished professorships," Frank cabled. "My plan is to allot one of these to you if you agree. Maybe a semester of residence and teaching prior to specific work on curriculum would solidify support and hasten results."[10] Increasingly impatient about his finances, Meiklejohn asked Frank to hurry before another offer came along. "I must tell you of the two factors in my own situation which led me to ask you to get a decision by December 15th," he explained. "The first is that a new prospect for the college was brought to me a few days ago. Mrs. Elmhirst [formerly Dorothy Straight] is interested and in itself it seems definitely worth considering. I said however that I was pledged to you and also Wisconsin seems better if our plan can be put through."[11] Two days later, Frank promised that everything would soon be settled. "I think you are entirely safe in turning down all other proposals with full assurance that the special professorship at special salary will be open to you beginning next semester." Scarcely able to hide his enthusiasm, Frank exclaimed at the end of his letter that, together, he and Meiklejohn would make their new college "the most thrilling adventure in America!"[12]

As Meiklejohn's partner in the new college endeavor, Glenn Frank had traveled a rather circuitous path to prominence in American higher education. Born in Queen City, Missouri, in 1887, he had attended the Kirksville State Teachers College and later earned a bachelor's degree at Northwestern. After graduating, he toured the country as a circuit rider with renowned revivalist Billy Sunday. Following brief stints as a Chatauqua lecturer and an administrator in Northwestern's Office of Alumni Affairs, he eventually landed a position as the personal secretary to Boston retail magnate Edward A. Filene. As Filene's secretary, Frank gained valuable experience as a publicist, spokesman, and speech writer. In his free time, he wrote two books, *The Stakes of War* (1916) and *The Politics of Industry* (1917), notable mainly for their deep concern with spiritual renewal in a secular industrial age. In 1918, he left Filene to take a job as associate editor of *Century* magazine in New York. Rising rapidly through the ranks, he became editor-in-chief in 1921. As head of one of the nation's most popular literary periodicals, he used his monthly column to share his views on a variety of social issues, such as the evils of market speculation, the irrationality of fundamentalist religion, the immorality of racial separatism, the dangers of gangster violence, and the problems of corporate control in higher education. At *Century*, he quickly built a national reputation for his commitment to educational reform. Then, in 1925, at the age of thirty-seven, he succeeded Edward Birge as president of the University of Wisconsin.[13]

Frank had not, however, been Wisconsin's first choice for the presidency. When Birge, a seventy-four-year-old limnologist who had served on the faculty for decades, retired in 1924, Robert La Follette, Jr., son of Wisconsin's famed Progressive governor, followed his parents' advice by recruiting Meiklejohn, along with Chicago English professor Robert Morss Lovett and Harvard Law School dean Roscoe Pound, to serve as part of an administrative triumvirate, with one man employed as president, one as dean of the college, and one as dean of students. The regents, however, offered the job exclusively to Pound, who declined after realizing the extent of legislative politicking over his nomination. It was at this point that Zona Gale, a fiery Pulitzer Prize–winning regent whose fiction appeared regularly in *Century*, thought of Frank. At first, Gale's fellow regents doubted Frank's ability to succeed as president of a major midwestern research university. They pointed to his youth, his lack of an advanced degree, his dearth of educational experience, and his "big-city ways" as marks against his candidacy. The fact that Frank dared to wear pin-striped pants and spats did not soften his image as an arrogant East Coaster. Chief among

Frank's critics was George Clarke Sellery, dean of the College of Letters and Science and a close confidant of the outgoing Birge. Despite Sellery's initial misgivings, Gale managed to persuade her fellow regents that Frank's paucity of academic credentials was actually an advantage, freeing him from entrenched university procedures and promoting a spirit of genuine liberal reform.[14] So, even though Frank struck many as an academic outsider, he got the job.

When Frank arrived in Madison in the fall of 1925, the University of Wisconsin ranked as one of the largest and most progressive universities in the country. Its beautiful thousand-acre campus sat a mere mile from the state capitol building on a high hill overlooking two large lakes. As Frank wrote to Meiklejohn shortly after the latter arrived, the University of Wisconsin seemed a prime setting for an experimental college or, in his words, a "laboratory for higher education in which the most radical hypotheses may be tested and tried."[15] Indeed, as one of the foremost research institutions in the Midwest, the University of Wisconsin boasted a long and illustrious history of educational innovation. In the early part of the century, guided by the leadership of its dynamic president, Charles Van Hise, the university had initiated its famous Wisconsin Idea, a program designed to facilitate greater cooperation among the educational, governmental, and commercial interests of the state. Between 1910 and 1925, despite the disruptions of war, its enrollment had nearly tripled, growing from three thousand to eight thousand in fifteen years. In the spring of 1925, in an effort to house its rapidly expanding student population, the university had secured funds for the construction of two new dormitories and a student union along the southern shore of Lake Mendota. These facilities, Adams Hall, Tripp Hall, and the Memorial Union, alleviated the university's overcrowded residential situation, but they did not ease the overcrowded classroom situation, where introductory courses swelled beyond the seating capacities of most lecture halls. In the summer of 1925, the Board of Visitors concluded that the university had "become somewhat disarticulated" with a "huge heterogeneous mass of students and faculty," and the University Committee similarly criticized "the large courses of the first two years, in which it is claimed that the students do not get as good teaching as is reasonably possible to give."[16]

By the time Frank settled into the president's house in September of 1925, Wisconsin's faculty, students, and regents were all virtually clamoring for change.[17] Seeking ways to improve instruction for ever-increasing numbers of undergraduates, the university looked to Frank for bold leadership, which he promptly delivered. Almost immediately after taking of-

138

Glenn Frank, president of the University of Wisconsin (on the left) ignoring George Clarke Sellery, dean of the College of Letters and Science, at the Freshman Welcome, 1925 (University of Wisconsin Archives, X25-1931, 3/1)

fice, he established the All-University Study Commission to investigate "the first two years of liberal college work" and to offer concrete proposals for reform.[18] In words reminiscent of Meiklejohn's inaugural at Amherst, he condemned the disintegration and agnosticism of modern research universities and called for a new synthesis of knowledge in American education. With plans for a new college in the back of his head, he promised great things for the University of Wisconsin during his tenure. "I venture the prophecy," he—somewhat furtively—announced, "that somewhere, before long, all these years of disillusionment and constructive thinking will come to a flowering. And when some one institution has deliberately brought its own evolution under conscious control, when some institution has dared to go beyond the tinkering with the minutiæ of curriculum-building and face freshly the fundamental problems of education in light of the wholly new intellectual stage of our time, all the clocks will strike twelve, the other institutions will hitch along, and we shall be in a definitely new educational era."[19] While Frank did not state his plans explicitly, he clearly hoped his All-University Study Commission would endorse the idea of a new college under the direction of Alexander Meiklejohn, and it was not long before it did just that.[20]

On January 20, 1926, two weeks short of his fifty-fourth birthday, Meiklejohn moved into the University Club in Madison and accepted the Thomas E. Brittingham Chair in Philosophy at a salary of nine thousand dollars a year.[21] Three weeks later, he taught his first class. "I abominate lectures," he told an auditorium full of undergraduates. "The only way to really learn this subject is by having you talk; and if you won't discuss, we'll just have to wait until somebody does talk."[22] Impressed by Meiklejohn's fresh and provocative style, students cheered. Before long, they dubbed him one of the most extraordinary teachers on campus. His fame, however, did not stop with the students. According to an article in the Madison *Capital Times,* Meiklejohn's arrival at the University of Wisconsin had "literally startled the educational world."[23] His appointment seemed particularly exciting because it came so soon after Glenn Frank's inauguration as president. "With Dr. Frank and Dr. Meiklejohn, two of the nation's most liberal educators, putting into practice their advanced views on teaching," the newspaper announced, "it is freely predicted here that the University of Wisconsin will become one of the leading laboratories of the nation in educational procedure."[24] As the *Times* astutely observed, Glenn Frank and Alexander Meiklejohn had come to Madison as a team with a shared vision of reform and a joint plan to put their ideas into action. Four days before Meiklejohn moved into the University Club, Frank sent him a note. "Would you be shocked," he asked in a letter written more for posterity than anything else, "if I told you that I think I have found a way to create and sustain 'an experimental college of liberal arts' inside the university? I am confident that such an experimental laboratory set up inside one of our great universities will more quickly and effectively provide leadership for the whole system of education in America."[25] With this letter, the new college became the Experimental College, and the name stuck.

By mid-April of 1926, Meiklejohn had a proposal ready for Frank's All-University Study Commission.[26] Following almost exactly the outline he published fifteen months earlier in *Century,* Meiklejohn's proposal for the Experimental College was unique in the history of American higher education.[27] A two-year program of required studies, it avoided the compartmentalization of academic subjects by concentrating on the interdisciplinary study of two civilizations, ancient Athens in the first year and modern America in the second.[28] Teachers, called advisers instead of professors, would hold weekly tutorials with individual students and give periodic collegewide lectures in their specific areas of scholarly expertise. Students, whose attendance at tutorials and lectures would be entirely voluntary, would read books from a prescribed syllabus and write short essays on topics of their choice. Everyone in the college, including advisers, would live and work in a common residence hall to foster maximum social and intellectual interaction. The college would have no fixed daily schedule, but everyone in the college would read the same material during the same week so that all could participate in group discussions outside of individual tutorials. After completing the program, students would take a comprehensive examination (their only graded assignment), then transfer with junior standing into the College of Letters and Science or to another university, where they would eventually earn bachelor's degrees. To many, Meiklejohn's proposal seemed full of contradictions—voluntary yet required, general yet specific, comprehensive yet coherent. Indeed, Meiklejohn's plan was nothing if not complex, but its very complexity captured the central paradox of liberal democratic education: the attempt to construct a unified learning community without sacrificing student freedom in the process.

The faculty of the College of Letters and Science hesitated to embrace Meiklejohn's plan. Some expressed concern about its vagueness. Others noted its lack of any control group to test the validity of its results. Still others criticized the high expense of such an individualized scheme of tutorial instruction. A few worried that the Experimental College would diminish the popularity of courses in the College of Letters and Science. Many feared that Meiklejohn and Frank would try to impose their reforms on the rest of the faculty without explicit approval. As professor of history Paul Knaplund recalled, Frank's All-University Study Commission seemed intended "to rig us up a ship, provide captain, crew, and passengers, but take chart and compass away and send it into a fog guided by a fog horn."[29] After a great deal of debate, the College of Letters and Science reluctantly agreed to support the Experimental College but insisted that its detailed setup, when completed, be submitted to the faculty for approval and, further, that periodic reports on its progress be subject to university review. It was clear that the College of Letters and Science viewed the Experimental College, as well as the All-University Study Commission that created it, as a threat. "I hope the appointment of this Commission means that we are setting up the instrumentalities and giving proof of the existence in this university of a spirit of continuous and constructive self-criticism of our own purposes and procedures," Frank said in a speech to allay faculty concerns. "No one is under the delusion that you desire to create a sort of corporate academic Mussolini who would undertake to dictate the future educational policies of the university."[30] Somehow, though, Frank's allusion to Italy's Fascist dictator seemed apt, especially after he dissolved the All-University Study Commission immediately upon its endorsement of the Experimental College plan.

Once the faculty had approved Meiklejohn's proposal, news of the Experimental College spread fast. "Every institution in the land wishes well to Dr. Meiklejohn and his alluring experiment," announced the *Providence Journal-Bulletin*. "If the experiment lives up to the high hopes of its promoters, then it may be extended to all the academic undergraduates and soon after, we may be sure, in its Wisconsin form or some other form based on it, will receive confirmation of outside acceptance and adoption."[31] Similar stories ran in the *Christian Science Monitor, Detroit Free Press, St. Louis Post Dispatch, Omaha Bee, Dallas News, Kansas City Post, Chicago Sun-Times, Minneapolis Tribune, Tulsa World, Houston Post-Dispatch, Salt Lake City Telegraph, Boston Transcript, Brooklyn Daily Eagle, Cleveland News, San Francisco Chronicle,* and countless other dailies.[32] In the mid-1920s, a time when new experiments in American higher education seemed more the rule than the exception, all eyes were fixed on Meiklejohn's work in Madison. Editors at the *Ashland Daily Press* in northern Wisconsin, on the shore of Lake Superior, announced their enthusiasm for the Experimental College. "If we were a high school student graduating this year, we should make a tremendous struggle to be one of those enrolled in the new Experimental College at the University this fall."[33] With two years of financial support guaranteed by the Wisconsin state legislature, everyone looked eagerly toward the opening of the Experimental College, slated for the fall of 1927.

Between the spring of 1926 and the fall of 1927, the planning of the Experimental College kept Meiklejohn extraordinarily busy. Not too busy, however, to get married. On June 9, 1926, after a long-distance courtship, Meiklejohn married Helen Everett, the youngest daughter of Walter Goodnow Everett, his former colleague from the Department of Philosophy at Brown. Intelligent, outgoing, red-headed, and twenty years younger than Meiklejohn, Helen had known Meiklejohn when she was still a child in Providence. Despite their difference in age, Helen and Alec were an excellent intellectual match. With a bachelor's degree from Bryn Mawr, a master's degree from Radcliffe, and a doctorate in labor policy from the Brookings Graduate School of Economics in Washington, D.C., Helen shared Meiklejohn's liberal social and scholarly outlook. An article in the *Springfield Daily Republican* in Massachusetts announced Helen's engagement, making special note of her intrepid investigations of factory labor conditions during World War I. "Miss Everett's knowledge of economics is far

Dr. Meiklejohn Weds Miss Helen Everett

"Dr. Meiklejohn Weds Miss Helen Everett," June 10, 1926 (State Historical Society of Wisconsin, WHi [X3] 52140)

from theoretical," the *Republican* commented. "During the war, she worked in the Norton Grinding company at Worcester. She used a false name and seemed no different from the rest of the workers. Her college training and influential friends were never suspected by her fellow laborers. Nor did she feel any different when she crawled into bed after ten hours at the machines."[34] After their wedding at Old South Church in Boston and a honeymoon in Maine, the new Mr. and Mrs. Meiklejohn moved into a large home at 2002 Chamberlain Avenue in Madison. They enjoyed nothing more than spending time with one another. "As companions and lovers," a friend later recalled, "they complemented each other in an inseparable mutual dependence, inspiring to all who touched their lives."[35] Theirs was a deeply caring relationship that continued to flourish for nearly forty years.

Of course, as Meiklejohn's second wife, Helen instantly became a stepmother to his four growing children, aged nineteen, seventeen, fifteen, and nine. Kenneth, the oldest, was enrolled as a sophomore at Swarthmore College, where President Frank Aydelotte had gained national attention for educational reforms of his own. Donald, the middle son, followed his father to the University of Wisconsin, where he matriculated as a freshman in the fall of 1926 and later served as a part-time adviser in the Experimental College. Gordon, the youngest son, continued as a boarder at the Taft School in Connecticut until 1927, when he enrolled in the first class of the Experimental College. Anna, much younger than her brothers, attended the Edgewood School in Madison, Wisconsin, before traveling to Dartington Hall, an innovative new boarding school located in a fourteenth-century abbey in the south of England. Dartington's progressive educational philosophy was well known to Meiklejohn. In 1927, just before the opening of the Experimental College, Leonard and Dorothy Elmhirst—formerly Dorothy Straight, the publisher of the *New Republic,* who had offered to sponsor Meiklejohn's "new college" two years earlier in New York—bought Dartington Hall and transformed it into a unique experiment in rural education. Though Meiklejohn did not keep in close contact with the Elmhirsts while Anna attended Dartington, he did follow their work, praising especially the activities of Britain's Political and Economic Planning Committee, which Leonard Elmhirst chaired.

Shortly after his wedding in the summer of 1926, Meiklejohn began to search for a faculty for his Experimental College. He received hundreds of applications from teachers throughout the United States, Canada, and England, but he and Frank had a very specific idea of the instructors they wanted.[36] "Frank wants me to get the Amherst group so far as possible,"

144

Meiklejohn wrote to John Gaus in April of 1926. "Now, if so, first in line comes one J. Gaus, noted tea-drinker and lover of English literature whose only aberration is a feline infatuation."[37] A few days later, he contacted Gaus again. "Frank wants me to get as many as I can of the Amherst men. That means five or six. We should have Saunders and Sautchard, surely, I think, if we can get them. Other possibilities are many: Agard, May, Gordish, Sharp, etc."[38] Meiklejohn briefly considered such figures as Sidney Hook, Lewis Mumford, Jacques Barzun, and David Riesman to help him in the work of the Experimental College, but he eventually chose ten of his closest friends. Six of the ten came from Amherst, two from Brown, and one from Scotland. Three studied idealist philosophy, while four had done graduate work in labor economics. All but one were under the age of thirty-five.[39] They included, in no particular order, John Gaus, Walter Agard, Laurance Saunders, Carl Bögholt, Malcolm Sharp, Paul Raushenbush, Samuel Rogers, John Walker Powell, William Phillips, and Percy Dawson. Meiklejohn also hired his father-in-law, Walter Goodnow Everett, to handle daily business while he concentrated on larger administrative duties. As he explained in his initial article for *Century,* he wanted a faculty both personally and intellectually compatible, a group that could operate as an intimate fellowship. "I am presupposing, of course, a certain like-mindedness in the group," he wrote. "But, more than this, I am presupposing that the members of the faculty would know and understand one another."[40] A necessary precondition of a unified college community, he decided after his disastrous experience at Amherst, was a faculty consisting of friends.

Meiklejohn's faculty, all of whom shared the title "adviser," were energetic, optimistic, and, like Meiklejohn himself, tremendously idealistic about the possibility of higher-education reform. "I can still remember our meetings at Meiklejohn's house," Walter Agard later recalled. "We had to plan this program from scratch, and it was a radical departure, certainly, from the ordinary methods of freshman and sophomore training." Convening regularly throughout the winter of 1926 and the spring of 1927, the advisers developed a strong sense of camaraderie. "I . . . remember one member of the faculty," Agard mused, "who would be rather silent during our discussion until about 1:00 a.m., and, then, as we were getting our coats to leave, he would say—this was Malcolm Sharp—he would say, 'I think it's more complicated than you understand, and we ought to go into it further.' "[41] Inspired by the excitement of their bold new venture, the young advisers drew their enthusiasm primarily from Meiklejohn himself. Even though he was twenty years older than most of

The advisers of the Experimental College, 1927. From left to right, they are: Walter Agard, Malcolm Sharp, (unknown), Paul Raushenbush, William Phillips, Alexander Meiklejohn, Carl Bögholt, Glenn Frank, (unknown), Laurence Saunders, and Samuel Rogers. (University of Wisconsin Archives, Meuer volume 14, p. 120, 3/1, M48)

his colleagues, he seemed to have twice their energy. "Meiklejohn was ahead of his time," Agard declared. "He was a prophet. He had a genius for teaching and for stimulating intellectually. He had great charisma, of course, and he *always* had a great following among young people, among students and younger faculty." Yet, as Carl Bögholt noted, Meiklejohn's charisma had negative aspects as well. "I think, probably, that the discussions and the ultimate conclusions of those discussions went in the direction that [Meiklejohn] had planned," Bögholt recalled. "[H]is whole method was such as to make you believe that you had actually had a very strong part in the formation of these . . . community judgments."[42] As chairman, Meiklejohn fostered open deliberations about the organization and operation of the Experimental College, but, in the end, he personally expressed the "shared" decisions of the group.

Meiklejohn hired his advisers at salaries ranging from three thousand to five thousand dollars, a step above the standard for junior professors at the University of Wisconsin. In an effort to satisfy the College of Letters and Science, he agreed to split his advisers' appointments on a two-thirds basis with their respective university departments. This arrangement meant that Meiklejohn's staff would spend two thirds of its time teaching in the Experimental College and the remaining third teaching in the College of Letters and Science. For example, John Gaus held a joint post in the Experimental College and the Department of Political Science. Laurance Saunders divided his time between the Experimental College and the Department of History. Percy Dawson gave one out of every three lectures in the Department of Biology. Even Meiklejohn—whose salary of nine thousand dollars, plus an extra thousand for directing the Experimental College, placed his income second only to Glenn Frank's—officially held a joint position with the Department of Philosophy. From Meiklejohn's perspective, this division of labor was not ideal. It undermined the autonomy of the Experimental College and reinscribed the disciplinary compartmentalization he sought to overcome. Yet, from the perspective of the College of Letters and Science, the chance to share Meiklejohn's staff increased its ability to monitor his work. Eschewing Meiklejohn's desire for a college set apart from the rest of the university, the College of Letters and Science kept close watch over the "Ex-College."

In the summer of 1927, Meiklejohn and his advisers began to look for a suitable collection of students for the Experimental College. They did not advertise the program, choosing instead to rely on newspaper articles, magazine features, personal speeches, and Meiklejohn's own celebrity status to attract applicants. Fully half of the students who applied to the Experimental College for the fall of 1927 did so explicitly because they wanted to study under Meiklejohn. Even Franklin D. Roosevelt, then governor of New York, considered sending his youngest son, Elliott, to "Meiklejohn's College," but Elliott opted for a career in ranching and therefore did not pursue a college degree. Meiklejohn hoped to have 125 students in his first freshman class. Above all, he did not want to turn any students away. Fortunately, he received only 119 applications and thus admitted every student who applied. The Experimental College, he proudly announced, would be an entirely self-selected and therefore truly democratic community of learning. As he told one newspaper reporter, revising statements he had made at Amherst and Brown, "We do not feel that a 'selective system' of admissions is a satisfactory answer to the problem. We do not agree with the pessimists who think that only half of one percent of America's youth is capable of receiving an education, nor do we think that there would be any hope for the future if this were true. The future of the nation depends upon the general quality of the body politic, and it is our problem to educate the general run of students."[43] Shifting his perspective from a private to a public institutional setting, Meiklejohn declared that the Experimental College would be a genuine democracy, accepting *all* who chose to participate.

The Experimental College attracted a remarkably diverse group of students—much more diverse than the general population of undergraduates at the University of Wisconsin. Only 32 percent of the students in the Experimental College came from Wisconsin, compared with almost 90 percent in the university at large. Twenty percent came from New York, and an additional 10 percent came from other states along the eastern seaboard.[44] In the fall of 1927, only forty-five students came from Wisconsin; twenty-three came from Illinois, nine from New York, six from Pennsylvania, four from Minnesota, three from Connecticut, two each from California, Ohio, Indiana, Iowa, and Washington, D.C., and one each from Maryland, New Jersey, Nebraska, Colorado, Mississippi, South Dakota, and Tennessee. While a majority of students at the University of Wisconsin came from rural towns throughout the state, most of the students in the Experimental College came from large urban centers. In the first class, 28 percent came from cities with more than a million inhabitants; 51 percent came from cities with populations over fifty thousand.[45] Besides their notable geographic diversity, the students in the Experimental College showed significant national diversity as well.[46] Though immigration restriction laws had recently curtailed the flow of southern and eastern Europeans into the country, more than a third of the students in the Experimental College had parents who had emigrated from Italy, Greece, Russia, Poland, Romania, Lithuania, Latvia, and the Ukraine. In Meiklejohn's view, he and his advisers had a unique opportunity when it came to these students. If liberal education aimed at the construction of a unified democratic community, then the Experimental College had an obligation to meet the diverse needs of *every* student, regardless of cultural differences.

Adding to the diversity of the Experimental College was its large number of Jewish students. At a time when discrimination against Jews was reaching new heights in American higher education, Meiklejohn estimated the proportion of Jews in the Experimental College at 40 percent of the total. One Jewish student from New York described his decision to apply to the Experimental College. "I virtually found myself an outcast as far as New York colleges went," Nathan Berman explained in an essay written for a half-English, half-Yiddish newspaper in Manhattan. "For Columbia I was too low. For New York University (because of some commercial subjects) I was half a point too short. City College of New York

was overcrowded. It was then that 'Meiklejohn's School' welcomed me."
Arriving in Madison, Berman wondered how, or if, he would fit in. "A
Jew and a New York boy, I had never been away from home; in fact, I mis-
trusted any place outside of New York. Again, I had been repeatedly told
that life in a Middle-Western town would be a bore; I would miss the
places of amusement, even the subways!"[47] On the contrary, Berman discovered that several of his classmates also came from Jewish neighborhoods on the Lower East Side. "At least 60% of my fellow students were
from the New York area," one midwestern Protestant student recalled.
"They were largely Jewish. They were, on the whole, well versed in various languages, were well acquainted with what was then current in magazines and papers and books, with good backgrounds in literature. In fact,
they knew far more of, say, the New Testament of the Bible than did most
of the Middle Western Christian boys. They had a far better idea as to
why they had made the trip to Madison and the Experimental College and
wished to make the most of it."[48]

By and large, the students who applied to the Experimental College
scored above average on standardized college entrance exams. For example, on the Scholastic Aptitude Test, which had become almost ubiquitous
as a measure of high school preparation by the mid-1920s, the students
entering the Experimental College consistently outperformed their counterparts in the College of Letters and Science. With a median of 50 percent,
students in the Experimental College scored an average of 82 percent,
while the students in the College of Letters and Science posted an average
of only 54 percent.[49] Similarly, on a national test of English usage, Experimental College students scored near 70 percent, while students in the College of Letters and Science scored closer to 50 percent.[50] Despite their consistently high scores, however, students entering the Experimental College
did not post particularly good grades in high school. Eighty-five percent
of students in the Experimental College attended public secondary
schools, but their grades tended to be much lower than the grades of students entering the University of Wisconsin at large. Evidently, many students entering the Experimental College had not performed up to their potential. According to one analysis, "[T]hese contrasting records of high
aptitude rankings and relatively low academic achievements raise the
question as to whether a number of the Experimental College students
were maladjusted academically in their preparatory schools, that is, not
working up to their capacity as evidenced by their aptitude standings."[51]
This situation presented Meiklejohn and his advisers with a clear chal-

lenge, namely, to see whether or not the Experimental College could "encourage the students to 'run at full capacity.' "[52] The challenge, in other words, was to inspire students to *want* to learn.

Taken together, Meiklejohn's records painted a vivid picture of the Experimental College students. They were highly intelligent but underachieving, non-Anglo-Saxon, non-Protestant, lower-middle-class, often second-generation immigrants, generally from large urban areas outside Wisconsin. They were *not*, in other words, typical undergraduates at the University of Wisconsin. For Meiklejohn, the task of the Experimental College was to get this diverse array of students to join a unified, self-governing, self-motivated educational community. He knew that the task would not be easy. "Our student body is to a quite unusual degree made up of different types, coming from different social groups, different geographical sections, and different kinds of training," he wrote in an annual report to the College of Letters and Science. "All these factors make difficult the task of welding the students together into a group which will feel and take responsibility for the conduct of its own affairs and the control of its own members. But it is also true that the difficulties here involved are a measure of the greatness of the educational values to be gained if the end can be achieved. To try to organize such a group is to get a glimpse of the wider problems of American life as the nation attempts to fuse its variegated groups into a national unity."[53] In Meiklejohn's view, success in the construction of a democratic college community gave hope for success in the improvement of American democracy at large. "It may be," he wrote, "that the educational program presupposed by a democracy is an illusion. It may be that it is the one significant insight and hope in all our modern social theory. But, to decide between the two is, in my opinion, to make the most important social decision now appearing in American life. In the last resort, it is our schools which must decide whether or not we can have a democratic scheme of life, and it is time that they were about the making of that decision on the basis of actual study and experimentation."[54] Starting with a diverse group of students, each of whom chose voluntarily to enter the Experimental College, Meiklejohn aimed to teach democracy, or at least to try.

It was precisely the link between diversity and democracy that led Meiklejohn to regret the absence of women from the Experimental College. In the spring of 1928, a year after its opening, Meiklejohn received a letter from Zona Gale, the writer-regent who nominated Glenn Frank for the university's presidency. Gale wrote that she had been "much stirred" by the exclusion of women from the Experimental College.

"Why, in a state university, should an experimental school be devoted to men?" she demanded. "What about the tax-paying parents of women students? Why should these distinctions be made in a state which has the equal rights law?"[55] Meiklejohn replied sympathetically to Gale. "I wish something could be done about extending our project to include girls next year," he wrote.[56] "I can find no adequate reason for defining in different terms the liberal education of women and of men. As persons attempting to understand the modern world, there is no significant difference between them. It seems to me that, for the same reasons, they should study the same things and in the same ways."[57] Unfortunately, the Experimental College was limited to men by the availability of dormitory space. "When we first started working on the idea of an experimental college there were three possibilities open to us," Meiklejohn explained. "It could be for men, for women exclusively, or it could be coed, since Wisconsin is a co-educational institution. The men's dormitories were available to us as a site, so we started with men students." Meiklejohn granted that a women's experimental college was a possibility "for the indeterminate future" but noted that, "until the officials are satisfied that the present venture is successful, no plans will be laid for another."[58] While Meiklejohn expressed his personal commitment to the idea of coeducation, Gale's fellow regents refused to put men and women together in the same dorm.

And what a dorm it was. The Experimental College occupied the east wing of Adams Hall, one of the new structures built in 1926 as part of the university's effort to accommodate expanding enrollments. Sitting on the southern shore of Lake Mendota just down the hill from the university's observatory, Adams Hall consisted of an Italian Renaissance–style quadrangle divided into eight sections, each capable of housing thirty students, two advisers, and a resident "fellow." Each section was a separate unit with its own entrance, commons room, shower facilities, and den. The den was the social center of each section, with a Victrola phonograph, an upright piano, a small library, and several lounge chairs. The nearby Van Hise Refectory served breakfast, lunch, and dinner to all students in the complex. Next door was a new intramural athletic field, providing ample space for football, baseball, hockey, and other sports. Students also had access to eight tennis courts as well as a new field house with facilities for basketball, boxing, and wrestling. Lake Mendota, in the "backyard" of Adams Hall, afforded opportunities for swimming, sailing, skating, and iceboating. The university ski jump was only a short distance away, and the Black Hawk golf links were accessible "by an interesting walk along the willow drive bordering the lake and through the attractive suburbs of

151

Adams Hall at the University of Wisconsin with Lake Mendota in the background, ca. 1928 (University of Wisconsin Archives, X25-2749, 26/1)

College Hills and Shorewood."[59] Situated in a secluded wooded area on the western edge of the campus, Adams Hall sat far away from both the university and the town.

Even before the creation of the residential college system at Yale and the house system at Harvard, students and advisers in the Experimental College lived and worked together in Adams Hall. Following the lead of Woodrow Wilson's preceptorial program at Princeton, Meiklejohn believed that group living could promote closer personal and intellectual ties between members of the college community.[60] "One of the most urgent needs of the American college—one might almost say 'a desperately urgent need'—is that of fusing together the intellectual and social activities of the students," he asserted. "[I]f the whole group is engaged in the same attempt at learning, then every aspect of the social living becomes steeped in the common purpose. Men breathe it in, eat it in, play it in, smoke it in, study it in, laugh it in, discuss it in, until education becomes what it ought to be—not a set of imposed, demanded, external tasks, but a form of human living and association, the natural and inevitable growth of a healthy organism in a congenial environment."[61] Evidently, Meiklejohn's plan worked, because the students in the Experimental College formed an extremely tight-knit community. "The very first night," one freshman recalled, "I met two of my future classmates carrying on an ardent discussion, on what subject I don't know but in a brilliant manner, with gesture and light. The three of us heard the sounds of Beethoven's 7th Symphony sounding from somewhere above." Climbing the stairs to the fourth floor, he found another group of students sipping fragrant tea. "This," the student declared, "was romantic and heady stuff to start off one's college career!"[62] The task of the Experimental College, Meiklejohn believed, was to direct students' various activities toward a shared social purpose, to guide them toward a common educational goal, and, ultimately, to gather them around a unified curriculum based on books.

Books were central to the work of the Experimental College. Recognizing that education could take place in many different kinds of institutions, from the family to the workplace to the church, Meiklejohn insisted that the liberal college was unique as a place dedicated to providing general education through books. "The college does not build up maturity by the same methods as those employed in a mill or an office," he wrote in an attempt to distinguish liberal colleges from other, more vocational institutions. "Its chosen material is literature; its chosen instrument is the book. The intention of the college is that, in the case of those favored young people who are allowed to study after the high-school period, minds shall be fed, and trained, and strengthened, and directed by the use of books." Of course, the specific choice of books, like the choice of any other pedagogical tool, was, on some level, arbitrary. Students in a liberal college could read comic books, romantic novels, or technical manuals just as easily as they could read philosophical treatises or poetry. They could *not,* however, read everything, so choices had to be made. It was essential, therefore, that colleges choose what they considered the best books without losing a sense of the coherence of the curriculum as a whole. "[I]t has been taken for granted," Meiklejohn wrote of the Experimental College curriculum, that "the books selected should be 'great,' should represent the human mind in its highest quality as well as in relation to its more significant themes."[63] In the Victorian tradition of Matthew Arnold, whose work Meiklejohn admired, the Experimental College held that the purpose of reading Great Books was to observe human intelligence in its most magnificent forms and, thus, to understand the ways in which brilliant thinkers had come to terms with the profound and timeless questions that *every* generation and *every* civilization inevitably faced.

Yet, how was one to measure the greatness of a book? In the 1920s, this question stood at the center of serious and sometimes bitter controversy. Ever since John Erskine and his colleagues at Columbia devised a canon of "the Great Books of the Western World" for their course "Contemporary Civilization" in 1919, the idea of picking Great Books had provoked widespread debate. Did the selection of certain books imply a critical judgment about the superiority of certain subjects, themes, or literary styles? Did the choice of Homer over Herodotus suggest the aesthetic preeminence of poetry over prose? Did the choice of Martin Luther over Thomas Aquinas imply the religious supremacy of Protestantism over Roman Catholicism? Did the choice of Adam Smith over Karl Marx prove the ideological dominance of capitalism over communism? For Meiklejohn, such questions seemed absurd. They confused the particular contents of each book with the more general principles of the curriculum as a whole. On some level, Meiklejohn believed, Great Books were interchangeable, so that Homer and Herodotus, Luther and Aquinas, Smith and Marx, while obviously different in many ways, nevertheless raised the same essential questions, the same enduring problems, the same basic ideas: What is good? What is just? What is true? General questions, not particular titles or authors or ideologies, formed the heart of liberal education. For Meiklejohn, the notion that liberal education involved a limited body of knowledge, a specific list of books, or a certain level of familiarity with discrete facts, missed the point. Rather than a random conglomeration of chronologically ordered Great Books, a curriculum gave a "scheme of reference" through which students could encounter and compare ideas in a reasonable and systematic way. "A college," Meiklejohn wrote, "is a group of people, all of whom are reading the same books."[64] Put another way, a college was a group of people, all of whom were asking the same questions. By this definition, the group of students and advisers living and working together in Adams Hall formed a genuine liberal college community, because all were reading—and discussing and debating and criticizing and trying to come to terms with— the same essential questions derived from the same long list of books.

And the list was very long indeed. The first year of the Experimental College curriculum focused exclusively on the civilization of ancient Athens, especially as it existed in the Periclean Age from 490 to 429 B.C. Despite the fact that only one adviser, Walter Agard, had specific training in Greek history or language, readings from Aeschylus, Aristophanes, Aristotle, Demosthenes, Epictetus, Euripides, Hesiod, Herodotus, Hippocrates, Homer, Lucian, Pindar, Plato, Plutarch, Sophocles, Thucydides, and Xenophon all found their place on the first-year syllabus. Meiklejohn joked that he and his advisers had assigned these authors, some of whom were extremely difficult for freshmen, "in the hope that greatness of mind may be contagious." Over time, the emphasis of the first-year curriculum shifted back and forth from the texts themselves to the broader civilization they represented, from the basic information contained in each book to the general questions raised in the excerpts assigned. "Our first thought had been that the student should see the Great Age as a set of objective achievements," Meiklejohn noted. "But later it became clear that for us the significance, the meaning, of those achievements is to be found not so much in them as such as in the thinking about them in the minds which they stirred to action." When it came to a choice between specific information and general questions—or, as he had called them in his Social and Economic Institutions curriculum at Amherst, essential problems—Meiklejohn always chose the latter. Yet, as his words about the steady evolution of the curriculum implied, the Experimental College curriculum did not emerge fully formed or completely coherent in a flash of educational insight. Rather, it developed slowly over time. As Meiklejohn put it, both teachers and students collaborated in a "never-accomplished but never-to-be-abandoned enterprise of the human spirit—the search for unified understanding."[65] Deliberation, not dogma, was the goal.

For some students, the Experimental College curriculum at first seemed bewildering and odd. Wilbur Cohen, who later became U.S. secretary of health, education, and welfare, described his initial encounter with the world of Pericles. "It was a heady experience for a young high school graduate of seventeen when I entered Adams Hall and was catapulted back twenty-five centuries and exposed to the challenging issues of fifth-century Greek Athens," Cohen remembered. "Yet we were counseled under those difficult circumstances to ponder the basic questions posed by Pericles, Epictetus, Plato, Aristotle, Socrates, and Thucydides, such as the issues involved in determining what is truth, knowledge, being, becoming, causality, free will, justice, freedom, and a host of other overpowering and overwhelming ideas." The focus of the curriculum was not the particular texts it assigned but the general questions it raised. "To me," Cohen noted in retrospect, "Dr. Meiklejohn was deeply concerned about conserving and interpreting the essentials, the basics, the universals in human thought and action. He focused on the conservation of some of the timeless concerns of Western Civilization and especially on the views of the great penetrating minds and books of the world. He urged us to discover what the great questions were and to try to discover the answers which various great thinkers had proposed."[66] Many students struggled before grasping the ideas of unity and coherence at the heart of the Experimental College curriculum. Indeed, the notion of studying Athenian civilization as an organic whole might have been lost had it not been for the constant oversight of the Experimental College advisers, particularly that of Meiklejohn himself.

"For me," one student later recalled, "the most enduring experience of the college was Alexander Meiklejohn: his presence, his personality, his friendliness, his kindliness, his intellect, his understanding."[67]

In order to make their study of Athenian civilization more manageable, Meiklejohn and his advisers divided the first-year curriculum into eight interconnected segments: politics, literature, art, economics, law, religion, science, and philosophy. While a slight concession to the discipline-oriented learning that Meiklejohn hoped to avoid, these phases aimed to give a synthetic overview of ancient Athenian thought and culture as a whole. They also gave a glimpse of Meiklejohn's own social, political, and intellectual concerns. For example, when the students studied ancient warfare, Meiklejohn assigned a few favorite supplemental texts, including Remarque's *All Quiet on the Western Front,* Tolstoy's *War and Peace,* and Zola's *La Débâcle.* When the students started ancient philosophy, Meiklejohn added George Berkeley's *Principles of Human Knowledge,* William James's *Will to Believe,* and John Dewey's *Quest for Certainty.* When they studied ancient politics, Meiklejohn suggested Walter Lippmann's *Public Opinion* and George Santayana's *Character and Opinion in the United States.* When they read ancient drama, Meiklejohn inserted Ibsen's *Brand* and O'Neill's *Hairy Ape.* Finally, when the students approached ancient economics, Meiklejohn recommended Marx's *Communist Manifesto* and R. H. Tawney's *Acquisitive Society.* These supplementary texts made implicit connections between ancient and modern civilization, between the problems of the past and the problems of the present.

Of all the texts assigned in the first year of the Experimental College curriculum, Plato's *Republic* emerged as the most important. For Meiklejohn, *The Republic* represented the apex of literary and philosophical achievement in ancient Athenian thought.[68] Much to Meiklejohn's delight, the students actually enjoyed reading Plato. One freshman reported that he and his classmates had "stayed up at all hours of the night arguing philosophical questions, calling one another Sophists, and acquiring that questioning attitude and that love for learning which we consider to be the most valuable contribution of the Experimental College."[69] Toward the end of the first year, Meiklejohn and his advisers asked the students to summarize what they had learned in their study of ancient Athens. "So far we have been making a phase-by-phase study of the various activities of Athens," he wrote. "But there is an important question, as yet only suggested, which should be faced squarely before the end of the year: To what extent were these different activities interrelated in the experience of the individuals and of the community as a whole?"[70] In this assignment, Meiklejohn indicated the purpose at the heart of his curriculum: to present

Greek civilization as an organic and living whole and, thus, to suggest the common cultural elements essential to the construction of *any* unified democratic community. To grasp the meaning of Plato's *Republic* was to understand the meaning not only of ancient Athens but also of modern America. One student articulated this connection particularly well. "The first year with the Greeks got me far enough away from myself and my day-to-day world for a bird's-eye view of a great civilization," remembered Walker H. Hill, "but again and again I found myself forced to search my own judgments and prejudices and to examine the values of our contemporary civilization."[71]

Meiklejohn's grand attempt to understand Western civilization as a synthetic and living whole seemed to many a preposterous educational undertaking. Indeed, Meiklejohn himself was unsure that the Experimental College could achieve such a lofty curricular goal. In 1929, however, he found ample justification for the attempt. In the spring of that year, Robert and Helen Lynd published their landmark work, *Middletown: A Study in American Culture*. Selecting what they considered to be a typical American community "in the east–north-central group of states that includes Ohio, Indiana, Illinois, Michigan, and Wisconsin," the Lynds examined the various social, political, legal, economic, residential, religious, commercial, and cultural aspects of everyday life in the small city of Muncie, Indiana.[72] Without telling their readers that "Middletown" actually existed, the Lynds used Muncie to draw wide-ranging conclusions about the nature of American civilization in general. In many ways, *Middletown*'s sweeping anthropological survey of a single city represented precisely what Meiklejohn hoped to accomplish with his study of ancient Athens. As soon as the book appeared in print, he assigned it to his freshmen and then, upon the suggestion of John Gaus, asked them to conduct similar regional studies of their own hometowns during their summer vacation. The value of the regional study, he asserted, lay "not only in gaining more knowledge and awareness of one particular community, but also in greater ability to understand and evaluate any concrete situation the student may confront in American life."[73] The students in the Experimental College embraced the idea of the regional study. Their papers, submitted at the beginning of the sophomore year, often ran to more than a hundred pages in length. They completed analyses of such varied localities as Chicago, Cleveland, Hartford, New Orleans, and the Mesabi iron range in northern Minnesota.[74] One student compiled a study of the Hawaiian Islands. Another did a study of Manitowoc, Wisconsin, which his father serialized in the *Manitowoc Daily Herald*.[75]

The culmination of the curriculum came in the sophomore year, which, Meiklejohn believed, constituted the last year of formal liberal education. By the beginning of the sophomore year, the time had come for students to take responsibility for their own learning, to step away from the college and begin the process of truly teaching themselves. "In whatever ways it can be done," he explained, "our purpose is to demand that [sophomores] shall take the lead in the making of their own education. In a real sense, we hope to lead by refusing to lead." But how? How could the college motivate sophomores to take responsibility for their own education? As Meiklejohn put it, "[H]ow shall minds be led or stimulated or driven or allowed to achieve activity and independence?"[76] Insofar as Meiklejohn's educational philosophy rested on the assumption that liberal learning must *precede* democracy, the sophomore year marked the pivotal point at which each student, finally possessing the ability to govern himself, left the moral guidance and institutional structure of the college behind. "The time has come for him to ask for and to take self-direction in an actual world," Meiklejohn wrote. "He must share in the thinking which is now being done or, perhaps better, in that which ought to be done." Armed with a critical interpretive scheme of reference, he had to conceive of his culture as an organic and living whole, an extension of his own consciousness. He had to see himself as both a subject and an object in the world, to know himself *simultaneously* as both the creator and the critic of his own understanding. By the end of the sophomore year, he became his own teacher. Yet, at the same time, Meiklejohn and his advisers carefully controlled the process by which this delicate transition took place. As he noted in a key statement on the structure of the Experimental College, "[T]he advisers have transformed their teaching method in such a way as to keep for the student the sense of his primary responsibility for the making of his own education."[77] In this way, the sophomores in the Experimental College, like the youth in Socrates' ideal republic, believed they were independent, even if, in a strict pedagogical sense, they were not.

Meiklejohn received a great deal of assistance in designing the sophomore curriculum, especially from John Gaus. Of all the books Gaus assigned in the sophomore year, the most important was *The Education of Henry Adams*.[78] According to Gaus, Henry Adams's turn-of-the-century autobiography seemed an ideal culminating text for the Experimental College. Not only did its splintered style convey the dizzying complexity of contemporary American culture, but its intense self-criticism modeled precisely the kind of intellectual autonomy that sophomores needed to acquire. Indeed, the final sophomore paper asked students to review Adams's

Education as "a study of the emergence of Modern America in particular and of the Modern World in general."[79] As an attempt to run "order through chaos, direction through space, discipline through freedom, unity through multiplicity," *The Education of Henry Adams* in many ways mirrored Meiklejohn's own attempts to construct a coherent curriculum in the Experimental College. Like Adams's autobiography, Meiklejohn's curriculum looked backward for the comfort and consolation of a distant and more unified past. Like Adams, Meiklejohn lamented the destructiveness of modern technology and the moral emptiness of modern science. And, like Adams, Meiklejohn searched for ways to anchor his subjective apprehension of the world in an objective reconstruction of modern experience. The Experimental College curriculum was Meiklejohn's response to the modernist agnosticism represented in *The Education of Henry Adams*.

The parallels between Adams's autobiography and Meiklejohn's curriculum did not escape the notice of students in the Experimental College. Sophomore David Parsons compared Meiklejohn's Athens-America curriculum to Adams's "device of trying to get perspective on our culture by finding some other point in history which was very much the opposite, very much a contrast."[80] Just as Meiklejohn used ancient Greece as a reference point for modern America, Adams selected twelfth-century France, specifically the building of the great cathedral at Chartres, as the reference point for his own analysis. Pointing to the veneration of the Virgin Mary as a symbol of mystical cultural unity, he cast religion as an overwhelming force demanding intense loyalty and devotion from kings and queens as well as artisans and peasants, all of whom were oriented around the building of the cathedral. The most striking feature of modern America, Parsons wrote in his final essay, was the absence of such unity and the rise of cultural multiplicity—"the whole change throughout science and economics, different attitudes, where you found not one, but many, many demands for different kinds of loyalty, different kinds of interests, and no one force, moral or intellectual." The aim of Adams's autobiography, like the aim of Meiklejohn's curriculum, was to highlight the tragedy of lost spiritual and intellectual unity. As another student explained in his final essay, "[T]he very nature of [Adams's] purpose in writing the *Education*—to fix himself as an intellectual and spiritual unit in the flux of multiplicity and to establish an historical relationship between himself and the unity of the medieval ages—imposed upon him the necessity of hypostatizing, as it were, his experience."[81] The curriculum of the Experimental College, like the text of *The Education of Henry Adams*, aimed to reconstruct modern experience, to represent the essence of modern consciousness, albeit momentarily, as a synthetic intellectual achievement in a particular time and place. Meiklejohn's curriculum, like Adams's autobiography, aimed to "hypostatize" the modern self as both subjective feeling and objective form and, thus, to enable students, like Adams's readers, to draw connections between their literary and lived experiences. To master Adams's autobiography as the culminating text of the Experimental College was to learn the meaning of modern self-criticism.

Some advisers worried that their students might be "baffled and defeated" by the deeper implications of Adams's work, but Meiklejohn vehemently disagreed. "In *The Education of Henry Adams*," he argued, "one finds a very powerful and sophisticated mind, thoroughly at home in the processes of American civilization, finding itself thwarted and defeated only because it goes out to meet every actual shock and to face every real problem." Meiklejohn encouraged his students to study Adams's message as a historian, a philosopher, an economist, a medievalist, a scientist, and an artist. Taken together, Meiklejohn insisted, these various and interrelated aspects of Adams's autobiography provided windows into the modern American psyche and illustrated, more vividly than any other book, the need for unifying liberal education in an almost overwhelmingly chaotic modern world. For Meiklejohn, the philosophical idealism at the heart of liberal education, whereby students applied their critical intelligence to the task of creating a shared social meaning, constituted a powerful antidote to the intellectual despair expressed in *The Education of Henry Adams*. To read Adams's third-person narrative, to understand its moral and philosophical complexities, to appreciate its fractured style, and then to emerge from the experience not baffled and defeated but determined to overcome its sense of alienation and estrangement was, for Meiklejohn, a truly educational process. "There can be no doubt," he concluded, "that if a student does succeed in mastering the book, he has made a long step forward in the process of his education."[82] To comprehend Adams was to understand the problems inherent in educating the modern self.

Among the most lively extracurricular groups in the Experimental College was the Philosophy Club, which held weekly meetings at Meiklejohn's house. One of the club's first meetings focused on the weighty question, What is the self? as a way to understand Henry Adams's convoluted psychology and his unusual narrative voice. "It was a laborious evening, traversing this uncharted region of the unseen," one student recalled. "Not only did we become aware of our 'selves' but of almost the whole gamut of metaphysical speculation: the one and the many, the dualism of mind and matter, freedom, determinism, appearance and reality, 'Where nothing

160

is, but all things seem,' and, perhaps most important of all, the vitality of logic in modern thinking." In another meeting, Meiklejohn offered a "penetrating exposition" of Kantian idealism. In direct opposition to those who held that morality was relative, Meiklejohn explained, Kant had argued that truth, justice, and beauty were universal, a priori, and absolute. "The fact that we have not as yet attained them does not disprove their existence," Meiklejohn argued. "Education helps us to approach them. That is the aim of education." Eventually, the Philosophy Club turned to Meiklejohn's favorite topic—the contest between philosophy and science in modern ethical thought. Meiklejohn invited his friend from Amherst, Clarence Ayres, who had recently published a book on this subject, to address the club. The young philosophers gasped when Ayres suggested that both philosophy and science were simply variations on myth or folklore. "It was perfectly amazing," one student recalled, "to learn that the fundamental difference between science and philosophy was only a difference of degree."[83] As another student put it, "[E]ven Mrs. Meiklejohn's dialectical cookies could not make us forget that modern philosophy has, indeed, a terrific problem before it."[84]

In addition to the Philosophy Club, students in the Experimental College participated in the Law Group and the Forum. The Law Group, under the guidance of Malcolm Sharp, advertised such varied legal topics as "The Problem of Liberty," "The Limits of State Action," "The Principle of Laissez Faire," and "The Liberty of Contract under the Constitution." The Forum, a bit less focused than the Philosophy Club and the Law Group, announced meetings covering such current events such as "War and Peace," "The Evil of Imperialism," "The Theory of Behaviorism," "The Coal Industry," and "Sex Problems." In addition to student-initiated discussion groups, Meiklejohn brought several noted visitors to Adams Hall. Bertrand Russell, who was closely acquainted with Leonard and Dorothy Elmhirst's work at Dartington Hall, told students about his attempt, in cooperation with William Butler Yeats, to establish communities of classical education in rural Ireland.[85] Other visitors included writer Lincoln Steffens, architect Frank Lloyd Wright, attorney Clarence Darrow, artist Morris Topchevsky, sociologist Edward A. Ross, and Meiklejohn's close friend, critic Lewis Mumford. Shortly after leaving the Experimental College in the spring of 1929, Mumford told Meiklejohn how much he had enjoyed his visit. "My feet are in Chicago," he wrote, "but my head is still in the College. The experience has thrilled me and given me new confidence. You have gone much further than I dared to hope. The students have the foundations of their maturity laid."[86]

Often, it was difficult to distinguish between curricular and extracurricular activities in the Experimental College. For example, the Experimental College Players, organized by Victor Wolfson, who went on to become a successful Broadway playwright, staged several classical theater productions complete with elaborate costumes and sets. The students performed Aristophanes' *Lysistrata,* a ribald comedy about a group of Athenian women who boycott sex in an attempt to end the practice of war, as well as Aristophanes' *Clouds,* a lampoon which characterizes Socrates as a wily Sophist who so befuddled a farmer and his son that they finally set fire to Socrates' house. The students also performed Sophocles' *Antigone* in a translation by Maurice Neufeld, a sophomore who studied ancient Greek independently with Walter Agard, as well as Euripedes' *Electra.*[87] Over time, the Experimental College Players developed a reputation for indecency. Their staging of *Lysistrata,* in which male students played both male and female roles, even in erotic scenes, raised eyebrows as far away as Ohio. "What Are They Learning?" cried the *Cincinnati Enquirer,* which reported that several young co-eds had been scandalized by the "Ex-College" performance. Louise Nardin, famously prudish as Wisconsin's dean of women, called Meiklejohn's decision to stage *Lysistrata* with an all-male cast a deplorable mistake. "I know from the hostesses in our dormitories," Nardin wrote angrily to Glenn Frank, "that some girls who attended the play were amazed and shocked at its coarseness."[88] Meiklejohn, however, did nothing to apologize for his students. In his view, their performances were not only historically authentic but also sincere in their attempt to make the process of liberal education relevant and "real." The students' decisions to perform *Lysistrata* showed their willingness to engage in provocative cultural criticism and, ultimately, their ability to govern themselves.

All of the extracurricular groups in the Experimental College, from the Philosophy Club and the Law Group to the Forum and the Players, were entirely student-run. The voluntary nature of these activities was perfectly in keeping with Meiklejohn's educational philosophy. On a basic level, he and his advisers assumed that students must choose freely to be educated. All too often, students finished college without ever taking responsibility for their own learning. Especially in the 1920s, when speakeasies, football games, and bob-haired co-eds seemed far more interesting to most undergraduates than literature or philosophy or classical drama, the notion that students would actually *choose* to study and take their learning seriously seemed almost laughable. "It is perhaps a strange thing to say," Meiklejohn wrote, "but we are hoping that students will get a drive toward personal initiative by finding themselves members of a community every member of which is embarked on the same enterprise."[89] Rather than resorting to coercion, force, or bribes in the form of grades, the Experimental College relied on the intrinsic value of learning to serve as the motivation for academic work. "Freedom is not merely the absence of external restraint," he said. "Freedom is rather the life of mutual agreement and understanding. There is no freedom except in the life of a community."[90] Meiklejohn took this idea a step further to argue that, if students chose freely to enter the college community, then its authority over them was *ipso facto* democratic, free of external disciplinary or coercive force. "In a very real sense," he wrote, "one can say that in the field of education discipline is effective only when it is unnecessary." In a statement to summarize his entire philosophy of democratic education, Meiklejohn added that any "purpose voluntarily accepted by the group has in itself authority over the desires and inclinations, the activities and wearinesses, of the separate individuals."[91] No other words so succinctly captured the essence of Meiklejohn's theory of liberal democratic education. To teach students how to be democratic was, ultimately, to teach them to teach themselves.

By the summer of 1929, after two full years of operation, the Experimental College had achieved impressive renown. Its first class of students transferred to a wide variety of first-rank schools, including Harvard, Princeton, Yale, Columbia, Brown, Northwestern, and Duke, as well as the Universities of Chicago, Pennsylvania, California, Michigan, Illinois, Virginia, Texas, and North Carolina. "The Experimental College was a chief topic of discussion at the session of summer directors held at Cornell University," reported Scott H. Goodnight, Wisconsin's dean of men, in 1928. "I was questioned extensively about our new Experimental College and had to explain it, for it was a source of great interest to all the directors."[92] The positive reputation of the Experimental College extended throughout the United States and even to Europe. A commission from England ranked the University of Wisconsin as one of the five best schools in America, noting in particular its reputation for lively debate and political ferment.[93] According to the registrar at the University of Wisconsin, the Experimental College received considerable attention in Oxford, the site of the university tutorial class movement that had so inspired Meiklejohn a decade earlier. "Not long ago I was talking with one of our Rhodes scholars," the registrar wrote to Meiklejohn, "and asked him whether he had heard any comments regarding the Experimental College while at Oxford. [He] replied that it was perhaps the best known American educational experiment and that, when he received literature concerning it, his English and American friends at Oxford were eager to read about it and discuss it."[94] Even on the other side of the Atlantic, the Experimental College seemed a smashing success. All this publicity was good for Meiklejohn and good for the University of Wisconsin, but, in many ways, it was not so good for the Experimental College. Already by the summer of 1929, trouble was beginning to brew.

6

"A Most Lamentable Comedy"

1929–1932

W HEN THE SCHOOL YEAR OPENED in the fall of 1929, students at the University of Wisconsin enjoyed the best of undergraduate life. Not only were they attending an internationally acclaimed research university, but they also reveled in almost unprecedented economic prosperity. They could, if they wanted, leave their dormitories and walk—or, better yet, drive—a short distance to any one of four movie theaters in Madison where, for fifteen cents, they could see Douglas Fairbanks in *The Careless Age*, Maurice Chevalier in *Innocents of Paris*, or dashing Elliott Nugent in *So This Is College?* If they happened to catch *Anna Christie* at a matinée, they could swoon over Greta Garbo, whose sultry voice survived the transition to cinematic sound. Stopping by the Ward-Brodt Music Store on State Street after the show, they could buy the latest orchestral recordings from the Columbia label and then return to their fraternities to dance the shimmy, the toddle, or the Charleston to phonographically recorded jazz. In their coonskin coats and cashmere sweaters, they embraced the unabashed consumerism of the 1920s. Such proliferation of material wealth—in ten years, annual radio sales jumped from $15 million to $338 million, purchases of other electrical appliances rose from $46 million to $976 million, and consumer credit climbed to $7.1 billion—delighted undergraduates, but it worried Meiklejohn. Instead of unifying America around shared standards of moral excellence, the mass culture of the 1920s seemed to divide the country into millions of disconnected lifestyle enclaves, each isolated from the next by the very goods and services that were advertised to bring them together. Meiklejohn called the frivolous youth of this giddy generation Young Barbarians, a reference not to their experience of war—for they had none—but rather to their apparently shameless ignorance of it.

In the spring of 1929, the *New Republic* sponsored an essay contest for college students. The topic, "College as It Might Be," attracted more than seven hundred entrants. After much deliberation, the panel of three judges, including Meiklejohn, selected Howard Jay Graham of the University of California, Berkeley as the winner. Graham opened his first-prize essay with a wry description of youth in the 1920s: "Seldom do even nicknames achieve the laconic perfection of Dr. Meiklejohn's reference to us as 'Young Barbarians,'" Graham wrote. "But is it any wonder that we are led astray? 'Culture' is vague and foreign to the majority of us, brought up on Sunday comics, movies, and Saturday Evening Posts, in drab and smug middle-class homes. . . . Truly," Graham announced, "we are 'intellectual barbarians.'"[1] A few months later, Graham's words were echoed by Justin Silverstein, winner of the Experimental College Freshman Oratorical Contest, who similarly lamented the spiritual emptiness of his teen-age peers. "We know not why we are living, nor how, and we can find no satisfying justification for continuing to live," Silverstein lamented. "We can see neither the end nor the purpose, and we find ourselves overwhelmed with an unspeakable depression and hopelessness."[2] Yet, according to Silverstein, the Experimental College had done well to fill the desperate void in its students' lives. "For intelligently and boldly striking out into uncharted educational fields in order to help us in our adolescent years of distress," he concluded, "the Experimental College finds justification a thousand fold."[3] For Silverstein, the Experimental College provided a much-needed antidote to the cultural decadence and moral aimlessness of *The Great Gatsby*'s America.

Meiklejohn agreed. On October 15, 1929, he traveled to Jacksonville, Illinois, to deliver a speech at the centennial celebration of Illinois College, a small school located just west of Springfield—and, coincidentally, not far from the neighboring towns of Glasgow and Manchester. Perhaps inspired by memories of his childhood in Rochdale, Meiklejohn spoke on the perils of a prosperous society. "We are a newly rich people," he proclaimed, "and we are in serious danger." Looking out at his audience of several hundred fur-collared women and tweed-suited men, Meiklejohn called for a revival of intellectual excellence in American institutions of higher learning. "All agencies of enlightenment are failing because we are rich," he declared. "Riches and education are in conflict with one another. Material wealth blinds men's eyes." Asserting that affluence led inexorably to moral apathy, Meiklejohn called for a renewed sense of ethics in American life. "I would not destroy this newfound wealth," he explained. "I would destroy the confusion it has caused and learn how to use the wealth to make us a truly great nation."[4] It was time, he said, to launch "an educator's war" on the power of money. But his message came too late. Exactly two weeks after Meiklejohn delivered this address, the stock market crashed. Prices plummeted and panic spread as fearful traders leaked news of impending financial disaster. Nearly eight billion dollars worth of inflated paper wealth vanished in a single week. Within a month, a deep depression gripped the nation, and it only got worse. Over the next three years, more than 100,000 businesses failed. Corporate profits dropped by 90 percent. The gross national product split in half. Banks closed. Farms folded. In Wisconsin, the dairy and grain industries suffered huge losses. With the economy collapsing all around them, scores of students in Madison could not afford their tuition, and, after the credit-crazed 1920s, few had savings sufficient to sustain them through the hard times. The Great Depression, the longest and most demoralizing economic downturn in American history, had begun.

In January of 1930, Meiklejohn received a letter from Ralph Crowley, a part-time adviser in the Experimental College who had gone on to medical school at Northwestern. "I am enclosing a check for $500," Crowley wrote. "The money is for the college to use and administer as a loan fund in any way it pleases."[5] Crowley's timing was impeccable. "Your letter," Meiklejohn replied, "brought joy and relief untold. I have already told one or two of the advisers about it, and they, out of their experiences with students in trouble, could tell you how much this gift will mean in specific cases."[6] A few months later, Meiklejohn established the Experimental College loan fund, which distributed interest-free loans to needy students, some of whom had pared their expenses down to fifty cents a day.[7] Later, Meiklejohn expanded the loan fund with donations from his advisers and wealthier students. "Members of the Experimental College will be asked in January to subscribe to an Experimental College Loan Fund," he declared in December of 1931. "A number of the students are already in poor financial condition. Probably twenty of them, while able to get along without aid, will be able to give very little to the fund."[8] For the Experimental College, the depression came as nothing short of disaster. Several students had to withdraw, and few applied to replace them. In the midst of overwhelming economic hardship, when Wisconsin's legislature tightened budgets in every part of the state, the notion of an experimental "college within a college" suddenly seemed superfluous. Between 1929 and

167

1932, under the severe economic and emotional strain of the Great Depression, Meiklejohn's Experimental College slowly fell apart.

Students remaining in Adams Hall during the depression did not escape its effects. Campus jobs grew scarce, and instructional budgets shrank. Books became a luxury, and extra expenditures dwindled fast. Signs of economic struggle were visible all around. David Parsons, who moved into Adams Hall in the fall of 1930, described his encounter with hoboes who passed through Madison on the railroads. "Every freight train that went by was loaded with people, refugees, you might say, looking for work," Parsons recalled. "There were grandparents and babies and all in between, with dogs and cats and other animal life that the family might possess, so that, sometimes, a train might carry as many as 125 people on those flat cars and box cars." Once, a group of students from the Experimental College decided to join the hoboes for an adventure on the trains. "A group of the sophomores got together and they decided they were going to explore this," Parsons remembered. "And so they broke up into teams of two and headed out without telling anybody where they were going, putting on old clothes, and some of them went up into Minnesota, others over to Iowa, some into Michigan, Illinois, and ending in Wisconsin. Riding the freight trains and looking for work, they tried to experience what these people were experiencing in their looking around and trying to find some way of supporting themselves." Living a life of boxcar transience, the vagabonds from Adams Hall considered their travels a sort of mixture, or conflation, of actual and academic experience. According to Parsons, they left for about two weeks and then returned to write papers on their trips.[9] Meiklejohn admired his students' self-critical search for an authentic experience of nomadic joblessness, particularly when it took the form of an academic essay. To draw meaningful connections between life and literature, between adventures and books, between the world of experiences and the world of ideas—that was, after all, the basic purpose of a liberal education.

Not every student in the Experimental College opted to ride the rails, however. Some translated their academic work into more concrete political activism. For example, Carroll Blair, a resident of rural Redgranite, Wisconsin, became an agitator for the Communist Party.[10] After finishing at the Experimental College, he took a job as a labor organizer at the International Harvester plant in Milwaukee.[11] There, in the summer of 1930, he accosted an unarmed police officer at a labor demonstration and received a one-year jail sentence for his crime. Meiklejohn appealed to Governor Walter Kohler for Blair's release, but Blair did little to help his own case when, from his prison cell, he launched a gubernatorial campaign against Kohler on the Communist ticket.[12] Another student, David Gordon, who entered Adams Hall with Blair in 1927 on a creative writing scholarship sponsored by Zona Gale, was even more controversial than his classmate. Even before he came to Madison from New York City, Gordon, the son of Russian Jewish parents, published a sexually explicit poem about capitalism in the Communist *Daily Worker*.[13] Gordon's poem resulted in a conviction for obscenity, which prevented his return to the Experimental College for his sophomore year. Meiklejohn, together with the American Civil Liberties Union, eventually won Gordon's release, but his radical activities did not end.[14] In May of 1930, he organized a march of unemployed factory workers and Experimental College students under the auspices of the Communist National Trade Union Unity League in Madison. When a group of varsity athletes and police disrupted the march and harassed Gordon's comrades, he accused them of "fascist terror." The *Capital Times* described the ensuing scuffle as "a battle between bearded 'Experimenters' and brawny members of the Wisconsin Club, a group of athletes who were bent on 'smashing the heads of the Reds.' "[15] In 1931, police arrested Gordon and two other Experimental College students for participating in a socialist march in Chicago. The judge dismissed the charges on a technicality, but, according to one account, "proceeded to berate the three at great length and placed the blame for their current state on the Experimental College, calling it 'a hotbed of radical activity.' "[16] As the depression deepened, Meiklejohn and his advisers received increasingly negative publicity for the radicalism of students such as Gordon and Blair.

At a time when most college and university students mimicked the cultural and political conservatism of their parents, the students in the Experimental College seemed revolutionary, or at least unorthodox. In reality, though, the radical image of Meiklejohn's College emanated from a relatively small group of bohemian or avant-garde students or from occasional well-publicized incidents, which, because of the extraordinarily high visibility of the college, attracted disproportionate attention from the press. Meiklejohn said repeatedly that there was too much publicity attached to the "supposed radicalism" of Experimental College students— publicity which only exacerbated the problem of mischievous behavior. "The much-misunderstood announcement that the methods of the college would be those of freedom attracted young men who were regarded by their fellows as 'red' and 'radical' and 'communistic,' " Meiklejohn later wrote. "My guess is that it was those who found us 'queer' and 'radical' who chiefly caused the over-stimulation of the students along those lines. Perhaps it would be truer to say that we did try a radical departure, and, perforce, we had to take its consequences, but it was very pleasant, as the years went by, to see these difficulties grow less." By the fall of 1930, he concluded, "[W]e had a pretty well-balanced and normal community."[17] Yet, Meiklejohn's own political affiliations did little to allay suspicions of leftism in the Experimental College. Throughout the 1930s, he belonged to the socialist League for Industrial Democracy as well as the League for Independent Political Action, which had united liberal intellectuals against the conservative Hoover administration.

Politics, however, were not Meiklejohn's main concern. As director of the Experimental College, he devoted the bulk of his attention to the task of curricular reform. In the spring of 1930, he held a series of meetings with his advisers to discuss his program's progress and, more specifically, to consider changes. These meetings, spurred by a university faculty review of the Experimental College led by Paul Knaplund, generated a number of important questions about the Athens-America curriculum and the extent to which it advanced the overall aims of the advisers. One adviser asked, for example, if the work of the first year should be used "as a means to an end (i.e., a better understanding of contemporary civilization), or as an end in itself (i.e., the appreciation of Athenian civilization and its problems, many of which are perennial)." Another wanted to know if the books on the syllabus should be read "simply as 'Great Books'" or as "material specifically dealing with the problems with which the college is concerned." A third adviser summarized these two questions and asked if the curriculum should place its emphasis on "(a) civilizations, (b) problems, or (c) Great Books." Meiklejohn, for his part, believed that the emphasis should fall on general intellectual problems rather than discrete civilizations or specific Great Books per se. He agreed that books were the special tools of a liberal college but maintained that books, and the curriculum they constituted, were ultimately secondary to broader ideas. As he put it, "[T]he securing of detailed and remembered information about Athens has seemed . . . quite secondary in relation to a more important purpose which the study of that civilization can serve. That purpose, it need hardly be said, is the fashioning of a 'scheme of reference' which a student may bring to his study of later civilizations."[18] For Meiklejohn, the process of learning was a process of drawing connections between the specific and the general, between the particular and the transcendental, between the individual example and the universal essence. Liberal education, in other words, tried to interpret the meanings of human civilization through the major problems and intellectual controversies presented in books.

The question remained, however, which specific course the college should follow in order to impart a useful and coherent scheme of reference. Which problems should the curriculum emphasize? Which civilizations should it study? Which books should it assign? These were difficult questions. Meiklejohn admitted that the choice of problems, civilizations, and books was always on some level open to variation and debate. For example, in the spring of 1930, he listened carefully as John Walker Powell suggested a curriculum based on the late eighteenth-century transatlantic Enlightenment. Emphasizing the intellectual and cultural problems posed by democracy, science, capitalism, and modern rationalism, Powell drew assignments from Voltaire, Rousseau, Hume, Smith, and Locke, as well as Montesquieu, Beaumarchais, Adams, Franklin, and Jefferson. "My principal justification for emphasizing problem material and minimizing the factual background," Powell wrote, "is that I felt our teaching is less and less the imparting of information, more and more the personal attempt to help each boy face the problems involved in his personal relationship to the past, to the future, and to his fellows."[19] Although the advisers rejected Powell's proposal, they considered various alternatives to a curriculum based on ancient Athens, including Europe in the Middle Ages, Europe in the Renaissance, and England during the Industrial Revolution. In the end, however, none of these options seemed as compelling as the civilization of Pericles and Plato. "Other minds have excelled the Athenian in the breadth and scope of acquired knowledge," Meiklejohn concluded, "but at least as far as the remaining literature reveals, no other mind has equaled it in the liveliness, the determination, the precision of its effort to 'make sense' out of the human enterprise, to understand what men are and what they are doing—in a word, to be liberally educated."[20]

Given that Athens had secured a place as the basis for the first-year curriculum, one adviser inquired whether the Experimental College had fallen into the trap of educational dogmatism. "Is it desirable," he asked, "for the college to have an educational dogma, and, if so, what is the educational dogma of the college?"[21] Here, of course, was a question Meiklejohn had long sought to answer. On the one hand, he wanted the Experimental College to find alternatives to free electives and, in the process, to discover a new educational "dogma." On the other hand, he wanted the Experimental College to avoid the dangers of curricular stagnation, always leaving itself open to continual educational innovation. By the spring of 1930, when the Experimental College was three years old, Meiklejohn found himself, once again, torn between two worlds. He hated the curricular relativism that had been enshrined in the "modern research university." He despised the open-ended pragmatism of so-called progressive education theory. He hoped to recover the intellectual certainty and cultural stability of an older educational milieu. Yet, at the same time, he hesitated to assert, at least in any *authoritative* way, the ultimate value, lesson, or truth of the Experimental College. He viewed Adams Hall and the Athens-America curriculum as laboratories for educational criticism but not as the essential components of a perfect college in final form. Did the Experimental College have a dogma? Was dogma ever desirable in education? Unsatisfied with the Deweyan dogma of "instrumentalism," contingency, and change, Meiklejohn leaned toward the Reconstructionist school of educational theory under the leadership of Dewey's colleague, George S. Counts, who focused on moral and aesthetic values in the hope that curricular choices could somehow be intelligently, albeit tentatively, made. Even Counts wondered, however, if modern education could expect its lessons—assuming it *had* lessons—actually to be learned.

The important question for Meiklejohn was how to balance the dogma of a prescribed curriculum with the freedom of voluntary participation in the work of learning. In the spring of 1930, still searching for answers to this question, he traveled to New York City, where he addressed a capacity crowd at the Park Avenue Presbyterian Church. Standing in the pulpit of Dr. Albert Parker Fitch, his former colleague and compatriot from Amherst, Meiklejohn confessed to being somewhat discouraged by the apparent futility of modern educational reform. "Why," he asked, "are our educational institutions so ineffectual? . . . Why are we all so failing to hit the mark?" Why were colleges doing so little to alleviate the "unhappiness, inequality, poverty, misery, and sorrow" increasingly pervasive in depression-era America? For Meiklejohn, these were critically important questions. How could institutions of liberal education train students to seek a common understanding of their collective problems and then work cooperatively toward mutually agreeable solutions? How could liberal education impart a sense of social consciousness, cultural coherence, or civic responsibility without resorting to a particular dogma or ideology? Much to his listeners' dismay, Meiklejohn could not answer his own questions. "I don't know the answer," he sighed before an audience that included several Amherst alumni. "I leave the question to you." To many who heard it, Meiklejohn's speech seemed to abandon hope for critical educational reform, even in the Experimental College.

According to the *New York Herald Tribune,* he spoke "so feelingly that some in his congregation wondered whether he were not referring with disappointment to the results achieved at his experimental school in Wisconsin, which, when he founded it, embodied his dreams for 'the university of tomorrow.' "[22]

Meiklejohn denied that his words reflected any kind of failure in the Experimental College, but his claim was somewhat disingenuous. As the depression deepened, he began to doubt that the lessons of rational self-criticism would ever be possible to *teach.* Judging from the rebellious behavior of his more "radical" students, Meiklejohn had plenty of reasons to be doubtful. Besides their penchant for political radicalism, students in the Experimental College took full advantage of their freedom and sometimes forgot, or at least ignored, traditional rules of decency and decorum. Excessive noise, practical jokes, and food fights were a regular part of life in Adams Hall.[23] Students were known to vandalize their rooms and leave piles of debris in their dens, a habit that severely tested the patience of university custodians. As one janitor recalled, the Experimental College students were "an ulcer of bad conduct" from the start. "Three times as much breakage in windows, doors, plumbing, fire hose, and furniture occurred as in other dormitory units."[24] Few looked askance when one artistically inclined student painted a large and colorful Dadaist mural on his dormitory wall.[25] Meiklejohn was aware of this destructive behavior but did nothing to stop it. "Uncouth behavior in the dining rooms is considered evidence of intellectual nonconformity," one dormitory proctor griped to President Frank. "This would apparently explain why the Experimental College fellows do not attempt to restrain food-throwing or excessive noise in the dining rooms."[26] Far more permissive than he had been as chief disciplinarian at Brown, Meiklejohn waited for his students to develop their *own* sense of self-government in the Experimental College. Unfortunately, though, they talked a great deal about citizenship and its duties without ever creating a stable democratic community on the shores of Lake Mendota.

In January of 1930, a student committee convened to address issues of collective discipline and concluded that students in Adams Hall displayed a disturbing lack of loyalty to the principles of self-government. "Quiet hours are flagrantly violated, lectures are poorly attended, conferences cut, vacations extended, and little attention paid to work," the committee reported. "This college, instead of sponsoring individual responsibility, is engendering selfishness, lack of social unity, and utter lack of ambition." The committee cautioned that, if Experimental College students could not learn to govern themselves, then their advisers might have to intervene. "There are certain minimum requirements without which no group can satisfactorily live together, and this group is by no means exempt from restriction. In fact, we are more than ever restricted by ourselves because of the very absence of external compulsion."[27] The threat of faculty reprimand alarmed many of the students, who jealously guarded their freedom and chafed at the thought of outside discipline or control. One sophomore argued that it was "the place of the college to get cooperation and interest, group consciousness, homogeneity, and sensibility concerning trivial matters, not by means of discipline, not by means of investigation and check, not by means of private remonstrances, but by the virtues of its own methods. If the students cannot see that the work of the college is to their own interest, then the college fails in that respect."[28] Evidently, this particular student overlooked the fact that, in the end, he and his fellows *were* the college and had a responsibility to regulate *their own* behavior for the sake of the community as a whole.

As it happened, the issue of student self-government had arisen at the very beginning of the Experimental College. In the fall of 1927, Meiklejohn asked his first class of freshmen to discuss the possibility of organizing a formal student government. Some suggested a town meeting form of government. Others recommended a coalition of representative councils. A number advised a city manager plan—complete with initiative, referendum, and recall—while a few thought the students should try a different form of government each semester. In the end, however, none of these plans could muster a majority. The students voted forty-nine to forty-six against the creation of *any* formal student government. So far as they were concerned, the only government appropriate to the Experimental College was "communistic anarchism" or "anarchistic communism."[29] Apparently, the idea of a democratic college community, with its emphasis on mutual understanding and shared responsibilities, did not sink in. Unable to see themselves as a part of a larger educational whole, the students valued their individual freedom more than their institutional connections. Meiklejohn did not hide his disappointment with the students' refusal to form a government. "I must admit that I gasped with astonishment and even dismay when the no-government decision was made," he later confessed.[30] Just as the undergraduates at Brown had abandoned the amateur athletic code, so, too, the students in the Experimental College had rejected the idea of a student government. Once again, they voted "democratically" to undermine the democratic college ideal. As soon as Meiklejohn gave his students the freedom to make their own decisions, they made what he considered to be a bad choice. Instead of forming a democracy, they opted for anarchy.

Ties of solidarity were loose within the Experimental College, but they were even looser between the Experimental College and the College of Letters and Science. To many students up on the Hill, it seemed that students in the Experimental College actively *tried* to be strange, odd, or somehow queer. They referred to the isolated residents of Adams Hall as lab rats or, more fondly, guinea pigs. At a time when most students wore tweed suits and polished shoes to class, the carefree men in the Experimental College donned T-shirts and dungarees. Some dressed up as sailors, farm hands, or women. Others affected the garb and air of poets. A few grew beards. One student admitted that it was "easy to see why we were thought queer," admitting that a number of friends "did rather revel in that reputation." "Our hair probably did grow longer than necessary at times, we probably did leave our trousers unpressed as added atmosphere, we did undoubtedly dramatize a studied casualness, a false indifference, a feigned superiority, an air of indolence. We felt the weight of the world's problems on our shoulders, and that we would solve them all by the end of two years we seldom if ever doubted. Our queerness was all stage setting."[31] Perhaps the most conspicuous display of Experimental College queerness was the Ex-College blazer that many students wore as a symbol of their membership in the group. Dark blue with pearl gray trim, the blazers had the Owl of Athena embroidered on the left breast pocket. According to one student, "[T]he men who originated the idea of the college blazer believed it would contribute, in some degree at least, to developing a spirit of fellowship, by distinguishing the college as a unity, apart from the rest of the university."[32] Acknowledging that the blazers separated them still further from their counterparts on the Hill, students in the Experimental College did not seem to mind—or care.

In the spring of 1930, an article in the *Daily Cardinal* listed a series of vital statistics to "disprove 'Ex-College' queerness." According to the article, 64 percent of the students had participated in some athletics. Thirteen students had been in varsity competition, eighteen had gone out for freshman squads, and sixty-one had joined intramural teams. Twenty-five sophomores and fourteen freshmen had pledged Greek letter societies, and a large number of Experimental College students belonged to the university newspaper staff, the literary magazine, the debating society, the marching band, and the glee club. And yet, the *Daily Cardinal* could not ignore the peculiarities of life in Adams Hall. By and large, students in the Experimental College chose books over other activities. The average stu-

Experimental College students, many wearing their "Owl of Athena" blazers, in front of the entrance to Adams Hall, 1930 (University of Wisconsin Archives)

dent in the Experimental College read sixteen unrequired books every semester. "One individual read two hundred books other than his assignments during the period between September and February," the newspaper reported. If Experimental College students spent so much time studying, the paper guessed, then they must have had very little time left for other worthy activities, such as drinking or, more important, dating. "The average Experimental College man had only two dates a month," the editors crowed. In fact, thirty men in the Experimental College had had no dates at all during the entire period of their enrollment in the university. Embarrassed to speculate on the implications of such bewildering statistics, the author of this article suggestively surmised that "seven dates and eighty books must appear scandalous to 'pink-tea' Wisconsin."[33] Indeed, by the fall semester of 1930, some conservative Wisconsinites began to wonder if Meiklejohn and his advisers might be harboring a disproportionate number of homosexuals in Adams Hall. Especially after the students' shocking performance of *Lysistrata,* suspicions about the Experimental College as a bastion of bohemianism grew.

In 1930, accusations of homosexuality in the Experimental College became so common that Meiklejohn hired Dr. Frankwood A. Williams, a noted Freudian psychiatrist from New York, to examine the psychosexual habits of his students.[34] In an attempt to aid Williams in his study, the

Publicity photo for Experimental College production of Aristophanes' *Lysistrata*, 1930 (University of Wisconsin Archives)

advisers submitted a list of questions for his consideration. Paul Raushen-bush asked, "Should discussion of sex have a definite place in the curriculum? Is this more important for our boys than normally, due to our living conditions?" John Gaus, much more blunt, wondered, "Which is to be preferred, masturbation or going to a prostitute?" and "Which set of problems is to be preferred: (a) the boy by himself, with a minimum of contact with girls, and the consequent difficulties of later social adjustment and the active temptation of masturbation and homosexuality, or (b) the boy in free contact with girls and the consequent and natural progression into 'petting' and from petting to the desire and need for sexual intercourse?" Carl Bögholt asked if there was "any justification for the charge made that the Experimental College 'coddles' or 'mothers' its students too much?" Williams took these questions under consideration and, after two weeks of interviews, offered his diagnosis. "These have been the most extraordinary two weeks I have lived in a long time," he told the advisers. "Psychologically, these boys are warped and twisted." Williams added, however, that the psychoses of the Ex-College students were actually quite normal for boys their age. "Of the boys I have seen," he assured the curious advisers, "their problems were created outside, and this situation has been a Godsend for them. They would have gone to pieces in a dozen different ways. This situation has not solved their problems, but it has kept them from breaking completely."[35] In short, Williams concluded, the Experimental College had helped rather than hindered the psychosexual development of the average undergraduate male.

But Meiklejohn had more questions. Always concerned about the role of personal freedom in the college, he inquired whether the required curriculum and tutorial instruction fostered too much emotional, intellectual, or even physical dependence on the advisers. In response to Meiklejohn's concern, Williams shared three case studies, each representing a different form of sexual maladjustment within the student body. "One boy is taking himself apart, separating the biological drives, is intellectualizing, speaks of his desire to 'create,' " Williams explained. This student isolated himself from both boys and girls, turning inward to the comfort and security of his own imagination. In his case, masturbation provided sufficient sexual release. The second boy was "a very hungry, lonesome lad" who spent his time daydreaming and "wishing he could go over and talk to 'John Jones.' " "He would like to know him," Williams wrote, "but, on grounds of Jones's disliking him or 'I am a Jew,' he doesn't, but sits and wishes about it, remaining lonesome. His mind is full of fantasies." The third boy Williams judged to be a homosexual. "Nothing you could do about this problem," he said. "I can tell him what friendship can mean short of homosexuality—working out his needs in that direction at the same time trying to make a heterosexual adjustment. The problem may solve itself. If it does become a problem, it isn't even then fatal." At a time when Freudian analysis commanded considerable respect in American intellectual circles, such theories perhaps impressed Meiklejohn. Given the homosexual subtexts of many of the ancient Greek works assigned in the first year of the Experimental College curriculum, the advisers tried to help their students make a successful "heterosexual adjustment" over the course of the second year.[36]

At the end of his report, Williams put his finger on the heart of the psychological problem, namely, that the Experimental College might hope to foster emotional and intellectual independence while, in actuality, it fostered a deep dependence on the charismatic appeal of the advisers. "What we really want to gain," Williams suggested, "is a real emotional independence so that they are not dependent on father, mother, school, but can stand on their own emotional legs. The success of that depends on how much we, as advisers, really want the boys to be independent. We have got to watch ourselves, because it is possible that we may say we want these boys to be independent intellectually and emotionally, but it may be that we are so constituted that we like to have people dependent on us. If that is true, we will never make them really independent."[37] Here Williams cut to the heart of the matter. Meiklejohn and his advisers espoused intellectual independence but, at the same time, encouraged emotional and psychological subservience to their collective educational will.[38] They allowed the students to *think* themselves autonomous, even if, as members of a larger college community, they ultimately were not. The advisers led the students to imagine themselves as self-governing individuals when, in fact, they still felt subordinate to the authoritative demands of their teachers. The varied implications of this profound pedagogical dilemma—stated explicitly by Socrates in book III of Plato's *Republic*—were difficult to overstate, especially in light of the emphasis on individual subordination to group obligations in Meiklejohn's theory of democratic education. Was it ever possible to teach people to be free without compromising their subjective autonomy in the process? In the early 1930s, Meiklejohn was acutely aware of this question, but he had not yet formulated conclusive answers.

In the meantime, rumors of strange and immoral behavior as well as dangerous political radicalism in the Experimental College circulated widely in the regional and national press. In the summer of 1930, Meiklejohn received a letter from A. C. Kinsford, the superintendent of schools in Baraboo, Wisconsin, a small town northwest of Madison. "I think that your school tends to attract individualistic, unorthodox boys of every sort," Kinsford declared. "Perhaps these tend to set the pace, dominate the whole, and set their stamp on the institution. So, the ordinary student who just wants a degree, who wants to join a 'frat' and afterwards go into business, practice a profession, and worship at the Methodist or Presbyterian Church, is somewhat inclined to look askance at the Experimental College." Consequently, Kinsford continued, a significant number of Wisconsinites were steering their sons away from the Experimental College. "The normal parents with normal boys hesitate to let their boys go to a college where such influences are supposed to prevail. . . . They say they do not want their boys to be put on the road that leads to socialism or anarchism or pacifism or any other particular sort of 'ism.' "[39] Similarly, Judge Evan Evans, also of Baraboo, informed Meiklejohn that the reputation of the Experimental College was "adverse in Wisconsin State." Noting the arrest of Carroll Blair in the summer of 1930, Evans condemned the radical atmosphere of the Ex-College as a threat to domestic tranquillity. "The boy who is aliasing as a so-called Communist in Milwaukee today is ('*of course*,' says the typical Wisconsin citizen) an Experimental College student." Since the advisers had attempted "neither to explain nor to correct" Blair's actions, Evans observed, "the *public thinks* they were *proud* of the notoriety the college has won."[40] Indeed, by September of 1930, the combined effect of political radicalism and educational nonconformism had seriously damaged the reputation of the Experimental College. Meiklejohn's complacence in the face of student misbehavior only strengthened the suspicions of traditionally conservative Wisconsinites, who instinctively kept their sons away from Adams Hall.

As early as August of 1928, Glenn Frank had warned of impending enrollment shortfalls in the Experimental College. "The outlook for new registrations in the Experimental College is far from good," Frank wrote to Meiklejohn shortly before his second group of freshmen arrived. "The explanatory material, this year as last year, did not get into the mails until long after most students had made up their minds on the school they were to enter. . . . Unless some of you take the matter in hand, next year may be very embarrassing and see the whole experiment jeopardized." "If your registration falls far short," Frank added, "it will virtually doom the experiment as far as faculty approval or acquiescence is concerned."[41] Fearing for the future of his experiment, Meiklejohn sent a delegation to Dean Sellery to inquire if he might stand in support of the venture before the people of Wisconsin. Sellery said he would do so, but only if Meiklejohn's advisers agreed to standardize disciplinary procedures and impose regular final exams on students in the Experimental College. Meiklejohn refused, insisting that the whole aim of the Experimental College was to see if students would choose *voluntarily* to participate in the work of a self-governing college community without such external incentives as attendance rules and tests.[42] Consequently, enrollments continued to drop. In the fall of 1928, the Experimental College admitted only 92 new students. Sixteen withdrawals from the freshman class left Meiklejohn with a total enrollment of 195. In 1929, the number of freshmen decreased to 79; with another 16 withdrawals, the total was 155. In the fall of 1930, burdened by the hardships of depression, the number of freshmen fell to 74, leaving a total, after 15 withdrawals, of 138. Within three years of opening, the Experimental College was running at less than half capacity.

In April of 1929, in an effort to reverse this downward trend, Meiklejohn launched a concerted public relations campaign. He sent a letter to every high school in the state asking fellow educators to promote the Experimental College among their students. "The outside impression of the college is that it is fitted only for students of superior ability and intellectual interest," he wrote. "But this is quite contrary to the spirit and intention of the college."[43] Meiklejohn noted that the Experimental College welcomed every type of student, including those who were not Protestant, midwestern, native-born, or even white. Unfortunately, in conservative "pink-tea" Wisconsin, where parochialism reigned, such radical "openness" only exacerbated his enrollment problems. Meiklejohn's worst fears of public misunderstanding were verified when a well-meaning hog farmer from Crystal Lake, having read about the Experimental College in his local newspaper, offered to contribute his "entire stock of guinea pigs" to the school. Noting that his animals were "not hothouse varieties but real healthy farm-raised stock," the farmer explained that he was willing to sell his furry friends outright or, if Meiklejohn preferred, to trade them for "some musical instruments or what have you."[44] Frustrated by such responses to his letter, Meiklejohn sent part-time adviser John Bergstresser on a tour of high schools around the state.[45] Driving the backroads of Wisconsin through Appleton, Eau Claire, Chippewa Falls, Green Bay, Fond du Lac, Menasha, Oshkosh, Sheboygan, Stevens Point, and Wausau, Bergstresser began to see why Meiklejohn's College was failing to attract applicants. The prospect of a traditional college experience was so thrilling to a majority of young people that "the explanation of a college experience that might transcend the traditional falls flat." Moreover, Bergstresser discovered, "most high-school seniors are definitely vocationally-minded."[46] The predominantly intellectual orientation of the Experimental College seemed irrelevant to the employment aspirations of most high school students in Wisconsin. When Bergstresser returned to campus after his trip, he informed Glenn Frank that "not a single student was found" who had decided to enter the Experimental College the next year.[47]

After 1930, parents of students in the Experimental College increasingly complained about the school's unfavorable reputation. One mother found her son's thinking abnormal. Another felt the Experimental College was "developing a lot of loafers."[48] A third thought the workload was too heavy. These complaints were not entirely new. As early as 1927, Alfred Harcourt, chairman of Harcourt, Brace, and Company Publishers in New York, wrote to Meiklejohn about the excessive book list assigned to his son. "I think the reading is entirely too stiff for boys of the maturity you are apt to have, both in the difficulty of the text (I am referring particularly to Plato's *Republic*) and in the likelihood that few if any of the freshmen have enough background to handle as abstract material as this in anything but a woozy fashion."[49] Another father feared that the total intellectual freedom of the Experimental College might later inhibit his son's success in regular university classes. His "antagonism to 'courses' and 'requirements' is so pronounced at present as to interfere with a sober choice of further college work," the father worried. Perhaps the Experimental College was too unstructured for its students' good. "If the young radical, even the young liberal, finds the problem of personal adjustment to actual conditions so difficult as to interfere with his larger social aims, is there not danger that the serried ranks of conservatism may gain recruits even from the nurseries of light and liberalism?"[50] The idea that Meiklejohn's college was simply too radical for its own good occurred to many of his detractors. An editor at Harper & Brothers phrased the issue particularly well, asking "[F]or what are you preparing the young men of your college, to live in the community, or in spite of it?"[51]

Charges of cultural contrariety were difficult for Meiklejohn to accept, but they were also difficult for him to escape. His educational program rested on the notion that a liberal college should stand apart from the mainstream as a cultural "critic." Indeed, his whole response to World War I depended on the idea that institutions of liberal education should stand in tension with their society as representatives of critical discourse and the quest for moral ideals. Framed this way, the mission of the Experimental College was not to prepare students for a life *in* or *in spite of* their community but rather for a life of dialectic and idealistic hope for reform. The liberal college, in other words, operated in a realm that George Santayana had recently called the realm of essence. Its aim was to encourage abstract contemplation and, in so doing, to transcend the "illusion" of the realm of everyday existence, the realm of war, death, and depression. The purpose of the liberal college, Meiklejohn believed, was to imagine *alternatives* to the world as it was and to inspire students to pursue those alternatives in collective institutional forms. Yet, the very idealism underlying Meiklejohn's educational philosophy led him to the status of an outsider at the University of Wisconsin and made the integration of his ideas into the wider scheme of higher education practically impossible. So long as his theory retained its critical intellectual autonomy, it necessarily remained a minority perspective. Students could pursue ideals, but they could never fully realize them. Once, when a student asked Meiklejohn if he should ever "refuse to conform to or be coerced by the world," Meiklejohn answered yes. However, when the student pressed further and asked how individuals could know when to conform and when to rebel, Meiklejohn shook his head, conceding that he had "no formula for that."[52] Meiklejohn's position was one of intellectual criticism, not intellectual commitment. He often suffered from the same ambivalence and agnosticism that he condemned so vigorously in his opponents.

Not surprisingly, Meiklejohn remained an outsider among the faculty of the University of Wisconsin. His closest companions were his young advisers, though, unlike them, he did not live in Adams Hall, preferring instead his large house several blocks away. He and Helen invited students to their home for cookies and tea, but they rarely invited professors from the Hill or people from the surrounding Madison community. The Meiklejohns' best friend outside the Experimental College was Glenn Frank, whose lavish lifestyle, even in the midst of the depression, reminded observers of Meiklejohn's own improvident habits at Amherst. Together, Meiklejohn and Frank did little to lessen the estrangement of the Experimental College. In speeches on behalf of the Ex-College, they often disparaged the older professors in the College of Letters and Science, calling them mossbacks and too much dead wood.[53] To Madison's more established residents, both Meiklejohn and Frank seemed like interlopers from the East. Meiklejohn's faint Scottish accent seemed somehow manipulative. His dry wit seemed deceptive. His indefatigable cheeriness seemed superficial. And, particularly as the economy deteriorated, his left-leaning political associations seemed subversive. Meanwhile, Meiklejohn's wife, Helen, a confident woman who dared to hyphenate her last name, also distanced herself from the conservative townspeople. Putting her economics background to use, she met regularly with individuals from the Madison Summer School for Workers in Industry, the Madison Federation of Labor, the Madison Woman and Child Labor Committee, and the Milwaukee Machinists' Union.[54] In parochial, pink-tea Wisconsin, the Meiklejohns' politics placed them far beyond the pale.

Leading the crusade against the Meiklejohns was George Clarke Sellery, the "scholarly yet crusty" dean of the College of Letters and Science and one of the most influential members of the university faculty.[55] Almost from the time of Meiklejohn's arrival in 1926, Sellery had considered him an intruder brought to the university to show his faculty how to teach. As early as March of 1929, Sellery had publicly criticized the Experimental College for its lack of attendance rules, its attempt to study whole civilizations, its use of nonexpert teachers, its avoidance of exams, its cursory treatment of foreign languages and science, its insistence on self-contained residence halls, and its raucous, impudent student body. His remarks made headlines. "SELLERY DECLARES 'EX-COLLEGE' IDEAS WRONG," printed the *Capital Times* in 1929. "EXPERIMENTAL COLLEGE TECHNIQUE ASSAILED BY DEAN G. C. SELLERY," cried the *Daily Cardinal*.[56] Sellery defended his admittedly provocative speech in a note to President Frank. "My purpose," he curtly explained, "was to say some kind, encouraging, and deserved things about the alumni and faculty of the College of Letters and Science and to give their recent critics the salutary—even if novel—experience of a little taste of their own medicine."[57] A few months later, Sellery snubbed Meiklejohn again, this time by forbidding students from other universities to transfer into the Experimental College. Given his precarious enrollment situation, Meiklejohn was outraged by Sellery's move and tried to reach a private agreement on the matter with President Frank. Sellery, however, rallied the faculty against Meiklejohn, who was forced to back down.[58]

In some respects, Sellery's hostility toward Meiklejohn stemmed indirectly from his ill will toward Frank. "We all felt that he was just getting back at President Frank through Meiklejohn," one student recalled. "Rumor had it that Sellery would have been next in line for the presidency if Frank hadn't stepped into the picture."[59] Indeed, Frank's relationship with Sellery had been sour from the start. Even before Meiklejohn arrived in Madison, Frank had hired a private investigator to gather information on leading political and educational figures in the state, including Sellery. For some inexplicable reason, Frank showed the detective's reports to the dean, who commented that they "were not always complimentary; mine wasn't."[60] In the spring of 1929, just when Sellery started to criticize the Experimental College, Frank had tried to fire him, but professor of philosophy Max Otto, realizing that faculty support lay with the dean rather than the president, persuaded Frank to drop his well-publicized plan.[61] Much of the antagonism between Sellery, Frank, and Meiklejohn centered on issues of a financial nature. Advisers in the Experimental College received higher salaries than professors in the College of Letters and Science, and the disparity provoked considerable resentment and envy. The fact that Meiklejohn's salary of ten thousand dollars exceeded Sellery's by more than 30 percent did not elicit much sympathy, especially during the depression, when newly elected governor Philip F. La Follette instituted a statewide policy of wage waivers to save money.

The controversy over salaries reached a peak in 1930 when Thomas E. Brittingham, Jr., threatened to withdraw his support for the professorship Meiklejohn held. Brittingham bristled at the supposed radicalism of the students in the Experimental College and tried to reclaim the endowment his father had originally pledged. Fearful for his financial future, Meiklejohn asked Frank about the situation. "Several times recently in conversation you have intimated that there is some difficulty with regard to my holding of the Brittingham Professorship," he suggested. "This difficulty has also been referred to now and then in the public press and has been mentioned to me by members of the faculty. I am writing to ask if you would give me a written statement as to just what the difficulty is and what action with regard to it has been taken or is under consideration."[62] Frank deliberated over his reply to Meiklejohn. He did not want to offend his friend, but, burdened by the effects of the depression, he needed Brittingham's support. He felt he could no longer endorse the controversy-laden Experimental College to the extent he once had. In the end, Brittingham withdrew his family's funds from Meiklejohn and transferred them to Professor Karl Link in the Department of Biochemistry. Meiklejohn thenceforth received his paychecks from Sellery, which meant that the expenditures for the Experimental College came directly out of the budget for the College of Letters and Science. At a time when the University of Wisconsin faced budget cuts exceeding $600,000 a year, conflicts between Meiklejohn and Sellery became virtually inevitable.[63]

At first, Meiklejohn tried to ignore Sellery's antagonism and constant lobbying for an end to the Experimental College. He joked with the dean in much the same way that he had joked with Professor Churchill, his old nemesis at Amherst. But the situation did not improve. Even a month's vacation in England in the summer of 1930 did not quell the hostilities.[64] "[T]he rumors that the college would be discontinued were constant and very disturbing," he later recalled. "It is enough to say that they were present, that they were freely expressed, and that such expressions added enormously to the burdens of those who were responsible for the carrying on of the experimental venture."[65] By November of 1930, the controversy surrounding the Experimental College had reached a fever pitch. One close observer noted that "the air was thick with flying verbiage, brickbats which ranged from antiquated objections on the grounds of atheism, bohemianism, and assorted symptoms of pseudo-radicalism to really astute and valuable points to which several of the keener minds had given air as justification for their position."[66] The question of justifying the existence of the Experimental College was crucial. Too often, Meiklejohn distanced himself from the rest of the university, keeping the activities of his advisers secret from anyone who might be inclined to criticize them. "On coming to the College," wrote graduate student H. H. Giles, who divided his time between the Experimental College and the English department, "one finds something of this attitude among the advisers: 'We need not justify ourselves. Our business is to make the thing work.'" Such an aloof stance, Giles argued, "denies the fact that the experiment is set up in a democracy and is subject to democratic interest and judgment. Any democracy feels that it has a right to be informed in terms which it

185

can understand."[67] According to Meiklejohn, however, the college had no duty to answer to the University of Wisconsin faculty. As he had tried to explain after his dismissal from Amherst, the liberal college was beholden only to the truth as its members—or, more accurately, its self-governing students and advisers—saw it. It was *not* responsible to critics, particularly those outside the Experimental College community.

Frustrated by Meiklejohn's philosophical abstractions, annoyed by his administrative indifference, and perhaps wondering why the right to criticize was not reciprocal, Dean Sellery increased his assault on the Experimental College. In his own subtle and backhanded way, he stopped at nothing, not even spying, to end Meiklejohn's stay in Madison. In February of 1931, he received a surprising letter concerning Meiklejohn's second son, Donald, and his relationship with a young woman on campus. According to the letter, the young woman's neighbors had witnessed, through an unshaded window, what appeared to be "unseemly conduct" between her and Donald Meiklejohn. The landlord had come over to the neighbors' apartment in response to their complaint, and, while he was there, "saw a young man take off all [the woman's] clothing, saw the two roll on the bed together for some time, and still later saw [her] sitting entirely nude on the young man's lap." The landlord told Sellery that he "readily identified the young man as Donald Meiklejohn."[68] A few days later, Sellery received a second letter. This time, Donald, who was at the time a doctoral student in the Department of Philosophy and a part-time instructor in the Experimental College, visited the young woman together with his friend, Maurice Neufeld. "Neighbors of 124 North Orchard Street saw a young woman they understood to be a student entertaining in her room two different young men," the second letter stated. The spies recognized one of the men as Donald Meiklejohn. "They had seen him tuck [the woman] into bed, kiss her goodnight, put up the window, and immediately after appear in his own room. The other young man visitor the neighbors had seen in [her] room Sunday night, January 25th, as late as 2:00 a.m. They had seen him participate in 'petting' scenes with [her], etc."[69] Since it was the university's usual policy to expel students caught having sex, Sellery pursued the same penalty for Donald.

Meiklejohn, greatly distressed by these letters, discussed them with his son, who confessed to having an illicit relationship. Meiklejohn promptly wrote to Sellery and enclosed a letter from Donald asking for leniency in his punishment. "The enclosed letter from Donald will give you the outcome of my conference with him as we tried to find some way of meeting your suggestion as to action which he might take. I cannot send the letter without again expressing the hope that you may find it possible to bring the matter to fair and impartial settlement without the doing of the things which Donald proposes. In my own opinion, an official reprimand would be an adequate dealing with the offense involved." Donald's letter was more obsequious than his father's. "I wish again to express my regret at the indiscretion which led to the present situation," Donald wrote in an attempt at conciliation. "However, your plan for expressing this regret in action seems to me too severe for the situation in question. I should therefore like to offer the following alternative scheme. It can be arranged, if satisfactory to you, (1) that I withdraw from the graduate school, (2) that [the woman] leave the community, and (3) that my graduate credits of last semester be canceled. Any or all of these possibilities will be acceptable to me and to [her]. I hope they may seem sufficient to you."[70] Unfortunately, Donald's plan did not satisfy Sellery, who called for immediate expulsion. "The alternative scheme which you offer in your note is in my judgment unacceptable," Sellery wrote. "I am convinced that it is to your interest as well as to that of the university that you should voluntarily 'take your medicine,' the same that others in like circumstances have had to take."[71] Needless to say, Donald was disappointed. His father, however, was furious. Writing hurriedly to Frank, Meiklejohn requested an appeal of Sellery's decision in a closed meeting of the executive committee of the Board of Regents. He did not succeed, however, and Donald was expelled.[72]

By this point, the antipathy between Meiklejohn and Sellery had become too much to bear. A week after Donald's failed appeal for mercy from the dean, Meiklejohn asked his advisers to end the Experimental College.[73] News of his astonishing decision spread rapidly throughout the United States. "This is perhaps the most inauspicious moment to write on the Experimental College," announced philosophy professor Eliseo Vivas in the *Nation*. "The day the editor of the *Nation* requested an article on it, its chairman, Dr. Alexander Meiklejohn, offered a motion . . . proposing that no freshmen be admitted in the next academic year." Unaware of Donald's recent tangle with the dean, reporters speculated wildly on the causes of Meiklejohn's move. Some pointed to student radicalism and disciplinary problems, while others saw administrative conflicts and financial disputes as the main reasons for the college's demise. According to Vivas, the chief failure of the Experimental College was its avoidance of grades as necessary incentives for students to work. Meiklejohn seemed to have an "unqualified faith in human nature," Vivas wrote. "He wishes to place the responsibility altogether upon the student and stands on his principle that the only way to make him work in a really valuable way is to interest him in some task 'which is so important that everybody is going to throw himself heart and soul into the doing of it.' " In some cases, Meiklejohn had successfully inspired his students to work up to their potential. "But," Vivas asserted, "in a larger number of cases, the freedom granted has worked instead toward a scattered picking up on smatterings of facts."[74] Such words cut deep, exposing a central nerve of Meiklejohn's educational theory. If the Experimental College could neither teach students voluntarily to learn nor give them more than a smattering of facts, then it merely duplicated the coercion and fragmentation of more traditional university methods—the very evils Meiklejohn sought to avoid. If Vivas was right, then the Experimental College was all wrong, a total failure as an institutional expression of Meiklejohn's liberal educational ideal.

A month after Vivas published his article in the *Nation*, Professor Grant Showerman, a long-time critic of the Experimental College and a close friend of Sellery, published an even more scathing screed in the progressive education journal *School and Society*. Writing under the title "A Most Lamentable Comedy," Showerman unleashed a series of vituperations against Meiklejohn's program, claiming that it "did not command the approval of the faculty of Letters and Science in the beginning, and it has not won the approval or commanded the respect of that body during the four years of its existence." Like Vivas, Showerman believed that the main reason for the failure of the Experimental College was the unchecked freedom of its students. "The student was under no compulsion or conviction to work," Showerman wrote, "or even to comport himself with decency, except as the light from heaven shined round about him." Showerman argued that education was, and always would be, a matter of *forcing* students to learn. "School education," he contended, was always "a forcing of experience."[75] Quite clearly, Meiklejohn and Showerman disagreed when it came to the goals and methods of liberal education. Whereas Meiklejohn viewed requirements as necessary but secondary to a cohesive learning community, Showerman viewed them as essential to educational discipline. Meiklejohn may have seemed conservative in comparison with educational progressives like John Dewey, but he appeared radical when compared with traditionalists like Grant Showerman. The line between Meiklejohn and Showerman was the ambiguous line between freedom and authority in the liberal college.

At least two alumni of the Experimental College agreed with Showerman. "I have not got over a feeling that education ought to be strict," wrote Phillip Garman, who entered the Experimental College in the fall of 1929 and finished in the spring of 1931. "[B]right boys (and we were many

188

A spoof on Meiklejohn's "guinea pig college" in the St. Patrick's Day parade at the University of Wisconsin, ca. 1931 (University of Wisconsin Archives)

bright boys) especially need management because there is otherwise no inducement to read with discipline or insight or to read difficult material in so permissive an environment. Only single-minded, verified, incontrovertible geniuses should be free to run on their own reins." Garman realized that his words sounded like heresy to Meiklejohn but insisted that the principles behind the Experimental College were simply too idealistic to work. "Lovely a man as Alec and the others were," he concluded, "I came to think of their educational theory as benighted."[76] Arthur Justin (formerly Justin Silverstein, winner of the Freshman Oratorical Contest in 1929) agreed with Phillip Garman, not only in his assessment of the weaknesses of the curriculum, but also in his high regard for the advisers' abilities as teachers. "For myself," Justin wrote to Meiklejohn after transferring to Brown in the fall of 1930, "the Experimental College . . . did me damage in only one respect. I was allowed complete freedom to form my own study habits when I wasn't sufficiently strong enough to take myself in hand." Nevertheless, Justin wrote, he would remember his Madison years fondly. "Aside from the freedom allowed at the Experimental College—and I think it might have been restricted without seriously altering the general approach of the school—I am still wholeheartedly in favor of the method there. Especially am I grateful for your teaching example. I have never seen anything to compare with your capacity to arouse thought in students. When I imagine myself as a teacher some years from now, it is always with the hope that I may in small degree at least be able to pattern myself after you."[77] Justin failed to realize, however, that Meiklejohn's teaching example was the very essence of discipline in the Experimental College. His relationship with his students embodied both discipline and freedom simultaneously in its attempt to teach *self*-government.

Despite such comments, Meiklejohn did not lack defenders. Ernest L. Meyer, a part-time adviser in the Experimental College and later a columnist for the Madison *Capital Times,* pointed to the mean-spirited articles by Vivas and Showerman and asserted that "the patronizing attitude of the College of Letters and Science becomes ludicrous under scrutiny. The errors of the Letters College are less obvious because they have been dignified by a hundred years of consistent mistakes, and deified under the name of System. It is difficult to uproot and perhaps foolhardy to combat any mistake that is whiskered by custom and widely believed by intelligent men whose name-cards bristle with imposing degrees." According to Meyer, the future of American higher education depended on the ability to distinguish between truly liberal educational programs like those of the Experimental College and conservative programs like those of the College of Letters and Science. "On the outcome of the experiment may hinge the verdict whether our youth will flock to college and come to grips with vital problems affecting themselves and the world or whether as now they will put on their bearskin coats and leave home to go into a four-years' hibernation."[78] The *New Orleans Tribune* echoed that the real lesson of the Experimental College was that "not all of our educational stagnation and inertia is due to the influence of regents and alumni; the vested educational interests, pedagogical superstitions, departmental jealousies, and college politics of the faculties are very often a greater menace to education."[79] Editors in Minneapolis concurred. "From the standpoint of intellectual illumination," they asserted, "Meiklejohn's experiment in the University of Wisconsin proved a success. But this apparently is not the essence of university endeavor. At Amherst, enlightenment was sacrificed to tradition and clique. At Wisconsin, economic considerations and departmental politics are said to have dominated."[80]

Meiklejohn thought he could avoid an Amherst-like outcome by setting the Experimental College apart from the rest of the university, but his strategy of a college within a college did not succeed. In May of 1932, the faculty and regents of the University of Wisconsin voted to end the Ex-

190

perimental College for good.[81] A few weeks later, Meiklejohn hosted a closing banquet for 250 students, advisers, and guests. It was a poignant event, paralleling in many ways the final alumni luncheon at Amherst nine years earlier. Glenn Frank, appearing painfully "stiff and cold and nervous," delivered a short address before making a "hurried exit" from the banquet hall. Meiklejohn then rose to speak. As usual, he spoke quietly at first, gradually warming to his theme. His remarks were brief—no more than twenty minutes in duration—but they were powerful. The Experimental College, he said, marked a rare moment in the history of American higher education, a moment unlikely ever to be repeated. It had been the highlight of his career, the pinnacle of his experience as a teacher. But now, because of circumstances beyond his control, it had to end, and he was sorry that the moment could not last longer. By the time Meiklejohn turned away from the podium and reclaimed his seat, his audience was in tears. "I don't know to this day what he said," one listener recalled. "It doesn't matter much. His appeal always affected my emotions more than my intellect. . . . The picture I remember is of the room when he had finished talking. Everyone was on his feet. For a moment there was tremendous clapping. Then silence, and for several moments nobody moved. Everyone watched that little man. It was almost a spell. A spell that broke slowly and, when it finally broke, found us staring embarrassedly, red-faced, at one another. Embarrassed and red-faced because every person in that room knew that the gulping in his throat and the mist in his eyes were in the eyes and throats of everyone else, too. We shuffled about for a few minutes, muttered gruffly to one another, then stampeded for the door."[82]

The first to leave had been Glenn Frank. According to an eyewitness, Frank had finished his speech and then "suddenly bolted from the room, really ran out and down the hall, and, at the end of the hall, he stopped and took out a handkerchief and wiped his brow and seemed to utter a great sigh and walked away defeated, his head down, utterly exhausted from the experience." The students and advisers in the Experimental College had very little sympathy for Frank. "We felt that he was a traitor," one recalled, "and had betrayed us."[83] Indeed, for Meiklejohn's adoring students, Glenn Frank was their Judas Iscariot. An administrative pragmatist who yielded to popular opinion at a time when true leadership was needed, he became for them a symbol of educational treason. Contrarily, Meiklejohn became a messianic redeemer bearing the weight of personal sacrifice for the salvation of a fallen world. "As I see it," Governor Philip La Follette noted in a letter to his wife, "Alec has the psychological twist where he personally identifies the college with himself; consequently, he cannot fight for it be-

191

cause he senses or feels that he is fighting, to put it crudely, for his meal ticket."[84] The closing banquet of the Experimental College was not the first time that Meiklejohn had played the role of spiritual martyr. He had assumed the same identity in his final baccalaureate sermon at Amherst. Then, as now, Meiklejohn cast himself as the "minority man" who spoke the truth for the redemption of humanity. To descend from the realm of ideals, the realm of pure essence, into the realm of reality, the Platonic "cave" of ignorance, was to lose the spirit of liberal understanding and to fall, as it were, from holiness, light, and grace. To try to save the Experimental College from its own worldly failings—or its petty practical problems, as Meiklejohn seemed to view them—was to surrender the battle for human intelligence, a battle he expected his students and faculty ultimately to win for themselves. Meiklejohn closed his final address by completing the messianic metaphor. George Sellery, his Pontius Pilate, he said, had "crucified" the Experimental College.[85] His beloved community of learning was now dead.

In the spring and summer of 1932, Meiklejohn devoted himself to a retrospective study of the Experimental College, published by Harper & Brothers, which John Dewey reviewed in the *New Republic*. "The book is fundamentally a discussion of the place and function of the college of liberal arts in the entire scheme of American education," Dewey wrote. "If I may say so without frightening anyone away from an extremely lucid and readable book, it is a contribution to the philosophy of American education." In Dewey's opinion, Meiklejohn's work was all "the more pointed and the more significant because, unlike most such discussions, it comes to us as the philosophy of an actual undertaking, not as a full bolt from the blue of abstraction. Moreover, the educational ideas presented are tied up with a clearly thought-out conception of the nature, the defects and promise, of American culture and life." According to Dewey, the Experimental College embodied the true purpose of liberal education—the cultivation of a genuine capacity for rational deliberation and honest self-criticism. "The experiment was conceived in terms so remote from the complacency and aimless drift of much of our social life, it was such a challenge to the accidental empiricism which so controls our college studies and teaching methods, that it is not surprising that it evoked bitter opposition or that it failed of achieving its supreme purpose. For it faced frankly that which is the great difficulty in the American college because it is the great defect in American life outside the college. Anyone who claimed that the problem could be solved in any term of five years, or of double or treble that time, would be a quack—and Mr. Meiklejohn is no quack."[86]

In the end, Dewey judged Meiklejohn's work a profoundly tragic success. "At every point, the experiment in Madison ran counter to the weight of precedent and tradition," he observed. Its commitment to cultural criticism was its greatest strength but also its greatest weakness. It succeeded in teaching its students to challenge social mores, but it did not succeed in explaining the value of that challenge to the wider community in Madison or the University of Wisconsin as a whole. Dewey's assessment of the Experimental College and its basic meaning in the history of American higher education could not have been more accurate. In the final analysis, Meiklejohn's Experimental College advanced an extreme interpretation of the meaning and purpose of modern liberal education. Conceived as an attempt to run order through chaos, direction through space, discipline through freedom, and unity through multiplicity, the Experimental College started from the assumption that reasonable individuals engaged in collective deliberation about common social problems could achieve mutual understanding and, moreover, that democracy depended on the validity of that assumption. It took seriously the belief that democracy involves the construction of a single, unified, self-governing community, the individual members of which choose voluntarily to subordinate their personal interests to the larger interests of the group. But the majority of the faculty in the College of Letters and Science could not understand, or at least could not accept, the reformist meaning of Meiklejohn's work. Neither, at times, could the College's own students. At the end of his review, Dewey posed the question most crucial to assessing the success of the Experimental College: "Is there an American college which is willing and able to carry its self-criticism to the point demanded by the Meiklejohn experiment?" to which he answered bluntly, "I doubt it."[87]

In a letter to educator and philanthropist Frederick P. Keppel, president of the Carnegie Corporation in New York, Meiklejohn looked back on the Experimental College and offered his own somber assessment of its work. "We had no real hope of establishing a permanent venture in the midst of this community," he acknowledged. "To do that one would have had to go much more slowly, cut much less deeply than we did. But to do that would have given a quite different result." The purpose of the Experimental College was to test an alternative, to strike out in a new direction, to act as a critic and a prophet in an age of educational aimlessness. "You see," he continued in a tone of serenity, "I believe in radical departures, but I am also conscious of their limitations. They should not be expected to provide sober and finished plans of action ready for immediate adoption. Their true function is that of abstractions which are useful in the discussion of principles but not immediately in the management of specific situations." The Experimental College, like every truly critical liberal college, was destined to cultural marginality. "We did try a radical departure," Meiklejohn concluded, "and, perforce, we had to take its consequences."[88] In a similar vein he had written to a friend at Mount Holyoke College back in May of 1923 (almost as if to foretell his dismissal from Amherst a month later), "it is quite impossible ordinarily to be a radical and also to be in the majority. I do not think that one fails because one doesn't get one's program adopted or even tried. Our task is that of bringing pressure to bear toward the reconsidering of points of view and modes of procedure which are not commonly adopted. If one is making the pressure felt, that is, I think, success."[89] The students in the Experimental College understood their leader's adversarial role as a minority man striving for cultural criticism and educational reform. "The place of Dr. Meiklejohn was not in the American college," they decided. "He belonged—like Socrates and all true educators—outside the pale."[90]

After the closing of the Experimental College, Meiklejohn's first concern was to help his former graduate-student advisers find jobs. In the dark days of the Great Depression, he implored Sellery to hire them as teaching assistants in their respective university departments, but Sellery refused. Finally, Meiklejohn appealed to President Frank for help. "For months I have tried to get from you some decision, some expression of attitude as to the men for whom you and I are jointly responsible—and I cannot get it. . . . It seems to me—I may be wrong—that you do not realize the position in which you have men who are dependent on your action. I say that *wholly* out of regard and solicitude for you. If you will let me, I *must* tell you more fully what is on my mind."[91] Meiklejohn wanted to watch out for his advisers, but he also wanted to protect himself. In June of 1932, on the advice of the Wisconsin State Emergency Board, Frank slashed all salaries over seven thousand dollars by 20 percent. Meiklejohn, who had no retirement pension from either Brown or Amherst, was outraged.[92] "I came here in good faith a few years ago at the invitation of the regents and with the agreement that my salary would be fixed at $10,000," he complained to Frank. "You know, of course, how eager I was that, when the time of depression came, higher salaries should be reduced to help in meeting that emergency." Arguing that a disparity between salaries was no reason, in itself, to cut his pay, Meiklejohn pleaded with Frank to preserve his high income. "I assure you that I write this note not in a spirit of controversy. I am concerned for the welfare of the University of Wisconsin and for our academic morale in general more than I am for my own immediate financial interest." At the end of his letter, however, Meiklejohn revealed a deeper source of his distress: "Helen has had a miscarriage," he wrote, adding that he was leaving at once for her hospital in New York.[93]

At the end of July, after a two-week respite with his recuperating wife at the MacDowell Colony in Peterborough, New Hampshire, Meiklejohn returned to Madison. No longer busy with the Experimental College, he turned his attention to the work that his friend Joseph Hart was doing in the adult education program of the University of Wisconsin Extension Division.[94] Founded on principles borrowed from the Experimental College, Hart's program aimed to provide Madison's adult residents with the rudiments of a liberal education. Meiklejohn took a keen interest in the growing adult education movement. Drawing on his experience with workers' training in Holyoke, Springfield, and Amherst, Massachusetts, he sat on Hart's advisory board and offered his assistance in planning for adult education in Wisconsin. In 1931, his former student, David Gordon, started a school for workers in Cleveland, Ohio, modeled closely on his experience in Adams Hall. "The method of teaching is the 'question-discussion' form," Gordon told Meiklejohn in February of 1933. "In this manner, the instructor draws from the student himself the logical explanation of a problem."[95] This idea of adult reading and discussion groups was spreading rapidly in the mid-1930s. In addition to Hart's work in Wisconsin and Gordon's work in Ohio, Meiklejohn followed the activities of Myles Horton's Highlander Folk School in the mountains near New Market, Tennessee. "Adult education is a necessity," Meiklejohn told a newspaper reporter in 1933, "and, to give it the start toward a development appropriate to the conditions of the adult, special institutions will have to be founded."[96] After the demise of the Experimental College, the adult training movement seemed the next frontier in American educational reform. Indeed, Meiklejohn already had his own new "special institution" in mind.

In September of 1932, Meiklejohn received a letter from James A. Blaisdell, head of the recently affiliated Claremont Colleges in California and a long-time admirer of the Experimental College. "It has seemed to me that a state university was an extremely difficult place in which to make this venture," Blaisdell wrote. "The question has often risen in my mind as to whether we had not, here at Claremont, an almost ideal environment for carrying forward your ideals of education, in which I myself deeply believe." Noting the beautiful setting and modern facilities of the five Claremont Colleges, Blaisdell invited Meiklejohn to visit and, possibly, if adequate financial resources could be found, to become the direc-

Alexander Meiklejohn, Stanley King, Arthur Stanley Pease, and Calvin Coolidge (appearing from left to right) gather for an uncomfortable photograph at King's inauguration as president of Amherst College in 1932 (Amherst College Archives and Special Collections)

tor of some kind of successor to the Experimental College in California. Meiklejohn thought seriously about Blaisdell's offer but doubted whether another college within a college would work. If he had learned anything at the University of Wisconsin, it was that experimental education could not succeed within the confines of established university procedures. A truly liberal college, conceived as a site for cultural criticism from an idealist intellectual perspective, needed to move *outside* preexisting educational institutions. Indeed, the very idea of liberal education involved an ambivalence about the "reform-ability" of established institutions and the complacent mainstream majorities that controlled them. As Meiklejohn had put it ten years earlier at Amherst, "I am a believer in democracy, but my query is whether institutions of learning should be in the hands of majorities."[97] The time had come to see if liberal learning could succeed *beyond* the bounds of traditional higher education as an organic process of small-group deliberation among adults. California promised just the right setting for such a venture—not in Claremont, but in Berkeley.

BERKELEY

1933–1947

7

"Adult Education: A Fresh Start"

1933–1940

I N THE SPRING OF 1933, Meiklejohn took a sabbatical from teaching and moved to Berkeley. While retaining a half-time appointment in the philosophy department at the University of Wisconsin, he rented a large house in the hills near the campus of the University of California. There, surrounded by pines and palms and cooled by a steady bay breeze, he found a relaxing and hospitable work environment. "Life here is very pleasant," he wrote to Glenn Frank. "The university crowd is very friendly. They have given me a fine office in one of the buildings so that I am well equipped at this point. I use the library and have use of the faculty club and the president's tennis court."[1] Besides reading, writing, and playing tennis, Meiklejohn also took time to help in the development of a new school. "A group in San Francisco has been trying to start an adult education school," he told Frank at the beginning of June, "and they have wanted to know if I would and could get leave of absence for a year to help them with the starting of the project."[2] Frank was delighted to hear of Meiklejohn's latest pursuits and agreed to grant him two semesters' leave for the 1933–1934 academic year. In the meantime, plans for the so-called San Francisco School developed rapidly. "Once more," the editors of *Newsweek* wrote, "Alexander Meiklejohn, stormy petrel of American education, wings his way westward. Professor Meiklejohn is on leave from the University of Wisconsin and has gone to San Francisco to organize an Adult Center for Social Studies to be opened on the Pacific Coast this fall. There, for the third time, he will put into practice his two favorite ideas— a small faculty with a limited number of students and instruction in the problems of modern society against a background of ancient civilization." While the details of this report proved only half accurate (the new cur-

Alexander Meiklejohn with Henry A. Wallace, Elmer Griffin, a nationally ranked tennis star, and Oren Root, Jr., the campaign manager for Wendell Willkie (appearing from left to right), ca. 1940 (State Historical Society of Wisconsin, WHi [X3] 52139)

riculum did not deal with ancient civilization), two things were certain: Meiklejohn had gone to California to start a new school for adults, and his reputation had preceded him. "For a man whose career in education has occasioned so much controversy, Professor Meiklejohn is amazingly mild and unassuming," *Newsweek* noted. "In appearance, he is still vigorous and young, though his hair is touched with gray. Soft-spoken and mild in manner, his steady eyes gleam almost diffidently behind his glasses."[3] Indeed, even at the age of sixty-one, Meiklejohn remained sanguine about the possibility of liberal educational reform.

In Berkeley, Meiklejohn worked for the first time outside academe. Shifting from a university-based to a community-based approach to liberal education, he announced a plan to educate a whole city through a loose network of locally organized adult discussion groups. In these groups, citizens from all walks of life could come together and, using a shared syllabus of Great Books, study the enduring questions of liberal democratic society. Reiterating the need for a place set apart from daily life for the sake of cultural criticism, he aimed to teach the methods of democratic deliberation to as many adults as possible. As *Time* magazine reported in June of 1933, "Dr. Meiklejohn will help radicals, businessmen, teachers, artists, laborers, preachers, and scientists in scrutinizing contemporary civilization and its problems."[4] No longer limited by what he had perceived as rigid administrative procedures, capricious turf-guarding professors, or fickle money-minded trustees, he seized the opportunity to start a new program entirely from scratch. Unencumbered by traditional institutional structures, he saw community-based adult education as a way to foster a more direct democracy in which diverse individuals could think together about common social concerns. Others applauded Meiklejohn's vision and, before long, he had assembled an impressive list of donors to sponsor his school. The roster included Presidents Robert Sproul of the University of California in Berkeley, Ray Wilbur of Stanford, and Aurelia Reinhardt of Mills College for Women, as well as lawyer Albert Rosenshine, surgeon Thomas Addis, architect Irving Morrow, Judge Daniel Koshland, author Jesse Lillienthal, and banker James Moffitt.[5] Meiklejohn also recruited Wetmore Hodges, chairman of the General Foods Corporation, and Andrew Welch, the well-known shipping and sugar magnate, to underwrite his venture.[6]

From the earliest stages, Meiklejohn stated his intention to unite upper-class patrons and working-class students in a common educational enterprise. "What excited me first of all," he wrote to Welch in May of 1933, "was the sense that you and I, despite our differences of training, of experiences, of relationships, could yet find common ground on which to cooperate. . . . I am thought of as a 'radical' and you are regarded as belonging to the 'conservative' group, but it appears that you and I have something in common that cuts beneath such separations as those words express. If that is true, then it brings us down to the only solid basis on which any teaching institution can rest. Far more important to me than any special beliefs is the human attempt at mutual understanding, and I judge the same is true of you." Apparently it was, because Welch agreed to pay more than a quarter of the school's operating expenses in its first year while giving Meiklejohn complete control over administration. Meiklejohn thanked Welch for his generosity and asked if he might be able to persuade "three or four or five" wealthy friends to join him in covering the full amount. "If that were done and the group would take a large part in pushing the project, then we could give the city an object lesson in education that would be of enormous value. They would see men they regard as conservatives and radicals working together for a common purpose." Meiklejohn knew that such collaboration might raise eyebrows among the city's well-to-do. "All of us would be suspected in ways I need not explain," he predicted. "But my guess is that my independence is strong enough to stand some suspicion. People know pretty well that I will not submit to control or dictation. And they know, too, that you and your friends have keen judgment, that you will not advance money unless you are convinced that the cause and the work justify it."[7]

At the end of the summer, Meiklejohn outlined his plan for the San Francisco School of Social Studies in a letter to Morse Cartwright, chairman of the American Association of Adult Education (which Meiklejohn and Joseph Hart had helped to establish in 1928). "San Francisco offers an excellent field for such a venture," Meiklejohn wrote, "and the group which makes the application is a powerful and intelligent one." Citing San Francisco's high per capita income, its relatively large proportion of white-collar workers, its ethnic diversity and conscious tradition of labor activism, and its strong record of private philanthropy, Meiklejohn proposed a three-pronged approach to adult education in the city. First was a plan of "general teaching for mature persons who have not had higher education." Second was a proposal for "advanced studies for persons who are already trained in the use of books." Third was a program of "discussions and conferences between various groups in the city whose interests and beliefs center about common problems but who are not now intellectually acquainted with one another." Building on the structure of the Experimental College, Meiklejohn envisioned a faculty of three or four teachers who could lead weekly or biweekly meetings with groups of six to fifteen students. He also drew up a syllabus of Great Books for a curriculum, the Theory and Practice of Democracy in America. "I am certain, on the basis of experience in the Experimental College," he explained to Cartwright, "that, along the lines suggested, we could make a valuable contribution to the study of ways of providing instruction for mature people in our cities who, for one reason or another, have not had higher education but who are capable of taking it."[8] Cartwright whole-heartedly agreed. In September of 1933, he helped Meiklejohn secure a fifteen-hundred-dollar planning grant from the Elmhirst Fund in New York. Leonard and Dorothy Elmhirst had missed an earlier opportunity to support the idea of a "Meiklejohn College" in Manhattan in 1924, but they gladly aided him now.

In February of 1934, the San Francisco School of Social Studies opened an office on the eighth floor of the Liebes Building at 177 Post Street in downtown San Francisco. Its location, on the border between the northern and southern halves of the city, was important. Not long after the school launched its first discussion groups, the Community Chest Club of San Francisco sponsored a survey of adult education programs in the city and found that almost all of them centered in the more affluent district north of Market Street, the city's diagonal dividing line.[9] Meiklejohn aimed to see if his program could succeed nearer the southern part of the city, where economic conditions were much worse. His goal was to bridge the gaps between the city's disparate social groups in an effort to facilitate a common critical discourse among urban cohabitants. "What we should like to develop in the city is the sense that there are certain central problems with which every mind should be dealing," he explained in a promotional brochure. "We need, in our American cities, what might be called a common culture of ideas, interests, problems, and values. We need to be brought together into a unity of interests and understandings so that we might have the materials, the methods, and the acquaintance with ideas that will make possible the experience of genuine thinking together." To create an environment in which diverse individuals might come together as friends, even just briefly, was, in Meiklejohn's mind, to create the possibility of a more deliberative and cooperative democracy. "In such a city as San Francisco, there should be hundreds of such groups at work, and they should be linked together in active cooperation," he declared. "If that could be done, then it would have in it the beginning of the making of an American mind."[10]

Innovative as it was, the San Francisco School was not entirely unique. It fit into a much broader adult education movement flourishing throughout the United States in the 1930s. Lyceums, chautauquas, evening schools, extension classes, correspondence courses, and public libraries had grown rapidly since the turn of the century and even more rapidly since the start of the depression. The League of Women Voters and other women's clubs rendered a service increasingly mirrored by men's organizations, such as the Commonwealth Club of San Francisco. Churches, synagogues, and other religious organizations played a significant role, along with theaters, concert halls, art museums, lecture platforms, and radio stations in providing educational opportunities for adults. For the adult education movement, the depression proved to be an organizational boon. With unprecedented levels of unemployment, the demand for book clubs, reading circles, and other inexpensive leisure activities increased dramatically. By the mid-1930s, the American Association of Adult Education, the Adult Education Association of the USA, and the American Library Association all operated rapidly growing literary programs for "mature readers." Convening in both urban and rural areas to read preselected "books of the month," club members typically met in private homes to discuss texts and also share opinions on various social, political, and personal topics unrelated to books. The weekly ritual of book-club meetings functioned as a source of individual and group therapy for many Americans during the hard times of the depression. The San Francisco School of Social Studies similarly offered a forum for debating the controversial issues of the day.[11] In this respect, its aims were not unlike those of Meiklejohn's Social and Economic Institutions curriculum at Amherst two decades before.

When it opened in 1934, the San Francisco School employed a staff of four, including Helen and Alexander Meiklejohn, Charles Hogan, an unemployed professor of philosophy with degrees from Oxford and the University of California, and John Walker Powell, who worked with Meiklejohn at the Experimental College and had continued as secretary in the philosophy department at the University of Wisconsin. During his second year in San Francisco, Meiklejohn hired a third teacher, Myer Cohen, a specialist in international relations and constitutional law who had studied at Cambridge before completing a doctorate in government at Yale. From time to time, Meiklejohn also brought guest lecturers to lead sessions on specific texts. In 1934, for example, he invited his father-in-law, Walter Goodnow Everett, to direct a discussion on his best-known book, *Moral Values*. The staff of the San Francisco School, while perhaps not as unified or like-minded as the advisers in the Experimental College, gradually became a close-knit teaching force. Just as the Experimental College had been a place for philosophers to flourish, so, too, the San Francisco School was a place devoted to philosophy as a practical art. "The deepest commitment which held them together," Powell later recalled, "was the philosopher's devotion to and belief in the importance of ideas . . . the belief that, not only are human values intelligible, but to understand them is the primary task of human intelligence."[12] Not surprisingly, the curriculum of the San Francisco School reflected Meiklejohn's own philosophical interests, cataloguing its topics as "Social Ideals and Social Change," "Evolution and Economic Theory," "The Bearing of Anthropology on Current Ethical Standards," "Contemporary Literature as a Form of Social Criticism," "Law and Civilization," and, perhaps most suggestively, "The Coming Struggle for Power."[13]

Rather than attempt the study of whole civilizations, as the Experimental College had done, the San Francisco School limited itself to contemporary social problems in the United States. Three sets of questions guided the selection of texts. First were questions pertaining to social and economic institutions, which had interested Meiklejohn ever since his days at Amherst. Second were questions of moral and ethical action in a modern industrial society. And third were questions concerning the legal, political, and constitutional structures of modern American democracy. The staff of the San Francisco School used a series of Great Books to lend a critical and coherent framework to students' weekly debates. Among the 150-plus titles on the three-year syllabus were Plato's *Republic,* Aristotle's *Politics,* Machiavelli's *Prince,* Hobbes's *Leviathan,* Locke's *Essay on Civil Government,* Rousseau's *Social Contract,* Marx's *Communist Manifesto,* Lenin's *State and Revolution,* Beard's *Rise of American Civilization,* Dreiser's *American Tragedy,* and Dewey's *Public and Its Problems.* Meiklejohn also incorporated motion pictures into his curriculum, including three movies produced by the Farm Security Administration: *The River, The City,* and *The Plow That Broke the Plains.*[14] By far the most controversial, and therefore useful, texts on the syllabus were the Declaration of Independence, the Constitution of the United States, and Myer Cohen's edited set, *Selected Opinions of the Supreme Court.* Since the chief goal of the discussion groups was to foster critical deliberation and collective understanding of common social problems, the Constitution provided an ideal springboard for debate. "The problem that faces adult schools is not whether or not to use controversial books," Powell explained, "but how to choose and how to group those books so that they focus on the relevant factors in a given issue." The purpose of the San Francisco School was not to create unanimity on solutions to social problems but rather to create a shared framework for discussing those problems. Intellectual controversy was the very heart of a deliberative democratic community.[15]

Initially, Meiklejohn hoped to enroll at least a hundred students in his new school. Interest was so overwhelming, however, that, within a few months, he had more than three hundred adults meeting in dozens of groups throughout the Bay Area. As Powell later recounted, "[F]rom the first week of registration, there were more people applying for entrance than the small staff could put into groups of convenient size. Because it was important to keep the groups within a limit of about fifteen regular members, there was generally a waiting list even after some had been rejected and others had dropped out."[16] To enroll, a student needed only to meet the approval of the faculty in a personal interview. Helen Meiklejohn, who worked closely with her husband in the operation of the school, asked three questions of each applicant: "Do you have the inclination to study?" "Can you come regularly to group meetings?" and "Will you participate in the discussions?" "These are the entrance requirements," Helen stated, "and the only ones."[17] Although the school accepted students regardless of their prior educational experience, it drew mainly from the city's young professional community. Half the school's students held white-collar jobs; another 17 percent held other office positions. Much to Meiklejohn's disappointment, only 11 percent were laborers. A mere 5 percent classified themselves as unemployed, including those who worked for the Civilian Conservation Corps and (after 1935) the Works Progress and National Youth Administrations. Sixty percent of the students were women, and 15 percent were foreign born. Although Meiklejohn's original plan had stressed the inclusion of students without previous higher education, more than half had college experience, and 22 percent had graduate degrees. On the other hand, 13 percent held only a high school diploma, and 2 percent had finished their education before the sixth grade.[18]

The San Francisco School attracted students from the both ends of the political spectrum. The proportion of social workers, young professionals, and recent college graduates was closely correlated with the prevailing "Left-New Deal" tenor of the discussion groups, but, according to Powell, there were also archconservatives "who under group pressure to choose between Socialism and Fascism frankly chose the latter." The largest number of students came from middle-class families living in secure neighborhoods with good public schools. They were, by and large, "stable citizens who held jobs and kept up homes and families; predominantly American for two generations or more; quiet, decent, middle-class, intelligent people, who kept up with the world through books and magazines; movie-goers and club members, educated in public schools, state universities, and places like Harvard and Princeton and Wellesley and Carnegie Tech, many of them going back to college or to extension classes for further training." In contrast with the open enrollment policies of the Experimental College, the San Francisco School chose its participants carefully. "Extremes of mind and personality were weeded out by the requirement of a personal interview at registration," Powell noted. "Many types of potential misfit were avoided by this necessary device."[19] Still, the challenge of the San Francisco School was essentially the same as that of the Experimental College—to bring a diverse group of students into a unified educational community and inspire them to take responsibility for their own education. The aims of liberal education were the same among average adults as they were among anarchistic adolescents.

In the summer of 1934, at the end of his first full session, Meiklejohn described the work of the San Francisco School in an article for the *New Republic*. Under the title "Adult Education: A Fresh Start," he outlined the basic purpose of his new school: to create a "learning cooperative" in which each student assumed personal responsibility for the educational success of the whole. Just as the advisers in the Experimental College had attempted "to lead by refusing to lead," so the teachers in the San Francisco School endeavored to teach by refusing to "preach."[20] In both cases, the school and its staff prescribed the curriculum, arranged times and places for weekly meetings, and set the tone of the debate, but the students had to choose *on their own* to learn. Meiklejohn clarified this all-important "paradox of teaching" in a memo to his instructors shortly after the discussion groups began. "In one sense, the leader must do nothing," he wrote. "His students cannot be educated by him; they must educate themselves. But, in another sense, leadership is the prime requisite of all group activity. Nothing is more helpless, more inept, more sure to go astray, than a group of people meeting for a common purpose but with no arrangement for focusing that purpose in some single mind which assumes responsibility for its realization. Here is the fundamental paradox of teaching, and nowhere does it appear more vividly, with greater force, than when the members of the group are mature persons capable of forming their own ideas and facing situations with which they must deal not as children but as responsible participants in the making of a social order." The essential point, Meiklejohn argued, was that teachers could not presume to control their students in any external or arbitrary way, but neither could they shirk their responsibility to guide, inspire, or even impel them to engage in the cooperative and dialectical process of learning. "The teacher in a democracy must make heavy, severe, rigorous demands upon his students, but it must be clear, to them as well as to him, that these demands come, not from him, but from themselves—from the enterprise which, together with him, they have freely chosen to follow."[21]

In order to make the San Francisco School as democratic as possible,

Meiklejohn insisted that registration should be free of charge for all interested adults. This meant that Meiklejohn spent a great deal of time raising money. The annual cost per student was approximately $40, not including books (which the students purchased on their own), and overall expenditures ranged from $6,000 in 1933 up to $25,000 in 1940.[22] Rent amounted to $2,000 a year. Utilities cost $1,500; office supplies cost another $1,500; and faculty salaries, which averaged $2,400, totaled $13,400. Meiklejohn's personal pay was $5,000, an enormous sum during the depression.[23] Most of the school's funding, after the initial investment of Andrew Welch, came from the Max Rosenberg Foundation of San Francisco, which contributed almost $10,000 a year. In 1935, Meiklejohn won a supplementary grant from the Workers' Education Bureau, and in 1936 he received additional support from the Carnegie Corporation in New York, which gave more money in 1937 and 1938.[24] Over time, the San Francisco School received significant assistance from individual private contributors. In 1939, ninety-seven separate donors, many of them students in the school, gave $6,425, mostly in small gifts of $5 to $20 over the course of a year.[25] Twice, in the spring of 1936 and again in the spring of 1937, in an effort to relieve the school of his own "disproportionate share of the budget," Meiklejohn withdrew temporarily from the staff and returned to teaching in Madison.[26] In order to boost his income during the depression, he supplemented his salary with a busy schedule of public speeches arranged by his agent at World Celebrities, Inc.[27] Each time Meiklejohn delivered a speech, he received a much-appreciated honorarium.

As it happened, finances were the least of Meiklejohn's concerns during the San Francisco School's first year of operation. On May 9, 1934, just three months after opening, the school found itself sitting quite literally in the middle of a serious labor crisis. After weeks of intense negotiations, the International Longshoremen's and Warehousemen's Association launched a general strike against the West Coast shipping industry. Led by union organizer Harry Bridges, the strike extended from Seattle to San Diego and involved more than 300,000 workers.[28] On July 2, riots erupted in the infamous Battle of Ricon Hill. A bloody contest of rocks, bottles, billy clubs, and bullets injured more than a hundred people and killed two. Meiklejohn followed the violence from his home in Berkeley. With the offices of the San Francisco School just blocks away from the wharves along Embarcadero Drive, his staff and students were under constant surveillance by "red hunters" who suspected them of spreading Communist propaganda among the strikers.[29] Meiklejohn commented on the strike in a letter to his friend John Gaus. "The strike here was quite tremendous," he wrote shortly after Congress imposed binding arbitration on both sides in the dispute. "My impression is that the labor group, largely through the set-up furnished by the government, won a great victory. All questions are to be arbitrated; then, I think, labor will make great gains. Most important are (1) the fact that labor now looms up as a united, powerful force such as no one dreamed of in this individualistic place and (2) the fact that the government arrangements make impossible the mere crushing of labor protests as has been done before." Expressing his support for organized labor, Meiklejohn wondered how the strike might affect his infant San Francisco School. "Radicals and liberals are suffering for the time, everyone finding satisfaction in blaming them and taking vengeance on them," he wrote. "I fear that our school may be one of the victims and that needed money will not be forthcoming, but we'll see."[30]

In the late summer of 1934, at the height of the longshoremen's strike, socialist muckraker Upton Sinclair won the Democratic Party nomination for governor of California. His campaign slogan, "End Poverty in California," alias EPIC, worried more moderate voters who accused the Democrats of Communist Party infiltration. Students at the University of California in Berkeley rallied for Sinclair, only to be vilified as political subversives. When Berkeley's president Robert Sproul attempted to silence student debates on such topics as whether or not Communism was fit for America, Meiklejohn expressed disdain for the state's increasingly reactionary political atmosphere. "The election here was confusing and difficult," he wrote to Gaus in December. "I voted Sinclair, much in your state of mind. Had decided not to, until the last week, when the abominable campaign against him turned me to him again. I wasn't sorry at his defeat, however. The politics here beats anything I ever saw for sheer frontier irresponsibility."[31] Meiklejohn sent a similar note to Sproul, listing several lessons that could be learned from the recent chaos. "In the midst of all the tempests of passion and misunderstanding which have been dominating the state in connection with the strike and the election," he wrote, "my mind has, of course, been fixed upon the educational opportunities and responsibilities which they offer. Seldom, if ever, have I seen such violations of the principle of freedom." When frustration with the depression gave way to reactionary political suppression, institutions of higher education had a responsibility to protect the freedom of speech. If they did not, Meiklejohn warned, then their own freedom might be compromised in the future. Reiterating his view that colleges and universities should transcend partisan politics in order to speak critically for the sake of democratic ideals, he denounced the university for its weakness in this

209

regard. "Someone in this state must speak for freedom," he told Sproul in 1934, and increasingly, that someone would be himself.[32]

In the winter of 1934, in response to the rash of political suppression during the governor's race, Meiklejohn helped to establish a regional chapter of the American Civil Liberties Union in San Francisco. The impetus for the new chapter, besides the silencing of radical student opinion during the election, was a schism within the union's membership over the Wagner Bill, which aimed to secure unions' right to bargain collectively. For those who had witnessed the violence of the longshoremen's strike, the right to unionize seemed essential to the fight for civil liberties. However, the national office of the ACLU disagreed. Led by its chairman, Roger Baldwin, the national office opposed the Wagner Bill on grounds that unions limited the autonomy of their individual members and thus skewed the freedom of wage negotiations.[33] As a result of this disagreement with Baldwin and the national office, Meiklejohn petitioned for a chapter of the ACLU based in northern California. Early in 1935, his petition was granted. Among the first projects of the northern California branch was the defense of seventeen members of the Cannery and Agricultural Workers Industrial Union who had been indicted under a new "criminal syndicalism" law. The trial of the cannery workers received national attention when the lead defense attorney accused farmers of resisting the work of the federal Farm Security Administration. The farmers, in turn, blamed the FSA for harboring Communist subversives in their ranks. When the cannery workers went on strike, police arrested them, along with their FSA sponsors, on charges of criminal syndicalism or seeking to promote the collectivization of agriculture by force. A veritable witch-hunt ensued, and several labor organizers were jailed as Communists. By the mid-1930s, a cloud of anti-Communist suppression was creeping, slowly but surely, across the California landscape.

As a local leader in the defense of civil liberties, Meiklejohn supported the workers' cause and took steps, through adult education, to curb their exploitation. In June of 1935, he and Helen collaborated with Florence Wyckoff and Brownie Lee Jones of the San Francisco Young Women's Christian Association and Jennie Matyas of the International Ladies Garment Workers Union to develop a month-long summer school for workers. Operating as an independent branch of the San Francisco School, the Pacific Coast School for Workers, originally called the Western Summer School for Workers, held classes just a few blocks from the Meiklejohns' home on the grounds of the Pacific School of Religion in Berkeley. The workers' school received funds from the University of California Extension Division, which Wyckoff's father directed, as well as the Workers' Education Bureau of the American Federation of Labor, which, fifteen years earlier, had sponsored Meiklejohn's workers' education program in Amherst. Through seminars, workshops, and forums, the Pacific Coast School trained students not only in the methods of critical deliberation and democratic debate but also in the practical methods of labor organization, from bookkeeping and arbitration to wage contracts and collective bargaining. As Myer Cohen told Meiklejohn a few years after the Pacific Coast School opened, regular informal sessions with local labor leaders provided "a useful tie-up between the labor movement in the raw and its stepchild, the workers' school."[34] For Meiklejohn, workers' education linked the immediate economic and political needs of the unemployed to the more abstract intellectual demands of democratic citizenship. As he told a crowd of two thousand at the California State Conference for Social Workers in 1935, "[T]he only democracy is one in which all people beyond school age are studying. This ideal is our only hope of emerging from our present state, of remedying present conditions."[35]

Throughout the 1930s, Helen Meiklejohn joined her husband in a wide variety of liberal causes. In addition to her work with the Pacific Coast School for Workers and the San Francisco School of Social Studies, she also served as a research associate with the Consumers' Division of the National Recovery Administration and volunteered as an academic assistant in the newly created Social Security Administration. Each summer, when Meiklejohn headed back to Madison to teach his fall-term philosophy courses at the University of Wisconsin, Helen traveled to Wellesley, Massachusetts, where she participated in the Summer Institute for Social Progress, a program for women workers hosted by Wellesley College. The Summer Institute not only gave Helen a chance to see family and friends back East but also enabled her to share her expertise in the fields of adult education and labor economics. "What are the factors in American life today that are giving such an impetus to this movement for adult education?" she asked at an institute roundtable with Max Lerner and A. J. Muste in 1934. "Is it an accident that the acceleration of interest in adult education has come in America during the depression? Time of privation and trouble always stimulate people to think."[36] Meiklejohn agreed with his wife's assessment that the depression had inspired Americans to reevaluate their social and political priorities. Moreover, he felt that the depression had exposed serious problems within the present economic order, not least of which were the moral problems involved in an ideology of laissez-faire capitalism. In Meiklejohn's view, unregulated economic competition had gradually distorted the meaning of the word *freedom* in America. Citizens, in their single-minded pursuit of financial gain, had lost their capacity for the kind of cooperative, even collective, political deliberation on which democracy ultimately depended. Soon, Meiklejohn feared, confusion between the freedom of economic competition and the freedom of political deliberation would tear the nation apart. What did *freedom* really mean in the United States? In the mid-1930s, Meiklejohn spent a considerable amount of time and energy seeking an answer to this abstract, but also deeply practical, question.

In the late summer of 1935, Meiklejohn took a break from his busy schedule of classes at the San Francisco and Pacific Coast Schools and turned his attention to writing. Working from his office in the Department of Philosophy at Wisconsin, he submitted a brief but wide-ranging essay to *Harper's Monthly* magazine. Published under the title "Liberty—For What?" the article noted that America's five-year depression had revealed a disturbing gap between the nation's relentlessly competitive economic practices and its otherwise honorable egalitarian political ideals. The cause of the gap, he asserted, was a deep-seated confusion over the meaning of the word *freedom,* or *liberty,* in modern liberal thought. "In recent years," he noted, "a great array of practical men and scholars have interpreted for us the Spirit of America, and their conclusion can be summed up very briefly. The freedom which Americans worship, in terms of which they live, for the sake of which they are willing to die, is, these men tell us, the freedom to manage their own property without interference from their fellows." Unfortunately, Meiklejohn noted, the ideal of unrestrained economic liberty had slowly undermined two other important liberal ideals—the ideals of political equality and social fraternity. All three of these ideals—liberty, equality, and fraternity—were essential to the spirit of liberal democracy, and none could be sacrificed without undermining the others in the process. "These three principles are still, for us, I am sure, three different aspects of one mode of life which we choose as our own," Meiklejohn argued. "To tear them apart is to tear our spirit to shreds."[37] Hinting at a possible distinction between the *political freedoms* of the First Amendment and the *economic liberties* suggested in the Fifth Amendment to the Constitution—a distinction that became increasingly important to him over the next three decades—Meiklejohn argued that the only way to overcome the pervasive malaise of the Great Depression was to bridge the spiritual gap between free-market capitalism and self-governing democracy.

The ideas for Meiklejohn's *Harper's* article came from a series of six

212

lectures he had delivered more than a decade earlier at Northwestern University. In Madison in 1935, Meiklejohn revisited these lectures—originally titled "The Crisis in American Institutions," then "Education for Democracy"—rewriting them for publication as a book, which he released nationwide under the rather ambiguous title *What Does America Mean?*[38] In many ways, the material contained in this book summarized Meiklejohn's intellectual development since his departure from Amherst in 1923. Specifically, it blended his interest in moral virtue and philosophical idealism with his increasing concern for civil liberties and economic justice. It was a transitional text, and as Meiklejohn himself acknowledged, its mix of ideas was not altogether clear. "When the task of publishing these lectures was faced," he admitted in the foreword, "I found that the problem running through them, though keenly felt, was not well formulated." Even after the book went to press, Meiklejohn conceded that he still had not framed his thesis well. "Some of my friends who have read the book in manuscript tell me that Part I bewilders them," he warned, referring to his opening section on Kant's dichotomy between mind and matter. Yet, after countless revisions, he concluded that the difficulty could not be removed. It was precisely the conflict between mind and matter, between spiritual and material interests, that had crippled America's liberal institutions. "I am convinced," he wrote in chapter 1, "that to speak of America, in terms of its spirit, as against the terms of material welfare, is to use that form of speech which, among all our ways of speaking, is most significant. To see American life in terms of aspiration and disappointment, to measure it as admirable or contemptible, to think of it as meeting or failing to meet its obligations—that is the one really important approach to understanding the nation."[39] Seeking the moral meaning of America, Meiklejohn set out to define the nation's deepest spiritual ideals.

What were America's deepest ideals? Returning to the argument of his article in *Harper's Monthly,* Meiklejohn argued that America's deepest ideal was liberty, but not at the expense of equality, fraternity, or justice. In two chapters reprinted verbatim from his earlier article, he distinguished the material freedoms of private property and economic possession from the spiritual freedoms of public expression and political belief. He drew a stark line between the internal freedoms of mind and the external freedoms of matter, noting the hollowness of attempts to define the spiritual meaning of America in terms of the material "liberty" of a competitive economic marketplace. It was futile, in other words, to seek spiritual comfort in capitalism. As he put it, "[I]t is chiefly for the sake of ex-

213

posing the tragic fallacy underlying that absurd [capitalist] interpretation of America that I have tried to make clear the distinction between Spirit and Matter. Only a mind which is utterly confused as to the relations between these two could so interpret the ideals of a person or a nation." Meiklejohn devoted the remainder of his analysis to restoring a relation of *complementarity* between mind and matter, between spiritual and material aspiration, in his interpretation of American liberty. His fear was not that the conflict between spiritual and material interests might cause America to collapse under the weight of economic depression, but rather that capitalism's inherent tension between ethics and profit might become a permanent feature of modern liberal thought. "My terror," he wrote, "is that laissez-faire may meet the external test of happiness, of material success, and may at the same time lead us to such inner madness that the excellence of the spirit will be lost, that men, as human beings, will be destroyed."[40] Meiklejohn did not doubt capitalism's ability to produce material wealth; he doubted its ability to provide spiritual *meaning*.

What, then, was Meiklejohn's solution? What institutional structure or ideological system did he propose to fill the gap between the inner and outer ideals of the American spirit? His answer was both simple and straightforward. In his last chapter—bearing the Leninesque title "What Shall We Do?"—he suggested what he considered to be a better doctrine of freedom for the United States: the doctrine of socialism. Defining socialism in explicitly moral rather than economic or political terms, Meiklejohn stressed the need for ethical cooperation among groups who shared common interests and concerns. "When people join together in the production of goods, not for a competitive market, but for the use of the community as a whole, when the scheme of distribution is not that of the blind play of conflicting desires and capacities, but that of reasoned planning for the human needs of all the members of the community, decisions must, in both fields, take on a directness, a simplicity, which brings them within the general understanding of all of us," he wrote. "In such a society, men and women could be bound together by the sharing of common purposes, common ideas, which would make them, in some real sense, members of a community." Here was the main idea of Meiklejohn's book, the central spirit and inner meaning of America. "The essential trouble with the outer view of life and of the world," he asserted, "is that it does not mean anything. It does not make sense. If a man devotes his energies solely to the making of a fortune, his life is, in the end, foolishness. If a nation takes as its goal the acquiring of wealth and power, that goal slips and slides away into incoherent and self-destructive acquisitions which serve no essential purpose. The outer world, taken by itself, has no meaning." The only way to give life meaning was to infuse external behavior with internal—that is, ethical—conviction. Harkening back to his study of Kant, Meiklejohn located the essence of a transcendental human community in the institutions of liberal democracy. "A democracy is not a multifarious collection of human bodies seeking satisfaction of their desires," he argued. "It is a unity of the spirit among a multitude of persons who are made one by common ties of admiration and devotion to common ideals. It is a people which knows itself to be one in purpose, whatever may be the multiplicities and variations in the midst of which its many lives are lived. The essential mark of any democracy is the domination exercised over all of its members by a single spiritual intention."[41] In a democracy, he asserted, self-governing citizens voluntarily subordinated their personal interests to the overarching welfare of the whole.

Here, in embryonic form, was Meiklejohn's theory of an idealist ethical community in a secular democratic state. In *What Does America Mean?* Meiklejohn translated his long-standing theory of liberal democratic education into a more complex and comprehensive political and intellectual framework. Highlighting the disintegration of moral and aesthetic excellence in the years after World War I, he condemned Americans' failure to see why material decadence would eventually lead to spiritual bankruptcy. The only hope for salvation, he claimed, was the recovery of a national conscience in the form of a renewed commitment to democratic education on a mass scale. "[I]f we try," he wrote, "we can make a democracy—a society in which every member is in process of education for the highest forms of behavior of which he is capable." Pointing to his work with adult education in California, Meiklejohn asserted that the key to spiritual renewal in the United States would be a nationwide network of community-based discussion groups. "We are, I think, just beginning to see, here in America, what the possibilities of a national planning of adult education really are," he declared. "We have upon our hands the task of making a national mind, a national spirit within which each individual mind and spirit shall find its own peculiar work to do in proper relation to the whole."[42] Only when Americans regained their sense of ethical obligations, their sense of a common spiritual enterprise, through adult education would they be able to rebuild their broken economy and reconstruct their shattered national will. Indeed, only when the general will of the people found expression in a truly democratic state could America recover the integrity of its most admirable liberal ideals. It took Meiklejohn three decades and two additional books to grasp the abstract political implications of *What Does America Mean?*—

215

particularly its implications for the state as an ethical educative community—but a new direction was beginning to emerge in his thought. In order to restore the complementarity of spiritualism and materialism in modern definitions of freedom, America needed to rediscover the ethical core of its own liberal ideals.

When it appeared in November of 1935, Meiklejohn's book attracted national attention. Author Florence Kelly, writing for the *New York Times Literary Supplement,* called it "a book of fine and worthy purpose, nobly felt, argued with keen and cultured intelligence, and written with an ardor that glows through its words and now and then touches them with flame."[43] Joseph Smith, in the *New York Herald Tribune,* added to Kelly's praise. "Perhaps the most outstanding feature of Professor Meiklejohn's argument is a devastating attack on the philosophy of *laissez-faire* as it manifests itself in the United States today," Smith wrote. "His reasoning has the appearance of orthodox Marxism until we read that his objections to capitalism are based on moral rather than economic grounds."[44] In addition to these laudatory reviews, Meiklejohn received positive words from friends. Raymond Fosdick, president of the Rockefeller Foundation and a member of the powerful General Education Board, announced that he had read the book "with rare delight." "It contains one of the best definitions of liberty I have ever seen," he wrote.[45] Supreme Court Justice Louis Brandeis agreed, commenting that Meiklejohn had "said to Americans the things they most need to hear."[46] Sociologist David Riesman was thrilled to see Meiklejohn's ideals "courageously expressed against the tide," even if the notion of a socialist democracy required "a faith in human nature" that Riesman himself could not accept.[47] Henry Wallace, U.S. secretary of agriculture, commended the work as well. "Apparently the only place we have a marked difference of opinion is with regard to the possibility of salvaging some good out of capitalism," Wallace noted. "The vital point is to have the individual incentive oriented in considerable measure toward the general welfare. You claim this cannot be done under the capitalistic system. I claim it can be done, provided capitalism can be sufficiently democratized."[48] Wallace, however, had missed the point. For Meiklejohn, to democratize capitalism was to change it into socialism.

Perhaps the most intriguing response to Meiklejohn's book came from Emma Goldman, the Russian-born anarchist who had been deported back to the Soviet Union in 1919. "I dare say," Goldman wrote to a niece who had attended the University of Wisconsin during the Ex-College era, "that Meiklejohn is, like so many other advanced men in the universities of America, if not an out-and-out anarchist, then, at least, very strongly inclined towards it. . . . I am convinced that anarchist ideas are playing a great part in the minds of a considerable number of men and women in the universities, though they may not be aware of the fact." Meiklejohn was indeed unaware of any anarchist tendencies in his book, though it was not hard to find evidence of radicalism in his thought. He openly suggested, for example, that the Soviet Union had usurped America's place as the symbol of social, political, and economic emancipation in the world. "[T]he plain and simple fact remains," he asserted in *What Does America Mean?* "that Russia, whether she be right or wrong, is now in the place which we had thought to be ours. . . . It is to Russia rather than to us that the wretched and oppressed of the earth are now turning as they dream of escape from age-long tyrannies and despairs."[49] Meiklejohn chose not to respond to accusations of anarchism in *What Does America Mean?* but he often found himself misinterpreted along "extremist" lines. His sympathy for state-sponsored adult education placed him solidly in the leftist camp. Even though his book took an explicitly moral stance with respect to social reform, he could not escape the communistic political undertones of his work.

Not long after the publication of *What Does America Mean?* Meiklejohn came under suspicion as an agent of the Communist Party. Several right-wing watchdog groups branded his San Francisco School a conspiratorial organization seeking to undermine the domestic loyalties of its students. Meiklejohn's chief critic was Ivan Francis Cox, a member of the American Legion of California. In the spring of 1936, Cox filed a complaint against Meiklejohn with the San Francisco County clerk's office, alleging that Myer Cohen belonged to the American Communist Party. In his affidavit, Cox charged that the entire curriculum of the San Francisco School was "predicated on the introduction and use of Communist literature."[50] A few months later, Harper Knowles, chairman of the Subversive Activities Committee of the American Legion, added the San Francisco School to his list of seditious organizations. "Because of the extremely liberal record of Dr. Alexander Meiklejohn," Knowles reported, "it was felt advisable to place this organization under observation." After sending spies to participate in adult discussion groups, the American Legion concluded that Meiklejohn did indeed pose a threat to national security. "The result of this investigation convinces us beyond all doubt that the activities of this organization are not in keeping with the principles of patriotism and Americanism and that, to the contrary, the San Francisco School of Social Studies is a breeding ground for Communists." Identifying Myer

217

Cohen as an active radical, Knowles also reported that his wife, Elizabeth Elson, was head of the Federal Theater Project, which staged "many plays of Communistic and otherwise questionable character."[51] By mid-1936, the staff of the San Francisco School, along with the federal government's own theater project, were labeled as distinctly "un-American" groups.

In the mid-1930s, Meiklejohn did little to distance himself from implied connections with the Communist Party. Although he never officially joined any political party, he received mailings from various leftist organizations and openly predicted the likelihood of radical revolution in the United States. In May of 1936, the *San Francisco Chronicle* reviewed a speech in which Meiklejohn asserted that the country would need to decide between communism and capitalism "sometime within the next twenty-five years."[52] A week later, he told the California State Teachers' Union that schools "must see to it that there is a sufficiently large body of teachers who believe in Communism to give that side adequate representation—teachers who are definitely on the 'Left.' "[53] Meiklejohn believed that teachers of all levels should play a leading role in adjudicating the controversy between communism and capitalism. "If you suppress teachers," he argued, then "you have chosen the way of violence—you have departed from the fundamentals of American life—and the decision will be made in blood."[54] Here, in short, was the essence of Meiklejohn's oft-misunderstood position regarding teachers' role in a possible Communist revolution in the United States. The issue was not *whether* Americans would choose communism but rather *how* the choice would be made. As he noted in a corrective letter to the editor of the *Pacific Coast Weekly*, "[T]he 'burning question' of the next twenty-five years . . . is not whether America will choose Capitalism or Communism, but whether that choice will be made by violence or by free discussion." The primary difference between the United States and the Soviet Union was that the United States adhered to the ideals of political freedom while the Soviet Union used methods of state-sponsored violence. "I am not saying that violence of another kind is absent from America," he wrote. "But I do say that we have a chance—our best chance—to solve our problems in the ways of freedom. The constant appeals to the methods of Russia do not help us in realizing that chance."[55] Teachers, therefore, must be free to address controversial questions, including the merits of communism, in class.[56]

Despite occasional appearances to the contrary, Meiklejohn never ascribed to Communist Party doctrine. He did, however, insist that all citizens, including Communists, should have access to open debates in a democratic society. Even within the increasingly turbulent political climate of the mid-1930s, he clung to his idealist conception of democracy as a self-governing arena for voluntary deliberations between mutually respectful individuals and groups. To his critics in 1936, however, Meiklejohn's political idealism seemed increasingly naïve. As Italy and Germany formed the Rome-Berlin Axis and Japan and Germany established the Anti-Comintern Pact against the Soviet Union, the notion of "voluntary discussions between mutually respectful individuals and groups" sounded either empty or obtuse—even more so after Spain plunged into bloody civil war, with Adolf Hitler and Benito Mussolini backing the Fascist rebels of Francisco Franco and Joseph Stalin supporting the Loyalist republican regime. Meiklejohn was not oblivious to this growing turmoil abroad. In the summer of 1937, he received two letters from David Gordon, the young radical from the Experimental College who, along with three thousand other Americans, had joined the Abraham Lincoln Battalion of the International Brigade in hopes of fighting in the Spanish Civil War.[57] Even before Gordon departed for Spain, Meiklejohn received a note from Rabbi Irving Reichert of the Temple Emanu-El in San Francisco asking if he might be able to help secure employment for German Jewish refugees filtering over to the West Coast.[58] In 1936 and 1937, Meiklejohn could scarcely ignore the escalating hostilities abroad.

Yet, at the time, he had seemingly more pressing concerns on his mind. Two weeks prior to Gordon's first letter from Spain, his father-in-law, Walter Goodnow Everett, suffered a fatal heart attack while visiting Berkeley.[59] Everett's sudden death came as a shock, not so much because it happened when it did (he was seventy-six years old and his health had been failing for months), but because it left the Meiklejohns in an awkward financial position. When Everett died, his substantial estate reverted to his second wife, who, impaired by senility, failed to release her stepdaughters' inheritances.[60] In itself, the postponement of Helen's patrimony would not have caused a serious problem, but its timing upset a far more precarious financial situation. In the spring of 1938, Meiklejohn received a letter from Dean Sellery at the University of Wisconsin explaining that the state legislature had decided to cut faculty salaries by 25 percent in order to alleviate depression-era strain. Since Meiklejohn still held his half-time appointment in the Department of Philosophy and depended on the additional income of $4,500 a year, he was dismayed by Sellery's recommendation that his salary be reduced to $3,263—still the highest in the university.[61] "Such a reduction of an individual salary . . . would seem a direct violation of my understanding with the university and also of the essential principles of academic tenure," Meiklejohn wrote in an angry letter to the dean. Standing on principles that he had not applied to his own faculty eighteen years earlier at Amherst, Meiklejohn sharply demanded that Sellery reinstate his salary. "My salary was placed as exceptional when I was asked to come to Wisconsin," he declared. "The fact that no other salary in the College of Letters and Science is now above $7,500 does not justify [the slated reduction]."[62] While recognizing the need for budget cuts, Meiklejohn insisted that his own salary should nevertheless remain immune to limitation.

When Sellery declined to withdraw his recommendation, Meiklejohn impetuously resigned. He immediately wrote to Max Otto, chair of Wisconsin's Department of Philosophy, attributing his abrupt resignation to ill health. "As I think I wrote you, I was wholly unfit for work in February and March," he claimed. "My blood pressure jumped sixty-five points, and I am still pretty bad when it comes to carrying strain." These claims were partly true; Meiklejohn did indeed suffer from high blood pressure. Despite his occasional bouts of hypertension, however, he continued teaching for financial reasons. "We felt on financial grounds that I simply had to do it if it were at all possible," he sheepishly confessed to Otto. When Sellery moved to reduce his salary, however, Meiklejohn looked for other options, and, as he told Otto, his search had been successful. "I have now," he informed Otto, "an invitation from another institution to give one course in the second semester—the kind of arrangement that professors emeriti commonly make. That will, I think, enable us to get along, and the work will involve little strain. With that option, it seems essential that I retire."[63] The invitation to which Meiklejohn referred had come from Dartmouth College. On the very day he sent his letter of resignation to Wisconsin, he received a letter of appointment from Dartmouth, promising a salary of thirty-five hundred dollars per semester to teach one philosophy course in the spring of 1938 and another in the spring of 1939.[64] This income, added to the five thousand dollars he earned from the San Francisco School of Social Studies, would sustain him—at least for awhile.

In 1938, at the age of sixty-six, Meiklejohn began to think for the first time about retiring. From his post at Dartmouth, he corresponded frequently with Mark Ingraham of the University of Wisconsin Retirement Board. After discussing several pension plans, he decided to take a monthly annuity from his retirement account, which, in the years since his initial Madison appointment in 1926, had accumulated a paltry $7,924.37. Beginning in the summer of 1938, he received monthly checks for $67.52—barely enough to cover his grocery bills.[65] At a time when the

Social Security Administration was only three years old, Meiklejohn found himself in a difficult spot. What made his financial situation particularly troublesome was his lack of any pension from either Brown or Amherst. By the 1930s, most colleges and universities relied on pension support from the Carnegie Foundation for the Advancement of Teaching and its successor companies, the Teachers Insurance and Annuity Association and the College Retirement Equity Fund (TIAA/CREF). Unfortunately, Brown had refused to join the Carnegie Foundation in 1905 for reasons of sectarian affiliation, and Amherst had forced Meiklejohn from its presidency in 1923, thus rendering him officially ineligible for a Carnegie pension at any time in the future. Shortly after Meiklejohn left Amherst, a friend wrote to Carnegie, pleading on Meiklejohn's behalf. "Recently, Dr. Alexander Meiklejohn spent a night at my house, and I had opportunity to ask him about his future," the discreetly anonymous letter began. "He told me that, amid various disappointments, his heaviest blow was the discovery that he would lose all right to a retiring allowance from the Carnegie Foundation if he remained for even a single year outside academic life. . . . Of his need there can be no doubt. In the case of his sudden death, I would judge—though he did not say so—that his wife and four children would be left entirely without resources."[66] For years, Meiklejohn had exchanged letters with various officials from the Carnegie Foundation, begging them to reconsider their policy denying him a pension.[67] Each time, however, they refused.[68]

Making matters worse was the fact that Meiklejohn continued to live beyond his means. His spacious home in the Berkeley Hills, complete with a cook, carried a significant mortgage, and each summer after classes ended at Dartmouth and Wellesley he and Helen rented a vacation house in the picturesque beachside community of Oak Bluffs on the resort island of Martha's Vineyard.[69] There, in the company of Meiklejohn's grown children, they relaxed and enjoyed time with family and friends. As a father and, now, a grandfather, Meiklejohn enjoyed nothing more than spending time with his children. Kenneth, aged thirty-five, had married and become a successful attorney in New York. Donald, after withdrawing from the graduate program at the University of Wisconsin, had earned a doctorate in philosophy at Harvard in 1936. Gordon graduated from the University of Wisconsin and earned a medical degree at McGill University, in Montreal.[70] Ann finished boarding school at Dartington Hall and graduated from the University of California, where she stayed for a doctorate in psychology before marrying, having three children, and working at Berkeley's Institute for Human Development.[71] Meiklejohn was proud of

Ken, Don, Gordon, and Ann. As he once put it, "[T]he primary duty of parents is to enjoy their children."[72] But his financial difficulties persisted. During the depression, his agent had a hard time collecting fees for his speeches. "We have had heavy losses this season and do not have the money to pay you," Walter Ricks confessed in 1935. "We will pay as soon as we can. If forced out of business, we have no assets to meet this obligation."[73] Meiklejohn must have been concerned by such news, but he did not despair. He had other—or, in his view, larger—issues on his mind.

In the fall of 1938, Meiklejohn opened a remote rural branch of the San Francisco School in Santa Rosa, sixty miles northeast of the Bay Area. A town of fifteen thousand residents in the heart of Sonoma County, Santa Rosa served as an agricultural distribution center for wine, fruit, lumber, poultry, and dairy products. It was an ideal location to test the methods of adult education in a nonurban setting. With a two-year grant from the Carnegie Corporation (as opposed to the previously mentioned Carnegie Foundation), Meiklejohn started Great Books reading and discussion groups among the farmers of the Sonoma Valley. Like their urban counterparts, the students in Santa Rosa turned eagerly to America's founding documents, including the Declaration of Independence, the Articles of Confederation, the Constitution, and the Federalist Papers, for discussion. At a time when President Franklin Roosevelt was talking of expanding the Supreme Court to make it more amenable to his legislative agenda, students in Santa Rosa debated the implications of judicial autonomy by reading Myer Cohen's edited work *Selected Opinions of the Supreme Court*. Just as students in San Francisco examined the general problems of modern industrial society, so, too, students in Santa Rosa studied the social, intellectual, moral, political, and constitutional controversies of rural life. Their chief concern was the structure and spirit of a democratic *community*. The discussion topics were listed in their course syllabus as "The Philosophy of the Community," "The Community and Its Institutions," "The Role of Women in the Community," "Labor, the Unions, and the Community," "Human Nature and the Democratic Process," and "Alternative Patterns for an American Economy."[74]

Meiklejohn hired two additional teachers to lead the Santa Rosa discussion groups: Ernest Beaglehole, an economist from Victoria University College in New Zealand, and Pierce Williams, a former member of the National Bureau of Economic Research and the Federal Emergency Relief Administration.[75] Myer Cohen also helped with the development of rural adult education, mostly for migrant workers. Noting a particular need for educational programs in the shanty towns near Fresno, Marysville, Stockton, Watsonville, Salinas, and Santa Cruz, as well as in Kern and Tulare Counties, Cohen suggested that Meiklejohn sponsor adult reading groups in these areas. By January of 1939, the San Francisco School had 1,500 students meeting in 120 different discussion groups in San Francisco and Santa Rosa as well as Sonoma, San Jose, Berkeley, Oakland, Petaluma, Healdsburg, and Windsor.[76] As Meiklejohn had hoped, the groups brought people from diverse backgrounds together to consider questions of common social concern. In one meeting, George Kidwell of the Bakery Wagon Drivers Union, who later became director of industrial relations for the state of California, addressed Jack Shelley, who later became mayor of the city of San Francisco, in a heated debate about the Constitution. In another group, a longshoreman from Embarcadero Drive extolled the virtues of Plato, and a stockbroker from Montgomery Street championed the views of Marx.[77] According to John Walker Powell, Meiklejohn's school had a dramatic effect on the intellectual life of the entire metropolitan area. "With such interests mingled in the groups," he noted, "Meiklejohn was necessarily involved in the dialectic of faction, party, and pressure groups within the city. Here again, he was at the top of his dialectical bent in arguing that democracy is not 'unanimity' but 'a creative use of diversity'; that what is important is not whether men argue, but whether they argue about the same things; and that the price of freedom is mutual responsibility of thought, of thinking together about whatever is vital to the common body."[78]

Always striving to reach more people, Meiklejohn and his colleagues in 1938 launched the Social Studies Roundtable, a series of biweekly radio broadcasts transmitted from the Columbia station in San Francisco. Building on the discussion format of the weekly discussion groups, the radio programs aimed to give listeners a critical perspective on current events and news headlines. Meiklejohn's staff devoted several days of work to each hour-long broadcast, but the results were not always satisfactory. "What emerged over the air was but a pale shadow of the fury that had gone into its preparation," Powell recalled. The broadcasts generally failed to reach large numbers of listeners, and those who heard them often failed to grasp their meaning. When Powell and Cohen produced a particularly hard-edged program on the growing aggressiveness of Nazi Germany, they discovered that many listeners missed the point. One lunchcounter proprietor evidently perked up when he heard the issue was war: "What do they say?" asked a sandwich customer. "I dunno," the dull proprietor answered. From this rather demoralizing anecdote, Powell concluded that radio was better suited for political propaganda than democratic deliberation. It was "no accident," he noted, "that the Nazi masters of public solicitation have made huge uses of the lecture platform and the radio nor that they have utterly forbidden the study circle and discussion group. Their weapons are those whereby one message can be given to all men and no outlet left for men to think together."[79] Critical discussion as an antidote to reactionary politics was precisely the idea behind the San Francisco School of Social Studies.

By 1938, the idea of democratic deliberation as an antidote to illiberal politics had gained new poignancy, not only in Europe, but also in the United States. In May of 1938, the U.S. House of Representatives created the Special Committee on Un-American Activities, later called the House Un-American Activities Committee but widely known as the Dies Committee after its chairman, Democratic representative Martin Dies of Texas. The Dies Committee had wide-ranging powers to investigate "subversive" activities throughout the United States, particularly the activities of Nazis and Communists. Given his experience two years earlier with Ivan Cox and the American Legion in California, Meiklejohn immediately recognized the Dies Committee as a threat to civil liberties and, more specifically, a danger to free and open debate in schools, colleges, and other institutions of democratic education. Less than two weeks after the Dies Committee convened for its first meeting in Washington, D.C., Meiklejohn sent an article to *Harper's Monthly* denouncing the climate of fear and suppression that, in his opinion, jeopardized the integrity of the nation's liberal ideals. Writing under the title "Teachers and Controversial Questions," Meiklejohn asked if public school teachers should be free to espouse politically controversial views in their classrooms. He wondered again if teachers should be free to discuss communism "as a possible alternative in America for our way of dealing with men and their possessions." Inasmuch as communism, socialism, and other forms of "state-controlled social planning" aroused such intense hatred and fear among so many Americans, Meiklejohn wondered how the country would handle ideological challenges to its most sacred ideals. "What do we, as Americans, propose to do about opinions which many of us deeply and passionately condemn?"[80]

This question brought the connections between democratic education and civil liberty into sharp and penetrating focus. How could liberal education preserve the integrity of open debate and at the same time allow for the free participation of antidemocratic groups? How could teachers create an environment in which *all* ideas, controversial or not, had equal access to the debate? In order to be democratic, Meiklejohn asserted, education needed to be free not only to address controversial questions but also to seek solutions to shared social problems, including problems of communism and fascism. "Teachers must, so far as they honestly can, take sides on the issue," he claimed. "The teacher must appear before his pupils as one who is struggling with the essential problems of his time and who is in his own way forming conclusions about them. He must be going left or right. To be a teacher, a leader, he must be . . . a believer in some plan of human living." Democratic education, Meiklejohn argued, needed to teach students how to disagree with one another without abandoning the possibility of mutual agreement, or at least open debate, altogether. "Young Americans must be taught to think independently, but they must also learn to think together," he declared. "They must reach conclusions while at the same time recognizing that other men for whom they have respect and affection are reaching opposite conclusions." Surely, Meiklejohn argued, public school teachers needed to be able to raise controversial questions, but they also needed to do so in ways that demonstrated the ultimate superiority of democracy as a moral and political ideal. "So far as minds are concerned," he concluded, "the art of democracy is the art of thinking independently together."[81]

When it appeared in June of 1938, Meiklejohn's article seemed oddly, even dangerously, out of touch with recent developments in world affairs. Just a month earlier, Hitler had ordered his Nazi storm troopers into his homeland Austria and had annexed the vulnerable Sudeten region in Czechoslovakia. Shortly after the Anschluss, Meiklejohn received a letter from Horace Kallen, who asked if he might have any room for political and intellectual exiles in Berkeley. "Is there a chance that the Far West could absorb any Austrian or German philosophical refugees?" Kallen wondered. Earlier in 1938, Kallen had searched desperately for a way to help a Czech friend escape the mounting persecution of Jews. "I am especially concerned to find some opening for Dr. Maximilian Beck of Prague, Czechoslovakia, whose discussion of the philosophy and anthropology of Nazi racist theory has made his position very precarious."[82] Whether or not Meiklejohn agreed to host any Jewish refugees, by March of 1939 it was already too late: Hitler conquered the rest of Czechoslovakia in a single crushing blow. A few weeks later, Meiklejohn heard from Walter Agard in Madison. "International affairs seem to grow worse daily," Agard wrote. "We dread hearing the radio or seeing the paper, apprehensive as to what will happen next."[83] What happened next shocked the world. In August of 1939, Germany disavowed its Anti-Comintern Pact with Japan and signed a bilateral treaty with the Soviet Union. Then, with

Stalin on his side, Hitler launched a devastating blitzkrieg in Poland. Meiklejohn hoped the Nazi-Soviet alliance would bring an end to Hitler's aggression, but Agard had no such faith. "While it may block Hitler in some ways," Agard predicted, "it will help him in others—enough to smash Europe pretty well to pieces. I'm especially sad about the Scandinavian countries."[84] Indeed, in the spring of 1940, Hitler's armies invaded Norway, Denmark, Belgium, Luxembourg, and the Netherlands. By the middle of that year, Nazi forces crossed the Somme and established a puppet government in Vichy, France. The Soviet Union, meanwhile, pressed into the Baltic, subjugating Latvia, Estonia, and Lithuania. Militarism was quickly enveloping the world.

In 1936, when Hitler, Mussolini, and Franco formed their Fascist alliance, Meiklejohn had become distracted by the death of his father-in-law in Berkeley. Now, three years later, as the Axis powers pursued their rapid conquest of northern and eastern Europe, his attention was once again diverted by a personal crisis, this time involving his wife. In the summer of 1939, after teaching his last class at Dartmouth, Meiklejohn caught a train back to Berkeley. Helen, in the meantime, finished her work at the Wellesley Summer Institute and spent a few extra days in Oak Bluffs before taking a separate train back to California. The first three days of Helen's journey proceeded without incident, but then, racing through the arid desert of southwestern Nevada, her engine jumped its track and tumbled off a trestle. The details of the crash appeared in the *Providence Journal-Bulletin*: "MRS. MEIKLEJOHN HURT IN WRECK; WIFE OF FORMER DEAN SUFFERS BACK INJURIES IN NEVADA ACCIDENT; ON WAY TO CALIFORNIA; RETURNING FROM OAK BLUFFS WHEN STREAMLINER PLUNGES FROM BRIDGE."[85] More than fifty people sustained serious injuries in the accident. Helen's wounds were severe, especially the strain to her back and the harm done to her nose, throat, and respiratory system. Hospitalized for several days, Helen made a slow recovery that was never quite complete. She suffered breathing problems for the rest of her life. Scar tissue in her neck continued to impair her speech, and she was highly susceptible to lung infections. Fortunately, Meiklejohn's own health was excellent, so he was able to care for his ailing wife. After a check-up in February of 1939, he received a flawless report. His blood pressure had stabilized at 145 over 98, and other tests proved "normal in every respect." His physician had made a few suggestions for longer life, noting that both he and Helen could stand to "do many more foolish, useless things with an easy conscience" and ending with a general notation for the Meiklejohns to "slow up, particularly on sex."[86]

226

Throughout the winter of 1939, Meiklejohn attended to Helen's injuries, but in the spring of 1940, he turned his attention back to the San Francisco School, which had recently begun to falter. Just when it seemed that adult education had gained a permanent foothold in northern California, the flow of private funds had suddenly stopped. With the growing hostilities in Europe, the Rosenberg Foundation and Carnegie Corporation shifted their philanthropic priorities, and other sources of support were not forthcoming. A full year earlier, Myer Cohen had asked what Meiklejohn planned to do if the Carnegie grant expired. "When I say things look bleak financially, you may discount it because of my perpetual pessimism on this score," Cohen wrote, "but, *really*, if the Carnegie $4,000 is not available again, as is most probably the case, then we are going to be in a desperate spot next November or so."[87] Though the nation's economy had improved slightly in 1939, public funds went increasingly to other concerns, especially preparations for war. Indeed, in the summer of 1940, California's shipbuilding industry roared back to life as President Roosevelt authorized the construction of two hundred new destroyers. Dockworkers and longshoremen were elated by the prospect of huge federal contracts, but their new jobs left little time to join in local reading and discussion groups. The San Francisco School, which flourished under the conditions of depression in the 1930s, when unemployed workers had extra leisure time, buckled in the burgeoning economy of the 1940s. As Cohen had predicted, by the fall of 1940, the San Francisco School of Social Studies had become a "dispensable luxury" in a wartime economy.[88]

In November of 1940, the school's board of directors, which consisted almost entirely of students who had participated in discussion groups, met to consider dismantling their program. John Powell recounted the emotional events of that last gathering. "At the final Board meeting, a man came and asked for a hearing for a plan . . . to keep the School open by changing some of its content and more of its method, giving it closer ties with front-page topics, and making it a big popular institution inside of which a little quiet experimenting went on." As the eleventh-hour visitor sketched his proposal to make the San Francisco School more profitable by making it more popular, Meiklejohn and his teaching staff listened silently. "The staff quite deliberately said nothing," Powell wrote. "It was the Board—the citizen-students who had staked on the School their time and interest and belief and sometimes their standing with their friends and had the most to gain from its success—it was they who refused, who explained their refusal on educational grounds and analyzed for their visitor the issues of survival versus integrity of method and aim." For those who had participated in the discussion groups and wanted earnestly for them to survive, the idea of selling their program to the highest bidder seemed unconscionable. To submit to the external authority of money-making interests would be to undermine the school's freedom and autonomy. The virtue of the San Francisco School was its independence, its ability to foster democratic debate without interference from dominating financial, political, or other special-interest controls. "To the staff," Powell proudly stated, "that was perhaps the supreme climax of the seven years, watching the Board magnificently answer a proposal which they themselves might have made a few years earlier and answer it with articulate understanding of what they meant."[89] According to the students of the San Francisco School, it was better to close than to compromise their self-governing ideal.

For the first time in his career, Meiklejohn felt that he had succeeded in his effort to teach the meaning of democracy. Unlike the undergraduates at Brown, who sacrificed the democratic rules of amateur athletics for professional pay; unlike the students at Amherst, who abandoned the democratic college community for the unreasoning passion of war; unlike the guinea pigs at the Experimental College, who refused the democratic structure of a student council for what they called anarchistic communism; the adult citizen-students of the San Francisco School had truly grasped the meaning of self-government. Rather than choosing the path of compromised survival, they chose the more difficult path—the path of virtue, excellence, and moral integrity—even though it ultimately resulted in the demise of their learning community. Accepting the tragedy of their position, they defended the ideal of an educational institution set apart from the popular concerns of a commercialized society, an institution free from material interests, an institution where truth emerged from democratic cooperation instead of economic competition. At the moment when self-government marked the difference between continuation and collapse, the San Francisco School remained true to its highest principles. It was better to fold than submit to external domination. Edward Lamb Parsons, a colleague of Meiklejohn's from the northern California branch of the ACLU, grasped the symbolism of the students' decision. "This is just a note to you and Mr. Powell to tell you how sorry I am that the School of Social Studies has had to close. It seems particularly sad at this time when it is precisely the things for which the School stands that we need to emphasize in America today."[90] Walter Agard expressed similar regrets. "We were sorry to hear of the school's shutting down," he wrote from Madison. "Hope it will be only temporary."[91] Unfortunately, deteriorating international circumstances and the rejuvenation of the American economy meant that the closing of the San Francisco School would be permanent.

The closing of the San Francisco School was disappointing for Meiklejohn, but he did not lack other activities to fill his time. As former chairman of the local branch of the American Civil Liberties Union, he began to assume a key position in the fight for free speech. Beginning in 1940, the Dies Committee redoubled its probes into allegedly seditious activities in the United States. In June of that year, Congress had passed the Alien Registration Act, popularly known as the Smith Act, which made it illegal to advocate the violent overthrow of the U.S. government. The Smith Act, which became one of the most controversial laws of the next twenty years, required all citizens who joined revolutionary or subversive organizations to register with a federal agency; consequently, it came perilously close to violating the First Amendment. Yet, in the tense political atmosphere of the early 1940s, few dared to challenge the provisions of the new law. Even the national office of the ACLU attempted to comply with the Smith Act by excluding all members of "totalitarian organizations" from its executive board of directors. According to a press statement, the ACLU barred all "persons affiliated with any political organization which supports 'totalitarian dictatorship' or who publicly sympathize with its principles." Within this category, it included all who directly or indirectly supported "the totalitarian governments of the Soviet Union and of the Fascist and Nazi countries (such as the Communist Party, the German-American Bund, and others) as well as native organizations with obvious antidemocratic objectives or practices."[92] According to the ACLU, citizens who advocated totalitarianism posed an intolerable threat to democracy.

As a long-time member of the American Civil Liberties Union and vice-chairman of its northern California branch, Meiklejohn held a seat on the national board of directors. He shared this post with a number of leading liberals, including John Dewey, Felix Frankfurter, Norman Thomas, A. J. Muste, and others. None of these men, however, responded to the ACLU's attempt to purge "totalitarian sympathizers" from its ranks. In this regard, Meiklejohn stood alone. Two weeks after the announcement of the union's new policy, he submitted a petition in protest. "Once the line is drawn against any minority's rights, no liberties are safe," he declared. "The heart of democracy is civil liberty for everybody without distinction up to the point of unlawful activities, committed or attempted." Predicting that the Smith Act would soon be found unconstitutional, he noted that the suppression of controversial ideas violated the most basic principles of democratic self-government. "Suppression of propaganda, even totalitarian, is contrary to democratic principles. . . . If for any reason our democracy suppresses totalitarian minorities or fails to protect their rights, we are on the road to dictatorship ourselves."[93] In the sensitive and volatile political atmosphere of the early 1940s, Meiklejohn staked his claim on the absolute inviolability of public expression, even for members of politically unpopular or potentially subversive organizations. In his mind, the need to preserve and protect the civil liberties of totalitarians at home was part and parcel of the need to fight totalitarianism abroad. To suppress freedom in the United States in order to save it in Europe was the very definition of hypocrisy.

Three weeks after registering his protest, Meiklejohn received an angry response from his good friend, Roger Baldwin, chairman of the ACLU. "We have to have a 'line,'" Baldwin cried. Excluding Fascists and Communists from the national board of directors was, in his opinion, "a policy based on such common sense that I should hardly think it admitted a reasonable attack."[94] Ernest Besig, head of the union's northern California branch, agreed with Baldwin. "I honestly feel," Besig told Meiklejohn, "that no Communist, Trotskyite, Nazi, Fascist, Ku Klux Klanner, Silver Shirt, etc. has any business directing an organization that believes in and seeks to maintain the idea of civil liberties for all in the United States. Such persons are disqualified by their refusal to grant civil liberties to all in the United States without discrimination." For Besig and Baldwin alike, the idea of allowing Communists to participate in the union's national leadership constituted a tacit endorsement of totalitarianism. "The heretics shouldn't be governing the orthodox," Besig declared, "and it constitutes no denial of civil liberties to throw them out."[95] But Meiklejohn was not so sure. It was difficult to distinguish between the heretics and the orthodox if both groups used the same tactics to silence their opponents. In 1940, Meiklejohn and Baldwin spent long hours debating this issue at Baldwin's summer home on Martha's Vineyard. It was not simply a matter of purging heretics; it was a matter of defending their civil liberties. How could a democracy protect the freedom of all speakers, no matter how controversial, without jeopardizing the very idea of democracy in the process? This was a question that ran through Meiklejohn's entire professional career. How could a democracy trust its citizens to make decisions on their own without risking the possibility that they might decide to reject democratic virtues altogether?

Not long after his exchange with Baldwin and Besig, Meiklejohn saw that his worst fears were already beginning to come true. In October of

1940, the University of California, Berkeley, fired a professor who supported and talked openly in his classes about the Communist Party.[96] Meiklejohn was shocked to see an institution of liberal learning dismiss a member of its own faculty using the same reactionary methods employed by Nazis and Communists. "The dismissal of Kenneth May seems to me the most extreme violation of the democratic principles of university freedom that I have ever seen," he declared in a note to Professor George Adams. "What our universities should now be doing, especially in the fields of history, social science, literature, and philosophy, is to see the program of democracy in conflict with the programs of National Socialism and Communism. These latter programs are living challenges to our beliefs. They are, therefore, the very things which we must study. Their advocates, provided they meet the usual requirements for membership in a university, should be welcomed to the ranks of the faculty and student body. They should be heard eagerly and answered fairly. They should be shown, by our dealing with them rather than by mere assertions, that we believe not in their principles but in our own." In Meiklejohn's view, the University of California had betrayed its own principles in order to defend them. "My own judgment," he declared, "is that the dismissal of Kenneth May has done more to break down democratic faith and democratic understanding among the teachers and students of the university than can be off-set by all the teaching and studying of library and laboratory and classroom of the total year. It is no use preaching and teaching democratic freedom unless we practice it." Revisiting the argument of *What Does America Mean?* Meiklejohn noted a deep divide between the university's supposedly democratic ideals and its clearly undemocratic actions. The only way to make liberal education meaningful was to uphold its highest principles in practice. "Please forgive my speaking so flatly and unequivocally," he concluded in his letter to Adams. "The issue at stake is the most vital and urgent issue in our culture."[97]

Over the course of the next twenty years, Meiklejohn became increasingly sensitive to the importance of this statement. In 1940, however, he was only beginning to see its implications for civil liberties and democratic education in the United States. What was the link between individual freedom and institutional authority in democratic education? Though he had yet to develop a systematic answer to this question, in the early 1940s he grew increasingly preoccupied with the idea of *state*-sponsored democratic schooling. Starting in the spring of 1940, shortly after the Smith Act became law but before the University of California fired Kenneth May, he began to explore the notion of increased state authority over public edu-

231

cation in a series of letters to James Conant, then president of Harvard. Conant read a manuscript of Meiklejohn's most recent book project but disagreed with almost every argument it made. "It does not seem to me that it is necessary to have a socialized state with a high degree of control by government on individual initiative and enterprise in order to have an effective school system," Conant wrote.[98] Given the steady rise of fascism in Europe, Conant saw no redeeming value in encroachments of government control over public schools. "It seems to me that public education will be run in a democratic country first of all locally," he noted.[99] But Meiklejohn disagreed. To assume that democratic government automatically subverted individual freedom was to mischaracterize democracy as an inherently authoritarian system. In the early 1940s, as war spread overseas, Meiklejohn made a concerted effort to redefine the democratic state not as an oppressive government but rather as a self-governing ethical community. He reminded his fellow citizens that liberal democracy did not mean the total absence of all government but rather the pervasive presence of rational *self*-government. To Meiklejohn, this definition of democracy seemed obvious. Yet, as Hitler gained ground in both western and eastern Europe, he found himself fighting his own two-front war with liberals and conservatives over the relationship between democratic government and liberal education in America's schools. Could a democratic state provide a truly liberal education?

8

"A Reply to John Dewey"

1941–1947

I N OCTOBER OF 1941, after a relaxing summer of tennis and swimming at Windy Gates, Roger Baldwin's family estate on Martha's
Vineyard, Meiklejohn published a short article in a rather obscure
scholarly journal called the *North Central Association Quarterly*.[1] His
title, "Higher Education in a Democracy," was disarmingly nondescript
given the complexity of his argument. Reflecting on the cultural and intellectual implications of the growing war in Europe, he asserted that the
twin battles against Hitler's Nazism and Stalin's Communism were actually battles against the perversion of America's own most dearly held liberal ideals. Highlighting the two most fearsome dogmas of totalitarian
power—"Down with religion!" and "Up with the state!"—he noted a
striking similarity between these war cries and the ever-more-secularized
political culture of the United States. "My impression," he wrote, "is that
our society fears and hates those two dogmas or war cries or slogans because they are the strongest elements in our own society, because we, too,
are saying in our hearts, 'Down with religion,' and 'Up with the state,' and
we are afraid of ourselves." For Meiklejohn, these dogmas were especially
significant in their moral implications for modern liberal education. "In
the field of education, we Protestant Americans have dethroned the
church, have cut it off from all vital connection with education, and have
put in its place the state," he wrote.[2] But how could the state become a
moral teacher? How could the nation's public schools teach values based
not on sectarian faith but rather on purely secular reason? Conceding that
the secularization of modern education, like the secularization of modern
American political culture, had probably been inevitable, Meiklejohn asserted that America's newest educational challenge was to see if the polit-

233

ical authority of the state could somehow replace the spiritual authority of the church without abandoning moral discourse altogether. Could the state become a moral teacher?

In Meiklejohn's view, the issue of moral education in a secular democratic state was especially important as America contemplated entering another world war—a war in which moral leadership would play a central role. Without the possibility of shared values based on reason, could the United States survive? "One of the deepest and most active convictions just now in our Protestant society," he lamented in his article for the *North Central Association Quarterly*, "is this: that there is no common basis for men's reasoning; that at the bottom of all reasoning is irrationality; that every man starts from his own private designs; that, after all, reasoning is rationalizing; and that the old dream of a common truth, a common intelligence, a common intellectual inquiry, is gone, and gone forever." Such a crippling moral relativism—or intellectual agnosticism, as Meiklejohn had called it at Amherst—now presented American education with an urgent question: Was it even possible to create a "new intellectual synthesis" that could serve as a moral foundation for a modern democratic state? Was it possible to believe in a truly reasonable human community? As Meiklejohn put it, "[S]ince the mind of God has gone out of our calculations and our plannings and our meditations, [the question now was] whether, in purely secular terms, we can find a common basis, a common goal, and whether we can defeat this notion that reasoning itself is essentially irrational."[3] Was a democracy capable of moral educational authority?

Toward the end of his article, Meiklejohn identified what he considered to be the primary source of moral and intellectual agnosticism in the twentieth century, namely, the pragmatist philosophy of John Dewey.[4] According to Meiklejohn, Dewey's pragmatism, as an outgrowth of the Darwinian revolution of the late nineteenth century, had actively facilitated the disintegration of moral authority in the modern world. Recognizing that pragmatism had done well to expose the more dogmatic aspects of its philosophical predecessors, especially the Hegelian idealists of the mid-nineteenth-century, Meiklejohn nevertheless condemned pragmatism for failing to put anything beyond the scientific method in place of the religious belief it so effectively deposed. Rejecting the idea that science had any inherent moral purpose, he refused to believe that mere experimentation or technology would foster the development of democracy in a war-torn world. "In Germany," he observed, "life has been transformed by technology, but not into 'democracy.' No, technology has produced . . . the exact enemy and foe of democracy—dictatorship. We can no longer, in a technological world, take democracy for granted." According to Meiklejohn, Dewey and his fellow pragmatists had simply taken democracy for granted as an inevitable outcome of "evolutionary" social development. The results of this assumption had been morally disastrous for Western civilization. "I think the day of pragmatism has gone," Meiklejohn declared. The time had come to establish a new basis for liberal education, a new intellectual synthesis that neither abandoned the search for shared moral values nor feebly took them for granted. The time had come, in other words, to test the educational possibilities of *idealism*. Reflecting on the turbulent years since World War I, Meiklejohn warned America's educators not to be seduced by Deweyan pragmatism again. "If they are not ready this time with an understanding of what democracy is," he concluded, "then they will deserve to be damned forever."[5]

These were strong words, and their timing only made them stronger. On December 7, 1941, less than two months after Meiklejohn published his cautionary article in the *North Central Association Quarterly*, Japan bombed Pearl Harbor, and the United States entered World War II. With amazing speed, the entire nation mobilized for war. Industrial manufacturing surged out of its depression-era doldrums as the government poured millions of dollars into new factories, which, in turn, added hundreds of thousands of new jobs to the economy. No region felt the effects of increased war production more than the West Coast, where the defense industry boomed. California alone received nearly four billion dollars in federal contracts for military equipment, including planes, ships, and tanks. Not long after the first American troops landed on Guadalcanal in the summer of 1942, Meiklejohn himself joined the National War Labor Board as director of a twenty-seven member commission to regulate wages in printing, publishing, and the graphic arts. He commuted between his commission post in Washington, D.C., and his home in Berkeley, where other wartime issues soon arose, most notably the internment of Japanese Americans. In February of 1942, President Roosevelt signed an executive order demanding the evacuation of all individuals of "enemy ancestry" from designated areas along the West Coast. The Western Defense Command designated a "safety zone" more than a hundred miles wide extending from Canada to Mexico from which all Japanese Americans, whether foreign- or native-born, were categorically excluded. According to Roosevelt, Japanese internment was necessary to protect the Pacific Rim from those more loyal to the enemy than to the country of their citizenship—and Meiklejohn agreed with this policy.

Despite his long-time involvement with the ACLU, Meiklejohn believed reports that Japanese Americans might aid the enemy, and he defended the government's internment program on grounds of military necessity.[6] "To deny that the presence of Japanese in California, in view of all the bitterness of conflict and misunderstanding in the past, creates a peculiar situation is, I think, to push one's head down into the sand," he wrote to Roger Baldwin. "The Japanese citizens as a group are dangerous both to themselves and to their fellow citizens, and, that being true, discriminatory action is justified."[7] Meiklejohn's support for Japanese internment rested on the widespread assumption that a minority of Japanese Americans—perhaps as many as five thousand—were involved in subversive activities. He accepted reports of disloyalty within the Japanese American population and agreed that the government had legitimate authority to detain citizens suspected of direct threats to domestic security. At the same time, he concurred with Baldwin that imprisoning *all* Japanese Americans *solely* because of their ancestry almost certainly constituted a violation of civil liberties. "We have taken an enormous educational risk by evacuating 100,000 of them because, perhaps, 5,000 of them are disloyal," he wrote to John J. McCloy, an Amherst alumnus working in the War Department. "As you know, I don't quarrel with that action, because it was taken on grounds of military necessity. But, as a form of education for the 95,000, it was a dangerous procedure. If now we go further, if we use the camps not for relocation but for detention, we will reap the fruits of resentment and disloyalty."[8] Though Meiklejohn's view eventually changed, he agreed in 1942 with the prevailing opinion that the federal government had a right to defend itself against potentially seditious activity. He also agreed that suspicion on the basis of race was justified so long as real crimes were proven. And the Supreme Court backed him up.

In 1944, in the highly publicized case of *Korematsu v. United States,* the Supreme Court asked whether or not the government's relocation plan was constitutional and, if so, whether citizens had a right to refuse military orders in time of war. Justice Hugo Black wrote the majority opinion and upheld Fred Korematsu's conviction on both counts. He ruled that the government had a right to detain Japanese Americans until it determined if they posed a clear threat to national security. Justice Felix Frankfurter concurred in Black's opinion, finding "nothing in the Constitution which denies to Congress the power to enforce a valid military order."[9] Meiklejohn praised the ruling of his friend Frankfurter in a personal letter. "I am very glad to hear that you find yourself in agreement with my brief remarks in the *Korematsu* case," Frankfurter responded. "I do so all the more because I know that your feelings and your general direction, were they unguided by your critical faculties, would naturally see only the immediate case of hardship and disregard the division of responsibility in our scheme of society between the court and the other branches of government."[10] In the early 1940s, Meiklejohn wholeheartedly supported the "war powers" of the president and did not expect the Supreme Court to limit those powers in any way. He conflated legitimate investigations of subversive activities with illegitimate incarcerations of innocent civilians. It took several years for his position on these issues to change, but when it did, it changed dramatically.

In many ways, Meiklejohn's acquiescence to federal authority in the case of Japanese internment reflected his developing view of the state as a moral teacher—a view he had been working hard to articulate in a new book. The book, which had been the basis of his recent article in the *North Central Association Quarterly,* dealt with the subject of moral education and liberal democracy in a secular pragmatist age. On March 23, 1942, five weeks after Roosevelt's internment order, Meiklejohn mailed his five-hundred-page manuscript off to Harper & Brothers in New York. "My book has gone off to the publisher at last," he announced in a jubilant letter to John Gaus. "The fight with the pragmatic movement is thoroughly fought out, and now I feel, at least, that I've had my say. The argument has to do with 'The State' as taking the place of 'The Church.' That seems to me the essential transition. . . . I hope you'll have a look at it if it soon comes out."[11] When Meiklejohn's book went to press, it had no title. Meiklejohn thought it might be *Revolution in Education,* but, when it finally came out, it carried the subtler heading *Education Between Two Worlds.*[12] Either title would have worked to convey the book's central thesis, which concerned the shift from church to state in modern liberal society and the tension that resulted between individual autonomy and institutional authority in contemporary democratic education. *Education Between Two Worlds* contended that the success of liberal democracy depended on its ability to balance—or even to reconcile—these two equally important goals. Reconciling individual liberty with institutional authority seemed particularly important in 1942, when the threat of fascism seemed to jeopardize the very survival of democratic self-government in the modern world. "I have tried in this book to write about education," Meiklejohn stated in his preface. "But I find myself writing about the World War. Have I then wandered from my theme? I think not. The catastrophe which has come upon humanity is, in its deepest aspect, the collapse of human learning and teaching."[13] In many ways, *Education Be-*

tween Two Worlds marked the culmination of Meiklejohn's search for a new intellectual synthesis for liberal democratic education in the twentieth century.

In an attempt to clarify the tension between individual freedom and institutional authority in liberal democratic education, Meiklejohn returned to its origins in early modern Europe. He opened his book with an extended comparison of two prominent seventeenth-century educational and political philosophers—John Amos Comenius and John Locke.[14] According to Meiklejohn, Comenius and Locke illustrated the two worlds between which modern liberal education had come to exist. Comenius, a Czech bishop from the Moravian Church of the Christian Unity, represented the spiritual world of religious values. He represented the church. Locke, the paragon of Baconian science and the new learning in the British Enlightenment, represented the secular world of scientific facts. He represented the state. Comparing Comenius with Locke, Meiklejohn followed the transfer of educational authority from church to state, from religion to science, from medieval unity to modern multiplicity, and, finally, in the tumultuous diplomatic context of the early 1940s, from peace to war.[15] "Why," he asked in his chapters on Comenius and Locke, "are their teaching plans, at every point of essential human significance, so different? For Comenius, mankind is one fellowship, one society, bound together by the common purpose of using intelligence for the making of a common life. For Locke, mankind falls apart into groups, classes, sects, factions, nations, individuals, which, seeking each its own ends, inevitably tend to plunge into hatred and strife, one against another." Comenius represented cooperation and community. Locke represented competition and conflict. "Comenius brings men together," Meiklejohn concluded. "Locke tears them apart."[16] In Meiklejohn's view, the conflict between Comenius and Locke set the stage for a far more profound and complicated educational and political philosopher of the eighteenth century—Jean-Jacques Rousseau.

In 1762, nearly a century after Comenius and Locke wrote their greatest works, Rousseau published two famous books. The first was *Emile,* a treatise on education. Second was *The Social Contract,* a treatise on government and civil society. In many ways, *Emile* and *The Social Contract* perpetuated the dichotomies that had divided Comenius and Locke. Indeed, it was typical of Rousseau that, at least on the surface, the arguments of these two treatises seemed to contradict one another. *Emile* seemed to argue for the final autonomy of the individual in the educational process. *The Social Contract* seemed to argue for the absolute au-

238

thority of the state or "general will" in the political process. "But," Meiklejohn wrote, "one does not understand Rousseau, nor does one grasp the essential problem of modern culture, unless one sees that they are really one argument. In *Emile,* Rousseau preaches the gospel of individual freedom in teaching. But a careful reading reveals that freedom is to be found only in conformity to the demands of an authoritative society. In *The Social Contract,* Rousseau discovers the absolute authority of a General Will. But the purpose of that will is, we are clearly told, to make individual men free."[17] This duality between individual freedom and institutional authority, between personal autonomy and public order, between the liberty of a citizen and the power of a state, had fascinated Meiklejohn for decades. Now, in *Education Between Two Worlds,* a single question guided his analysis: What kind of educational authority could a democratic state legitimately exercise over its citizens? To answer that question would be to develop a general theory of democratic education.

For Locke, the answer to this question was "very little." In his view, all citizens possessed certain inalienable natural rights which were prepolitical and which no temporal government could ever revoke. Among these rights were the rights to life, liberty, and property. Yet, according to Rousseau, Locke's theory of natural rights was fundamentally flawed. In Rousseau's view, human beings living in a mythical state of nature had no rights at all. Without a society (or a state), human beings could have no government. Without a government, they could have no laws. And, without laws, they could have no rights. "Men living without government," Meiklejohn noted, "can have neither 'rights' nor 'wrongs.' They have neither 'laws' nor 'reason.' They can have no property since the owning of property implies a contract or an agreement as to the conditions under which it shall be held and used. And such an agreement can be made and enforced only by the will of a political state." For Meiklejohn, as for Rousseau, human beings living exclusively in nature had no state. Indeed, they had neither society nor government nor laws nor principles nor civilization nor reason to bind them together into a community of any kind. "When men have no government," Meiklejohn asserted, taking Rousseau's argument a step further, "they can have no morality."[18] In order to have rights, human beings needed first to have institutions and associations to represent their shared social interests. These institutions, taken together, formed a state. A state was not a secondary institution. It did not merely secure rights which individuals received from God prior to their citizenship. Once formed, Meiklejohn explained, "[g]overnment is primary. It creates 'rights' and 'wrongs.' They are meaningless and impossible without it. The state is the creator of mankind. It makes civilization, makes culture, makes human beings."[19] Here was the core of Meiklejohn's educational and political philosophy. The state, as the embodiment of its citizens' collective will, not only protected but actively *created* their rights, reason, laws, and moral code. For Meiklejohn, the ideas of personal freedom and individual autonomy had no meaning outside the context of an ethical (or "civil") society, which, he asserted, could be manifest *only* in the institutions of a democratic state.

Rousseau's theory of government, whereby states emerged as the original and organic expressions of their citizens' general will, had important implications for Meiklejohn's theory of democratic education. Building on Rousseau's concept of an original, and therefore authoritative, state, Meiklejohn advanced a preliminary definition of teaching. "*The purpose of all teaching*," he wrote, using italics to emphasize his point, "*is to express the cultural authority of the group by which the teaching is given.*"[20] This definition seemed irrefutable. Yet, even as Meiklejohn wrote it, he recognized its potential dangers. "As I look back at this statement and at the figure of speech upon which it rests," he confessed, "I am painfully conscious how dangerous they are, how absurd they may seem, how easily they may be misinterpreted. Authority is not, just now, as we watch events in Europe, and Asia, a favorite term among us."[21] Meiklejohn knew that his definition of teaching would provoke fears of fascism, communism, and totalitarianism in education. "And yet," he continued, "I am sure that the statement, properly interpreted, is essentially valid, both for life and for education. Especially is it valid as we try to make a democracy. A society which takes the democratic mode of life as its dominant aim is not living without pattern, without general will. It is attempting to create the most difficult, the most complicated, as well as the most sublime, of all social compositions. It can succeed only insofar as the authority of that purpose is accepted by every member of the group."[22] Meiklejohn acknowledged the links between Rousseau and fascism, particularly as they pertained to the role of an authoritative state. He maintained, however, that education was always, and unavoidably, an expression of cultural and moral authority. In Meiklejohn's view, education without authority was virtually inconceivable. The challenge was to ensure that modern liberal education would express the cultural authority of *democracy* as opposed to the cultural authority of *dictatorship*.

According to Meiklejohn, the great danger to democratic freedom in the United States was that liberal governments would surrender their moral authority to *teach* the meaning of freedom to their citizens. Nowhere was this danger more urgent than in institutions of progressive liberal education, which, Meiklejohn believed, had slowly but surely relinquished their capacity to teach democracy with any kind of moral conviction. Devoted merely to openness, tolerance, and experimentation, they had no principles for critical judgment and no stable values for ethical action. The source of this disappointing pedagogical weakness was none other than the pragmatic educational philosophy of John Dewey. In Meiklejohn's view, Dewey's commitment to detached scientific discourse and instrumental inquiry into consequences rendered his followers utterly incapable of asserting moral authority during the war. "The method of inquiry into consequences, as Dewey uses it, or fails to use it, does not, and cannot, give an adequate theory of political life," he noted.[23] Characterizing pragmatism as a sort of theory without a theory, Meiklejohn argued that Dewey's followers had concerned themselves exclusively with experimental processes and scientific means instead of firm moral principles or concrete political ends. Consequently, they had proven themselves totally inadequate in the fight against fascism. Given an ideological battle between democracy and dictatorship, would pragmatists simply identify the two combatants, describe their respective political programs, and leave the decision to students? "[T]o do that is not teaching," Meiklejohn declared (perhaps forgetting some aspects of his own work at the Experimental College, Amherst, and Brown). "In spite of all complexities, the first principle still holds. Teaching must find its roots in some active code of behavior. It must express some authoritative pattern of culture. It must believe something. Some social group must be speaking through it, impressing its way of life. Nothing short of that is education. But the question is, which code shall it be? In the midst of our shifting, uncertain, self-contradictory world, what shall we teach?"[24]

Out of his critique of Dewey, Meiklejohn constructed his own general theory of liberal democratic education.[25] In so doing, he summarized all his previous work on the theory and practice of teaching. "Modern education," he argued, "must teach its pupils to participate, not in an intelligence which makes and controls the universe but in an intelligence which men are inventing as they seek to create meaning and value in an otherwise meaningless world." The aim of modern liberal education was to renew the critical search for common social values, to resuscitate the possibility of shared moral principles and unified cultural ideals, even in the face of a civilization that seemed increasingly and often hopelessly fragmented. While liberal education could not control, coerce, force, or manipulate its students into learning, neither could it deny the need for educational authority altogether. Rather, it had to teach students to recognize their own authority to govern themselves. "All authority over human conduct or belief is human authority," Meiklejohn explained. "There is no court of judgment beyond ourselves to which appeal can be made for the controlling of our lives. And yet, the traditional imputation of that judgment to the universe as such may suggest to us how deeply significant our unconscious wisdom has felt it to be." Ascribing a quasi-religious dimension to the ideal of human brotherhood, Meiklejohn put his faith once again in the possibility of transcendental reason. Reason, he asserted, was the opposite of violence, selfishness, and war. It was the fundamental unifying principle behind all human communities. "When we have said, in the past, that God created men in His own image, that He cared for them, and that they, therefore, should care for one another, what we were really saying was that human insight has disclosed life to be such that it cannot be lived rightly or intelligently unless men deal with one another as if they were brothers."[26] The task of modern liberal education was to cultivate this transcendentally "reasonable" brotherhood, to construct this purely rational kingdom of heaven on earth.[27] The task, in other words, was to transfer educational authority from church to state.

The culmination of Meiklejohn's book came in his theory of democratic state formation, that is, the ways in which liberal education actually *created* the conditions necessary for a democratic state to exist. "The state is intelligence in action in its most inclusive form and, hence, at its highest level," he wrote. "It is the function of the state to organize, to harmonize, to make reasonable all the activities of its constituent groups and its individual members." Meiklejohn recognized that his definition of the state would invite reproach in time of war. He knew he would be accused of "exalting the state at the expense of the individual." He knew he would be vilified as a Nazi, a Communist, and a totalitarian. But he risked censure in order to plead his case for the educational authority of a moral state. "When men say that the exaltation of the state is hostile to the dignity and freedom of the individual they are making an assumption," he declared. "They are assuming that the state and the individual are enemies. They are taking it for granted that what the state gains, the individual loses, and vice versa. But those assumptions are false. Government by the consent of the governed is not hostile to the governed. Government of the people, for the people, by the people is not intended to destroy the dignity and freedom of the people. Democratic government cannot be too strong." According to Meiklejohn, it was precisely this assumption of hostility between individual autonomy and state authority that led to the rise of Nazism. "The task now facing our democracies is to show that a free people does not need a 'dictator' to make it strong. It can govern itself strongly, efficiently, wisely. That would be the real victory over Nazism. We must show it in war by being more efficient in war. But it is even more important, in the long run, that we show it in peace. The human will to freedom and equality must be so strongly expressed in the agencies of government that no selfishness of individuals or groups can prevail against it."[28] The only way to defeat fascism was to strengthen freedom in the self-governing institutions of a democratic state.

Appearing in bookstores in the summer of 1942, *Education Between Two Worlds* attracted instant critical attention. Max Lerner, the well-known political scientist, wrote a letter to Ordway Tead, editor of the *Nation,* expressing his keen admiration for the work. "Meiklejohn has written a book which is a blow between the eyes," Lerner exclaimed. "It explains why our educational effort has become fragmentized. It helps us to clear away what has become 'useless' in the history of educational thought, and it gives us a new and usable past in that history." Most of all, he added, "it compels us to see that if education is not a part of the state, then neither education nor the state has any meaning."[29] Ralph Preston, reviewing the book for the *Christian Century,* appreciated Meiklejohn's attack on pragmatism. "Perhaps no one has yet analyzed Dewey's writings with the understanding and penetration of Meiklejohn. Many have vaguely sensed the unsuitability in Dewey's approach without being able to get their hands on more than surface manifestations of it. With unimpeachable fairness, Meiklejohn successfully endeavors to discover why pragmatic plans of teaching provide for content lacking in unity and purpose."[30] Walter Agard agreed. "We were all delighted to get the copy of *Education Between Two Worlds,*" Agard wrote. "I've given it a first reading, with a glance at the start and enthusiasm steadily mounting as I read along. Your argument seems to me beautifully worked out, and I think the conclusion is a critically important one." Agard added that he was "especially pleased with the critique of Dewey."[31]

A few months later, Dewey himself sent a note to Meiklejohn. "I haven't seen your book yet, but shall do so," he scrawled in typically illegible handwriting. "I'm sure of your contribution, and, while of course I think fundamental criticism of my views (there are plenty of minor points to be criticized!) is wrong-headed, I'm sure in advance it will be fair." At the end of his letter, Dewey could not resist adding a few warnings about the dangers of totalitarianism in a war-torn world. "What troubles me about the present time is the extra-ordinary revival of reactionary ideas in philosophy and theology," he wrote.[32] "And I fear there is already under way a prospect for political-social reaction after the war. I know you are the last person in the country to be in that [group], and I hope your criticisms of empirical naturalism aren't going to give support to our common foe."[33] Lurking behind Dewey's words was a deep-seated ambivalence concerning Meiklejohn's definition of the democratic state. Given the emergence of fascism under supposedly democratic political conditions, Dewey and other liberals retreated from the idea of a strong state, especially during war. Unlike Meiklejohn, Dewey considered the state to be a distinctly *secondary* form of political association; it did not exist prior to other social groups, so it had no legitimate claims to over-arching authority. As he explained in *The Public and Its Problems,* first published in 1926, states existed primarily as instruments for adjudicating conflicts between competing social groups. Dewey's state was merely "a mechanism . . . for arranging terms of interplay among the indefinite diversity of groups in which men associate and through active participation in which they become socially minded."[34] Stressing the autonomy of the individuals who constituted various social groups, Dewey thought it best to minimize the size and scope of the state, lest it become despotic, as states, in his view, were always wont to do. "To become state-minded instead of socially minded," he believed, was "to become a fanatic, a monomaniac, and thus to lose all sense of what a state is."[35]

When it came to defining the democratic state, disagreements between Meiklejohn and Dewey were attributable largely to differences in terminology. Meiklejohn's state was roughly analogous to Dewey's group—or society or community or public—except that Meiklejohn's state had the added feature of institutional and organizational *form.* Dewey's groups were utterly formless until they entered the context of institutional control. Dewey himself acknowledged that citizens became socially minded only when they began to participate in cooperative activities which achieved their fullest expression in the functioning of a democratic state. He recognized that a democratic state, as an institutional manifestation of collective aspirations and ideals, gave meaning to all other kinds of group association; indeed, a democratic state created the very *possibility* of meaning—or culture or civilization—as a shared human construct. As Meiklejohn contended in *Education Between Two Worlds,* even Dewey, in his most insightful moments, conceded the cultural primacy of the democratic state. "The governing state is, as Dewey insists, unique among human associations," Meiklejohn wrote. "[I]t is unique, not as being secondary and negative and derivative, but as being primary among them

244

all."[36] According to Meiklejohn, it was the duty of the democratic state authoritatively to *teach* its citizens—or, more accurately, itself—how to be reasonable, how to be socially minded, and, thus, how to foster the collective deliberations that were essential to democratic self-government.

And yet, to criticize Dewey, America's high priest of liberal democratic principles, was inevitably to invite attack. Several strongly worded reviews placed Meiklejohn's book squarely in the reactionary camp. As Meiklejohn wrote to Lewis Mumford, many of Dewey's most fervent disciples had condemned his work as philosophical heresy. "A letter from New York told me of a meeting at which 'a group of Deweyites' were 'outraged' by the argument of my book attacking the master," he confessed.[37] Two days later, he recalled the same incident in another letter, saying that he regretted causing so much controversy. "I don't like that," he cringed. "I'm shrinking from it a bit."[38] Foremost among Meiklejohn's opponents was Sidney Hook, Dewey's most prominent student and a professor of philosophy in New York, who reviewed *Education Between Two Worlds* for the *Nation*. In Hook's view, Meiklejohn's state-centered thesis was tantamount to treason. "One has to read this book in order to believe that it could have been written by a liberal convinced he is defending democracy," Hook cried. "The most charitable interpretation of Mr. Meiklejohn's position is that he has written a defense, not of democracy, but of a benevolent dictatorship by those who know what we ought to want better than we know ourselves." In Hook's view, Meiklejohn's work came close to an apology for fascism. The book, he wrote in one stabbing sentence, was "the 'Mein Kampf' of all frustrated administrators whose enlightened projects have been shipwrecked in the processes of democracy, who would like to ram them down their colleagues' throats, make them like it, and still remain democrats." "In the pre-Hitlerian era," Hook sniffed, "it would be sufficient to say that this is a false and foolish book. In the era of Hitler, it must be characterized as false and dangerous."[39]

The most extended critique of *Education Between Two Worlds* came from Edward Strong, chancellor of the University of California and a close friend of Meiklejohn's. Writing a letter in six installments over the course of several weeks, Strong, a self-described Deweyan pragmatist, offered a lengthy commentary on Meiklejohn's thesis, emphasizing especially the complex relation between liberal education and the democratic state. Using Hitler's Third Reich as an example, Strong drew a sharp distinction between true (democratic) states, which legitimately expressed the general will of their citizens, and false (dictatorial) states, which restricted public liberty by violently suppressing dissent. For Strong, the distinction between true and false states corresponded to a parallel distinction between free societies defined as organic communal associations and authoritarian governments defined as arbitrary agencies of control.[40] Serious problems arose when authoritarian governments masqueraded as free societies, as was the case in Nazi Germany. In Strong's view, Meiklejohn had failed to distinguish his use of the term *state* meaning "an ideal society" from the more common use of the term *state* meaning "the mechanisms of government." As a result, he left himself vulnerable to misinterpretation, especially among pragmatists. "The whole intent and spirit of your book is missed or falsified by any supposition that it defends the totalitarian domination by some men of most men," Strong acknowledged. "Yet, your book does lend itself to such misappropriation. I think that, in your hope and eagerness for this better world to be fashioned, you tend to convert the 'ideal' to be realized into the 'real' that will bring the great event into existence. It is my opinion that some men must think and work very hard to establish institutions which will teach many men the reasonableness of cooperative living." Meiklejohn wholeheartedly agreed. If *Education Between Two Worlds* showed anything at all, it showed that "some men"—particularly philosopher-teachers—"must think and work very hard to establish institutions"—particularly institutions of liberal democratic education—"which will teach many men the reasonableness of cooperative living."[41]

Strong's letter pointed to the most complicated aspect of Meiklejohn's work, namely, his conflated definition of the state as *both* an ethical community *and* an institutionalized government. A number of critics thought Meiklejohn's authoritative state came dangerously close to describing a totalitarian regime. "You convinced me of the desirability of a strong, free state," wrote his good friend Morse Erskine just after Christmas in 1943. "But, without your painstaking explanation of Rousseau's philosophy, I would not have understood your terms. In conversation, when you use the word 'total' without any preceding remarks, people . . . are apt to get the wrong idea. Most of us Americans are so saturated with the Locke and Dewey concept of the state that we immediately rise in defense of our so-called liberties."[42] Erskine was right. For Meiklejohn, a state was an amalgam of civil society and institutional authority, a blending of ethical bonds and self-governing control. In *Education Between Two Worlds,* he commented repeatedly that Rousseau's state was neither exclusively a government nor simply a community but rather a mixture of both. As an association formed around shared moral ideals, Meiklejohn's state encompassed both the public *and* the private affairs of its citizens. "The state is 'the people' *in action*," Meiklejohn explained. "It establishes manners and customs. It builds roads, parks, hospitals, museums. It enacts statutes and enforces them. It issues currency. It makes war and peace. It sets up relations of collective bargaining between capital and labor. It conducts education. In all these things, as in a multitude of other ways, the people, as 'a state,' are expressing and making effective a general will toward the general welfare."[43] For Meiklejohn, a state was any group that actively governed itself. More specifically, it was the institutionalized *process* by which self-government occurred.

Meiklejohn's complex theory of the state confounded those accustomed to a traditional liberal separation of public government from private behavior. John Gaus, for instance, had a difficult time understanding Meiklejohn's conflation of these two spheres. "When you use the term 'state' so all-inclusively as to replace (apparently) *all* institutions such as churches," Gaus suggested in June of 1944, "I suspect you seek to convey by it the sense of our common humanity—once associated in Stoic terms with an ethical ideal of all humankind; whereas your readers will be looking for . . . the organization through government of collective services, the location of decision-making sanctions and coercions, etc." What Gaus failed to realize was that Meiklejohn's definition of the state encompassed *both* the ethical ideal of all humankind *and* the organization through government of collective services. According to Meiklejohn, ethical ideals were formless as well as meaningless outside of the context of governmental institutions. Only when a democratic state achieved institutional form did it have the ability—and the authority—to *teach* ethical ideals to its members, or, more accurately, to uphold and enforce those ideals within itself. Unfortunately, Gaus missed this point. Identifying the state with a more limited concept of government as coercive power, Gaus thought Meiklejohn should use the term *humanity* for his state, not only to clarify his analysis, but also to bring his work more into line with Dewey's. "I think I might have elaborated . . . on your use of the word 'state,'" Gaus wrote. "I feel that you did not meet on the same use-of-word plane with Dewey in his *The Public and Its Problems* precisely at that point; your *state* and his *mankind* are, I judge, about the same, and you can clarify to your readers (and I think for the good of cumulative understanding you should) by further treatment."[44] Again, though, Gaus misunderstood. Meiklejohn's *state* did not simply correspond to Dewey's *mankind,* nor did it align with Dewey's formless *public.* Meiklejohn's state was human intelligence in action. It was humanity voluntarily governing itself in concrete and explicit ways, above all in the institutionalized processes of liberal democratic education.

Meiklejohn acknowledged that, perhaps, he had exaggerated his conflicts with Dewey. "In a sense, I think you are right in finding me to agree with John Dewey," he wrote to Gaus in 1944. "Our social intentions are, I think, nearly identical. But his ethical theory seems to make 'public' action a *secondary* thing, derived from 'private' interest. Am I wrong in thinking he does that? If he does, I can't agree with him, and the opposition seems to me terribly important. But the more important matter is your saying that I am not clear about the 'state' and thinking I should try to do better. That's true, and I'm going to try or bust." It took many years for Meiklejohn to iron out the implications of his definition of an organic and ethical state, but he insisted on its importance for a general theory of democratic education. For Meiklejohn, a state derived none of its authority from private interest—a concept he considered anathema to the nature of civil society. Instead, the state was an original and organic expression of its citizens' public, or general, will. "I'm trying, you see, to say what I take it Rousseau means by the General Will," Meiklejohn concluded in his letter to Gaus. "The 'state' as I see it, is not simply a community. It is a community taking corporate action. But there is the further implication that *every* member of the community shares in the taking of that action. One has to keep both the 'group' and the 'individual' factors strongly emphasized. Any politically active group is thus a state, as a society or a community may not be if it has not focused a common mind and will on the making of decisions."[45] As a student of ethics, not politics, Meiklejohn defined the state as any group of individuals committed to shared principles and thus unified for the sake of self-government.[46] The crucial issue was how the authoritative purposes of a moral state could be translated into the lives of socially-minded citizens. The crucial issue, in other words, was just how values were *created* through the process of state-sponsored democratic education.

Like John Gaus, Clarence Ayres accused Meiklejohn of ignoring Dewey's terms and ideas. "What you are saying is precisely what Dewey has been saying or trying to say in many different ways over a period of many years," Ayres wrote to Meiklejohn in 1943. "Your primary concern is with values, but you don't even mention his 1939 *Theory of Valuation*."[47] Like Gaus, Ayres thought Meiklejohn had simply used different words to convey ideas that pragmatist thinkers had already espoused. Meiklejohn admitted that he and Dewey probably pursued similar goals, but he continued to insist that Dewey had no compelling theory to explain how values were *created* and thus no valid explanation of the educational *origins* of democracy. To many, however, it seemed that Meiklejohn's own vague theory of moral valuation was no more compelling than Dewey's. Indeed, when Meiklejohn tackled the subject of moral or ethical values, he sounded a lot like a pragmatist himself. "Our human inquiry has no 'absolute' or 'transcendental' knowledge or standards to which it may appeal to give it warrant for its validity," he wrote to Horace Fries, a colleague from the philosophy department at the University of Wisconsin, in 1944. "The only truth we have is what we ourselves find or make, and the only tests are our own."[48] The purpose of liberal education in a democracy, he believed, was to provide diverse individuals with the institutional means to address essential problems in a common social discourse. Without claiming that different viewpoints must eventually coalesce around a single perfect meaning, Meiklejohn nevertheless hoped that citizens from all walks of life could join together in mutual deliberation and debate. This dialectical process, he insisted, was the true value of democracy. "What objective social inquiry is driving at," he wrote to Fries, "is some common constructive planning in which so far as possible all men may agree or at least make intelligible their differences."[49] Dialectical deliberations in which different perspectives became intelligible to one another were the ultimate objective of liberal democratic education. These deliberations were, in and of themselves, the intellectual synthesis that Meiklejohn had long hoped to find.

In the summer of 1944, the debate between Meiklejohn and Dewey finally came to a head, though it took a major detour along the way. In June of that year, Dewey published an article in *Fortune* magazine condemning idealists for their reactionary views, especially their retreat from objective scientific *facts* into a realm of subjective moral *values*. His title, "A Challenge to Liberal Thought," conveyed his annoyance with what he considered the anti-intellectual dogmatism of neoconservative ideologues, especially those associated with what he considered backward-looking educational programs. Implicit in Dewey's article was an attack on the Great Books curriculum that Robert Hutchins and Mortimer Adler had recently instituted at the University of Chicago.[50] According to Dewey, Hutchins's Great Books curriculum rested on a blind appeal to dogma and tradition and, as such, constituted a wholesale rejection of the modern scientific method. "The contribution that the reactionary philosophy makes is to urge that technology and science are intrinsically of an inferior and illiberal nature!" Dewey complained, adding that modern "educational theory [must] break down the philosophy of fixation that bolsters external authority in opposition to free cooperation. It must contest the notion that morals are something wholly separate from and above . . . the scientific method." Criticizing Great Books programs for exalting literary over scientific pursuits, Dewey declared that modern educators must "accept wholeheartedly the scientific way, not merely of technology, but of life, in order to achieve the promise of modern democratic ideals."[51] To anyone familiar with educational debates during World War II, Dewey's *Fortune* article sounded a battle cry against Hutchins, Adler, and the Great Books group. Yet, with caustic phrases like "reactionary philosophy" and "the philosophy of fixation," he clearly stereotyped his opponents. In the tense political atmosphere of the mid-1940s, neither Dewey nor the idealists sought constructive dialogue on the major issues of contemporary liberal education.

But dialogue was precisely what *Fortune* wanted. Two weeks after Dewey's provocative article appeared, *Fortune* contacted Meiklejohn for a reply. He waffled for weeks, wondering if it would be possible to bring the debate out of the realm of angry rhetoric and into the realm of concrete educational practice. How could he show that a curriculum grounded in Great Books did not bolster external authority but rather focused undergraduate teaching on the methods of critical deliberation and debate, and that a curriculum rooted in classical texts was not in opposition to free cooperation but wholly devoted to that process? The answer, he concluded, was to base his reply on the Great Books program recently introduced at St. John's College in Annapolis. As early as 1925, Meiklejohn's close friend and former student, Scott Buchanan, had invited him to teach at St. John's. More recently, after the San Francisco School had closed in 1940, Buchanan again invited Meiklejohn to serve as a part-time lecturer in philosophy and a member of St. John's Board of Visitors and Governors. When St. John's officially launched its four-year Great Books curriculum in the fall of 1937, Meiklejohn enthusiastically endorsed the new program in a speech titled "The Classical Theory of Education and the Pragmatic Revolt against It." Now, in 1944, he prepared to defend the Great Books curriculum again. "A friend of mine on the staff of *Fortune* has sent me an article by John Dewey discussing the 'issue' in education with the suggestion that I write a reply," he wrote to St. John's president Stringfellow Barr in August of 1944. "I'd rather like to tackle the job, making the question relate directly to the teaching done at St. John's, but of course I can't do that unless you and Scott would heartily approve."[52] Barr and Buchanan approved, but they wondered if Meiklejohn's decision to focus on St. John's curriculum might sidetrack him from a more thorough critique of pragmatism. Their concerns were not unreasonable.

Meiklejohn worked on his response to Dewey for several weeks. "What I'm trying to do," he explained to Barr, "is simply to get the general philosophical attack which Dewey makes stated and then reply to that. I don't want to say that St. John's is good and that his program is (or would be, if there were one) bad. I only want to say that his argument, as stated, is nonsense."[53] Meiklejohn hoped that a detailed explanation of the St. John's curriculum might induce a more general philosophical rebuttal from the pragmatists. "The boys must change their ground, and, if they do, the attack will become a phase of good inquiry," he wrote to Buchanan. "That's optimism, I know, but, as you (one of few) know, I have no other wisdom than to follow after God." From the very beginning, Meiklejohn's "Reply to John Dewey" sought reconciliation with the pragmatists. He noted that he had much in common with Dewey but emphasized the ways in which they differed in their approaches to democratic education, particularly in their approaches to democracy as a *moral,* rather than a scientific, ideal. Noting that St. John's tried to place science in *dialogue* with the humanities, he showed how Pythagoras, Ptolemy, Copernicus, and Darwin all derived meaning within a context of moral values. Contrary to Dewey's fear that the Great Books curriculum ignored science altogether, Meiklejohn argued that St. John's integrated science into the rest of the liberal arts, thus creating a dialectical and interdisciplinary approach to the whole. "The makers of the St. John's curriculum have seen with unusual clarity that, unless one knows what science is and does, one does not understand the world or the society in which we live," Meiklejohn wrote.[54] St. John's goal was not to impart specific scientific facts but rather to cultivate a sense of general social values, particularly a respect for the value of critical deliberation and intellectual debate.

Turning to the heart of Dewey's criticism—the charge that a Great Books curriculum was prone to backward-looking dogmatism—Meiklejohn responded with a question. "Why should the study of the past, as carried on at St. John's College, lead to dogmatism?"[55] The central virtue of the Great Books curriculum lay precisely in its *lack* of any fixed or universal doctrine. Any intelligent student of the Great Books would realize that, taken as a group, these texts contained countless different interpretations of reality, value, and truth. "As he follows the sequence of ideas," Meiklejohn asserted, "the pupil will be confronted, not with one 'static' set of dogmatic beliefs, but with all the fundamental conflicts that run through our culture. He will find Protagoras at war with Plato, Kant at war with Hume, Rousseau at war with Locke, Veblen at war with Adam Smith. And he must try to understand both sides of these controversies. He is asked, first of all, not to believe, but to think, as a precondition of justifiable belief."[56] The controversies at the heart of a Great Books program, Meiklejohn asserted, were relevant at all times and in all places. To be familiar with the debates that produced them was not only to be prepared for participation in a life-long process of learning but also to be trained for the critical deliberation that was the essence of a democratic community. The only permanent principle of a Great Books curriculum was the principle of intellectual excellence in debate. Following Aristotle, the leaders of St. John's College assumed that every student must strive for intellectual excellence and, moreover, that the success and survival of democracy depended on the validity of that assumption. The central feature of the Great Books curriculum was not the particular texts on the syllabus but the collective deliberation those texts fostered. The goal was not dogma but dialectical debate.

At the end of his reply, Meiklejohn called for cooperation between the pragmatists and the idealists. "Mr. Dewey and his 'opponents' have a common belief and a common purpose," Meiklejohn asserted. "I am not suggesting that, as they may work together, the two groups will reach the same philosophy. I am only saying that they will be engaged in the same inquiry, will be discussing the same problem." According to Meiklejohn, the problem was not the presence of illiberal views but the attempt to silence those views. The only way to ensure the integrity of democratic debate was to ensure that all views, both liberal and illiberal, had access to the same discussion. "I wish that Mr. Dewey and his colleagues would not speak of those who differ from them as 'challenging liberal thought,' " Meiklejohn wrote. "I, for one, do not 'challenge liberal thought.' I do challenge Mr. Dewey's analysis of it. I cannot accept the pragmatic interpretation of the modern and the new. But that does not mean that my heart is fixed upon 'the past' rather than upon 'the future.' To many of us, Mr. Dewey's account of 'the scientific method' is very unsatisfactory, especially as it bears upon the difference between 'values' and 'facts.' But surely our opposition to a theory of science should not be taken to mean that we are hostile to 'science' itself. I find Mr. Dewey's interpretation of democracy misleading and incomplete. But that criticism does not indicate my lack of interest in 'democracy.' And, finally, if we find that an intellectual colleague has taken a view of American institutions different from our own, that need not mean that he is un-American."[57] Reminding Dewey that the two of them stood on the same side of the political fence, Meiklejohn called for a democracy in which disagreement did not have to mean disunity, a democracy in which supposedly illiberal ideas would not be met with equally illiberal attempts at suppression. Only then could a democracy discover just how values were created. Only then could a democracy become a truly deliberative community and, thus, a truly moral teacher.

The debate between Meiklejohn and Dewey, refracted through the Great Books curriculum at St. John's College, continued. Two weeks after Meiklejohn's reply appeared in the pages of *Fortune,* Sidney Hook published an article in the *New Leader,* provocatively titled "The Apologists for St. John's College." It was not the first time Hook had criticized St. John's, but it was the first time he explicitly connected Meiklejohn with the project. In his article, Hook accused Meiklejohn of intentionally distorting Dewey in order to support his own point of view.[58] Meiklejohn read Hook's article with dismay. "Two days ago I saw for the first time your article in the *New Leader,*" he wrote to Hook. "Your first paragraph has hurt me so deeply that I am driven, much against my will, to ask you whether or not something can be done about it. In the paragraph in question you publicly brand me as a liar. The charge is, so far as I know, totally false. I beg of you to write me frankly about this matter, whatever your mind about it may be, and to do so as quickly as possible."[59] Two days later, Hook replied. He explained that, three years earlier when reviewing *Education Between Two Worlds* for the *Nation,* he had noticed that Meiklejohn had misquoted Dewey's *Democracy and Education* in order to make an argument that pragmatism merely "*took for granted* the democratic criterion and its application in present social life." As Hook pointed out, Dewey had not italicized the words *took for granted* in his original text. "The italics are yours," Hook charged, "but you do not indicate that. You make a great play with these italicized words and present them as crucial evidence that for Dewey values are chosen, not by reflection, but arbitrarily 'taken for granted.' You use them . . . to tax Dewey with believing that we cannot rationally justify democracy, that we cannot reasonably reject dictatorship, that 'we simply (!) "take for granted" our way of life and fight for it with guns.' " In Hook's opinion, Meiklejohn's interpretation of Dewey was simply preposterous.[60]

Calling Meiklejohn's analysis a hair-raising distortion and an intellectual atrocity, Hook continued. "It seems to me that you are so strongly in the grip of a negative compulsion in respect to Dewey that your mind cannot dwell on what he writes without unconsciously distorting it," he wrote. "All this reinforces my impression that it is something over and above the theoretical differences between you and Dewey which accounts for the crude, wild, and persistent misrepresentations on your part." Reiterating his point that Meiklejohn's erroneous italicizations had skewed Dewey's meaning, Hook extended his harangue. "[B]efore an attack can reach the level of criticism, it must meet certain standards of fair statement. I am deeply sorry to say that I do not always find those standards met in your attack. And, since you are a personally honorable man and an intelligent one, I am at a loss to explain the facts I have cited."[61] A few days later, Meiklejohn sheepishly responded. "You have," he wrote, "missed the point of my note. May I state it again? You found in my book a quotation from Mr. Dewey which italicized words which were not italicized in his text. How that mistake occurred I do not know. You assert in the *New Leader* that you do know. You say that it was an attempt on my part to 'palm off' my italics as Mr. Dewey's own. My note informed you that that 'charge is, so far as I know, totally false.' "[62] Shortly after receiving this letter, Hook wrote again, using language even more petulant than before. "Precisely what do you think the issue is which, according to you, I have missed?" he snapped. "I did *not* call you a 'liar,' and I did *not* assert that you were 'not a personally honorable man.' Your failure to give a careful and scrupulous presentation of Dewey's views is evidence to me of a deep-seated bias. In other words, you are more anxious to refute him than to understand him."[63] Perhaps sensing that Hook was hitting too close to the mark, Meiklejohn finally ended the exchange. "I think we had better stop," he submitted. "Your review of my book in the *Nation* had made public discussion between you and me impossible. The same difficulty came from your *New Leader* article. It was in the hope that we might break down that impediment that I wrote to you. But we have made no headway whatever."[64]

Significantly, Dewey himself never accused Meiklejohn of mischaracterizing his views. He did, however, suggest that Meiklejohn misunderstood the purpose of his initial article in *Fortune*. "In spite of appearances to the contrary," Dewey remarked in a brief letter to *Fortune*'s editor, "I am confident that Mr. Meiklejohn's misconception is not due to desire to misrepresent my views. Why, then, did the misconception occur? I venture the following explanation. Mr. Meiklejohn devotes the greater part of his article to a spirited defense of St. John's College. This fact is understandable only upon the hypothesis that he supposed that St. John's was the main objective of my criticism." Denying that St. John's had been the target of his attack on reactionary programs in higher education, Dewey thought it significant that Meiklejohn had opened his article with a reference to his long-defunct Experimental College. "The implication is that, while I was directly attacking the educational program of St. John's, I was indirectly attacking his educational philosophy. As to the former, I can say that the philosophy I criticized is so current and so much more influential than is the work of St. John's that there are only a few sentences in my article even indirectly referring to St. John's." Moreover, Dewey added, "so far was I . . . from addressing myself to the educational philosophy and experiments of Mr. Meiklejohn that I had supposed there were pretty fundamental differences between his philosophy and that reigning at St. John's."[65] While Dewey did not accuse Meiklejohn of intentional misrepresentation, he did wonder why Meiklejohn had chosen St. John's as a vehicle for criticizing his initial article and, in a larger sense, for condemning all of pragmatist philosophy.

In fact, it was *Fortune*'s managing editor who had suggested that Meiklejohn respond *not* to Dewey's specific article but to his pragmatist philosophy more generally. "It seems to me your case would be better presented if it were more a rebuttal to Dewey in general and less a rebuttal to this particular Dewey article," Ralph Paine wrote in October of 1944.[66] Unfortunately, the effect of Paine's suggestion was to pit Meiklejohn "the idealist" against Dewey "the pragmatist" in a way that left many readers befuddled as to what the two philosophers were actually arguing about. The comments of one reader, Alice van Arsdale, showed just how poorly both men came off. "Regarding the letters in the March issue of *Fortune*," van Arsdale wrote to Meiklejohn, "I most humbly dare write you to suggest what is a very elemental observation on the part of one who is, perhaps fortunately, not too interested in which 'opponent' is right or wrong. . . . The suggestion is this: when two men who are as capable of clear thinking, as are you and Mr. Dewey, 'misconceive' the meaning of the other whose writing is really very clear, then it is simply a matter of something in yourselves wholly aside from the words written—ego-reaction, I suppose the psychologists would call it."[67] Van Arsdale had hit the nail squarely on the head. The problem was not that Meiklejohn had misconceived Dewey's meaning. The problem was that he had chosen the wrong medium—the Great Books curriculum at St. John's—to express his deeply personalized criticism of pragmatist philosophy. What might have been a constructive exchange on the pedagogical and curricular challenges of undergraduate education or even a useful discussion about the clash between scientific facts and moral values in a modern secular society became, instead, an embarrassing personal tiff. Rather than debating the philosophical problems of state-sponsored democratic education or the role of collective deliberation in the formation of cultural norms—a subject on which the two men almost certainly agreed—Meiklejohn succumbed to Hook's pettiness and reduced the discussion to a ridiculous squabble over italics.

Ultimately, Meiklejohn's decision to focus his reply on St. John's limited his ability to offer a complete, or even a coherent, response to Dewey. To many, it seemed he had tried to attack pragmatism without ever talking about philosophy. It seemed he tried to criticize progressive educational theory without really discussing education. It seemed as if he tried to challenge the moral significance of the scientific method without ever talking about science. Certainly, he could not address the entire corpus of Dewey's work in one brief article for a popular magazine, but the path he chose—that of portraying St. John's as somehow representative of his own idealist philosophy—was a travesty of his long career. The effect was to present an educational idealism that seemed both reactionary and weak. By April of 1945, the debate between Meiklejohn and Dewey had degenerated into a bitter exchange with both parties speaking past one another. Clarence Ayres scolded Meiklejohn for his intransigence throughout the dispute. "You baffle me!" Ayres cried. "Knowing you as I do—indeed, as anybody should who reads Parts I, II, and IV of *Education Between Two Worlds*—I just can't see how you can attack Dewey or defend St. John's." In Ayres's view, Meiklejohn's decision to filter his critique of pragmatism through St. John's instead of stressing the deep-seated philosophical issue of valuation—that is, just how values are created through the processes of liberal education and dialectical debate—had been a profoundly regrettable mistake. "I just don't get it," he concluded, "and I get the impression that Dewey is in much the same state of mind, though probably he does not care as much as I do. For I do. I always have and always will! You mean too much to me for me to let the whole thing go down with a shrug of the shoulders."[68]

Despite Ayres's exasperated tone, Meiklejohn did not let the whole thing go down with a shrug of the shoulders. For him, the debate with Dewey had tremendous significance, not only personally, but also philosophically. He cared deeply about the problems of moral valuation and dialectics in modern liberal education. Indeed, he cared about it more than Ayres ever imagined. In February of 1945, a month after his reply appeared in *Fortune,* he discussed the clash between pragmatism and idealism in a lecture to students at St. John's. Reiterating the connection between science and the humanities that had formed the heart of his reply to Dewey, he traced the distinction between facts and values back to Kant. In the *Critique of Pure Reason,* he explained, Kant had attempted to bridge the gap between phenomena and noumena, between the empirical world of sensory experience (facts) and the rational world of conscious ideas (values). Kant's great achievement was his ability to show the link between these two realms in the transcendental categories of pure reason. Reason was both the creator and the critic of its own impressions of the world. "The essence of reason," Meiklejohn noted, was "the activity of ordering the sensuous, which has no order in itself." And the ultimate proof of reason's existence in the world, the ultimate proof that reason could both create and criticize itself, was the existence of moral behavior. "Moral activity is the bringing of order out of chaos," Meiklejohn told the students at St. Johns.[69] Morality was proof that diverse human beings ultimately shared one mind, one ethical consciousness, one general will. This belief in the unifying power of mind was the cornerstone of Kant's—and Meiklejohn's—faith in education as a morally significant endeavor. A liberal college, as a deliberative democratic community, was an institutional manifestation of humanity's rational and moral mind. The challenge of liberal democracy, therefore, was to create institutions of liberal education throughout the world so that reason and morality could flourish on a global scale.

In April of 1945, two months after Meiklejohn lectured at St. John's, representatives from fifty nations gathered in San Francisco to charter the new United Nations organization. Meiklejohn cheered the event, viewing it as the first necessary step toward the establishment of a "world-state" founded on principles of reason and democracy. "The human task, so far as men are moral and intellectual, is that of extending the scope of reasonable cooperation to its widest and deepest limits," he had written in *Education Between Two Worlds* in 1942. "The final goal of that attempt would be the creation of a world-state in which the appeal to reason would have replaced the resort to violence in the relations of all men to one another." Meiklejohn predicted the creation of some kind of "nation to include all nations" long before the United Nations became a reality. In January of 1943, he wrote an essay for *Free World* magazine titled "Education as a Factor in Postwar Reconstruction," in which he outlined plans for an international institute of democratic education for adults.[70] With teachers and students drawn from around the world, the institute would train students in history, politics, economics, literature, and philosophy so that they might understand global civilization as a unified whole. "To arrange that a world government shall be conducted by the consent of the governed implies and requires a system of world education," he argued. "A free world government is possible only if, from one end of the world to the other, free men and women are engaged in widespread, well-organized, and persistent study both of the *ends* and the *conditions* which are favorable to its realization."[71] When Meiklejohn published these ideas in 1943, the United Nations did not exist. But, as one State Department official told Meiklejohn at the time, "[S]ome day it will happen, and then you will be a prophet."[72]

Between 1943 and 1945, the adult education movement had progressed slowly toward its goal of international cooperation. The creation of the United Nations organization in 1945 gave the movement a much-needed push. In October of that year, Meiklejohn received an urgent telegram from Assistant Secretary of State William Benton inviting him to participate in a "most important" international conference on the formation of an "educational and cultural organization of the United Nations." "We very much need you as one of the advisers on the delegation to give adequate and proper representation to the United States at this crucial conference and I hope you can arrange your plans on such short notice so as to make yourself available."[73] Meiklejohn enthusiastically agreed and, at the age of seventy-three, set sail for London as one of eight advisers to the American delegation to the United Nations Educational, Scientific, and Cultural Organization (UNESCO).[74] For sixteen days, three hundred delegates from forty-four nations met to draft UNESCO's charter. When Meiklejohn left London in early November, he was filled with hope for the new organization and its potential to foster world peace. "No one who attended the London conference could fail to feel the passion, the desperate determination, which ran through all its deliberations," he effused in article for the *New York Times Magazine*. "These devotees of education, of science, and of culture had enrolled themselves as willing servants of that tremendous undertaking of world-organization which is now afoot, upon whose success or failure now hangs the balance between world-order and world-chaos, between human peace and human catastrophe, between freedom and slavery, between love and hate."[75]

For Meiklejohn, the most striking feature of the UNESCO conference was the prevalence of pragmatist "instrumentalist" thinking among the international delegates. "The instrumental view of the 'practical' responsibility of knowing and, with it, an implied condemnation of the irresponsibility of much of our current scholarship, broke out into words whenever the conference faced a vital issue," he reported. "It was fittingly expressed by a woman delegate from Norway, a pupil of Madame Curie, when she said, 'In the past, we scientists have gone into the laboratory to find the "truth." And, as we entered, we closed the door behind us to shut out "the world of men." Never again will we do that. If we are to find truth, that door must be open. There is no truth in a laboratory which has cut itself off from communication with human living.' "[76] These words struck Meiklejohn like a bolt from above. No longer insisting that education should be detached or set apart from society as a refuge for abstract ideals, he acknowledged the need to make education more accessible to all citizens, regardless of their views. No longer committed to the notion of a college isolated from society as a haven "pure and true and clean and free," he accepted a union of knowledge and politics as an unavoidable feature of modern liberal social thought.[77] As his remarks after the UNESCO conference made clear, he realized for the first time in his life that educational idealism must operate within a thoroughly practical cultural context—a context in which the primary threat to democracy was not intellectual agnosticism so much as moral and political relativism in the face of competing value claims. The challenge of the future would be to ensure that diverse voices could *all* be heard, even if their ideological positions differed.[78] The challenge, in other words, would be to protect the existence of dialectical deliberation and debate.

Meiklejohn's intellectual outlook had shifted significantly during the war, and he knew it. In the spring of 1947, he delivered the annual Howison Lecture in Philosophy at the University of California, Berkeley. Choosing Kant's *Metaphysics of Morals* as his text, he reflected on the years since his departure from Amherst. "I am," he said, adopting Kant's persona, "an investigator by inclination. I feel a great thirst for knowledge and impatient eagerness to advance, also satisfaction at each progressive step. There was a time when I thought that all this could constitute the honor of humanity, and I despised the mob which knows nothing about it. [But] Rousseau set me straight. This dazzling excellence vanishes. I learn to honor men, and would consider myself much less useful than common laborers if I did not believe this purpose could give all the others value—to establish the rights of humanity."[79] Meiklejohn, like Kant, was an investigator by inclination, and he, too, had once despised the mob. But now, as he entered the final chapter of his life, he saw with renewed clarity the true meaning of Kant's idealism. In the aftermath of World War II, "dazzling excellence" had indeed vanished, leaving a more modest, more realistic, and ultimately more reasonable goal: to establish the rights of humanity. "In the last resort," Meiklejohn said, "that is the only thing worth thinking about, the only thing worth teaching about." Already in his midseventies, Meiklejohn set his dispute with pragmatism aside and prepared for a new challenge—the defense of civil liberties in an increasingly repressive postwar society. Fortunately, he was fit for the task. "Aside from the fact that you are seventy-four years old," his doctor wrote after his annual checkup in 1946, "there is no cause for alarm. The only alarming thing is the amount of vitality you have stored away and your inexhaustible supply of enthusiasm." Advising Meiklejohn to eat less, rest more, and take frequent warm baths, his doctor told him to relax. "You should slow down and conserve some of your energy," he wrote, "for the important things which you still want to do."[80] And, indeed, Meiklejohn still had much he wanted to do.

BERKELEY

1948–1964

9

"What Does the First Amendment Mean?"

1948–1954

I N JANUARY OF 1945, the House Un-American Activities Committee became a permanent standing committee in Congress. A year
later, Attorney General Tom Clark announced the infiltration of a
"sinister and deep-seated plot on the part of Communists, ideologists, and
small groups of radicals" to overthrow the U.S. government by force. It
was in the midst of this increasingly tense postwar atmosphere that Meiklejohn drafted a short article on the importance of free speech in the twentieth century. Writing under the title "Free Speech and Justice Holmes," he
examined the extent to which "revolutionary" speech was protected under
the First Amendment. In particular, he challenged the well-known "clear
and present danger" doctrine that Justice Oliver Wendell Holmes, Jr., had
outlined in the famous case of *Schenck v. United States* in 1919. Unlike
Holmes, who had claimed that the government could regulate speech if it
posed a clear and present danger to public safety, Meiklejohn insisted that
the First Amendment was absolute in its protection of the freedom of
speech. In his words, "discussion of the public welfare can under no circumstances be abridged, however 'clear' and however 'present' the 'danger' it may appear to present to the safety of the nation."[1] Certainly, it was
a provocative thesis. Given the agitated state of postwar political culture,
Meiklejohn was not even sure he should publish it. "You told me you were
not certain that you should publish your manuscript," wrote Philip Glick
of the Yale Law School. "Of course you should publish it! You are offering the most penetrating and illuminating criticism of the 'clear and pre-

sent danger' principle that has been suggested anywhere."[2] Yet, in April of 1946, when Meiklejohn sent his work-in-progress to Harper & Brothers in New York, editor Ordway Tead suggested he wait. "I hardly know what to advise about your manuscript entitled 'Free Speech and Justice Holmes,'" Tead wrote. "Isn't it a project you can defer . . . until 1947, when I am sure you can get more favorable consideration?"[3]

Given the mounting fear of Communist subversion in the mid-1940s, Tead's recommendation was not surprising, but the delay only heightened the impact of Meiklejohn's ideas. In October of 1947, he revisited "Free Speech and Justice Holmes," giving a series of three invited lectures on that subject at the University of Chicago. He later delivered the same set of lectures, in full or in part, at Dartmouth, St. John's, and Yale.[4] In December of 1947, Tead finally agreed to publish Meiklejohn's lectures as a book under the title *Free Speech and Its Relation to Self-Government*.[5] The purpose of this book—which eventually became the most influential of all Meiklejohn's writings—was, quite simply, to encourage all Americans to study the Constitution, especially the First Amendment. "Every loyal citizen of the nation must join with his fellows in the attempt to interpret, in principle and in action, that provision of the Constitution which is . . . regarded as its most vital assertion, its most significant contribution to political wisdom," he asserted in his book's foreword. "What do 'We, the People of the United States,' mean when we provide for the freedom of belief and of the expression of belief?"[6] With this question, Meiklejohn brought the debate on the meaning of free speech into sharp and penetrating focus. What were the limits of public debate in the United States? What were the constitutional standards for legitimate political expression in a self-governing democracy? Over the next decade and a half, Meiklejohn's "absolutist" interpretation of the First Amendment led scholars, judges, and lay people alike toward a new understanding of civil liberties and a more sophisticated awareness of the legitimacy of revolutionary speech in a democratic society.

The reference to loyal citizens in Meiklejohn's foreword was no accident. In the late 1940s, the difference between loyal and subversive citizens, between patriotic and communistic organizations, between American and un-American activities, constituted a pervasive social concern. The Truman Loyalty Program, launched by executive order in 1947, made distinctions between loyal and disloyal government employees a matter of explicit federal policy. Given the contentious state of cold war geopolitics, with the United States pitted against the Soviet Union in an ideological battle to the death, Meiklejohn felt an urgent need to establish a valid theory of the First Amendment—an interpretation that supported the advocates of democracy and peace without unconstitutionally suppressing those who spoke for totalitarianism and war. According to Meiklejohn, the only valid interpretation of the First Amendment was an absolutist interpretation based on total nonabridgment. "No one who reads with care the text of the First Amendment can fail to be startled by its absoluteness," he asserted. "The men who adopted the Bill of Rights were not ignorant of the necessities of war. Out of their own bitter experience they knew how terror and hatred, how war and strife, could drive men into acts of unreasoning suppression. They planned, therefore, both for the peace which they desired and for the wars which they feared. In both cases, they established an absolute, unqualified prohibition of the abridgment of the freedom of speech." For the Founders, Meiklejohn argued, the First Amendment was unequivocal. Its meaning did not change in the face of a clear and present danger, even if that danger threatened the future of democracy itself. "To be afraid of ideas, any ideas, is to be unfit for self-government," Meiklejohn declared. "Any such suppression of ideas . . . the First Amendment condemns with its absolute disapproval."[7]

Meiklejohn acknowledged that the Constitution did not guarantee a right to speak whenever, wherever, and however an individual might choose. It did not protect a right to slander, libel, or perjure, nor did it protect a right to incite violent crimes. Meiklejohn's absolutist interpretation applied *only* to political speech that was relevant to matters of public concern. "Conflicting views may be expressed, must be expressed, not because they are valid, but because they are relevant," he wrote in *Free Speech and Its Relation to Self-Government*. "If [such views] are responsibly entertained by anyone, then we, the voters, need to hear them." In an effort to illustrate his argument, Meiklejohn pointed to the example of a New England town meeting. "In a town meeting," he explained, "the people of a community assemble to discuss and act upon matters of public interest—roads, schools, poorhouses, health, external defense, and the like. Every man is free to come. They meet as political equals. Each has a right and a duty to think his own thoughts, to express them, and to listen to the arguments of others." In order to keep the meeting from disintegrating into anarchy, participants elected a moderator whose duty it was to enforce the rules of the house. The moderator called the meeting to order, identified each speaker in turn, and adjourned the meeting when its business was done. The most important function of the town meeting was its attempt to foster open debate, to encourage the exchange of ideas, and, ultimately, to *educate* the public about matters of common social concern.

"The welfare of the community requires that those who decide issues shall understand them, and this in turn requires that, so far as time allows, all facts and interests relevant to the problem shall be fully and fairly presented to the meeting."[8] The focal point, therefore, was not so much the words of the speakers as the minds of the hearers. Every citizen had a fundamental right to *hear* all opinions and ideas relevant to the making of public decisions, and none could legitimately be excluded from the debate.[9] It was the moderator's job to ensure that all hearers heard.

Central to Meiklejohn's analysis was his distinction between public and private speech. The First Amendment, he asserted, guaranteed the public right to hear, but it did not necessarily guarantee the private right to be heard. The distinction between these two rights was essential to Meiklejohn's conception of self-government. As he had argued in *Education Between Two Worlds,* the idea of self-government made sense only if an ethical public had the institutional authority to limit private action, or, put another way, if private individuals willingly allowed themselves to be regulated by a consensual public. Meiklejohn based his separation of public and private speech on a subtle reading of the Constitution, which, in his mind, clearly distinguished a First Amendment "freedom" of public deliberation from a Fifth Amendment "liberty" of private exchange. Whereas the First Amendment offered *absolute* protection to certain public activities—speaking, printing, assembling, petitioning, or believing—the Fifth Amendment offered only *limited* protection to other private activities—such as buying or selling personal property—which could legitimately be regulated by due process of law. "Individuals have a 'private' right of speech which may, on occasion, be denied or limited. . . . So says the Fifth Amendment," Meiklejohn argued. "But this limited guarantee of the freedom of a man's ['private'] wish to speak is radically different . . . from the unlimited guarantee of the freedom of 'public' discussion given by the First Amendment. The latter, correlating the freedom of speech . . . with the freedoms of religion, press, assembly, and petition for redress of grievances, places all these alike beyond the reach of legislative limitation, beyond even the due process of law."[10] American democracy, in other words, had no authority to abridge its citizens'—that is, its own—internal right to public deliberation. To do so would undermine the very idea of self-government.

Not surprisingly, Meiklejohn's separation of the public freedom of the First Amendment from the private liberty of the Fifth Amendment raised questions among constitutional scholars. How could judges tell the difference between public and private speech? Did the Founders, especially the anti-Federalists, ever intend to write such a distinction into the Bill of

Rights? Harry Kalven, professor of constitutional law at the University of Chicago, was one of many who doubted the validity of Meiklejohn's public-private dichotomy. Some years after reading *Free Speech and Its Relation to Self-Government,* Kalven asked Meiklejohn what would happen if a majority of the public voted to nullify the First Amendment, thereby denying itself the right to free speech. "I take it," Kalven wrote, "that your position is that the regulation of speech, whatever the popular views as to its dangers at any particular time, is, under our scheme of government, permanently beyond the competence of the majority and, hence, beyond the competence of the legislatures to experiment with." In response to this statement, Meiklejohn jotted a marginal note, "Yes." However, when Kalven took his question a step further and asked if Meiklejohn's absolutist interpretation "was made once and for all time when the Constitution was adopted and is not really open to re-examination as new problems appear," Meiklejohn scribbled "No."[11] Here, in the tension between Meiklejohn's two seemingly contradictory answers to Kalven, lay the heart of his interpretation of the First Amendment. For Meiklejohn, the First Amendment, like the Constitution as a whole, was *always* open to disagreement and debate. Such openness was its greatest virtue as well as its greatest vulnerability. Precisely *because* the First Amendment was open to dissent, it was also open to the possibility of its own demise. Citizens, exercising their right to free speech, might very well advocate non-democratic forms of government. They might even go so far as to establish a totalitarian regime in place of the democratic state that gave them the right to advocate such a "revolution" in the first place. In such a situation, self-governing democracy would indeed cease to exist. Yet, as Meiklejohn had learned over his years at Brown, Amherst, the Experimental College, and the San Francisco School, the risk of self-destruction was a risk every democratic community had to take. To limit the freedom of speech in order to protect the survival of democracy—as, for example, the House Un-American Activities Committee claimed to do—was to misunderstand the very foundation of self-government.

In the last section of *Free Speech and Its Relation to Self-Government,* Meiklejohn turned from an abstract discussion of constitutional theory to a more concrete discussion of legal practice. Returning to the argument of his original article "Free Speech and Justice Holmes," he identified what he considered to be the most damaging interpretation of the First Amendment in the twentieth century: Holmes's clear and present danger test in *Schenck v. United States.* During World War I, Charles Schenck, the general secretary of the American Socialist Party, had denounced military conscription in a widely distributed circular. He was convicted under the Sedition Act of 1918, and the Supreme Court upheld his sentence. Holmes's opinion, written for a unanimous Court, set a new precedent for First Amendment jurisprudence. "We admit," Holmes stated, "that, in many places and in ordinary times, the defendants, in saying all that was said in the circular, would have been within their constitutional rights. But, the character of every act depends upon the circumstances in which it is done. The most stringent protection of free speech would not protect a man in falsely shouting 'Fire!' in a theater and causing a panic."[12] Nor, Holmes reasoned, would the First Amendment protect those who incited insubordination among draftees during war, as Schenck purportedly had done. "The question in every case," Holmes claimed, "is whether the words used are used in such circumstances and are of such a nature as to create a clear and present danger that they will bring about the substantive evils that Congress has a right to prevent. It is a question of proximity and degree. When a nation is at war, many things that might be said in time of peace are such a hindrance to its effort that their utterance will not be endured so long as men fight and that no court could regard them as protected by any constitutional right."[13] According to Holmes, Congress had a legitimate right to suppress subversive speech if it threatened to cause a clear and present danger to public safety.

In Meiklejohn's view, Holmes's opinion had been a disaster for the freedom of speech in the United States. In his words, it had "led to the annulment of the First Amendment rather than to its interpretation." Above all, it had collapsed the distinction between the First Amendment and the Fifth Amendment, giving Congress the power to limit *all* speech, both private and public, so long as it followed due process of law. Searching for the source of Holmes's blunder, Meiklejohn cited his tendency to view human behavior as an expression of exclusively personal, private, or selfish interest. "Mr. Holmes sees human society as a multitude of individuals, each struggling for his own existence, each living his own life, each saving his own soul, if he has a soul to save, in the social forms of a competitive independence," Meiklejohn wrote. "Always, therefore, he tends to interpret the constitutional cooperation of one hundred and more millions of Americans, together with the past and future generations who belong to the same community, as if they had no fundamental community of purpose at all."[14] In Meiklejohn's view, Holmes had fallen prey to the pervasive laissez-faire mentality of late nineteenth-century American capitalism. Consequently, he equated the freedom of speech with an abstract "marketplace of ideas" in which autonomous individuals fought against each other in an ongoing struggle to control the production and dissemination of truth. In fact, Holmes made the idea of an intellectual marketplace explicit in the case of *Abrams v. United States,* which the Court decided shortly after *Schenck* in 1919. Like Charles Schenck, Jacob Abrams had been convicted of advocating the violent overthrow of the U.S. government, and the Supreme Court had upheld his conviction. This time, however, Holmes dissented, defending Abrams's right to free speech on grounds that "the best test of truth is the power of the thought to get itself accepted in the competition of the market."[15]

For Meiklejohn, the notion of an intellectual marketplace had troubling implications for a self-governing society. While admitting that social truths inevitably emerge from the give and take of public deliberation, he asserted that the notion of intellectual competition, as opposed to intellectual cooperation, could easily go too far. "We Americans, when thinking in that vein, have taken the 'competition of the market' principle to mean that, as separate thinkers, we have no obligation to test our thinking, to make sure that it is worthy of a 'citizen' who is one of 'the rulers of the nation.' That testing is done, we believe, not by us, but by 'the competition of the market.' " To equate political deliberation with intellectual competition—as many pragmatists, including Holmes, had long been inclined to do—was to misunderstand the essential meaning of a democratic public. "That dependence upon intellectual *laissez-faire*, more than any other single factor, has destroyed the foundations of our national education, has robbed of their meaning such key terms as 'reasonableness' and 'intelligence' and 'devotion to the general welfare.' "[16] The primary intent of the First Amendment was *not* to protect the private interests of individual speakers in a competitive marketplace of ideas, but rather to promote the public interests of all citizens in a shared discussion of common concerns for the sake of unified intelligence and collective action. "As against the dogma of Mr. Holmes," Meiklejohn declared, "I would venture to assert the counterdogma that one cannot understand the basic purposes of our Constitution as a judge or a citizen should understand them unless one sees them as a good man, a man who in his political activity is not merely fighting for what, under the law, he can get, but is eagerly and generously serving the common welfare."[17] Holmes, by setting the supposedly public interests of the majority against the supposedly private interests of minorities, had failed to see the common interest that both groups shared in the defense of unabridged freedom for all.

For Meiklejohn, the only way to justify a faith in democracy as a form of self-government was to trust in the essential goodness of human beings, to believe in their ability to abide by shared rules of deliberation, to protect their dignity as free and morally responsible citizens. In short, the only way to justify a faith in democracy was to believe in basic human rationality. Harkening back to the ethical arguments of *Education Between Two Worlds,* and, even further, back to the moral and epistemological idealism of Kant, Meiklejohn insisted on the essential brotherhood of humanity and the "generous spirit" that led to the formation of any social compact. "We, the People of the United States, are a body politic," he wrote in the closing pages of *Free Speech and Its Relation to Self-Government.* "Under the Constitution, we are agreed together that we will be, by corporate action, self-governed. We are agreed that, as free men, politically equal, we alone will make the laws and that, as loyal citizens, equal before the laws, we will obey them. That is our social compact—the source of both our freedoms and our obligations." Did the laws of a self-governing democracy include the right actively to destroy the social compact by revolutionary force or violence? Perhaps not. Did the laws include the right to *advocate* for the destruction of the compact by force? "Certainly, yes!" Meiklejohn declared. Democracies guaranteed civil liberties not only to those who enthusiastically endorsed their laws but also to those who, if they had the power, would alter the political structure entirely. As Meiklejohn had asserted in his letter to the editor of the *Pacific Coast Weekly* in 1936, democracies protected the political rights even of Communists, fascists, and totalitarians. "Our action must be guided, not by their principles, but by ours," he concluded. "We listen, not because they desire to speak, but because we need to hear. If there are arguments against our theory of government, our policies in war or in peace, then we, the citizens, the rulers, must hear them and consider them for ourselves. That is the way of public safety. That is the program of self-government."[18]

Like Meiklejohn's other books, *Free Speech and Its Relation to Self-Government* attracted widespread critical attention. Accolades came first from Max Lerner, who applauded Meiklejohn's efforts in a personal letter to Ordway Tead. "I count Alexander Meiklejohn's book . . . among the very small number of books published this year that will live," Lerner wrote. "It is a fresh, living, and important study of the most crucial single issue in American life today."[19] Lerner's praise for Meiklejohn was not new. Twenty-five years earlier, in 1923, Lerner had heard Meiklejohn deliver a Phi Beta Kappa lecture to his senior class at Yale. "Since then," he wrote in a review of *Free Speech* for the *New Republic,* "I have found, in his half-dozen books and his tart conversation, a quality of mind which I can best express by the nickname . . . 'sabra,' which means 'prickly pear.'"

Lerner was not surprised that Meiklejohn should be the one to redirect the nation's thinking on the First Amendment. "The man who caused a turmoil at Amherst in the twenties; whose Wisconsin Experimental College produced more than a flurry in the thirties; who later ran an Adult Education School in California where he taught workers by the Socratic method using a few great Supreme Court cases as his raw material; who has carried on a sharp feud with John Dewey's pragmatic-progressive concept of education; who has dared come out for the full assumption of educational responsibility by the state, Plato-wise, at a time when the *grande peur* of our era is the fear of statism; such a man, I suggest, is unlikely to worship the phantoms of our generation or to wear anyone's intellectual blinkers—unless perchance they be his own." Whatever blinkers Meiklejohn wore, Lerner judged them minor in their effect on his book's central thesis: "the basic distinction it makes between the freedoms of the individual as an individual, which a collective society has a right to whittle down, and the freedoms of the individual as part of the whole self-governing group, which cannot be cut down without an act of selective suicide."[20] Such a thesis, Lerner concluded, was sure to endure.

The one potential liability Lerner found in Meiklejohn's argument was his distinction between public and private speech. "Where Meiklejohn is weakest is in his statement that 'private speech, or private interest in speech, has no claim whatever to the protection of the First Amendment,'" Lerner wrote. "He suggests that if you are arguing for the interest of a lobby, a corporation, a pressure group, a trade union, or seeking the advantage of a private group, then you are not guaranteed free speech, but are protected only by the 'due process' clause of the Fifth Amendment." The trouble with such an argument was that few citizens would actually admit to pursuing only their own private interests. Meiklejohn's distinction between public and private speech fell flat not only in the realm of common sense but also in the realm of traditional liberal political theory, where personal liberty always trumped group solidarity. "It is clear that this is an effort to find a new basis for 'free speech' in the philosophy of an organic society," Lerner wrote, but "it reminds me of Jean-Paul Sartre's present effort to find a 'Fourth Force' which combines the idea of communism with the idea of complete freedom." "I, too, would like to have the best of both worlds. But in the theory of free speech, it is an effort like trying to square the circle. It can't be done."[21] Like other liberal theorists of the mid-twentieth century, Lerner saw a fundamentally irreconcilable conflict between individual autonomy and institutional authority, between the political freedoms of citizens and the governing powers of a state. Synthesizing these two forces he thought was impossible. Yet, it was precisely such a synthesis that Meiklejohn hoped to achieve.

The most sophisticated technical criticism of Meiklejohn's interpretation came from Zechariah Chafee, professor of constitutional law at Harvard and the author of two influential works on the First Amendment.[22] Chafee's acquaintance with Meiklejohn stretched back even further than Lerner's. "The first time I saw the author of this book," Chafee noted in a critique of *Free Speech* for the *Harvard Law Review*, "was on an October morning forty-five years ago. With other Brown freshmen, I was emerging from the daily chapel service to find a solid mass of sophomores waiting for us outside the door. A free fight was starting when Dean Meiklejohn suddenly appeared out of nowhere, right in the center of the fray, wearing a stiff derby hat. His good-humored display of authority stopped the fight, but in the process his derby got several bad dents." Now, once again, "with similar pluck," Meiklejohn had rushed in with great confidence to settle a dispute about the meaning of the First Amendment. "Once more, the courageous vigor with which Mr. Meiklejohn dashes at contending factions excites my admiration," Chafee noted, "but his derby is likely to get a good many dents."[23] As the nation's foremost proponent of Holmes's "clear and present danger" theory, Chafee—whose own highly litigious personality qualified him for Lerner's "prickly pear" designation—put several deep dents in Meiklejohn's legal "hat." Like Lerner, Chafee challenged the distinction between public and private speech, but he focused his attack on examples of literary, artistic, and other "aesthetic" expression. Did literature constitute public or private speech? Did art, drama, and poetry fall under the protection of the First Amendment or the Fifth Amendment? Was Meiklejohn prepared to deal with the issue of obscenity?[24]

Chafee doubted that Meiklejohn's interpretation could answer these questions. "The most serious weakness of Mr. Meiklejohn's argument," he explained, "is that it rests on his supposed boundary between public speech and private speech. That line is extremely blurred." Pointing to Lillian Smith's recent and controversial novel, *Strange Fruit,* published in 1944 and banned in Massachusetts, Chafee noted that the text did not address issues formally before voters but did address the undeniably public issues of racism and miscegenation. If a majority of citizens found the subject of miscegenation objectionable, Chafee asked, then should it be illegal to discuss, either in public or in private? How did Meiklejohn's "absolutist" interpretation of the Constitution propose to separate "offensive" or "obscene" (and thus arguably private) material on the one hand from "respectable" or "decent" (and thus allowably public) material on the other? Meiklejohn acknowledged that he had not addressed these dilemmas in *Free Speech and Its Relation to Self-Government*. In fact, he had intentionally limited his thesis to political expression in order to avoid the issue of obscenity. Nevertheless, he felt compelled to answer Chafee on this point. "You take me to mean that 'science, art, drama, poetry' or 'scholarship, art, and literature' are 'private' speech and, hence, not under the protection of the First Amendment," he replied. "I do not mean that. The essential quality of these activities is that they are 'public.' The First Amendment, I am sure, intends to protect not only the immediate process of political arguing but all the intellectual and aesthetic activities which make available to us arguers, understanding and appreciation, both of the universe and of society."[25] Despite its candor, Meiklejohn's response to Chafee carefully evaded the issue of obscenity. If pressed, he might have supported the freedom to show obscene words or images in public, but he would have opposed the freedom to sell such words or images for profit. Obscene expression was a permissible public activity, but expression for profit was subject to regulation by due process of law.

To most Americans in the late 1940s, the notion that the First Amendment should protect obscene or otherwise radical speech seemed antithetical to the fight against Communism. Most Americans supported the Truman Loyalty Program as well as the House Un-American Activities Committee and found nothing problematic, let alone unconstitutional, in measures to keep evidence of the "Red Menace" at bay. They had few complaints, for instance, when the government tried to purge Hollywood and the entire motion picture industry of suspected Communist activities in 1947—a purge Chafee tacitly endorsed. "Herein lies my main objection to Mr. Meiklejohn's book," Chafee wrote in the *Harvard Law Review*. "Whereas the supporters of [government probes] are genuinely worried by the dangers of Communism, [Meiklejohn] refuses to argue that these dangers are actually small. Instead, his constitutional position obliges him to argue that these dangers are 'irrelevant.' No matter how terrible and immediate the dangers may be, he keeps saying, the First Amendment will not let Congress or anybody else in the government try to deal with Communists who have not yet committed unlawful acts." As Chafee noted, most Americans were constitutional "pragmatists," equating ends with means and believing that Congress should do everything possible to shield the country from domestic subversion. "Since Mr. Meiklejohn as a philosopher is not a pragmatist," Chafee recognized, "he would probably reply that what has just been said does not matter. If he is right in his interpretation of the Constitution, then his view is not made wrong by the fact that nobody else agrees with him. He is not trying to frame arguments which will win votes, but is seeking for eternal truth."[26] Meiklejohn could not have said it better himself. The issue was not whether the danger of Communist subversion was clear or present; the issue was whether Congress ever had a right to keep citizens from discussing it. And, in Meiklejohn's view, Congress had no such right.

Before publishing his review of *Free Speech and Its Relation to Self-Government*, Chafee debated the issue of judicial "pragmatism" in a series of personal letters to Meiklejohn. "I shall have to reject your views of constitutional interpretations and still more your objections to the positions taken by Holmes," Chafee wrote a few weeks after Meiklejohn's book came out. "These are not philosophical treatises, but judicial acts, in which Holmes wrote as a member of a group and not as if he were Kant." According to Chafee, Holmes's first priority was "to get the majority of the court with him," not to state a grand philosophical truth. "If he had taken the positions which you do," Chafee argued, "he would have written in magnificent isolation, and the cause of free speech in American law would have been much worse off than it now is." Chafee reminded his old philosophy professor that the Constitution meant whatever the Supreme Court said it meant. Unlike philosophy, democratic law did not aspire to universal principles or transcendental ideals. It had no use for metaphysical absolutes. Instead, it was a distinctly pragmatic enterprise, operating in specific historical contexts for specific social purposes. "I feel that it is not arrogant for me to suggest in this letter that you would have a greater awareness of the serious difficulties involved in your position if you had read more widely in the legal materials before you wrote your lectures," Chafee wrote.[27] But Meiklejohn was not a lawyer. He was a philosopher, a teacher, and a cultural critic. His audience was neither judge nor jury but every reasonable and intelligent citizen in America. He defended freedom not because he sought a pragmatic solution to a particular political crisis—though he certainly hoped his book would contribute to contemporary debates over civil liberties—but because he sought the truth about the nature of self-government. Whenever lawyers told Meiklejohn his arguments would be better if he "had gone to law school" (as Felix Frankfurter often did), Meiklejohn countered that lawyers' arguments would probably be better if they had gone to philosophy school.[28]

Meiklejohn's distinction between public and private speech, particularly as it pertained to a parallel distinction between political and commercial speech, was ambiguous, but its full ambiguity was not apparent until Meiklejohn entered the fray surrounding the most visible First Amendment case of the late 1940s: the case of the Hollywood Ten. In October of 1947, the House Un-American Activities Committee, under the leadership of J. Parnell Thomas, had launched a series of highly publicized hearings on the extent of Communist Party infiltration in the movie industry. Targeting such films as Warner Brothers' *Mission to Moscow* and Metro-Goldwyn-Mayer's *Song of Russia*—both of which had been made when the United States and the Soviet Union were allies during World War II—Thomas's hearings aimed to purge Hollywood of Communist sympathizers. HUAC focused its probe on ten director-screenwriters—Alvah Bessie, Herbert Biberman, Lester Cole, Edward Dmytryk, Ring Lardner, John Lawson, Albert Maltz, Samuel Ornitz, Adrian Scott, and Dalton Trumbo—all of whom were eventually blacklisted by industry executives. A year after the witch-hunt began, Meiklejohn received a letter from Robert Kenny, chief counsel for the Hollywood Ten. "Although I have been living intensively with the problems of free speech for more than a year," Kenny wrote in October of 1948, "your book has done more to clarify my thinking than all the research that I have hitherto been working on." In Kenny's opinion, *Free Speech and Its Relation to Self-Government* was "this century's most important contribution to constitutional philosophy."[29]

Over the course of the next several months, Meiklejohn became increasingly involved in the case of the Hollywood Ten. In October of 1949, he and his good friend Carey McWilliams, editor of the *Nation,* submitted to the Supreme Court a "brief in amicus curiae on behalf of the cultural workers in motion pictures and other arts."[30] Noting that American movies reached an estimated eighty-five million people a week, Meiklejohn and McWilliams asserted that films constituted an important medium of public *education* and therefore should be free from the fear-driven censorship that federal investigations promoted. Expanding his definition of public speech to include all noncommercial speech, Meiklejohn contended that films were "less important as an economic institution than as a social institution." Even if studios made money on their films, their educational value superseded their commercial value under the terms of the First Amendment. So long as movies contributed to public understanding and political debate, Congress had no right to investigate them, at least not by unconstitutional means. Central to Meiklejohn's defense of the Hollywood Ten was his contention that the House Un-American Activities Committee aggressively abridged the public's right to hear, and thus to learn from, relevant ideas presented through film. When studios

Alexander Meiklejohn, ca. 1948 (University of Wisconsin Archives, X2-5, 737, 3/1)

blacklisted directors in order to avoid external sanctions by government agencies, the implications for educational speech were serious. "As rapidly as possible," Meiklejohn noted, "censorship is extended to the entire educational system which is 'coordinated' through an attack on the concept of academic freedom and a gradual denial to students and faculty of the right to entertain unorthodox views."[31] Judging from the experiences of the Hollywood Ten, educational freedom was in serious jeopardy in the United States.

Indeed, by the time Meiklejohn wrote his brief in support of the Hollywood Ten, his worst fears about the threat to educational freedom had already come true.[32] Several months earlier, in February 1949, the University of Washington in Seattle had dismissed three tenured professors and warned three others for their alleged associations with the Communist Party. In a move that became increasingly common during the 1950s, University of Washington president Raymond Allen turned the issue of academic freedom on its head, telling reporters that the dismissed professors had "jeopardized the academic freedom of the University of Washington by becoming secret members of a clandestine party dedicated to the overthrow of American institutions of freedom." He claimed that the Communist Party exercised thought control over its members and that the dismissed faculty were "incompetent, intellectually dishonest, and derelict in their duty to find and teach the truth." According to Allen, the only way to protect innocent students from the subversive activities of Communist professors was to fire such teachers and force all others to sign an oath of political loyalty. Observing this situation from his home in Berkeley, Meiklejohn recoiled in disbelief. It was not the professors who were derelict in their duty to find and teach the truth, but the regents who fired them. In March of 1949, Meiklejohn commented on Washington's debacle in an article for the *New York Times Magazine*. Asking with his title "Should Communists Be Allowed to Teach?" he insisted that scholars must be free to follow truth wherever it might lead. "The primary task of education in our colleges and universities is the teaching of the theory and practice of intellectual freedom as the first principle of the democratic way of life," he wrote. "Whatever else our students may do or fail to do, they must learn what freedom is. They must learn to believe in it, to love it, and most important of all to trust it." Under the current policy in Seattle, every professor in the university was officially "on probation."[33]

Shortly after publishing this article, Meiklejohn heard from Professor J. Harrison at the University of Washington. "I have just read your superb statement on Communism and education in the *New York Times*," Harrison wrote. "I hasten to join the many who must be congratulating you on it. It is a great boon to those of us here who are dissenting from the action of our university administration to be supported by so cogent and eloquent an argument from one who commands such an audience as yours. More importantly, it is a service to the nation and to democracy that one clear, calm, and nationally audible voice is raised in the midst of hysteria."[34] Not everyone, however, agreed with Harrison. Foremost among Meiklejohn's critics was Sidney Hook. Paraphrasing Meiklejohn's seemingly unassailable argument that "fair and unabridged discussion" should be the university's first priority, Hook countered in quintessential cold war rhetoric: "Dr. Meiklejohn does not feel called upon to explain how 'fair and unabridged discussion' can be carried on by those who are under instruction to inject and indoctrinate party dogmas and who have clearly expressed their intention to do so by virtue of their membership in an organization which gives them these instructions and does not countenance refusal to abide by them." In Hook's view, members of the Communist Party could not enjoy the freedom of speech because, as participants in a sinister network of worldwide suppression, their speech was never free in the first place. "Dr. Meiklejohn is as wrong as anyone can be," Hook charged. "It is loyalty to the Soviet regime and not 'a passionate determination to follow the truth' which leads the Communist Party member to teach specific Communist doctrine on any specific point. [A member's] 'integrity' is expressed only in his total commitment."[35]

Hook was Meiklejohn's most outspoken critic in the 1940s, but he was not alone. George Stone, who knew Meiklejohn from his days as an undergraduate at Amherst, suspected that his former "Prexy" had been co-opted by the Kremlin.[36] Similarly, Helen McNulty, a homemaker from Philadelphia, who read Meiklejohn's article in the *New York Times,* suggested that he "should be assigned to a mental institution."[37] Meiklejohn chose not reply to such comments, but he did respond to his friend Robert Hooker, a former teacher in the San Francisco School who had since taken a job with the U.S. State Department. Like Hook, Hooker believed that members of the Communist Party relinquished their autonomy to the all-powerful authority of the Supreme Soviet. Meiklejohn, however, insisted that Communist Party membership was no different from membership in any other political group. "The strength of [Communist Party] control cannot be greater than the strength of the motivation which prompts Party membership," he wrote to Hooker a month after publishing his *New York Times* article. In Meiklejohn's view, any member of any political association had the "double experience" of "(1) loyalty to the corporate decision of the group and (2) the freedom of mind which keeps open the question of whether or not that loyalty should be maintained."[38] The second factor always qualified the first. If a party—or group or association or state—ignored its own founding principles, then its governing authority became illegitimate, and its members had both the freedom and the right to withdraw from that association and give their loyalty—their "consent"—to establish another. The notion that Communists were free to obey their own consciences and discontinue their party membership at will was essential to Meiklejohn's defense of their right to civil liberties under the First Amendment. But Hooker disagreed. He continued to insist that Communists were slaves to party mind control.

In the fall and winter of 1949, the anti-Communist purge continued. Following the lead of the University of Washington, the regents of the University of California required all faculty and staff to sign an oath of political loyalty. Unlike the professors in Seattle, however, a large number of professors at Berkeley refused. More than half, in fact, condemned the oath as a violation of their academic freedom. Almost immediately, the Berkeley faculty began to receive support from colleagues at other schools. More than two hundred teachers and administrators at Stanford sent donations to their friends across the bay. The faculty at the University of Chicago voted to take a 2 percent voluntary pay cut to sponsor a Berkeley legal defense fund. Several scholars from the Institute for Advanced Study in Princeton, including Albert Einstein and Robert Oppenheimer, encouraged Berkeley professors to resist the oath. Twenty professional societies, including the American Association of University Professors, stated their disapproval of "test oaths." More than a thousand scholars from dozens of universities signed a petition denouncing California's loyalty probe. Even in the face of such overwhelming protest, however, Berkeley's regents did not back down. They dismissed twenty-six professors, bid farewell to thirty-nine others who voluntarily resigned, and fired more than a hundred teaching assistants without so much as a word of protest from President Robert Gordon Sproul.[39] After this purge had taken place, one administrator commented that "no conceivable damage to the university at the hands of the 'hypothetical' Communists among us could have equaled the damage resulting from the unrest, ill-will, and suspicion engendered by this series of events."[40]

Living virtually across the street from the Berkeley campus, Meiklejohn found himself in the eye of the storm. Was there a way for California regents to govern the university faculty without compromising academic freedom? Could the regents monitor professors without subjecting them to external ideological control? Meiklejohn, of course, had been asking similar questions for more than fifty years, and his answers had not changed significantly in all that time. Shortly after the turmoil in Berkeley, he drafted a brief pamphlet titled *Crisis at the University of California.* "We can assess scholars without enslaving them," he wrote, only "if the assessing is done by their colleagues, by their fellow members on the faculty." Harkening back to an argument he had first made in 1923 after his dismissal from Amherst, Meiklejohn insisted that ultimate academic responsibility rested with the faculty and its duty to pursue—and teach—the truth. Responsibility did *not* rest with the regents. "In dealing with the faculty," Meiklejohn asserted, "the regents are empowered to appoint or to dismiss, to promote or to refuse promotion, to fix salaries, to assign to each member of the staff his special tasks, to define the qualifications for degrees, and to award or to deny those degrees. But, over against this 'legal' authority of the regents is a prior authority, for the sake of which alone the 'legal' authority has been established. It is the 'academic' authority of the faculty."[41] Just as citizens in a democracy possessed an original and unabridgeable right to the freedom of speech, so, too, the faculty possessed an original and unabridgeable right to the freedom of thought and teaching. These were not legal rights. They were not even political rights. Rather, as the First Amendment to the Constitution made clear, they were *pre*political rights which lay beyond the power of government—or, in this case, the regents—to restrict. Regents could control the physical and financial health of the university, but they could not control professors' minds. Only professors themselves could do that.

Most Americans did not share Meiklejohn's faith in a freedom-loving faculty. Shortly after publishing his pamphlet, Meiklejohn received a letter from his long-time friend and intellectual sparring partner, Clarence Ayres, who criticized his failure to condemn the Communist threat. According to Ayres, the Communist Party posed a genuine danger to the United States—"the danger that our devotion to freedom and fair play will be used against us, perhaps fatally." Americans, therefore, needed to stand strong against subversion, drawing a strict line between Communist beliefs and Communist behavior that might lead to violent revolution. "I feel very strongly that we must clearly dissociate freedom of thought and utterance from participation—on however small a scale—in conspiratorial activities the intent of which is the overthrow of the present social order by force and violence and substitution of the 'dictatorship of the proletariat.' That is, we must distinguish between Communism as a way of thinking (which we must defend) and membership—dues-paying in support of overtly subversive acts—in the Communist Party (which, I feel very strongly, we must not defend)." Ayres's fears stemmed from his belief, typical among Americans in the late 1940s, that membership in the Communist Party was directly related to participation in violent crimes. "I think our only chance of coming through this crisis with the freedom of thought unimpaired is by the clear dissociation of Marxist ideas from USSR-dictated acts," Ayres wrote. "Granted the sincerity and dedication of [Soviet] leaders, they are still dedicated to the extermination of you and me—and I'm against that!"[42] Ayres's vague attempt to distinguish Communist ideology from Communist actions, to separate political advocacy from revolutionary incitement, became increasingly important to Meiklejohn's interpretation of the First Amendment in the years to come.

As Meiklejohn repeatedly pointed out, the Constitution protected both the freedom of speech *and* the freedom of association, and neither could legally be abridged. Nevertheless, to most Americans living in 1950, Ayres's fear of imminent Communist invasion seemed justified. By the fall of that year, the Soviet Union had detonated its first atomic bomb, China had fallen to the revolutionary forces of Mao Zedong, and North Korea had invaded South Korea with the expressed intent of bringing the entire Korean Peninsula under Communist rule. On the home front, Senator Joseph McCarthy had flaunted his list of "card-carrying" Communists in the State Department, Klaus Fuchs had admitted that he sold nuclear secrets to Soviet agents after World War II, and Julius and Ethel Rosenberg had been arrested for the capital crime of espionage.[43] In addition, Alger Hiss had confessed to perjury in a trial that Richard Nixon identified with the most serious series of treasonable activities in American history, and Congress had passed the Internal Security, or "McCarran," Act, forbidding the establishment of totalitarian dictatorship in the United States and forcing "Communist Front" organizations to register with the Department of Justice.[44] Then, in October of 1950, California's governor Earl Warren responded to the containment policy in Korea by signing the Levering Act, which converted state employees into civil defense workers, giving them thirty days to swear under oath that they had not, in the previous five years, advocated the violent overthrow of the U.S. government.[45] Twenty professors at Berkeley refused to sign the Levering oath, and California's Third District Court of Appeals eventually ruled in their favor. Two years later, in October of 1952, California's Supreme Court declared all test oaths unconstitutional, and the *Providence Journal-Bulletin* attributed the court's decision largely to Meiklejohn. "He is not a 'former liberal,' " the *Journal-Bulletin* noted. "At seventy-nine, his colors are still

Alexander Meiklejohn with Scott Buchanan, right, and Leon Mohill, left, at a meeting of Henry Wallace's Progressive Party in Pittsfield, Massachusetts, March 28, 1949 (State Historical Society of Wisconsin, WHi [X3] 52152)

nailed to the masthead, and they are the same philosophical beliefs in freedom, social progress, and the right of unterrified teaching which have kept him in academic hot water for nearly half a century."[46]

California's decision to repeal its test oath was remarkable given the fact that, in 1952, the rhetoric of anti-Communism had set the terms for a bitterly contested presidential election. Four years earlier, in 1948, Meiklejohn had voted for Henry Wallace, though he was relieved when Harry Truman defeated Thomas Dewey at the polls.[47] This time, Truman had opted not to seek reelection, and Illinois governor Adlai Stevenson was his replacement on the Democratic ticket. While Meiklejohn never officially endorsed any political candidate, he supported Stevenson in the battle against General Dwight D. Eisenhower. "I am supporting Stevenson as the lesser evil," a like-minded friend wrote to Meiklejohn just before the election. "I greatly fear what might happen if we get Eisenhower backed by Nixon, McCarthy, et al."[48] Stevenson, however, faced a barrage of criticism for being soft on Communism. The Republicans attacked

282

the Democrats for Truman's failure to purge the federal government of subversives as well as his apparent inability to end the stalemate in Korea. Fear of Communism set the tone for the entire election, and, ultimately, more than 80 percent of the electoral votes went to Eisenhower. On November 6, 1952, Meiklejohn received a melancholy letter from St. John's president Stringfellow Barr. "This is the Morning After," Barr wrote, "and not the pleasantest one I have endured. I must now sit down (as I imagine you may be sitting down) to do a brief comment for the *Nation.* I haven't made up my mind what oracular remarks I ought to make, but I suspect I shall point out that neither candidate had a genuine foreign policy, that Stevenson allowed himself to endorse the defective one we have been following, and that this left the voters hoping that the Republican messiah would find one either by visiting Korea or by opening the Bible at random."[49] Arguably the most important factor in the Republican landslide of 1952 was the perception that Eisenhower would be even tougher on Communism than Truman had been.

In the early 1950s, anti-Communism was the undisputed key to political success. Even the American Civil Liberties Union voiced its opposition to Communism, declaring that the Communist Party was "an arbitrary and disciplined organization exercising rigid totalitarian control over the lives of its members."[50] Meiklejohn, however, disagreed. Committed to the idea that freedom of membership involved freedom of belief, he insisted that Communists must enjoy the same freedoms of association and speech that every other citizen enjoyed. Just as he had been the lone dissenter against the exclusion of Communists from the ACLU's national board of directors in 1940, so now he railed against the union's "reactionary" cold war position a dozen years later. "Whether or not one objects to the beliefs and purposes of that Party," he wrote to the union's national leaders in 1953, "the fact remains that it is a voluntary body, brought together, not by compulsion or necessity, but by the acceptance of common beliefs and purposes. Its form of organization, like that of the Union, expresses merely the defined conditions under which a group of persons choose to join together in common action. It is based not upon a forced submission but upon a willing agreement. Under that agreement, every member may expect on occasion to become a 'minority' man. . . . But so long as there is open to him a genuine option of withdrawing from the group rather than of conforming to it, . . . there is no basis for the inference that, by joining the Party or the Union, he has forfeited his intellectual independence."[51] According to Meiklejohn, citizens could join the Communists just as freely as they could join the Democrats or the Republicans. To belong to any party was to abdicate a measure of personal autonomy for the sake of membership in the group. Every "democratic" organization worked that way. To accede to the authority of a party was not to succumb to totalitarianism; it was simply to enter a collectively self-governed community.

In this position, Meiklejohn found himself at odds, once again, with ACLU president Roger Baldwin. "It is hardly necessary to tell you that I dissent sharply from the whole basis of your argument," Baldwin wrote to Meiklejohn in the summer of 1953. "I found myself reading it by substituting the Ku Klux Klan for the Communist Party, and wondering if you would make the same argument. If you distinguished between them on the ground that the KKK is characterized by overt acts, it is a hardly tenable position in view of the divergent practices of the KKK in different areas—for in some it is as law-abiding as the Communist Party."[52] According to Baldwin, both the Communist Party and the Ku Klux Klan actively suppressed the freedom of their members, who, once pledged to the organization, relinquished their ability to reject its tactics or repudiate its doctrines. But, once again, Meiklejohn disagreed. As he had written in the *Progressive* in June of 1952, neither Congress nor the ACLU needed to protect Americans from allegedly dangerous ideas or groups. "Do we Americans wish to be thus 'mentally' protected?" he asked. "If so, we have abandoned our experiment of self-government. Any man or any nation which is afraid of ideas, of any ideas, is unfit for the great venture in freedom and independence which is ordained and established in the Constitution of the United States. In protest against all these attempts, political or educational, to protect freedom by suppressing it, I wish to declare my confidence in the shrewdness, the sanity, the practical efficiency, of our American plan of self-government."[53] If Americans could not think for themselves, inform themselves, or teach themselves in cooperative institutions of political association, then democracy *deserved* to fail.

Meiklejohn's theory of democratic self-government found its clearest and most comprehensive expression in 1953, when he published an article titled "What Does the First Amendment Mean?" in the *University of Chicago Law Review*. Reiterating his idea that democracy guaranteed the freedom of speech even for those who, if they could, might destroy the institutions and even the idea of self-government, he took as his target the verdict of Justice Felix Frankfurter in the case of *Dennis v. United States*. Two years earlier, in 1951, Frankfurter had upheld the Smith Act conviction of Eugene S. Dennis, general secretary of the American Communist Party, on grounds that he advocated the overthrow of the government by violent force. Pointing back to principles outlined by James Madison and Alexander Hamilton in the *Federalist Papers* of 1787, Frankfurter had argued that no government could reasonably recognize a right to revolution or a right to incite revolution among its citizens.[54] Every government, he insisted, had a fundamental right to self-preservation. It was on this point that Meiklejohn disagreed, and he returned to the Founders to support his claim. "The 'Federalist' finds, as basic features of our American plan of government, not only the right to 'advocate revolution,' but also the right of 'revolution' itself," Meiklejohn contended. As Hamilton himself had written, "[W]henever any . . . government becomes destructive of ends (for which it was instituted), it is the right of the people to alter or to abolish it and to institute a new government, laying its foundations on such principles and organizing its powers in such form as to them shall most likely effect their safety and happiness."[55] As Meiklejohn now retold the story, elaborating on arguments first advanced in *Free Speech and Its Relation to Self-Government* in 1948, the Founders never claimed that the institution of democracy precluded the right to revolution. Rather, the very essence of democracy was the people's right to deliberate among themselves and, thus, to establish "government by consent of the governed."[56]

Meiklejohn conceded that the right to revolution was not a political right per se. He acknowledged that no government could formally recognize a right to overthrow itself. Yet, he insisted that the right to revolution existed at the heart of the Founders', and particularly Hamilton's, view of democracy. The right to revolution was a *prepolitical* right, part and parcel of the freedom to construct a mutually agreeable social compact. Indeed, the right to revolution necessarily *preceded* the formation of a democratic state. "What he is here saying," Meiklejohn argued with respect to Hamilton, "is that, if a government exists by consent of its citizens, there is implicit in it an 'original' and 'pre-political' right without which the structure of consent would be meaningless. . . . If the grounds of consent are destroyed, then the obligations of consent are destroyed with them."[57] If and when a government became "external" to its citizens and unable to express their general will, then those citizens had a right to form a new state—by violent means if necessary. Such a revolution could not be political, because, for Meiklejohn, that term implied a peaceful process of rational deliberation among citizens unified for the sake of self-government. Rather, their revolutionary struggle was extrapolitical, because it involved the death of one state—a state which, in effect, was already dead before the revolution began—and the birth of another. The right to create a new state through revolution was prepolitical, because it indicated a right to "ordain and establish" the conditions necessary for free and open—that is, rational and political—debate. Hence the validity of the American Revolution. Through revolution, a democratic state emerged as the original and institutional expression of its citizens' collective will.

Even if revolution was extrapolitical—or prepolitical—the right to *advocate* revolution fell within the realm of legitimate political discourse. "Madison and Hamilton are both convinced that the right to advocate revolution, as contrasted with the right actively to engage in it, is clearly 'political' and gives expression to a valid constitutional principle upon which the very structure of political freedom rests," Meiklejohn wrote in his article for the *University of Chicago Law Review*. "That principle, which, in the judgment of the 'Federalist,' runs throughout the Constitution, is explicitly stated by the First Amendment." At this point, Meiklejohn summarized his entire theory of the First Amendment in two profound, but deeply complex, sentences. "What it says," he wrote, "is that a government is maintained by the free consent of its citizens only so long as the choice whether or not it shall be maintained is recognized as an open choice, which the people may debate and decide, with conflicting advocacies, whenever they may choose. If the time or the occasion should ever come—as by the decision of our courts it seems now to have come—when the people of this nation are prevented by their subordinate agencies from considering and advocating and deciding whether or not to maintain the present form of our government, then, in the opinion of the 'Federalist,' that form of government has already ceased to exist."[58] In other words, a government that limited its citizens' right to advocate changes in its basic structure or operation had *already* ceased to be a democracy. Certainly, a democratic government had a right to protect itself from subversion, but *only* in ways that did not compromise the integrity of democracy itself. A democracy's right to defend itself against attack did not include the right to abridge the freedom of political deliberation as guaranteed by the First Amendment.

Meiklejohn's argument rested on the prior consent or prepolitical authority of citizens to govern themselves. In his view, all citizens shared a basic and equal status as reasonable human beings; therefore, they had an essential and inviolable right to give their consent, voluntarily, to a state which guaranteed their freedom. In this sense, their freedom of consent *preceded* the formal institutions of their government, including the legislative, executive, and judicial powers that wrote, enforced, and interpreted their laws. To claim that the freedom of citizens preceded the authority of government was to pass within a hair's breadth of Locke's theory of natural law or Dewey's theory of an organic public, both of which entailed a vague political unity *prior* to governmental power. Meiklejohn, however, repudiated any such parallel, noting that both Locke and Dewey perceived the state merely as a mechanism for balancing competitive private interests of individuals rather than the cooperative public interests of truly reasonable human beings. Reiterating the thesis of *Education Between Two Worlds,* he argued that, in a reasonable human community, the public interests of the state always took precedence over the private interests of individuals. The crucial issue was "the way in which a 'public' is generated." For both Locke and Dewey, a public was generated out of the personal interests of individuals. For Meiklejohn, a public was generated out of the collective interests of a reasonable state. Revolution, therefore, was always a two-step process. It involved, first, a "declaration of independence" from an external tyrant and, second, a "constitution" expressing the collective will and institutional authority of its self-governing citizens. As Meiklejohn explained, "[C]ontrol by a self-governing nation is utterly different in kind from control by an irresponsible despotism and to confuse the two is to lose all understanding of what political freedom is." "Free men are not 'non-governed,'" he added. "They are governed by themselves."[59]

After the publication of "What Does the First Amendment Mean?" Meiklejohn received a note from Philip Glick, professor of constitutional law at Yale. "I have just finished reading your article in the *University of Chicago Law Review* on the meaning of the First Amendment," Glick wrote. "It is one of the finest philosophical essays I have ever read, and quite definitely the clearest legal article that this or any other law review has ever published. I think you have made, with this brief essay, a fundamental contribution to constitutional law and to the political theory of democracy."[60] Supreme Court Justice William O. Douglas concurred. "You have a sharp-edged mind, and your ideas cut deep," Douglas noted. "I thought the piece you did in the *Chicago Law Review* on our *Dennis* case was one of the best pieces we have on civil liberties. I took the liberty of quoting you in my new book, *An Almanac of Liberty,* out next month. All power to your mighty pen!"[61] But Clarence Ayres, still concerned about the threat of Communist takeover, disagreed. "As you surely realize," he noted, "I can't go along with your interpretation of the *Dennis* case. . . . Surely, it is unthinkable that we should wait until the Soviet Union has begun dropping bombs (encouraged, perhaps, by the impunity their Fifth Column enjoys under our Constitution), and until Dennis and his boys have actually begun to try to take over (under circumstances which at last do constitute a clear and present danger)!"[62] Ayres's concerns about imminent Communist subversion—first expressed in 1949 and now again in 1953—were far more closely attuned to mainstream America than the comments of Douglas or Glick were. The vast majority of Americans continued to believe that subversive speech should be silenced even before it started, and they were willing to tolerate a great deal of suppression in order to assure that it was. In 1953, Meiklejohn's absolutist interpretation of the First Amendment was still but a faint voice crying in the wilderness.

Even at the age of eighty, Meiklejohn maintained a busy schedule of reading, writing, and public speaking. In the winter of 1951, he had embarked on a five-week lecture tour that brought him from his home in California to Colorado, Kansas, Missouri, Illinois, Wisconsin, Ohio, New York, Connecticut, Rhode Island, Massachusetts, Maryland, and Washington, D.C. His motives for the long tour were three: to visit friends, to share his views on the First Amendment, and, most important, to earn additional income.[63] By the time he left on his tour, Meiklejohn had been in "retirement" for nearly two decades, and, without a pension, he often struggled to make ends meet. He had never been particularly frugal, and, unfortunately, when friends offered to help, he tended to minimize his financial difficulties, which only made matters worse. As Scott Buchanan explained in November of 1952, "Meiklejohn has one peculiar trait that I admire but that prevents his friends from helping him as they would like to do. He will not admit, even to himself, any reasons for worrying about personal finances." In the early 1950s, Meiklejohn's only income was eight hundred dollars a year from the University of Wisconsin plus twenty-five hundred a year from Helen's inheritance, finally released from her stepmother. As Buchanan told Ernest Brooks at the Bollingen Foundation in New York, "[T]hey were getting along proudly and happily until recently, when inflation and a change in . . . family financial arrangements indicated necessary cuts in their standard of living, particularly the elimination of travel. I noted the effects of this in their close figuring on lecture fees and expenses whenever I expected a visit from them. On questioning, I learned the facts stated above and also learned that they had begun to refuse invitations to lecture which did not meet the expense."[64] Before long, it was an open secret that Meiklejohn needed money.

In the summer of 1953, Buchanan suggested that Meiklejohn apply to the Bollingen Foundation—recently established by Paul Mellon to support research in the humanities—for a small study grant. "I wouldn't hesitate for a moment in making an application," Meiklejohn wrote excitedly to Buchanan. "The financial strain does diminish quite a lot our working efficiency."[65] In June, Meiklejohn met with Brooks at the Bollingen office in Manhattan. Laying his work on the First Amendment aside, he returned to his earlier interest in international adult education. His application proposed a six-month trip to Europe to examine the relationships among peace, politics, and adult education in the postwar era. His goal, he tried to explain, was to "write something philosophical about the current human need to establish peace among men" and, thus, to understand the processes of cultural, intellectual, and educational "reconstruction" in Europe after World War II. Unfortunately, his plan did not appeal to Brooks. "I don't quite see why Brooks let me come," Meiklejohn reported back to Buchanan, "since his mind was made up before I arrived."[66] But Buchanan did not lose hope. He returned to Brooks and suggested that Bollingen hire Meiklejohn as a paid consultant. Meiklejohn appreciated Buchanan's efforts on his behalf but refused to accept the idea of a paid consultancy. "Bless you for looking out for me!" he replied. "You are determined to take care of me, aren't you? Thanks! Thanks! But the Spirit of Socrates rises up in me to say that I can't accept pay for talking with you. That's out. If the Foundation would give me the status of 'consultant' with you, I'd gladly accept, but only on a non-fee basis."[67] As an eighty-one-year-old Scotsman, Meiklejohn was far too stubborn to accept financial handouts from friends.

Giving up on Bollingen, Meiklejohn looked for other funding sources. "As you know," he wrote to Buchanan in the late summer of 1953, "I have, for years, been lamenting that philosophy has lost 'direction' and, hence, motivation, and, so, is doing little worthwhile. But now, if I may be permitted a bit of 'megalomania,' I seem to have found the direction again, and I want very much to study it and write about it. Philosophy is for me now the overall planning for human welfare."[68] Recalling his enjoyable experience with UNESCO a few years earlier, Meiklejohn thought he might now try to put his theory of democratic education into a more international framework. He wanted to see if his core assumption about democracy—namely, that reasonable citizens could create common institutions of mutual deliberation to govern their collective political existence—was valid on a global scale. Perhaps, he suggested, the Foundation for World Government, run by their joint friend, Stringfellow Barr, might sponsor his work. "I'd like to take a six month's trip, let us say, to Italy, Yugoslavia, France (perhaps Germany and Scandinavia), and Britain to find out what people are 'planning' and how their minds are working," Meiklejohn wrote. "Helen would go along and we'd work together. Then we'd come back and I'd try to write a 'philosophy.'"[69] It seemed an ideal plan. "Would the Foundation take me as a consultant and pay travel expenses of the trip up to some fixed sum, but without other payment?" Meiklejohn asked.[70]

Indeed, Buchanan responded, the Foundation for World Government would be delighted to sponsor Meiklejohn's trip.[71] "We decided to make you a consultant to the Foundation concerning the matters you state in your letter to me, and we are appropriating $5,000 for your expenses. This is your travel fund, and you can draw on it as you please, but our advice is that you accept a check for the full amount right now, without advance estimate, and that you give us an account of your expenditures when you have finished the trip, breaking them down roughly into transportation and hotelling. This will give you full use of the fund without taxes and will meet the auditor's scrutiny adequately."[72] Meiklejohn, who convinced himself that this grant was not charity but a legitimate research fund, was elated by the news. "The telegram came last night and made us exceedingly happy," he declared. "You have given me the chance to work that I have long wanted, and I shall do my damnedest to make sure you don't regret it."[73] Within weeks, he had sketched an itinerary, renewed his passport, scheduled inoculations for smallpox and typhoid, and booked reservations on a transatlantic steamer. On December 3, 1953, he and Helen boarded the thousand-passenger S.S. *Independence* and sailed for Gibraltar.[74] After a few weeks of relaxation in Cannes, Marseilles, and Nice, they headed for the United Nations headquarters in Geneva and then spent most of January at the Vatican in Rome. In each location, Meiklejohn tested his assumptions about the viability of democratic self-government on a global scale. His objective was nothing less than the construction of a new intellectual synthesis of democracy and education to advance the purposes of world peace in the postwar era.

Thanks to generous letters of introduction from several well-connected friends, Meiklejohn enjoyed ready access to highly placed political and intellectual leaders throughout his trip. This was particularly true in Rome, where he had long lists of references from Jacques Maritain, the famed Catholic theologian from the Sorbonne, and many more from John McCloy, the American diplomat, who knew Meiklejohn from his undergraduate years at Amherst. McCloy gave Meiklejohn entrée into business and government circles while Maritain welcomed him into the Vatican crowd.[75] As Helen reported in a letter to Buchanan's wife, Miriam, she "could have had a whirl" in Italy if only her husband had not spent so much time with philosophers. And yet, despite his extensive conversations about the prospects for global peace and self-government, Meiklejohn found both the United Nations and the Vatican somewhat disheartening. "In both cases," he noted, "we were met with friendly and even eager attempts at understanding our purpose and at meeting our need. But, in both cases, the outcome for us was a keen and rather desperate sense of the obstacles which block the way toward an understanding of the principles of peace rather than the discovery that there is a clearly marked road along which men can march together toward that goal."[76] The ideal of a unified plan for international peace—which, for Meiklejohn, involved building institutions of liberal democratic education throughout the world—seemed distant at best. How could humanity synthesize its multifarious cultural perspectives in a single understanding of the whole? How could a world split by ideological conflict build institutions to create meaningful connections between otherwise isolated individuals and groups? By the time the Meiklejohns left Rome in late January, they began to doubt the feasibility of global peace education in a cold war context. Certainly, the frigid weather did not help their mood.

From Rome, via Venice, it was on to Belgrade. "We arrived in Belgrade one icy morning at 5:30 a.m., and our friends, the Cohens, met us," Helen explained to Miriam. The Cohens of Belgrade were the same as the Cohens of Berkeley who had worked with the Meiklejohns twenty years earlier in the San Francisco School of Social Studies. In 1952, Myer Cohen and his wife, Elizabeth, had assumed leadership of the United Nations Technical Assistance program in Yugoslavia, which was at that time an anti–Soviet Communist dictatorship under the rule of Josip Broz Tito. As Helen later reported, "Myer and Elizabeth were bound that we should get as close as possible to this *amazing* experiment in anti–Soviet Communism, and we are enormously grateful to them."[77] Throughout their three-week stay in Belgrade, the Meiklejohns observed Tito's "experiment" in close and intimate detail, and it renewed their faith in the future. Helen especially admired what she perceived as Tito's progressive economic reforms. "It isn't often you get a chance to see a country in the white-heat of transformation as we are doing here," Helen wrote. "Their guiding principle is decentralized and local autonomy, and their general watchword is 'whatever Russia does, let's do it differently.' "[78] Besides the social and economic issues that fascinated his wife, Meiklejohn took a keen interest in Yugoslavia's rapidly developing educational system. "Alec did a perfectly stunning job of stating the educational needs of the country as he sees them to Tito's *Chef de Cabinet*," Helen told Miriam.[79] As Meiklejohn saw it, Tito's greatest challenge was that of fusing six very different regions—Bosnia, Serbia, Croatia, Slovenia, Montenegro, and Macedonia—into a single unified state.

Scribbling in his notebook, he observed that Yugoslavia's political and educational success depended on its adherence to two complementary principles—the same complementary principles he identified with any self-governing community in which diverse groups coexist. First, he observed that every "individual, joining a group, must be willing to accept and support in action decisions with which he does not agree." Second, he emphasized that the "group must allow [each individual] to disagree freely."[80] These twin principles of state authority and individual liberty were essential to any democracy, but, in 1954, it was still too early to tell if they would take hold among the diverse peoples of Yugoslavia.

All in all, Meiklejohn expressed great enthusiasm for Tito's work. "The Yugoslav thing is intensely exciting," he commented in a letter to Corliss Lamont, an ardent supporter of international Communism. "We were brought at once in close and familiar touch with high government officials and with foreign ambassadors and the resulting conferences left us breathless but eager for more. They are trying to work out Communism with an amazing degree of flexibility, and their hatred of the Soviet regime colors everything they do." Meiklejohn admired Yugoslavia for its rapid progress but recognized that Tito's dictatorial leadership blocked the path to democratic self-government. Particularly troubling was the case of Milovan Djilas, who had urged Tito to promote "democratic" reforms, only to be purged from the party and, later, imprisoned. When Meiklejohn asked about Djilas's fate, a number of Yugoslavian officials turned the issue back on him and asked about Senator Joseph McCarthy's anti-Communist purge in the United States. "One of my best experiences," Meiklejohn reported to Lamont, "was a seminar with a Youth Organization group where we first discussed McCarthyism and then they asked me, as a philosopher, to criticize their Marxism. I did, and a free fight was had by all."[81] Meiklejohn mailed this letter just as news of the infamous Army-McCarthy hearings reached Europe. "We follow the 'McCarthy' news eagerly day by day, and the papers make much of it," Meiklejohn reported in a subsequent letter to Lamont. "It would seem (1) that the President must soon stand up and fight and (2) that, whether he does or not, the Republican Party's unity must be badly broken before the November elections. That's good, too!"[82] Much to Meiklejohn's disappointment, however, Eisenhower did not stand up to McCarthy, and the Republican Party did not suffer at the polls.

On February 3, 1954, Meiklejohn celebrated his eighty-second birthday with a vigorous hike through deep snow along the outskirts of Belgrade.[83] The outing was an adventure but also a mistake, because, a week later, Meiklejohn suffered noticeably from fatigue. Two months of traveling in freezing wet weather brought a painful case of bursitis to his right arm. "We arrived very tired," Helen reported to Miriam from France, "and Alec has been fighting a cold and sleeplessness, so we have to let up a bit. But we both agree that Yugoslavia was worth a setback. I must say, everything seems a bit flat after that experience."[84] In an attempt to regain some of their energy, the Meiklejohns stayed for seven weeks at the posh Hotel Castigliani in Paris, devoting most of their time to the Department of Philosophy at the Sorbonne. They heard several lectures about the emerging existentialist movement, particularly the works of Jean-Paul Sartre and Albert Camus. Meiklejohn appreciated existentialism's quest for freedom in the realm of subjectivity but suspected a "strange pair of assertions" in the existentialists' work. Noting Sartre's belief that the "freedom of the individual is subjectivity, belonging wholly to himself," he wondered how the existentialists could also claim that "to will to be free is to will that all men shall be free." Seeking to resolve this contradiction between subjective and objective human freedom, Meiklejohn thought Sartre's conception of a universal "Fourth Force" must involve "some theory of moral objectivity as present in subjectivity." For Meiklejohn, the most appealing part of existentialism was its tenaciousness and perseverance in the face of seemingly insurmountable obstacles. "Human nature has (effectively) more than desires," he jotted in his travel notebook. "It has the capacity of hanging on by its teeth, if need be, in dreadful agony, to a purpose which it does not 'desire' but does 'choose.'"[85] These words were appropriate, not only for Meiklejohn's continued insistence on the validity of liberal democratic peace education in a fragmented postwar world, but also for his insistence on the need to keep a strict schedule of activities even after twelve weeks of grueling winter travel.

In mid-March, Meiklejohn left Paris for London, where he promptly acquired a case of insomnia and an extended bout of nervous tension. "The strain of hotel life since December has been very heavy, and we are tired," he wrote to his friend Clark Foreman back in Berkeley. "Now, however, we have taken a little flat, and we are hoping for easier times."[86] But easier times did not follow. With his trip more than half over, Meiklejohn pressed on with a full calendar of visits, interviews, and other events. He met with Bertrand Russell, Isaiah Berlin, and Sir Richard Livingston in London, taking only a brief break to watch a cricket match between England and Pakistan. Returning to work, Meiklejohn kept his focus on the issues of peace education and social planning, following closely a proposal to combine elite grammar schools and open-enrollment state schools into one comprehensive system. "The London experience has been by far the richest," Meiklejohn commented in a letter to Scott Buchanan. "A good deal of our interest in recent weeks has gone to the lively discussion of school reform initiated by the 1944 Education Bill. A sharp fight is raging round the 'comprehensive school,' which is Labour's suggestion for bringing all classes into one school so that the division by exams between 'scholars' and others at eleven or a bit later can be overcome. It's all incredibly complicated, and the English will not, of course, formulate their purposes or convictions. So you have to watch what they do."[87] A few weeks later, after a brief trip to Oxford and another to Leeds, Meiklejohn's research was done. Although he had not found evidence of extensive political cooperation *among* nations, at least he had found evidence of active reform *within* nations, particularly in Yugoslavia. It was not the grand international synthesis he had hoped to discover, but neither was it the total negation of his vision for global democracy and world peace. What struck him most of all was the great distance still to be traveled before the meaning of self-government would be clear.

Boarding the *S.S. Atlantic* in June of 1954, Alec and Helen finally headed for home. A week later, they docked safely in New York, a half-year's journey behind them. Starting west by train, they took a northerly route through Montreal and Chicago en route back to Berkeley, where they hope to spend several weeks recuperating from an exhilarating but also exhausting trip. As it happened, they spent their time recovering from something else entirely. Helen related the story to Miriam Buchanan. "We left Chicago at 6:00 p.m. Thursday on the 'City of San Francisco,'" she wrote. "Alec felt fine and ate a good breakfast. During the morning, he said his abdomen felt sore, though there was no pain. He took only tea and soup for lunch. By evening, the situation was about the same—no pain, no nausea, no fever, only soreness. I thought it . . . wise to consult a doctor and we found one on board. He said at once, 'Appendicitis.' Alec and I were *amazed* and didn't trust his judgment, but we were taking no risks so we telegraphed our doctor to meet us at the station."[88] Waiting in the emergency room at Alta Bates Community Hospital in Berkeley, Meiklejohn phoned his son, Gordon, an internist, and asked his medical opinion. Gordon recommended that Meiklejohn see a certain Dr. Clausen, one of the top gastroenterologists in northern California. An hour later, Dr. Clausen arrived and, after a brief abdominal exam, concluded that Meiklejohn's appendix had to go. Despite Meiklejohn's advanced age, he came through the four-hour operation in fine form and was home within five days.[89] A few weeks later, he wrote to Scott Buchanan. "The recovery (physiological) has been perfect," he stated. "My muscles are fine, but my nervous tone comes back very slowly."[90] Even if Meiklejohn's physiological recovery was quick, his emotional recovery was not. The experience of emergency surgery after a major international tour only reminded him that, at the age of eighty-two, he was not getting any younger.

In December of 1954, six months after his return from Europe, Meiklejohn sat down to record his thoughts on the trip. His illness must have put him in a melancholy mood, because he had little optimism about the prospect for global peace. "I had been asked by the Foundation for World Government to try to write something 'philosophical' about the current human need to establish peace among men," he scrawled. "I was told that what was wanted was not a description . . . of actual or possible political, economic, or social arrangements among nations, but an attempt to discover—and so far as possible to make clear—the moral and intellectual presuppositions which must underlie any intelligent consideration of such arrangements." His aim, in other words, was to devise an educational philosophy for international peace, and it was a onerous task. He wrote page after page of draft material, trying to make sense of his travels, but found himself even more "helpless and inarticulate" than he had been before he left. Now that the time had come to clarify the "moral and intellectual presuppositions" of a "reasonable society," he began to question the basic usefulness of philosophy as a critical intellectual endeavor. How could individuals in such a diverse and divided world agree on the purpose of liberal education or the institutional structures most likely to promote its aims? How could nations agree on the best route to global self-government? These were questions Meiklejohn had asked before, but he still had not found conclusive answers. "Though the question presented had been my major concern throughout my long career of teaching," he confessed, "I could not find, when challenged to discuss the question, any clear or significant statement to make."[91] Asking if three major wars—World War I, World War II, and the cold war—had perhaps nullified his life's work, he wondered if he could ever regain a sense of idealist hope for the future. And yet, he refused to quit. He refused to abandon his search for a modern intellectual synthesis founded on the presumption of a rational humanity. He refused to turn his back on the need for collective deliberation in a self-governing democracy. At the age of eighty-two, he realized that his final task would be to rebuild his faith in the possibility of a truly ethical community in an increasingly, and perhaps irreversibly, fragmented world.

10

"The Faith of a Free Man"
1955–1964

MEIKLEJOHN'S EUROPEAN TOUR coincided with a series of important political events in the United States, foremost among them the Army-McCarthy hearings, which exposed on national television the arrogance, irresponsibility, and perhaps even drunkenness of Senator Joseph McCarthy. In November of 1954, the Senate condemned McCarthy, asserting that his reckless investigations of unproven subversion threatened "to bring the Senate into dishonor and disrepute, to obstruct the constitutional processes of the Senate, and to impair its dignity." Though McCarthy was allowed to keep his seat in the Senate, his fall from grace—and his early death three years later—opened new possibilities for the defense of civil liberties in the mid-1950s. In the spring of 1955, six months after the Army-McCarthy hearings began, the Senate Judiciary Committee began an inquiry into the ongoing abuses of the House Un-American Activities Committee. Senator Thomas Hennings, Jr., a liberal Democrat from Missouri, chaired the Senate's Subcommittee on Constitutional Rights and asked Meiklejohn and three other experts to testify on the meaning of the First Amendment, specifically as it pertained to HUAC's controversial work.[1] On November 14, 1955, Meiklejohn accompanied Zechariah Chafee—along with Thomas Cook, a law professor at Johns Hopkins, and Morris Ernst, an attorney who had reviewed Meiklejohn's *Free Speech and Its Relation to Self Government* for the *Saturday Review of Literature*—to a series of public hearings in the (ironically named) McCarthy Room of the U.S. Capitol building. The Hennings hearings gave Meiklejohn an opportunity to restate his absolutist interpretation of the First Amendment and, at the same time, to set the stage for a nationwide movement to abolish the House Un-American Activities Committee.

On the morning of his subcommittee appearance, Meiklejohn repeated his conviction that Congress had no right to silence citizens suspected of holding radical or revolutionary beliefs, even if those beliefs were associated with the Communist Party. "The most troublesome issue which now confronts our courts and our people," Meiklejohn stated, "is that of the speaking and writing and assembling of persons who find, or think they find, radical defects in our form of government and who devise and advocate plans by means of which another form might be substituted for it." The First Amendment, he continued, "does not protect either overt action or incitement to such action. It is concerned only with those 'political' activities by which, under the Constitution, free men govern themselves." Turning to the difference between *advocacy* and *incitement,* Meiklejohn drew a subtle line separating these two closely related categories of speech. "An incitement is an utterance so related to a specific overt act that it may be regarded and treated as a part of the doing of the act itself—if the act is done," he argued. Incitement, therefore, could be legally regulated if proven to be a direct cause of criminal action. "An advocacy, on the other hand, even up to the limit of arguing and planning for the violent overthrow of an existing form of government, is one of those opinion-forming and judgment-making expressions which free men need to utter and to hear as citizens responsible for the governing of the nation."[2] Advocacy, therefore, was completely immune to congressional investigation. Acknowledging that the line between incitement and advocacy, between planning and preparation, was almost inscrutably narrow, Meiklejohn nevertheless believed that a valid interpretation of the First Amendment depended fundamentally on the precision with which that line was drawn. In his view, the Constitution protected speech up to the point of advocacy so long as it did not incite overt violence against the state. Moreover, incitement was impossible to prove until *after* such violence had occurred.

Meiklejohn's distinction between advocacy and incitement, like his distinction between public and private speech, worried some constitutional scholars. Harry Kalven, for example, doubted the validity of Meiklejohn's distinction between words on the one hand and actions on the other. "I wonder how sharply you mean to distinguish between advocacy of revolution and incitement to revolution," he queried even before Meiklejohn testified in Congress. "In your analysis, could verbal conduct alone amount to incitement and, if it did, could it legitimately be punished by the state?"[3] To this pivotal question, Meiklejohn replied that words, or verbal conduct alone, never amounted to incitement as such. Only words linked directly to criminal action could be considered illegal under the First

Amendment, and, in Meiklejohn's view, such a *direct* linkage between words and actions was virtually impossible to establish beyond a reasonable doubt. Yet, according to John Frank, professor of constitutional law at Yale, Meiklejohn's narrow line between advocacy and incitement rested on the very "proximity" test that Justice Oliver Wendell Holmes used to establish his theory of clear and present danger in the *Schenck* case of 1919. "Your own suggestion," Frank wrote to Meiklejohn, "is that incitements should be controlled on a sort of 'time' or 'proximate' basis—i.e. 'incitement to violation of law can be punished . . . when the incitement is close enough to the act committed to become in effect a part of it.' As you yourself suggest, this is a theoretical statement because in no real sense is one 'act' part of another act with such precision that legal rights can be made to depend upon it. But, is not the fact of the matter that you are meaning to forbid speech which gives a 'clear and present danger' that lawlessness will result?"[4] In Frank's opinion, Schenck's antidraft circular was part of the act of criminal insubordination and therefore posed a clear and present danger to national security. But Meiklejohn disagreed. In his view, words were not punishable until they actually *became* violent actions—an ontological transformation he could scarcely imagine.

To some extent, Meiklejohn's distinction between words and actions derived from his undergraduate study of philosophy. Just as the medieval nominalists had rejected any direct ontological relationship between words—say, the words of the Holy Scripture—and actions—say, the Resurrection of Jesus Christ—so Meiklejohn rejected any direct metaphysical or legal connection between the words of Communist doctrine and the actions of Communist revolution. For nominalists, biblical words functioned only as *symbols,* expressing and signifying, but never actually being, the essence of divine action in the world. Words made actions intelligible, but words themselves were ontologically different from actions. Similarly, for Meiklejohn, language operated as a web of political meaning, referring to significant beliefs, hopes, and aspirations, but it did not constitute a physical activity per se. In Meiklejohn's view, language could be politically hateful or even emotionally hurtful in its meaning, but it could not, in and of itself, constitute violent physical force. Unfortunately, Meiklejohn never took time fully to articulate the philosophical origins of his distinction between words and actions. Consequently, he faced a barrage of questions from constitutional scholars. As John Frank wrote in 1949, "[I]t is this 'force and violence' problem, not the problem of truly peaceful advocacy, which seems to me to need your full attention. In short, what arguments have you to address to the honest citizen who believes, as a matter of fact, that Communists will overthrow the government by force if they get the chance?"[5] Meiklejohn probably would have replied that peaceful advocacy was a political right guaranteed by the First Amendment while revolutionary incitement, even to the point of promoting or encouraging overt violence, constituted a *pre*political right implicitly expressed in the Declaration of Independence. In either case, Congress had no authority to abridge citizens' freedom of speech.

Meiklejohn's attempt to resolve these interpretive questions was timely, for the Hennings hearings marked the beginning of a brief liberal revival in the mid-1950s. Buoyed by the condemnation of Senator McCarthy and the relative calm of global affairs after the Korean War, the Supreme Court took a mild stand against HUAC's most outrageous violations of the First Amendment. Two pathbreaking decisions, both issued in 1957, indicated a leftward shift in the political orientation of the Court.[6] The first involved Oleta Yates, California state secretary of the Communist Party. In the summer of 1951, the FBI arrested Yates and eleven other Communists for violating the Smith Act. Yates's case went all the way to the Supreme Court, where Chief Justice Earl Warren, who had been the governor of California at the time of Yates's arrest, wrote the majority opinion. Warren ruled that the Smith Act's prohibition against revolutionary advocacy pertained exclusively to actions and not to mere associations or beliefs. Therefore, Yates's membership in the Communist Party was deemed perfectly legal under the First Amendment, and her conviction was reversed. The second major decision of 1957 involved John Watkins, a labor organizer with the United Auto Workers. In 1954, HUAC asked Watkins to testify against thirty of his friends who were suspected of belonging to the Communist Party. Watkins refused. Consequently, in a move that became commonplace by the mid-1950s, HUAC held him in contempt and ordered him to pay a substantial fine. When the case reached the Supreme Court, Warren again wrote for the majority with Justices Black and Douglas concurring. He ruled that HUAC could investigate Watkins's political activities but had no right to *compel* his testimony with the threat of a fine. Overturning Watkins's conviction, Warren asserted that "there is no congressional power to expose for the sake of exposure."[7] As astute Court-watchers noted, Warren's distinction between revolutionary actions and political beliefs, particularly in the *Yates* case, set a new and virtually unattainable standard for proving criminal incitement in future Smith Act cases.

For Meiklejohn, the *Yates* and *Watkins* decisions marked a personal triumph and a high point in his effort to clarify the meaning of the First

Amendment. Even John Frank, who earlier challenged Meiklejohn's interpretation, conceded the correctness of his view. "In last Monday's Supreme Court opinions, in the case of *Yates,*" Frank wrote to both Helen and her husband, "Justices Black and Douglas for the first time expressly and in some detail adopted Alex's theory of the First Amendment with express reference to him by name. This pleased me very much. You may recall that my own review of Alex's book was inclined to be somewhat favoring the 'clear and present danger' approach. Upon more mature consideration, I am now much more inclined to think that you were right and I was wrong."[8] Unfortunately, however, the celebration did not last long. A few days after the Supreme Court released its opinions in the *Yates* and *Watkins* cases, Meiklejohn received a letter from Frank Wilkinson, a friend from the Emergency Civil Liberties Union of Southern California. Wilkinson noted that HUAC was paying very little attention to the Court's most recent rulings. "We must withhold our joy in the Supreme Court decision in California's Smith Act cases and in the *Watkins* case with the awful news that the brilliant cancer research scientist at Stanford, William K. Sherwood, took his own life after receiving a subpoena for tomorrow's San Francisco hearings," Wilkinson wrote.[9] Before Sherwood ingested the fatal poison, he left a suicide note asserting that HUAC's upcoming investigations at Stanford were "strewn with blasted lives, the wreckage of useful careers."[10] As Wilkinson correctly observed, many members of Congress, even if they opposed HUAC and its tactics, shied away from challenging its authority for fear that their own political loyalty might come under suspicion.

In the summer of 1957, Wilkinson began the National Campaign to Abolish the House Un-American Activities Committee. One of his first projects was to solicit from Meiklejohn a "petition for redress of grievances" against the committee.[11] "Yes," Meiklejohn wrote to Clark Foreman, one of Wilkinson's colleagues on the Emergency Civil Liberties Committee, "I agree that I had better have a try at writing an appeal to Congress to put an end to the Committee practices. It should be, I think, a very simple, direct statement, and brief. But the essentials should be in it, too."[12] Over the next few months, Meiklejohn put his petition through several drafts. "I'm surprised to find how easily my attempt is working out," he wrote to Foreman in July. "I only hope it is as good as it is quick."[13] Exercising his First Amendment right to solicit Congress for a redress of grievances, Meiklejohn focused his petition exclusively on HUAC's tendency to intimidate witnesses in order to compel their testimony. "The attempt to 'compel testimony' in the area of the First Amendment has proved to be in actual practice not only unconstitutional but also ineffectual or harmful," Meiklejohn argued. "In these cases, the Committee has known in advance of its inquiry that the information asked for would not be given. And, for this reason, the only significant outcome of the Committee's use of coercion has been that of 'exposing' to public calumny and to private disaster citizens of the United States against whom no charges of unlawful action have been proved or even legally made."[14] Citing *Watkins,* Meiklejohn asserted that HUAC's tactics had effectively undermined its charter of 1938 and rendered it undeserving of further congressional appropriations. He petitioned the House "either (1) to decide against continuing the mandate of the Committee on Un-American Activities or (2) to so modify that mandate as to deny to the Committee any authority to 'compel testimony' concerning the 'beliefs, expressions or associations' of its witnesses."[15]

Shortly after Meiklejohn sent the first draft of his petition to friends, Wilkinson went to Washington to gauge its potential effect in Congress.[16] One of the first people Wilkinson interviewed was Congressman Roy Weir of Minnesota, who had voted six times to cut the annual appropriation to HUAC. "Will it help if we organize a national campaign, if Dr. Meiklejohn and others initiated petitions to Congress?" Wilkinson asked. "Sure," Weir responded, "of course it will help." Weir added, however, that "you've got a very BIG job on your hands if you want ABOLITION. You've got my vote, of course, but remember the boys are thinking about self-perpetuation. Right now they think that a vote against HUAC is going to be used against them back home." Senator Joseph Clark of Pennsylvania was even warier than Wier. "The climate here is such that a petition—as fine as Dr. Meiklejohn's is—may be less effective because it comes from one who is somewhat controversial—than would be the case if it could come from a coalition of forces, say, with the ACLU and with labor." According to Clark, Meiklejohn's reputation was too radical to win the centrist support needed to abolish the House Un-American Activities Committee. Representative James Roosevelt, son of President Franklin D. Roosevelt, agreed with Clark. "Remember," Roosevelt told Wilkinson, "Meiklejohn, Robert Hutchins, my mother, and the people in the American Friends Service Committee—all do little more than 'prick' the public conscience. They can't organize an effective campaign of public movement because they are all too 'labeled.' " Roosevelt supported the abolition of HUAC but thought Meiklejohn's petition needed signatures of a more moderate bent. "Get a George Meany, not a Walter Reuther," he said, referring to the leaders of the recently merged AFL-CIO, "a Judge

Learned Hand," he added, mentioning the most respected member of the Second Circuit Court of Appeals, "not a Meiklejohn."[17]

Despite these warnings, Meiklejohn submitted his petition to Congress in December of 1957. The following April, he received a note from Howard Smith, chairman of the House Committee on Rules. "No action is scheduled by the Rules Committee on your petition at this time," Smith explained, "and, in view of the large number of measures pending before the Committee, it is very doubtful that any action will be taken."[18] The Rules Committee presented an obstacle to Meiklejohn's petition, but a much bigger hurdle was presented by the launching of the Soviet satellite *Sputnik* a few weeks earlier. Raymond Fosdick of the General Education Board noted that Meiklejohn's petition simply came at a bad time. "With the Russian satellite soaring overhead and a new wave of hysteria beginning to mount, there is now no chance that the House will abandon its Resolution of 1938," Fosdick observed. "The most we can hope for, I believe, is that the *Watkins* case will curb some of the excesses of the Committee. Do I sound pessimistic? I am. This is not my generation, and events are moving far too rapidly for easy orientation. While some of these [events] could open up a glorious future, I am not at all confident that human intelligence is geared to the task."[19] Fosdick, like most Americans, viewed the launching of *Sputnik* as cause for serious alarm, but Meiklejohn cheered the event. "Hurrah for *Sputnik!*" he exclaimed in a letter to Scott Buchanan. "We'll never get wise to ourselves until we suffer sharply and deeply, and I suppose our most secretive spot is on pride of achievement, our superiority in getting ahead and smartly taking the lead."[20] Perhaps, Meiklejohn hoped, *Sputnik* would show Americans how far they had to go before realizing their highest social and political ideals.

Disappointed, but not discouraged, by the failure of his petition, Meiklejohn turned his attention in 1957 to other matters. Shortly after celebrating his eighty-fifth birthday, he published a series of essays under the title *Education for a Free Society*. Then, that summer, he attended the twenty-fifth anniversary of the closing of the Experimental College, held on the campus of St. John's College, in Annapolis.[21] Meiklejohn took great pleasure in seeing his former students and advisers and hearing what they had done with their lives. He especially appreciated hearing how much they still valued their experiences in Adams Hall. They resumed old debates about Athens and America almost as if they were still in Madison. Not long after the "guinea pig" reunion in Annapolis, Meiklejohn continued his tour of the East Coast with a trip to Amherst, where he witnessed the unveiling of his presidential portrait in Johnson Chapel. Again

Alexander and Helen Meiklejohn at a reunion with advisers from the Experimental College held at St. John's College in Annapolis, Maryland, 1957. Delos S. Otis is in the first row; Paul M. Herzog, John Walker Powell, and Malcolm Sharp are in the second row; H. H. Giles, Paul Raushenbush, and Ralph Crowley are in the third row (all appearing from left to right) (University of Wisconsin Archives, 11/10/1)

he was delighted to discover that his ideas were still in action. Amherst's current president, Charles Cole, had recently established a new curriculum modeled closely on the interdisciplinary Social and Economic Institutions courses that Meiklejohn had initiated in 1915. For Meiklejohn, the opportunity to see Amherst incorporating so many of his reforms was deeply heartwarming. It showed him that, even as a "minority man," he had perhaps been a prophet, far ahead of his time in envisioning solutions to the enduring problems of liberal education. Others seemed to think so, too. As one Amherst alumnus noted, "[O]ne of the most important trustees admitted on his death bed that they had made a mistake. Twenty-three years after [Meiklejohn] left, the college adopted *his* curriculum."[22]

Alexander Meiklejohn with his son Donald, ca. 1955 (State Historical Society of Wisconsin, WHi [X3] 52011)

Besides witnessing the belated adoption of his educational programs, Meiklejohn also had a chance in 1957 to clarify his views on the First Amendment, particularly on the subject of censorship. In his defense of the Hollywood Ten in 1949, he had argued that Congress had no constitutional authority to investigate any medium of public education, including film. Now, eight years later, he turned his attention from Congress to the people, asserting that citizens, acting as individual participants in public debate, had a right, and even a responsibility, to criticize, denounce, and call for the suppression of any material they found objectionable. On this point, Meiklejohn stood in direct opposition to the ACLU, which asserted that *all* censorship, whether it was sanctioned by Congress or by individual citizens, violated constitutional rights. The ACLU, for example, took a strong stand against book bans imposed by local parent groups. But, once again, Meiklejohn disagreed. "The First Amendment is emphatic in its requirement that Congress as a corporate body shall do no censoring," he wrote. "But the Amendment, on its positive side, expresses the demand that citizens, as they engage in the give-and-take of free discussion, shall have unhindered authority, not only to express their own beliefs, but also to criticize and to condemn, as well as to approve of, the beliefs of their fellow [citizens]." Acknowledging that, in some cases, citizens might be foolish, ignorant, prejudiced, or even bigoted in their attempts at public censorship, Meiklejohn argued that "such acts of unwisdom by individuals and groups should [simply] be opposed and exposed by other individuals and groups with all the power which the freedom of discussion provides." To organize for the expression of public concerns was to demonstrate a capacity, however imperfect, for "the judgment-making authority upon which the entire structure of free institutions rests."23

Meiklejohn's reiteration of his basic faith in the sagacity of public deliberation came at a crucial moment. In 1959, the Supreme Court issued a decision that seemed to undermine all the progress that had been made in *Watkins* and *Yates*. This time, the trial involved Lloyd Barenblatt, a thirty-one-year-old professor fired from his position in the English department at Vassar College. In 1954, HUAC had summoned Barenblatt and asked him, under threat of imprisonment, if he had ever been a member of the Communist Party. Barenblatt, like Watkins before him, refused to answer, and his case eventually reached the Supreme Court. In a hotly debated five-to-four decision, Justice John Harlan, joined by Justices Clark, Whittaker, Stewart, and Frankfurter, concluded that HUAC had done nothing wrong in calling Barenblatt to the witness stand, even if the stigma of his summons resulted in the loss of his job. The query, Are you or have you ever been a member of the Communist Party? was deemed directly pertinent to the investigative powers of Congress, regardless of its effect on the professional well-being of the witness. Far more significant than Harlan's majority opinion in the *Barenblatt* case was the dissenting opinion of Justice Hugo Black, in which Justices Warren and Douglas concurred and which Justice Brennan supported in a dissent of his own. In Black's view, Harlan had completely missed the point of Barenblatt's defense. His refusal to answer HUAC's question rested *not* on a Fifth Amendment protection against self-incrimination but rather on a First Amendment protection of the right to free speech—or, in Barenblatt's case, the right to silence regarding his past political associations.[24] Under *Yates*, membership in the Communist Party was not illegal; yet, when HUAC asked, "Are you a member of the Communist Party?" any answer in the affirmative amounted to legal suicide. Barenblatt had chosen the only option available to him—silence. In this way, he intended to show that the First Amendment prohibited Congress from investigating, or at least openly asking about, citizens' political associations. Under the First Amendment, possible associations qua associations were *always* legal.

Barenblatt based his defense on the protections of the First Amendment rather than those of the Fifth Amendment because he wanted to show that Congress had no right to scrutinize political associations with the aim of exposing and then prosecuting activities deemed un-American. His defense was not about protection against self-incrimination; it was about clarifying the freedoms guaranteed by the First Amendment. As Black wrote in his dissent, Barenblatt's plea "was not that of a private individual defending his own interest. Quite the contrary was true. At great personal sacrifice, he spoke [or, more accurately, refused to speak] as a free citizen, sharing in the governing of his country and seeking to do his duty to the government as he understood that duty to be prescribed by the Constitution."[25] According to Black, the majority in the *Barenblatt* case was fundamentally mistaken in its belief that Congress had an unqualified right to protect national security. Rather, Barenblatt had a *prior* right to political association that he retained even if he used it to associate with the Communist Party. Moreover, Black argued, Barenblatt retained this prior right even if the leaders of the Communist Party openly advocated the overthrow of the U.S. government by force. The right to political association superseded the right to protect the nation from revolt, because, if Congress did not respect that prior right, then democracy would *already* have ceased to exist. Black concluded his dissent in terms drawn almost directly from Meiklejohn's *Free Speech and Its Relation to Self-Government*. "The only constitutional way our government can preserve itself," he wrote, "is to leave its people the fullest possible freedom to praise, criticize, or discuss, as they see fit, all governmental policies and to suggest, if they desire, that even its most fundamental postulates are bad and should be changed."[26]

Long before his *Barenblatt* dissent, Black had acknowledged his personal and intellectual debt to Meiklejohn.[27] "My dear Meiklejohn," he wrote in 1952, "I have read most of what you have written for publication, and I have also had the advantage of hearing you express many of your beliefs in person. Undoubtedly we agree on many, if not most, basic issues. There can be little if any dispute between us concerning the most basic of all rights, that of freedom to think, speak, and write."[28] Like Meiklejohn, Black insisted on the need for democracies to trust in the possibility of reasonable, and thus peaceful, public debate. "Our Constitution assumes that the common sense of the people and their attachment to our country will enable them, after free discussion, to withstand ideas that are wrong," Black explained in his *Barenblatt* dissent. "No number of laws against Communism can have as much effect as the personal conviction which comes from having heard its arguments and rejected them or from having once accepted its tenets and later recognized their worthlessness. . . . Unless we can rely on these qualities—if, in short, we begin to punish speech—we cannot honestly proclaim ourselves to be a free nation and we have lost what the Founders of this land risked their lives and their sacred honors to defend."[29] Not long after writing his *Barenblatt* dissent, Black invited Meiklejohn to his Washington home for dinner. Meiklejohn gladly accepted and enjoyed the occasion immensely. "I recently went to Justice Black's house for dinner and debate," he wrote to his friend Thomas Emerson of the Yale Law School. "It was, for several hours, a gay and spirited controversy in which we appeared to agree on all conclusions but differed continuously about all the reasons for them. He's a charming and stimulating person as well as a wise one."[30] Even in his late eighties, Meiklejohn still loved the rigor of a stimulating discussion and the excitement of philosophical debate.

In the winter of 1960, Meiklejohn published his own critique of the *Barenblatt* opinion in the *University of Chicago Law Review*. It was his last significant publication, and, in many ways, his final word on the relationship between free citizens and a democratic state. "I'm still struggling desperately with the Supreme Court and the First Amendment," he wrote to his friend and former student Seelye Bixler. "I can't be satisfied with anything until it seems simple and easy. But that means that every word is a puzzle and a torture and an agony. But it's fun, too."[31] Meiklejohn's article examined the constitutionality—or, rather, the unconstitutionality—of the question, Are you, or have you ever been, a member of the Communist Party? The trouble, he explained, was not that Barenblatt's silence represented a dishonest answer but that the question was wrong in the first place. When HUAC asked Barenblatt if he belonged to the Communist Party, it asked, in effect, six different and profoundly damning questions, including "(1) Do you believe that our present form of government should be fundamentally changed? (2) Have you joined with others in advocating such a change? (3) Have you engaged with others in violent action to bring about such a change? (4) Have you engaged in espionage to secure, for any enemy nation, information which might help it against us? (5) Have you incited others to criminal action against our government? and (6) Are you 'subject' to the directives and discipline of the Communist Party?" Confronted with such an array of incriminatory questions, members of the Communist Party—whose membership was perfectly within their rights, according to *Yates*—faced a difficult choice. They could either perjure themselves by denying their association with the party, or they could seal their own fate by admitting to full participation in an evil and sinister plot of global domination. In both cases, they were trapped. So long as the Supreme Court equated party membership with active participation in "multifarious activities directed toward the destruction of the freedom-loving governments of the world," protecting minority voices under the First Amendment was impossible.[32] The only defense against conviction for treason, sedition, or conspiracy was a Fifth Amendment defense against self-incrimination. On this point, the First Amendment was moot.

Meiklejohn's critique of the *Barenblatt* opinion won high praise from lawyers, scholars, and judges alike. Roger Traynor, associate justice of the California Supreme Court, considered it a masterpiece of democratic principles. "I am profoundly moved by the Meiklejohn Opinion on the *Barenblatt* case," he wrote. "I shall read over this lucid opinion, this valiant brief, many times . . . for its reminder that at least one philosopher cares deeply about the common health of philosophy and law."[33] Joseph L. Rauh, Jr., an influential liberal attorney, agreed with Traynor. "Here," Rauh remarked to Meiklejohn, "you seem to me to have hit upon the major civil liberties problem of the past ten or fifteen years, namely, the Court's preferment of the privilege against self-incrimination over the First Amendment. . . . If the Court had been in a mood to knock out the Smith Act prosecutions under the First Amendment, it would never have found answers to simple questions about Communism incriminatory."[34] Unfortunately, the majority of Supreme Court justices did not agree with Traynor and Rauh. Following the majority opinion in *Barenblatt* opinion were three related decisions: the first against a man named Willard Uphaus; the second against a man named Carl Braden; and the third against Meiklejohn's close friend and colleague in the campaign to abolish HUAC, Frank Wilkinson.[35] All four decisions—*Barenblatt, Uphaus, Braden,* and

Wilkinson—were essentially alike in stating that the First Amendment did not protect radical associations or speech. The *Wilkinson* decision, however, was the hardest for Meiklejohn to accept.

In 1958, HUAC had discovered Wilkinson in Atlanta, where he had gone to collect evidence for his abolition campaign. Accusing Wilkinson of inciting hostility to its work, the committee had summoned him to testify. Following Barenblatt, and Watkins before him, Wilkinson had refused to answer the committee's question about his past political associations. Like Barenblatt, he claimed that HUAC had no authority to ask such a question. Consequently, the committee found him in contempt and gave him a maximum sentence of one year in jail. The Supreme Court upheld Wilkinson's conviction, with Justice Stewart writing for the majority. Tying *Wilkinson* to *Barenblatt*, Stewart argued that the question, Are you a member of the Communist Party? was allowable under the First Amendment, because Congress had an "over-balancing interest" in regulating seditious speech as a way of preventing revolutionary conduct. In other words, Stewart interpreted association with the Communist Party not as a form of political expression, but as a criminal incitement to violent action. "As the *Barenblatt* opinion makes clear," he contended, "it is the nature of the Communist activity involved—whether the momentary conduct is legitimate or illegitimate politically—that establishes the Government's over-balancing interest. To suggest that, because the Communist Party may also sponsor peaceable political reforms, the constitutional issues before us should now be judged as if that Party were just an ordinary political Party from the standpoint of national security, is to ask this Court to blind itself to world affairs which have determined the whole course of our national policy since the close of World War II."[36] According to Stewart, the suppression of Communist speech was a matter of national, even international, security. Faced with a need to balance security against speech, Congress could overbalance the former in the interest of national self-preservation.

Hugo Black disagreed with Stewart and, once again, registered his dissent. "The result of all this," he wrote, referring to *Barenblatt, Braden, Uphaus,* and now *Wilkinson,* "is that, from now on, anyone who takes a public position contrary to that being urged by the House Un-American Activities Committee should realize that he runs the risk of being subpoenaed to appear at a hearing in some far off place, of being questioned with regard to every minute detail of his past life, of being asked to repeat all the gossip he may have heard about any friends or acquaintances, of being accused by the Committee of membership in the Communist Party, of being held up to the public as a subversive and a traitor, of being jailed for contempt if he refuses to cooperate with the Committee's probe of his mind and associations, and of being branded by neighbors, employers, and erstwhile friends as a menace to society *regardless of the outcome of that hearing.*" With such a powerful weapon in its hands, HUAC could weather all criticism, for few would have the courage to speak out against such a formidable foe. If HUAC could construe any opposition to its investigations as criminal activity, then its ability to suppress dissent was total and its survival assured. So long as the Court agreed that the committee's investigations provided a useful defense of national security, the number of dissenters would continue to shrink. "If the present trend continues," Black lamented, "then this already small number will necessarily dwindle as their ranks are thinned by the jails. Government by consent will disappear, replaced by government by intimidation, because some people are afraid that this country cannot survive unless Congress has the power to set aside the freedoms of the First Amendment at will."[37] As Black's dissent made clear, the *Watkins* victory of 1957 had been almost completely dismantled by the *Barenblatt* defeat of 1959 and, subsequently, by the *Braden, Uphaus,* and *Wilkinson* decisions of 1961.

Meiklejohn took these decisions extremely hard, not only because they undermined the progress that had been made in the mid-1950s, but also because they involved the imprisonment of his friends. "Life has been bad this week because of the blinding cruelty of the Supreme Court decisions on *Braden* and *Wilkinson,*" he confessed to an acquaintance, John Gill.[38] A few days later, he received a sympathetic letter from Harry Kalven. "I agree that the *Braden* and *Wilkinson* decisions are a mess and completely obliterate the hopes that were raised by *Watkins,*" Kalven wrote. "At times it seems to me as though the Court has forgotten that somebody will go to jail at the end of their opinion."[39] Meiklejohn winced at the thought of twelve months' incarceration for Barenblatt, Braden, and Wilkinson. "I feel a heavy responsibility for my part in getting these . . . young fellows into trouble," he wrote to Wilkinson's attorney, Rowland Watts. "I must do whatever I can to stand by them."[40] In the fall of 1961, Meiklejohn sought clemency for both Braden and Wilkinson. "In both cases," he pleaded in a series of letters to federal officials, "the record makes it clear that the offenses were motivated, not by hostility to the Government of the United States, but by a loyalty to it, especially to the First Amendment, which made the committing of the offense morally imperative, no matter what might have been the cost to the offender and to his family and friends. . . . the imposition of the maximum imprisonment upon these honest and loyal men is worse than cruel, worse than unjust. It is absurd."[41] Unfortunately, Meiklejohn's pleas went unheard. Braden and Wilkinson both served out their full terms in federal penitentiaries. While Wilkinson was in jail, his wife and children suffered tremendously. "The family," Wilkinson confided in a note to Meiklejohn, "has been threatened with great violence. Possibly you did not hear, but the family home in Los Angeles was bombed the night after I left; then, two days later, a swastika was painted on the door. Jo [Wilkinson's young daughter] narrowly missed being killed. . . . This is the second bombing we've had—you recall the office was bombed in September."[42] For Meiklejohn, such news was almost too much to bear.

Shortly after Wilkinson's release from jail in January of 1962, he sent a note expressing his heartfelt admiration and support for his friends. "Now that the immediate agonies are over, we can think more clearly about the great deed which you have done for your country and for yourself," he wrote, adding a favorite passage from Plato's *Apology* to illustrate the significance of Wilkinson's sacrifice. "Socrates," Meiklejohn explained, "was jailed by the Athenians, but he was not in prison, because he had freely chosen to be there. A prison, he argued, is a place where one is against his will. Socrates, then, was not in prison, because he was willingly there. That's true of you too, Frank. Facing incarceration, you said 'Base as that is, it is better than denying my own principles and those of my own country.' And, by making that choice, you preserved the freedom which, by submission to injustice and folly, you might have lost forever. This is a strange doctrine, Frank, but, in its way, it is true and terribly important. I am, therefore, writing to say 'Hats off!' to the man who has not been in prison!"[43] Even as he approached the age of ninety, Meiklejohn still took time for the emotional encouragement of a younger generation. Besides Wilkinson, he also helped Lawrence Speiser, staff counsel of the northern California branch of the ACLU, who narrowly avoided a conviction for contempt. Both of these men could have avoided tangling with HUAC if they had pleaded the Fifth Amendment, but each chose Meiklejohn's more difficult and idealistic path. Consequently, they became martyrs for a cause. Like the existentialists Meiklejohn had admired in Europe a few years earlier, these men showed a remarkable capacity for "hanging on by [their] teeth, if need be, in dreadful agony, to a purpose which [they did] not 'desire' but [did], in fact, 'choose.' "[44] Wilkinson and Speiser did not desire the agony they endured in their fight to abolish HUAC, but they did choose the purpose for the sake of which they suffered.

During the year that Wilkinson spent in jail, Meiklejohn endured some dreadful agonies of his own, not least of which was his close encounter with an anonymous gunman in Colorado. "My beauty of feature was marred in Denver," he later quipped to a friend, "because, as we drove to the airport, a lad shot a bee-bee bullet at the car window and a shower of glass splinters hit my cheek. One of them, hitting just beside my mouth, cut a small blood vessel, as a result of which I have from mouth to chin a great black mark of blood clotted inside." Grateful that his wound had been only minor, Meiklejohn reported that local authorities had apprehended his juvenile assailant, whose gunfire had simply been a prank. "We caught the plane, and the boy," Meiklejohn wrote to Lawrence Speiser, "and soon I'll be handsome again."[45] Two weeks later, Meiklejohn's face had healed. "I (my head) was bloody but unbowed," he told Speiser after the ordeal, "and there may be a glass splinter in my jaw yet. . . . You will be glad to hear that from beginning to end, though I bled quite a bit, I had no pain."[46] Though he may have added a few wrinkles as a result, Meiklejohn came through his accident remarkably well. Indeed, he remained in excellent health. He played tennis on a regular basis and kept a daily regimen of writing and correspondence, all of which he did by hand.[47] His doctor begged him to take a sampling of pills, mostly for high blood pressure and nervous tension, but he insisted that one was the limit. When he turned ninety in February of 1962, his physician started to make monthly house calls, but, hating to be monitored, Meiklejohn convinced the doctor to stay away. Besides, he claimed, doctors only insisted that his advanced age gave him "no right to be alive."[48]

In addition to his own intermittent health concerns, Meiklejohn worried a great deal about Helen, whose respiratory problems intensified after returning from Europe. In January of 1956, seventeen years after the train wreck that had caused her throat problems, Helen's physician discovered that it was necessary to remove one of her vocal cords. The operation, which took place in New York, was a success, but her recovery was painful and slow. "We have practical certainty that all is well," Meiklejohn told Corliss Lamont, "but Helen will have to re-learn speech-articulation and will not be allowed to begin that for some undetermined time." With only one remaining vocal cord, Helen could not speak without experiencing sharp pain. "Helen can only whisper," Meiklejohn explained, "and must do very little of that."[49] She communicated by writing messages on a toy Magic Slate erasable board. Her throat troubles worsened until 1961, when she had a tracheal tube inserted in her neck to prevent scar tissue from obstructing her breathing passage. The plastic tube involved a tantalum keel, or thin metal plate, to keep her trachea open, as well as a suction machine to keep the passage clear of dust and disease. In August of 1961, Meiklejohn wrote to W. H. Ferry at the Center for the Study of Democratic Institutions in Monterey. "The last two or three months have been pretty bad," he told. "We decided to have surgery on Helen's throat to improve breathing and, perhaps, voice. It has required three operations, the second over four hours long. She has to use a tracheal tube all the time and must still keep it for a couple weeks more. Her experience has been one of continuous pain, discomfort, and anxiety."[50] In September, Helen's doctors extracted the keel and found that her breathing aperture was a bit wider than it had been before. Still, she had trouble with phlegm, and speaking continued to require great effort. "She talks now," Meiklejohn told Buchanan, "but not with much tone."[51] In 1962, as if to make matters worse, Helen discovered a lump in one of her breasts. She endured a radical mastectomy to remove the cancer, and, while doctors found no metastasis, the whole experience weakened her—and her husband—considerably.[52]

Even while Helen was sick, Meiklejohn did not stop writing. "The hard work has helped to keep me sane," he told Glenn Burch, an old friend from the San Francisco School of Social Studies. [53] But sanity was difficult to maintain in the period between Helen's laryngectomy in 1956 and her mastectomy in 1962—a period that witnessed a whole string of dramatic national and international events. In 1960, an American U-2 reconnaissance spy plane crashed while taking top-secret pictures of Russian military bases in Siberia. President Eisenhower refused to apologize for the incident, thereby jeopardizing a U.S.–Soviet summit on the division of Berlin and the installation of American army bases in Turkey. Meanwhile, the election of 1960, pitting Vice President Richard M. Nixon against Massachusetts senator John F. Kennedy, produced the closest vote of the century. Among Kennedy's first acts in the White House was an effort to reverse Fidel Castro's Communist revolution in Cuba. In April of 1961, Kennedy endorsed an ill-fated invasion at the Bay of Pigs, but the covert plan was a disaster. Humiliated by defeat, Kennedy authorized Operation Mongoose, a secret naval mission to impede Cuban trade and assassinate Castro. In response to American hostilities, Castro asked for Soviet assistance, which promptly arrived in the form of nuclear weapons pointed at the United States. Suddenly, it seemed as if the world faced an imminent threat of war. In 1962, Kennedy assembled a team of experts to assess the possibility of global annihilation in the event of a nuclear standoff with Cuba. After several days of heated debate, he imposed a quarantine on the island, blocking further shipments of weapons from the Soviet Union. For a week, battleships patrolled the Caribbean while fighter planes prepared to repel a Soviet attack. "Have you ever known a time," W. H. Ferry asked Meiklejohn after the Bay of Pigs calamity, "when the human condition was so bleak and unpromising?"[54]

By all accounts, the danger in Cuba arose from its proximity to the United States. Not so the danger far away in Vietnam, which worried Americans for other, more abstract, reasons. Ever since the French withdrew from Vietnam after the disastrous Battle of Dien Bien Phu in 1954, the United States had been trying to prevent a Communist-supported nationalist insurgency in South Vietnam. However, rampant political corruption and incompetent military forces impeded efforts to establish a stable democratic regime. In 1963, Corliss Lamont asked Meiklejohn to sign a letter to President Kennedy opposing American involvement in Vietnam. Meiklejohn did not sign Lamont's letter, but he strongly backed its message. "I, too, am sorry that the news about Vietnam does not improve," he wrote after a series of Buddhist self-immolations and the assassination of South Vietnamese leader Ngo Dinh Diem in 1963. "There are, I fear, some very ugly moods in our government mind which would involve us in reckless and persistent wickedness."[55] Several months later, when the military situation deteriorated further, he elaborated: "Yes, yes, the Vietnam War is bad business," he wrote to his friend Otto Nathan, "and our being in it is extreme folly."[56] If Meiklejohn's hope for global peace had been low after his European tour in 1954, it was far lower after the Vietnamese atrocities of 1963. With the almost overwhelming confusion in foreign affairs, Lamont tried to keep Meiklejohn's spirits up. In February of 1963, he mailed a card to commemorate Meiklejohn's ninety-first birthday. "I believe February is your birthday month," Lamont cheered, "and I want to extend my cordial congratulations to you as you hit ninety-one. I think you are one of the great Americans and will go down in history as such."[57]

Four months later, Lamont's prediction came true, at least in some sense. On July 4, 1963, John F. Kennedy named Meiklejohn one of the first recipients of the Presidential Medal of Freedom, the nation's highest civilian honor.[58] Unfortunately, the announcement of the Presidential Medal became an occasion more for sadness than for celebration. On November 22, a few days before the Presidential Medals were scheduled to be bestowed, President Kennedy was assassinated in Dallas, and the entire nation plunged into a catatonic state of mourning. Exactly two weeks later, a recently sworn-in Lyndon Johnson presided over a solemn medal ceremony in the East Room of the White House.[59] Dozens of dignitaries attended the somber event, including all nine Supreme Court justices as well as Attorney General Robert Kennedy, whose deceased brother's name was added to the list of honorees. Not long after receiving his award, Meiklejohn wrote to Robert Kennedy to express his condolences. "Your brother, the President, was clearly present for all of us who were receiving the Medals of Freedom," he wrote. "May I add a word of personal sympathy and friendship? Fate has dealt you a bitter, nearly unbearable, blow. As we sat together [at the White House ceremony], my heart was sore at the sight of your suffering it so gallantly."[60] Indeed, the attempt to balance suffering with gallantry was becoming a theme for Meiklejohn, who came away from the awarding of his Presidential Medal with mixed emotions. "The agony and bewilderment of the assassination were in everyone's mind," he remarked after the ceremony in a letter to W. H. Ferry, "but 'We, the People' went marching on. Helen and I came away deeply stirred and more resolute than we had been before. There is something tough and enduring in this nation of ours, however negligent and slip-shod its thinking may be."[61] As he approached the age of ninety-two, Meiklejohn tried to maintain his idealism and hope for the future, even as the nation—and the world—seemed to be falling apart.

After receiving his Presidential Medal, Meiklejohn received congratulations from dozens of friends, including Roger Baldwin, Alfred Kazin, Henry Luce, John McCloy, Linus Pauling, Louis Schweitzer, and Norman Thomas, among others. Of his many admirers, however, none perceived his melancholy mood better than Lewis Mumford, who knew that the medal ceremony had been bittersweet. "History has certainly been made in the last month or so," Mumford wrote in a quiet and contemplative note, "and I hope we will have no more of it in our lifetime."[62] A few months earlier, before Kennedy's assassination, Mumford had written to congratulate Meiklejohn on being chosen for the award. Its presentation was appropriate, he judged, "not mainly because it reflects credit on you, but because the offering of it to someone like yourself symbolically redeems—or at least half-redeems—the many shameful acts our leaders have committed before and since the infamous McCarthy gave his name to them." More than anyone else, Mumford thought, Meiklejohn had led the nation in its defense of civil liberties and democratic rights. "Somehow, it is especially appropriate that I say these things today after the magnificent demonstration that took place in Washington yesterday," Mumford wrote, referring to the 200,000-plus participants in the Civil Rights March on Washington for Freedom and Jobs, led by Bayard Rustin and Martin Luther King, Jr., on August 28, 1963. "The very report of it brought tears of pride to my eyes, for the Negroes and for our fellow countrymen to whose best traditions they have given a new life. They have uncovered those potentialities of the human spirit that the best minds of the eighteenth century were so sure of and that our own desperate, disintegrated age had buried under the debris. Even the faint and the weary—and I confess I am sometimes one of them—can take heart again."[63]

With these tired but optimistic sentiments, Meiklejohn wholeheartedly concurred. "I hope you saw on television the March on Washington," he wrote to his friend John Gill. "It was magnificent in itself and, I think, full of significance for both whites and blacks in the future."[64] For Meiklejohn, the pursuit of racial toleration was part and parcel of the quest for civil liberties. Both were essential in a truly democratic and cooperative society. Noting the rise of separatist ideologies among civil rights activists before the March on Washington, Meiklejohn recognized that, in the short term, black and white Americans might need to work apart, each in their own communities, to achieve the goal of racial reconciliation. He hoped, however, that in the longer term racial differences would fade into irrelevance as integration became the norm. He shared these views with Grace Lee Boggs, a graduate student at Berkeley whose essays on the revolutionary nature of civil rights movement had appealed to him.[65] "On the one hand," he wrote to Boggs, "you say that the Negroes, as they win their way toward the freedom of self-government, do not ask for help from whites. They must fight and win their own battles. And the truth of that was magnificently shown in the August 28 March. . . . But, on the other hand, [your] argument . . . is directed chiefly at the redemption of whites, telling them both what they cannot do and what they must do in order to win their own dignity by devotion to a cause in which the contrast between black and white becomes irrelevant, becomes meaningless."[66] Encouraging Boggs to continue her work on American race relations, Meiklejohn emphasized the need for diverse individuals to seek common interests, to pursue common aspirations and common goals. He stressed the need for blacks and whites to work together to create a single cooperative community. In the meantime, he found his own ways to support racial justice in the early 1960s. Not long after the march on Washington, he joined the Alabama Legal Defense Committee, which had been formed to protest the recent bombing of Birmingham's Sixteenth Street Baptist Church.

Despite his encouragement of younger activists like Boggs—and Wilkinson and Speiser and Robert Kennedy—Meiklejohn increasingly admitted his own growing disillusionment with the possibility of progressive social reform. He especially admitted his hopelessness regarding the future prospects of liberal education. "We need to *transform* the schools," he wrote desperately to W. H. Ferry in 1962. "But, far more, we need happenings in our public life that will shock us into sanity, or, at least, out of insanity. I've been writing for fifty years, and it feels horribly futile."[67] For months, Meiklejohn had been struggling to make sense of the turmoil around him, especially the commotion in Berkeley over the civil rights movement and the recent military escalations in Vietnam. "I'm trying to start a paper on college education with some reference to the Cold War and the treason of the universities," he wrote to Scott Buchanan in February of 1963, alluding to Julien Benda's famous work, *La Trahison des clercs* (1927).[68] "I've been sunk deep, far below the surface, in an attempt to explain the liberal college, which is very ill, and to prescribe for it," he told John Frank. "It's been a long frustration, but I seem to be moving now."[69] By July, however, Meiklejohn once again conceded defeat. "Alas and alack," he complained to Ferry, "my writing prospects are even worse than I thought. I have just stopped trying to do anything on the interpretation of the college—for how long I do not know."[70] Abandoning the idea of producing something new, Meiklejohn asked Ferry if he should reprint *Education Between Two Worlds* with a more detailed critique of the fragmented modern research university. "I have been wondering," he wrote to Ferry, "if a new edition, perhaps paperback, omitting Book III on Dewey and pragmatism, would be usable. Our enemies are no longer the pragmatists (that incident is over); it's the pluralists who now threaten sanity and coherence and, hence, justice and freedom."[71] For Meiklejohn, pluralism had replaced pragmatism as the movement most directly opposed to intellectual and cultural unity in modern liberal education.[72]

Meiklejohn's concern over the dissolution of the modern university focused primarily on the institution closest to home—the University of California in Berkeley. Earlier in 1963, Berkeley's president, Clark Kerr, had delivered a series of lectures at Harvard in which he posed John Henry Newman's nineteenth-century classic, *The Idea of the University* (1852), against the idea of a modern scientific research university. In an age of increasing specialization, commercialization, and politicization, Kerr noted, the modern university had devolved into a "knowledge production plant," a so-called multiversity of competing academic and nonacademic interests.[73] No one dreaded the prospect of a multiversity more than Meiklejohn, who had devoted his entire career to the pursuit of intellectual *unity* in institutions of liberal democratic education. After reading advance copies of Kerr's lectures, Meiklejohn deemed them terrifying in their implications for the future. "The terror of which I speak arises from your finding . . . no academic autonomy," he wrote in a plaintive letter to Kerr. "The institution responds, bit by bit, as demands and pressures come along, and that is all. The outcome is that, apparently, academic autonomy disappears or disintegrates." Most appalling to Meiklejohn was the notion that the multiversity had no effective way to counteract external political and commercial demands. Devoid of critical autonomy, it relinquished its cultural independence to the capricious whims of partisanship and profit. The college was no longer the intellectual leader of its community. "I know that this is 'old stuff' to you and that you 'think' of it, however you feel, as an old-fashioned longing for days that are gone forever," Meiklejohn admitted to Kerr. "But I don't agree. The need of 'liberal education' for undergraduates is greater now than ever before."[74] The ideal of liberal education in critical tension with modern culture survived in Meiklejohn's mind, even if it had already vanished from the world around him. He could not help being disillusioned. "My writing situation is so desperate that I've begun to fear that my writing days may be over," he confided to Frank Wilkinson in the summer of 1963. "P.S." he added at the bottom of the page, "please don't tell anybody about my situation."[75]

The years between 1962 and 1964 were extraordinarily difficult for Meiklejohn. He tried to confront the cultural and political upheavals of his time with all the moral courage and spiritual conviction of his Kantian idealist roots, but events overwhelmed him. As his longtime friend Arthur Upham Pope observed, the early 1960s presented Meiklejohn with "a sea of troubles which he met with soul well-knit and all his spiritual battles won and against which he pitted as best as he could his faith in the power of critical intelligence armed by moral purpose."[76] But idealism was not enough. As race relations teetered warily on the brink of violence, as international events plummeted into a quagmire of guerrilla war, and, most painful, as the nation's political leaders alienated an entire generation of idealistic youth, Meiklejohn began to wonder about the victory of intelligence over ignorance, the triumph of wisdom over violence in the conduct of human affairs. What was the purpose of it all? What was the *meaning*? Toward the end of his life, he developed an increasingly tragic sense of his place in the world. As he wrote to Scott Buchanan in May of 1961, "[T]he use of 'tragedy' to express the quality of human behavior pleases me much. Life is, for us, a *spiritual* adventure."[77] These words echoed his undergraduate idealism with uncanny resonance, and yet the search for spirituality had never been easy for Meiklejohn. He tended to view the realm of spiritual belief as a realm of otherworldly abstraction, a realm of subjective imagination ultimately removed from the quest for rational ideals. To yield to spiritualism was to succumb to mysticism and, thus, to abandon the search for practical values in a Kantian sense. Meiklejohn yearned for transcendental understanding, but he was hard-pressed to find it in the chaos of the mid-twentieth century. His final task, which was really the abiding task of his entire life, was to recover the possibility of true belief in a fallen and faithless world. If he could still believe in the possibility of a rational humanity, then perhaps he could steel himself against modern skepticism and despair.

Throughout the 1950s and 1960s, Meiklejohn had tried to stay abreast of recent developments in contemporary philosophy, especially the works of the existentialists, whose efforts to join the rational and the spiritual fascinated him. He maintained an extensive and illuminating correspondence on the subject of existentialism with his friend, Seelye Bixler, the Amherst graduate who had gone on to become president of Colby College in Maine.[78] It was Bixler who encouraged Meiklejohn's interest in Jean-Paul Sartre, as well as Albert Camus and Paul Tillich. Meiklejohn exchanged a series of letters with Bixler on the questions of nothingness and meaninglessness that guided the existentialists' project. He found in these questions an opportunity for moral "reconstruction" and philosophical "synthesis" of the kind he had sought since his youth. "I am fully with you in the conviction that we need not live in anxiety and the depression of nothingness," he wrote to Bixler in September of 1963. "But, what is the 'something' in the universe, or society, or ourselves, or some combination of them, which makes life joyous and worth living?"[79] For Meiklejohn, finding something in existentialism meant bridging the gap between philosophy and religion, between rationalism and spiritualism, between agnosticism and belief. "As you know," he told Bixler at the outset of their exchange, "philosophy has to do for me what religion, together with philosophy, does for you. And so, it must answer for me, as well as it can, the questions, 'What should I do?' as well as 'What do I know?' "[80] Was it still possible to believe in a rational humanity?

In a series of candid letters, Meiklejohn consulted Bixler on the work of the twentieth century's most profound—and problematic—existentialist, Martin Heidegger. Bixler knew Heidegger personally from their days as graduate students under German phenomenologist Edmund Husserl in the 1920s. In his letters to Meiklejohn, Bixler did not conceal his disdain for Heidegger, who had accepted the rectorship of the University of Freiburg at Hitler's behest in 1933 and then supported Nazism throughout World War II. "I don't know quite why I have so much animus against

Heidegger except that I hated him so when I knew him," Bixler explained. "He was dogmatic, arrogant, conceited, a man who was willing to politick to get himself made rector of the University of Freiburg, one who ran the university arrogantly when he did run it, and one who led many youth, through his arrogance, straight down the road to Nazism. I remember one lecture in which he said that Plato and Aristotle received their culmination in Hitler! Also, Heidegger was most deliberately unfair, even mean, to Husserl, who made Heidegger what he was, and, of course, it was because of his anti-Semitism." In Bixler's opinion, Heidegger's fascism had completely undermined any integrity his philosophy might otherwise have had. He condemned Heidegger's best-known work, *Being and Time,* first published in 1928, as a pernicious ideological predecessor to National Socialism, and he doubted Heidegger's claim to "care" for humanity in a basic existential sense. "I think his [political] weakness gets in the way of his [philosophical] understanding of the nature of 'Being' and the 'Care' man should show as he reaches out to it," Bixler judged.[81] Heidegger was, in his view, a dangerous figure whose amoral philosophy was rotten at its core. Meiklejohn, however, was curious about Heidegger and thought there might be something salvageable in his work.

Without plunging too deeply into Heidegger's complex metaphysical theories, Bixler humored Meiklejohn by summarizing the fundamentals of Heidegger's argument, which hinged on the need to care for human existence in an original, authentic, and completely unmediated way. By caring for all existence, Heidegger had asserted, human beings could aspire to apprehend the *essential* nature of pure Being as such. "You ask what Heidegger is really trying to say," Bixler wrote to Meiklejohn. "It seems to be that we should get back of propositions and formalized statements to an original experience of Being itself. We are 'alienated' now and must restore our 'primitive' relation. We should understand man in the light of Being, not the other way round. Man is really 'Care' in Faust's sense, 'Care first shapes creation.' So, if we study 'Care,' we should find what man's relation to himself and all else really is."[82] Meiklejohn felt a strong attraction to Heidegger's belief that humanity could achieve a transcendental understanding of existence when it cared for, or reasoned about, the universal state of being in a completely nondualistic, unmediated way. His idealist epistemology had long focused on the culmination of critical intelligence in an ability to embrace knowledge as a unified whole, unfettered by dogma, ideology, or prejudice. Following Kant, he still believed in the synthetic power of mind to create its own meaning, to exist as both a subjective and an objective apprehension of itself, and he admired Heidegger for resisting the skepticism that had derailed so many modern philosophers. While recognizing the dangers inherent in any attempt to forge a single transcendental meaning out of diverse individual viewpoints, Meiklejohn nonetheless esteemed Heidegger's willingness to seek intellectual unity, the pursuit of which reflected the abiding idealism of Meiklejohn's entire philosophical career.

Meiklejohn expressed his appreciation for Heidegger in a letter to Vera Maslow, the author of several articles on *Being and Time*. "I can see that he is trying to do what I have always wanted to see done and, probably, what I would have been working at all these years if I had not been drawn into administration," Meiklejohn wrote after reviewing one of Maslow's articles. "In other words, [he takes] me back to F. H. Bradley's *Appearance and Reality*, which, in my earliest student years, thrilled me and set me to work. It is Kantian, of course, or seems so to me." Confessing his sympathy for Heidegger's account of caring for the world, Meiklejohn noted the difficulty of transforming such mystical care into a rational theory or institutional endeavor. Such a transformation, he knew from his own hard-fought experiences at Brown, Amherst, and the Experimental College, was "a terribly difficult and even dangerous task." "Yet," he added, "it is at least true that we should give much of our lives to . . . 'caring,' finding in [it] whatever 'meaning' our human experience is capable of having." To seek truth and yet to acknowledge its unattainability was a paradox that had guided Meiklejohn's thought since his earliest encounter with Kant. Now, at the age of ninety-two, he returned to this paradox as a basic feature of human existence. "There is, as you recognize, paradox in what I am saying," he wrote to Maslow. "And the insistence upon the validity of paradox makes human living very difficult. It may even keep us from . . . 'caring.' But there is, I think, a gladness in your work which saves you from that danger."[83] So, too, was there a gladness in Meiklejohn's own work which saved him from the "dangerous" side of transcendental idealism. His admiration for Kant might have led him toward fascism in the years before World War II, just as his affinity for Rousseau might have led him toward totalitarianism in the years thereafter, but in neither case did he succumb to the reactionary politics that had marred Heidegger's career. In neither case did Meiklejohn embrace authoritarianism. Instead, his gladness, his faith in the fundamental goodness of rational humanity, led him to one of the century's most profoundly liberal statements of the freedom of conscience and speech.

For Meiklejohn, the search for some sort of validity in paradox had been a life-long project. "What seems to me, reflectively, most significant about the human 'mind' or 'spirit,' " he wrote to Bixler at the end of their Heidegger exchange, "is that, besides being a unity, it is a bundle of different (may I say?) interpretations of the world, which must be correlated with one another, but which can never really be reduced to one another. This is a sort of doctrine of 'complementarities' around which, since my early youth, all my attempts at philosophy have always revolved."[84] Indeed, Meiklejohn had long struggled with the meaning of complementarity—with persistent dualities between facts and values, between actions and beliefs, between mind and matter. Complementarity and compromise, along with dialectics, had been the central concerns of his philosophical career. His strong rhetoric on behalf of absolutism and authority often obscured his underlying interest in collaboration and cooperation, but the basic theme of his life had been a search for dialogue between competing interests and groups. He knew that dichotomies and differences lay at the heart of liberal democracy, and he continually insisted on an ethical approach to resolving social conflicts and encouraging political debate. The genius of democracy, he maintained, was its ability to facilitate common aspirations and enforce common obligations within the collective institutions of a self-governing state. Believing that humanity must create its own meaning through both formal and informal associations and groups, Meiklejohn argued consistently that democracy must claim the cultural, as well as the educational, authority to perpetuate itself as the best—indeed, the only—way to bring diverse interests together for the sake of mutual deliberation and understanding. "The major, inclusive task of philosophy," he concluded in his last letter to Bixler, "seems to me to be that of taking mutually unintelligible complementaries and establishing such connections among them that there emerges, or is created, a way of life which, so far as possible, makes life worth living."[85] That way of life, he maintained, was democracy.

In August of 1964, at the age of ninety-two, Meiklejohn participated in a month-long seminar at the Center for the Study of Democratic Institutions in Monterey. The seminar's objective—to search for a philosophy of democratic education as a basis for a theory of the First Amendment—combined the two most significant intellectual concerns of Meiklejohn's life. "Your venture, in which you let me share, is a very difficult one," he wrote to Robert Hutchins, who had resigned from the presidency at the University of Chicago to direct the Center for the Study of Democratic Institutions.[86] "[S]o difficult that, even apart from all external hindrances, it must be hard to keep one's courage up. But, speaking now with the freedom of many years, you do and you must keep it up. Nothing in the study-

Alexander Meiklejohn and James Baldwin celebrating the 172nd anniversary of the ratification of the Bill of Rights at a dinner organized by the Emergency Civil Liberties Committee in New York City, December 1963 (photo by Arthur Swoger)

ing and thinking of the country has the same fundamental significance. I feel more pride and contentment in being connected with it than I could find in any other institutional procedure that is going on."[87] Scott Buchanan, who also participated in the seminar, recalled Meiklejohn's contribution to the discussion. "In the arguments of the summer," he recorded, "Alec always returned to one theme: a correct interpretation of the First Amendment presupposes the proposition that the liberal college is the key institution in a self-governing society. I knew that this—along with cricket—had been the theme of his whole life."[88] Indeed, at the end of the summer, Meiklejohn put pen to paper and composed his own edu-

Alexander Meiklejohn and Norman Thomas share a laugh at the Emergency Civil Liberties Committee dinner, December 1963 (photo by Russell Leake)

cational amendment to the Constitution. It was in many respects a summation of his entire career. "In view of the intellectual and cultural responsibilities laid upon the citizens of a free society by the political institutions of self-government," he wrote, "the Congress, acting in cooperation with the several states and with non-governmental organizations, shall have the power to provide for the intellectual and cultural education of *all* citizens of the United States."[89] Here, in a succinct addendum to the nation's founding document, Meiklejohn expressed his undying hope that American citizens might someday recognize their authority—indeed, their duty—to teach themselves how to be democratic. Only then could democracy, as an institutional manifestation of the country's highest ideals, survive.

Meiklejohn's lifelong idealism met its final test in the long hot summer of 1964. In June of that year, three white students were brutally murdered in Mississippi while registering black citizens to vote. One of those students, Andrew Goodman, had been a friend of Meiklejohn's for years. "I know that you have been very saddened by the death of my friend Andy in Mississippi," wrote Joseph Popper, one of Goodman's classmates from the City College of New York. "It is a terrible thing that a tragedy of this magnitude must occur in order that other people may again see the truth."[90] Overcome by emotion on reading Popper's letter, Meiklejohn responded with one of his own. As he often did in times of extreme grief, he ended with a quotation—this time from the German existentialist playwright Bertolt Brecht. It was a fitting choice. According to Brecht, human life was a lot like acting. "In the very nature of acting," Meiklejohn wrote, quoting Brecht's *Messingkauf Dialogues,* "there is an essential gaiety. If it is not lighthearted, it becomes absurd. You can achieve every shade of seriousness by means of ease [but] none of them without it. No matter how fearful the problems plays handle, they should always be playful." Meiklejohn took great comfort from this passage. Just as he had once viewed the liberal college as an enclave set apart for the contemplation of ideals, so Brecht viewed the theater as a sanctuary from the agonies of modern life. "In the theater," Meiklejohn continued, quoting Brecht, "we manipulate a pair of golden scales, meting out justice with elegance, indifferent to the earth that shakes beneath our feet. . . . Tomorrow our corpses may be pulverized and scattered, but here today we busy ourselves with the theater, because we want to evaluate our lives with its help." Meditating on the link between the theater and the liberal college, Meiklejohn connected the need to act with the need to teach, despite the existential inadequacies of both. "That's it, Joe!" he exclaimed. "To evaluate our lives is 'education.' Life is serious; so it has to be gay."[91]

Meiklejohn's optimism was the hallmark of his personality. As his friend Milton Mayer recognized, "[H]is gaiety was unshakable—even, I think, when it should have been shaken."[92] And, indeed, in the summer of 1964, Meiklejohn saw much that shook his gaiety and confidence. After the Civil Rights Act passed in July, the nation exploded in racial violence. White supremacists torched more than two dozen black churches in Mississippi. Harlem witnessed its worst race riots ever. Meanwhile, halfway around the world, the U.S. Navy baited North Vietnamese battleships in the South China Sea. In September, just after Meiklejohn returned from his summer seminar in Monterey, thousands of students flocked to Sproul Plaza at Berkeley to protest the war. When police arrested the nonviolent demonstrators, members of the fledgling free speech movement, including its bold young leader, Mario Savio, staged sit-ins that reverberated from coast to coast. In the midst of all this chaos, Meiklejohn tried to remain hopeful. He spent several weeks working with an archivist to catalogue his personal and professional papers.[93] The process of sorting through nine decades of hard-wrought materials was exciting, but it put him in a contemplative mood. "A woman is here arranging my papers," he wrote to

Alexander Meiklejohn receiving an honorary degree at the University of California, Berkeley, 1964 (University of Wisconsin Archives)

Alexander Meiklejohn wearing his Presidential Medal of Freedom, 1963 (State Historical Society of Wisconsin, WHi [X3] 52116)

W. H. Ferry. "It gives me intimation that the end is near."[94] Indeed, by November, Meiklejohn had slowed considerably. "I am not ill," he assured a friend. "I just get tired out more readily than I used to."[95] But, in fact, Meiklejohn was actually much sicker than he thought. By mid-December, when eight hundred activists from the free speech movement were arrested for occupying Sproul Hall and Governor Pat Brown dispatched state police to quell the protests, he was homebound with pneumonia. On December 16, he told Helen that he felt well enough to receive visitors, but his good health was just an illusion. Sitting in his living room engaged in an animated conversation about the Berkeley protests with his friend Barnaby Keeney, president of his alma mater Brown, Meiklejohn drew one last breath, quietly closed his eyes, and died.[96]

Afterword: Education and the Democratic Ideal— The Meaning of Alexander Meiklejohn

I N THE DAYS AND WEEKS following Meiklejohn's death, obituaries ran in virtually every major newspaper in the country.[1] "The death of Alexander Meiklejohn, at the age of ninety-two, robs the country of a national resource—a figure almost uniquely symbolic of its libertarian tradition," the *Washington Post* eulogized. "This ramrod-straight, sparse, spectacled philosopher was at once a scholar and polemicist, a man of learning and a champion of freedom. An implacable foe of every restraint on expression, an inveterate champion of underdogs and lost causes, he was, nevertheless, a man of extraordinary sweetness, gentleness, and tolerance." According to the editors at the *Post*, Meiklejohn had been a man ahead of his time. "He pressed incessantly for educational ideas and practices which were not to win general acceptance for nearly half a century," they observed. "All of higher education in the United States is today indebted to him for his theories and innovations."[2] In subsequent weeks, friends, family, and admirers gathered for memorial services in Berkeley, San Francisco, Providence, New York, and Washington, D.C. In San Francisco, more than four hundred people attended the event. In Washington, guests heard reflections from Justices Hugo Black and William Douglas, as well as Randolph Burgess, ambassador to NATO; Calvin Plimpton, president of Amherst; and Thomas Corcoran, a prominent attorney and adviser to President Roosevelt who knew Meiklejohn from his childhood in Pawtucket.[3] In New York, remembrances came from Roger Baldwin, Seelye Bixler, Carey McWilliams, Thomas Emerson, and Peter Weiss, a graduate of St. John's.[4] "Here passed Alexander Meiklejohn," Weiss noted, "with a twinkle in his eye, the truth by his side, freedom in his bones, conviction in his heart, and scorn for no man."[5]

Meiklejohn's legacy was perhaps most evident in the varied careers of his many students. The Experimental College, for example, yielded a remarkable number of leaders in government, journalism, teaching, and the arts. Wilbur Cohen became President Johnson's secretary of health, education, and welfare. Phileo Nash became the United States commissioner for Indian affairs and chair of the Wisconsin State Democratic Committee. John Scott served as assistant to the publisher of *Time* magazine. Merlyn Pitzele became the labor editor of *Business Week*. Sidney Hertzberg was editor of *Common Sense*. Sam Burger became vice ambassador to Korea in the 1950s and Vietnam in the 1960s. Michael Sapir became an economic adviser to the World Bank. Irving Fein became the executive producer of *The Jack Benny Show* and vice president of CBS-TV. Victor Wolfson found fame as a major Broadway playwright, and R. Freeman Butts became a distinguished professor of education at Columbia's Teachers College.[6] Few professors evoked such lasting emotional bonds as Meiklejohn did. Nearly twenty years after the Experimental College closed, he received a long letter from a student who had withdrawn before the end of his sophomore year because of financial troubles brought on by the Great Depression. "Quite simply," Saul Brahms wrote to Meiklejohn, "the college, the teachers, my fellow students, the environment which you and the men around you created—[constituted] the most important intellectual experience in my thirty-six years on this earth. My thinking, my feeling, my wanderings, my dreaming, yes, my living, could not have been so rich and vivid had I not been associated with the college. And I have recognized this for many years. Yes, I was confused. But, how I wish I could be so internally agitated with ideas, ideals, hopes, and loves again!"[7]

From his earliest days as an instructor at Brown, Meiklejohn played the role of a Socratic teacher. He insisted on the merits of learning through discussion and enjoyed nothing more than a vigorous classroom debate. "All of his friends must have at times drawn the analogy to Socrates," Harry Kalven observed. "But the comparison to Socrates has its limits. I have always suspected that Socrates, however wise and admirable, would have made a trying and difficult companion. 'Alec' was a Socrates who wore well, a Socrates it was fun to be with, a Socrates for all seasons."[8] The words Meiklejohn used to describe his own favorite teacher, E. Benjamin

Andrews at Brown, also described himself: "[H]e was a maker of men, because he had a mad, impetuous vision of what a man may be."[9] Indeed, as a life-long idealist, Meiklejohn was convinced that both education and democracy rested on the assumption that all people shared an equal potential for reason and virtue. To teach freedom was not to coerce or manipulate students; rather, it was to cultivate the interests and powers already latent within them. The origins of democratic education always lay with students who chose *voluntarily* to learn, to enter a process of critical deliberation, to be initiated into the ways of rational self-government. "Education," Meiklejohn explained in 1919, "is not the giving of knowledge. It is the process in which a young mind, fascinated by the activities of an older one, imitates it, accepts its values and its own criticisms of them, catches its methods, becomes caught up in all its enterprises. A college is a place where minds well trained for studying human problems are doing so and where younger minds, by association, are getting the feel of what the thinking process is, are getting started in the work of carrying it on. In a word, education is not the receiving of instruction; it is a contagion of the spirit."[10] The only way to teach freedom *democratically* was to persuade students to believe in their own capacity to teach themselves, even if the impetus for this belief came inevitably from external institutions of liberal education.

As his friends observed, Meiklejohn shared much in common with Socrates. His decision to assign Plato's *Republic* as one of the central texts of his Experimental College reflected his abiding interest in the dialectical relationship between education and democracy and his desire to contribute to the construction of an ideal republican state. Like Socrates, Meiklejohn believed that education could *teach* citizens how to be democratic, though he constantly questioned the role that teachers—or "philosopher-kings"—must play in that process. The crucial lesson of liberal education, he consistently argued, was the lesson of self-criticism— the lesson that knowledge is above all a humble awareness of one's own ignorance. "A genuine liberal attitude is as old as human self-criticism," he asserted in *Education Between Two Worlds*. "If an individual or group will hold fast both to custom and to intelligence, then its experience will be inevitably paradoxical."[11] No one expressed this paradox of liberal self-criticism, and the even deeper paradox of cultivating such self-criticism in student-citizens, better than Socrates. In book VII of Plato's *Republic*, Socrates tells his famous Parable of the Cave. Conversing with his companion, Glaucon, he describes an underground den inhabited by prisoners who know nothing of daylight. Shackled and unable to turn their heads, the prisoners see only faint shadows on the cave walls cast by the

331

flicker of fires burning behind them. One day, a group of philosophers re-
leases several prisoners and leads them outside the cave to see the dazzling
light of the sun. Blinded by the light, they flee in terror, refusing to believe
that the outside world is any more real than the shadows inside the cave.
When the philosophers try to explain that the cave dwellers have mistak-
enly believed in mere shadows, the prisoners call them liars. The Parable
of the Cave captured perfectly the difficult relation between teachers and
students in a process of democratic education. For Meiklejohn, the challenge of democratic education was neither to push students out into a
light so dazzling they could not bear it nor to pull teachers into a darkness
so deep they would forget the light. Rather, democratic education required cooperation between both forces. The task of teaching freedom demanded, first, a willingness on the part of students voluntarily to consent
to education and, second, a willingness on the part of philosophers to
leave the light and enter the cave as teachers.

The greatest danger to democracy, Socrates claimed, was not that citizens would refuse to seek a liberal education or would ridicule the deliberative process when it was presented to them. Rather, the danger was
that philosophers would shirk their duty to serve as examples of critical
intelligence in the world. When teachers refused to teach, Socrates argued,
virtue was in jeopardy of disappearing from the state. Herein lay the lesson that Meiklejohn had tried to teach throughout his long career—the
lesson that democracy rests on a set of common assumptions and shared
ideals that need to be taught actively and authoritatively by citizen-
philosophers. "The founders of a state," Socrates says, must "compel the
best minds to . . . ascend until they arrive at the good." They must *not,*
however, remain in this realm of dazzling excellence forever. They must
"descend again among the prisoners in the den and partake of their labors
and honors, whether they are worth having or not." Philosophers, in
other words, must become kings in order to teach their fellow citizens
how to be reasonable and virtuous rulers of themselves. Only then could
the process of *creating* democracy continue in perpetuity. When Glaucon
asks if philosophers must relinquish their "absolute autonomy" in order
to enter the cave as teachers, Socrates answers affirmatively. "Yes," he
says. "You have forgotten the intention of the philosopher, who did not
aim at making any one class in the state happy above the rest; [rather,] the
happiness was to be in the whole state, and [the philosopher] held the citizens together by persuasion and necessity, making them benefactors of
one another. To this end, he created them not to please themselves, but
rather to be his instruments in binding up the state."[12] As Meiklejohn dis-

covered over the course of his long career, philosophers had a fundamental obligation to aid their fellow citizens in the search for truth. The paradox of their educational authority lay in the fact that they did not teach for their own private or personal gain; rather, they accepted their role reluctantly and wielded it carefully for the sake of the democratic ideal.

When Glaucon asks if Socrates can guarantee that cave dwellers will consent to be educated, or even if philosophers will consent to teach, Socrates concedes that he cannot offer any such assurance. "If beggars, men hungering for want of private goods, go into public affairs supposing that in them they must seize the good, then it isn't possible," Socrates admits. But, "if you discover a life better than ruling for those who are going to rule, then it is possible that your well-governed city will come into being."[13] Socrates' ideal republic was exactly that—an ideal. It was profoundly vulnerable to dissent, disagreement, and debate. It always risked the possibility that citizens might choose ignorance and prejudice over reason and self-criticism. It could not teach democracy if students refused to learn. Meiklejohn, as much as anyone, recognized this tragic vulnerability of modern liberal democratic education. As he wrote in 1961, "[T]he primary social fact which blocks and hinders the success of our experiment in self-government is that our citizens are not educated for self-government. We are terrified by ideas rather than challenged and stimulated by them. Our dominant mood is not the courage of people who dare to think. It is the timidity of those who fear and hate whenever conventions are questioned."[14] And yet, despite these obstacles, Meiklejohn never abandoned his hope for a more unified human understanding. "Humanity," he contended at the peak of World War II, "has one intelligence. That intelligence, it is true, is only 'in the making.' Its making is a difficult and precarious venture. It may at any time collapse. And yet, the statement that all men may share in a common enterprise is both true and significant. It tells us, in part, what the world is. It tells us, in part, what men are. And it is upon that basis of fact that any proper plan of education must be based."[15] Here, in statements such as these, lay the meaning of Alexander Meiklejohn. Throughout his life, he maintained that the true purpose of liberal democratic education was to teach citizens, all citizens, how to deliberate reasonably and cooperatively about issues of common public concern. His goal was not to force citizens to think alike but to persuade them to think together. "So far as minds are concerned," he wrote in a statement that summarized his lasting contribution to the theory and practice of liberal democratic education, "the art of democracy is the art of thinking independently together."[16]

Notes

Bibliography and Suggestions
for Further Reading

Index

Notes

The vast majority of the research for this book came from the archival collections of Meiklejohn's many personal and professional papers, including the Alexander Meiklejohn Papers (abbreviated as AMP throughout) at the Brown University Archives, John Hay Library, Providence, Rhode Island (BUA); the Alexander Meiklejohn Papers at the Amherst College Archives and Special Collections, Amherst College Library, Amherst, Massachusetts (ACL); the Alexander Meiklejohn Papers at the State Historical Society of Wisconsin, Madison, Wisconsin (SHSW); the Experimental College Papers at the University of Wisconsin Archives, Madison, Wisconsin (UWA); and the Meiklejohn materials at the Meiklejohn Civil Liberties Institute, Berkeley, California (MCLI). Besides contemporary published books and articles, these archival collections contain all of the sources cited in the following notes.

PREFACE: MEIKLEJOHN, SOCRATES, AND THE PARADOX OF DEMOCRATIC EDUCATION

1. Benjamin B. Goldman, ed., "The First Year of the Experimental College: An Informative Résumé Published by the Pioneer Class of the Experimental College" (1928), 10–11, Experimental College Departmental Folder, 7/37, University of Wisconsin Archives, Madison (hereafter designated UWA).

2. Plato, *The Republic,* trans. Benjamin Jowett (New York, 1944), 177.

3. "Education the Salvation of Democracy," *Portland Spectator* (1923), box 34, folder 2, Alexander Meiklejohn Papers (hereafter designated AMP regardless of the depository), MSS 64, State Historical Society of Wisconsin, Madison, Wisconsin (hereafter designated SHSW).

4. *The Amherst Student* (February 23, 1920), Amherst College Library, Amherst, Massachusetts.

5. Alexander Meiklejohn, "Inaugural Address" (October 16, 1912), Non-Alumnus Biographical File—Alexander Meiklejohn, Amherst College Archives and Special Collections, Amherst College Library, Amherst, Massachusetts (hereafter designated ACL).

6. The closest attempt to write a comprehensive biography of Meiklejohn's

life was Margaret G. Frantz, "Radical Visions: Alexander Meiklejohn on Education, Culture, Democracy, and the First Amendment" (unpublished Ph.D. dissertation, University of California, Santa Cruz, 1984). Only one book on Meiklejohn, an annotated collection of his writings, exists. See Cynthia Stokes Brown, *Alexander Meiklejohn, Teacher of Freedom* (Berkeley, 1981).

7. Theodore Crane to Lawrence Cremin (July 19, 1965), MSS 95-180, Theodore R. Crane Papers, SHSW. See also Scott Abbott to "Mr. Edmunds" (December 22, 1965), Theodore R. Crane Papers, SHSW. "I happen to know that Meiklejohn was not anxious to have a biography done—as a matter of fact, it was his wish that it not be written."

8. Alexander Meiklejohn to W. H. Ferry (September 25, 1961), box 12, folder 27, AMP, SHSW.

CHAPTER 1. "A VOYAGE ACROSS THE ATLANTIC," AND "KANT'S ETHICS," 1872–1899

1. George Jacob Holyoake, *Self-Help by the People: Thirty-three Years of Cooperation in Rochdale, in Two Parts* (London, 1882), part 1: 11–29, quotation from 11.

2. Alexander Meiklejohn, "I'm an American" (August 10, 1941), transcript of an interview broadcast on WBZ-FM radio in Boston, box 35, folder 3, AMP, MSS 64, Archives Division, SHSW.

3. Meiklejohn, "I'm an American." "From boyhood to old age," Meiklejohn added, "my father worked as a color-designer in the textile industry. My mother and father were early members of the Rochdale Cooperative. I played cricket and soccer with the boys and men from the mills."

4. Holyoake, *Self-Help by the People*, part 1: 48–57. Quotations come from the Rochdale declaration of principles, written in 1855 and contained in Holyoake's *Self-Help by the People*.

5. Holyoake, *Self-Help by the People*, part 1: 22; part 2: 78.

6. Holyoake, *Self-Help by the People*, part 1: 20.

7. Meiklejohn, "I'm an American."

8. Holyoake, *Self-Help by the People*, part 1: 11.

9. Arthur Upham Pope to Theodore Crane (March 30, 1966), Theodore Crane Papers, MSS 95-180, SHSW.

10. Meiklejohn, "I'm an American."

11. Pope to Crane (March 30, 1966).

12. "Photographs and Brief Description of the Establishment of the Conant Thread Company, Pawtucket, R.I., Intended as a Souvenir of the Visit of Sir Peter Coats during the Winter of 1877–78" (Pawtucket, R.I., 1878), Pawtucket Coats and Clark File, Pawtucket Public Library, Pawtucket, Rhode Island.

13. Alexander Meiklejohn, "A Voyage across the Atlantic" (n.d.), box 60, folder 7, AMP, SHSW.

14. *Pawtucket–Central Falls Directory* (Pawtucket, R.I., 1884), 250; all the Pawtucket–Central Falls directories cited are housed in the Pawtucket Public Library.

15. "Dr. Meiklejohn Dies; Liberal Educator Lived in Pawtucket," *Pawtucket–Central Falls Gazette* (December 17, 1964), Meiklejohn newspaper clippings, AMP, Brown University Archives, John Hay Library, Brown University, Providence, Rhode Island (hereafter designated BUA).

16. Robert Grieve, *An Illustrated History of Pawtucket, Central Falls, and Vicinity* (Pawtucket, R.I., 1897), 154. See also *Pawtucket Past and Present, Being a Brief Account of the Beginning Progress of Its Industries and a Resume of the Early History of the City* (Pawtucket, R.I., 1917), 28.

17. See advertisement in the *Pawtucket–Central Falls Directory* (Pawtucket, R.I., 1886), 52.

18. *Leading Manufacturers and Merchants in Rhode Island* (New York, 1886), 163, Rider Collection, BUA.

19. "William Meiklejohn, 85, Dead at Pawtucket Home; Store's President Was City's Oldest Active Businessman," *Providence Journal-Bulletin* (February 17, 1947), Meiklejohn newspaper clippings, AMP, BUA.

20. *Pawtucket–Central Falls Directory* (1884), 250. See also "William Meiklejohn, 85, Dead at Pawtucket Home; Store's President Was City's Oldest Active Businessman," *Providence Journal-Bulletin* (February 17, 1947), Meiklejohn newspaper clippings, AMP, BUA.

21. United States Bureau of the Census, *Historical Statistics of the United States: Colonial Times to 1970* (Washington, D.C., 1975), part 1, 117.

22. Stephan Thernstrom, ed., *The Harvard Encyclopedia of American Ethnic Groups* (Cambridge, Mass., 1980), 913.

23. *Pawtucket–Central Falls Directory* (Pawtucket, R.I., 1890), 536.

24. Joshua Little to Alexander Meiklejohn (September 23, 1919), box III, folder 23, AMP, ACL.

25. See Alexander Meiklejohn to William O. Douglas (November 18, 1960), box 11, folder 21, AMP, SHSW. For more information on the Pawtucket Congregational Church, see *The Providence Plantations for Two Hundred and Fifty Years* (Providence, R.I., 1886), 380, BUA.

26. *Pawtucket–Central Falls Directory* (1886), 52.

27. See Alexander Meiklejohn, "Recreation" (n.d.), box 60, folder 7, AMP, SHSW.

28. See "Cricketing Meiklejohns," *Providence Journal-Bulletin* (July 28, 1935), box 59, folder 2, AMP, SHSW.

29. Alexander Meiklejohn, "Foreign Immigration" (n.d. [pre-1889]), box 60, folder 7, AMP, SHSW.

30. Meiklejohn, "Foreign Immigration."

31. "The Courses of Study in Pawtucket High School" (1888), box 265, number 14, Rider Collection, John Hay Library, Brown University.

32. Alexander Meiklejohn, "Campaigning" (n.d.), box 60, folder 7, AMP, SHSW. Despite his opposition to raucous parading, Meiklejohn was not unpatriotic. See, for example, his "Essay on the Declaration of Independence for George Washington's Birthday, 1889" (n.d.), box 60, folder 7, AMP, SHSW.

33. Alexander Meiklejohn, "Oration on Prohibition" (April 1, 1889), box 60, folder 7, AMP, SHSW.

34. Pawtucket City Death Records, 1763–1900, book 3: 55.

35. Grieve, *An Illustrated History of Pawtucket, Central Falls, and Vicinity,* 154. See also *Pawtucket Past and Present, Being a Brief Account of the Beginning Progress of Its Industries and a Resume of the Early History of the City* (Pawtucket, R.I., 1917), 28.

36. Robert Perkins Brown, Henry Robinson Palmer, Harry Lyman Koopman, and Clarence Saunders Brigham, eds., *Memories of Brown: Traditions and Recollections Gathered from Many Sources* (Providence, R.I., 1909), 435, 367.

37. Alexander Meiklejohn to Chesley Worthington (November 28, 1950), Chesley Worthington Papers, BUA.

38. For more information on Andrews, see James E. Hansen, "Gallant, Stalwart Bennie: Elisha Benjamin Andrews (1844–1917): An Educator's Odyssey" (unpublished Ph.D. dissertation, University of Denver, 1969). See also James E. Hansen, "Students and the Andrews Legend at Brown," *Rhode Island History* (August 1971): 75–85.

39. Walter Bronson, *History of Brown University* (Providence, R.I., 1913), 431.

40. Brown University course catalogues, 1889–1893, BUA.

41. Alexander Meiklejohn to John Gaus (April 10, 1963), box 14, folder 3, AMP, SHSW.

42. See Lucien Price, *Prophet Unawares: The Romance of an Idea* (Boston, 1924), 22.

43. Meiklejohn to Gaus (April 10, 1963).

44. James Seth's works included *Freedom as Ethical Postulate* (1891); *A Study of Ethical Principles* (1916); and *Essays in Ethics and Religion* (1926).

45. *Annual Report of the President to the Corporation of Brown University* (1890), 21–22, BUA.

46. *Annual Report of the President to the Corporation of Brown University* (1890), 21–22.

47. See Elisha Benjamin Andrews, "A Hundred Years of Immanuel Kant," *Baptist Quarterly Review* (winter 1882): 121.

48. See Andrew Seth, *Scottish Philosophy: A Comparison of the Scottish and German Answers to Hume* (Edinburgh, 1890). Andrew Seth was the brother of James Seth.

49. Alexander Meiklejohn, "A Defense of Empirical Knowledge" (n.d. [1889–1893]), box 60, folder 9, AMP, SHSW.

50. Meiklejohn, "A Defense of Empirical Knowledge."

51. See Alexander Meiklejohn, "Synopsis of the *Critique of Pure Reason*" (n.d.), box 60, folder 8, AMP, SHSW.

52. See Meiklejohn's class and paper notes (n.d. [1889–1893]), box 61, folder 2, AMP, SHSW.

53. Notes for "History of Philosophy, Leibnitz to Kant" with James Seth (n.d. [1889–1893]), box 61, AMP, SHSW. "A perfect (divine) understanding would be creative," Meiklejohn scribbled in his notebook. "Our understanding is discursive," he added. "It relates, arranges, and forms the given matter. It does not create."

54. Meiklejohn, "A Defense of Empirical Knowledge."

55. Alexander Meiklejohn, "Nominalism and Realism" (n.d.), box 61, folder 1, AMP, SHSW.

56. Meiklejohn, "Nominalism and Realism."

57. For a complete summary of the lectures in this course, see James Seth, *Essays in Ethics and Religion, with Other Papers* (Edinburgh, 1926), 134–179.

58. Alexander Meiklejohn, "Plato" (n.d.), box 61, folder 1, AMP, SHSW.

59. Alexander Meiklejohn, "Kant's Ethics" (n.d.), box 61, folder 3, AMP, SHSW.

60. Johann Wolfgang von Goethe, *Faust,* ed. Cyrus Hamlin, trans. Walter Arndt, Norton Critical Ed. (New York, 1976), 83–86.

61. "Orations Delivered at the Class Tree—Humorous Words for the Undergraduates," *Providence Journal-Bulletin* (May 1893), Brown University Scrapbook, vol. 4, number 195, BUA.

62. Alexander Meiklejohn to Frederick Pierpont Ladd (June 25, 1904), box 1: "Material on, about, or by Alexander Meiklejohn," Meiklejohn Civil Liberties Institute, 1715 Francisco Street, Berkeley, California (hereafter designated MCLI).

63. Alexander Meiklejohn, "The Value of the Evolutionary Method, as Applied to Ethics" (n.d.), box 61, folder 1, AMP, SHSW.

64. Alexander Meiklejohn, "The Significance of the Scientific Movement of the Nineteenth Century," unpaginated typescript (n.d.), box 61, folder 1, AMP, SHSW.

65. "Philosophical Club Meeting: Ethics of Evolution with Reference to Huxley's Romanes Lecture," *Brown Daily Herald* (January 12, 1894), 1, BUA.

66. John Harland to Alexander Meiklejohn (January 10, 1917), box III, folder 1, AMP, ACL.

67. Meiklejohn to Ladd (June 25, 1904).

68. Meiklejohn to Ladd (June 25, 1904). See also "Speech of President Meiklejohn Recorded by Eric S. Erickson for Cornell University Records" (n.d.), box 34, folder 3, AMP, SHSW.

69. Alexander Meiklejohn, "Hockey Pioneers," *Brown Alumni Monthly* (April 1951): 5–6. For more information on Meiklejohn's role in bringing hockey

to American colleges and universities, see "Harvard Makes a Poor Debut in Hockey," *Boston Herald* (January 20, 1898); "When They First Brought Hockey to This Country" and "The Strange Beginnings of the Sport, First Played in the States by Brown," *Providence Journal-Bulletin* (January 22, 1933); "Pioneers in College Hockey," *Brown Alumni Monthly* (March 1957): 6–11; and the "Hockey" subject file, BUA.

70. See Alexander Meiklejohn, "Kant's Theory of Substance" (unpublished Ph.D. dissertation, Cornell University, 1897), box 63, folder 1, AMP, SHSW.

71. See Alexander Meiklejohn to John Gaus (May 9, 1952), box 14, folder 3, AMP, SHSW.

72. Meiklejohn to Ladd (June 25, 1904).

73. Brown University course catalogue, 1898–1899, BUA.

74. Arthur Upham Pope, "Alexander Meiklejohn," *American Scholar* (fall 1965): 641–645.

75. Louis I. Newman, untitled piece, *Jewish Community Bulletin of San Francisco* (n.d.), Meiklejohn newspaper clippings, AMP, BUA.

76. J. Irving Manatt to William B. Greenough (April 15, 1912), box X, folder 9, AMP, ACL.

77. Frank J. Goodwin, "The New President of Amherst College," newspaper unidentified (n.d.), miscellaneous newspaper clippings, Non-Alumnus Biographical File—Alexander Meiklejohn, ACL.

78. Alexander Meiklejohn, "Competition in College," *Brown Alumni Monthly* (November 1909): 75–78, BUA.

CHAPTER 2. "COLLEGE EDUCATION AND THE MORAL IDEAL," 1900–1911

1. "Annual Reports of the School Committee of Pawtucket, Rhode Island" (1899), box 371, numbers 10 and 15, Rider Collection, John Hay Library, Brown University.

2. Cornelius Kruse to Alexander Meiklejohn (October 21, 1938), box 2, folder 10, AMP, SHSW.

3. Alexander Meiklejohn to "Professor Beck" (October 11, 1949), box 11, folder 1, AMP, SHSW.

4. Alexander Meiklejohn to Frederick Pierpont Ladd (June 25, 1904), box 1: "Material on, about, or by Alexander Meiklejohn," MCLI.

5. See Scott Abbott, "Philosopher and Dean: Alexander Meiklejohn at Brown, 1901–1912" (unpublished Ph.D. dissertation, University of Denver, 1967).

6. "New Dean Chosen," *Providence Journal-Bulletin* (July 10, 1901). See also "Annual Meeting; Corporation of Brown University Did Important Business; Professor Alexander Meiklejohn Elected as Dean," *Providence Journal-Bulletin* (September 5, 1901). Both in Brown University Scrapbooks, vol. 7, numbers 160 and 161, respectively, BUA.

7. See the *Brown Alumni Monthly* (July 1902): 43, BUA.

8. Some of La Villa's wealth apparently came from stock in the U.S. Steel Corporation. See M. D. Howell to Alexander Meiklejohn (October 10, 1951), box 11, folder 19, AMP, SHSW.

9. Meiklejohn to Ladd (June 25, 1904).

10. See "Mrs. Meiklejohn Dies in Hospital," *New York Times* (February 14, 1925), miscellaneous newspaper clippings, AMP, BUA.

11. Meiklejohn to Ladd (June 25, 1904).

12. Alexander Meiklejohn, "Hockey Pioneers," *Brown Alumni Monthly* (March 1951): 35, BUA.

13. Morris J. Wessel to the Amherst College Board of Trustees (April 12, 1912), box X, folder 9, AMP, ACL.

14. See Alexander Meiklejohn, "Report of the Dean of the University," *Annual Report of the President to the Corporation of Brown University* (1903), 29, BUA.

15. See Alexander Meiklejohn, "Report of the Dean of the University," *Annual Report of the President to the Corporation of Brown University* (1910), 46, BUA.

16. These figures represented 2 or 3 percent of the nation's population aged eighteen to twenty-four. See U.S. Department of Commerce, Bureau of the Census, *Historical Statistics of the United States from Colonial Times to 1970* (Washington, D.C., 1975), part 1: 383–386.

17. Colin B. Burke, *American Collegiate Populations: A Test of the Traditional View* (New York, 1982), 217–218.

18. See the Carnegie Foundation for the Advancement of Teaching, "A Practical Illustration of the Use of College Requirements for Admission," *Fourth Annual Report of the President and the Treasurer* (New York, 1909), 141. See also Carnegie Foundation for the Advancement of Teaching, "The Function of College Requirements for Admission," *Second Annual Report of the President and Treasurer* (New York, 1907), 66–75.

19. Alexander Meiklejohn, "Report of the Dean of the University," *Annual Report of the President to the Corporation of Brown University* (1911), 34, BUA.

20. Meiklejohn, "Report of the Dean of the University" (1910), 51.

21. Interview with Meiklejohn conducted by Theodore R. Crane (October 19, 1963), BUA.

22. See Alexander Meiklejohn, "Report of the Dean of the University," *Annual Report of the President to the Corporation of Brown University* (1902), 35, BUA.

23. See "University Scholarships," *Brown Alumni Monthly* (January 1904): 132–133, BUA. In 1904, the Brown trustees appropriated more than $15,000 for university scholarships, which fell into three groups: "(1) a small number yielding each $50 a term or $150 a year, paying the whole college bill for tuition and incidentals, awarded to a few juniors and seniors of specially high scholarship, (2) a

number yielding each $35 a term or $105 a year, (3) a number yielding $20 a term or $60 a year, used in part to supplement the smaller endowed scholarships, and also for those needing relatively less assistance."

24. Brown University, "Accounts of Students" (1904–1907), 1–4; (1908–1910), 26–29, BUA.

25. Brown University, "Accounts of Students" (1904–1907, 1906–1909, and 1908–1910).

26. William E. Witham to Alexander Meiklejohn (May 4, 1903), box I, letters regarding scholarships, L–Z, AMP, BUA. For more examples of financial aid requests, see letters of recommendation for potential students, AMP, BUA.

27. Samuel B. Huey to Alexander Meiklejohn (June 18, 1901), box I, letters regarding scholarships, L–Z, AMP, BUA.

28. F. Childs to Alexander Meiklejohn (January 14, 1903), box I, letters regarding scholarships, A–K, AMP, BUA.

29. Charles J. Blomberg to Alexander Meiklejohn (March 21, 1912), box II, folder B, AMP, BUA.

30. "Alexander Meiklejohn," unpaginated typescript (n.d.), box 53, folder 3, AMP, SHSW.

31. See Meiklejohn, "Report of the Dean" (1902), 30–31.

32. "The Dean Took a Hand: Now Some Brown Students Are Wondering What Will Result," *Providence Journal-Bulletin* (April 17, 1902), Brown University Scrapbook, vol. 7, number 181, BUA.

33. J. Ralph Honiss to Alexander Meiklejohn (September 10, 1907), box 1, folder H, AMP, BUA.

34. Alexander Meiklejohn, "Report to Presidents of the Freshman and Sophomore Classes" (April 13, 1908), box II, letters regarding bills paid and unpaid, AMP, BUA. See also "Damage Report" (March 4, 1907), box II, letters regarding bills paid and unpaid, AMP, BUA.

35. See "Letter of Apology" (n.d.), box II, "Student Life Activities" folder, AMP, BUA.

36. W. H. P. Faunce, "Report of the President of the University," *Annual Report of the President to the Corporation of Brown University* (1905), 12, BUA.

37. Albert A. Bennett to Amherst College Board of Trustees (April 22, 1912), box X, folder 9, AMP, ACL. The Amherst board solicited opinions from Brown students when considering Meiklejohn for the Amherst presidency.

38. Charles E. Hughes, Jr., to Amherst College Board of Trustees (April 22, 1912), box X, folder 9, AMP, ACL.

39. Mrs. O. L. Altdoerffer to Alexander Meiklejohn (January 21, 1910), box II, letters concerning students' dismissal, AMP, BUA.

40. "Brown 6; Manhattan 5; in a Game Marred by Unsportsmanlike Conduct, Brown Downs Her Opponents," *Brown Daily Herald* (October 10, 1901), 1, BUA.

41. Lester E. Dodge to Alexander Meiklejohn (October 24, 1903), box II, folder D, AMP, BUA.

42. R. W. Swetland to Alexander Meiklejohn (October 15, 1904), box II, folder M, AMP, BUA.

43. M. H. Buckham to Alexander Meiklejohn (October 15, 1904), box II, folder M, AMP, BUA.

44. Archibald Freeman to Alexander Meiklejohn (December 2, 1905), box II, folder E/F, AMP, BUA.

45. Alexander Meiklejohn, "The Evils of College Athletics," *Harper's Weekly* (December 2, 1905): 1751–1752.

46. Fred J. Cox to Alexander Meiklejohn (August 19, 1903), box II, folder C, AMP, BUA.

47. See the *Boston Globe* (August 17, 1903).

48. See "The Athletic Situation at Brown; Statement of the Athletic Board," *Brown Alumni Monthly* (February 1904): 146–153, BUA.

49. See "Absolutely Amateur Athletics," *Brown Alumni Monthly* (March 1904): 171–173, BUA.

50. Hammond Lamont to Alexander Meiklejohn (October 21, 1903), box II, folder L, AMP, BUA.

51. Chester S. Allen to Alexander Meiklejohn (n.d.), box II, folder A, AMP, BUA.

52. "Keep Up the Bars!" *Brown Alumni Monthly* (February 1904): 154–156, BUA.

53. See the *Providence Journal-Bulletin* (February 6, 1904), Meiklejohn newspaper clippings, AMP, BUA. "To emphasize their dissatisfaction with the action of the board and the publication of the reasons for this step, which have already been broadcast through the country and are now the subject of comment in all the leading universities, the two dissenting members of the board tendered their resignations."

54. "Position of Minority of the Board, Professor John E. Hill," *Brown Alumni Monthly* (February 1904): 152–153, BUA.

55. Meiklejohn, "The Evils of College Athletics," 1751–1752.

56. Meiklejohn, "The Evils of College Athletics," 1752.

57. "Amherst's New Leader: Dr. Meiklejohn and What He Has Done" *Boston Transcript* (May 18, 1912), miscellaneous newspaper clippings, Non-Alumnus Biographical File—Alexander Meiklejohn, ACL.

58. Alexander Meiklejohn, "Report of the Dean of the University," *Annual Report of the President to the Corporation of Brown University* (1907), 37, BUA.

59. Alexander Meiklejohn, "Report of the Dean of the University," *Annual Report of the President to the Corporation of Brown University* (1908), 37, BUA.

60. Meiklejohn, "Report of the Dean of the University" (1908), 37. See also Alexander Meiklejohn, "Competition in College," *Brown Alumni Monthly* (November 1909): 75–78, BUA.

61. Alexander Meiklejohn, "College Education and the Moral Ideal," *Education* (May 1908): 552–567.

62. Meiklejohn, "College Education and the Moral Ideal," 560.

63. Meiklejohn, "College Education and the Moral Ideal," 566.

64. See Meiklejohn, "Report of the Dean of the University" (1907), 35.

65. Meiklejohn, "Report of the Dean of the University" (1910), 33.

66. See Meiklejohn, "Report of the Dean of the University" (1911), 28.

67. Meiklejohn, "Report of the Dean of the University" (1910), 34. See also "Report of the Advisory Committee on Fraternities," *Annual Report of the President to the Corporation of Brown University* (1910), 32–33, BUA.

68. Despite his objections to fraternities, Meiklejohn did not seek to abolish them altogether. See Meiklejohn, "Report of the Dean of the University" (1907), 36.

69. See Meiklejohn, "Report of the Dean of the University" (1910), 40.

70. See Meiklejohn, "Report of the Dean of the University" (1910), 45. See also Alexander Meiklejohn, "Fraternities and Scholarship," *Brown Alumni Monthly* (November 1910): 89–91, BUA.

71. *Providence Journal-Bulletin* (November 11, 1910).

72. Alexander Meiklejohn, "Report of the Dean of the University," *Annual Report of the President to the Corporation of Brown University* (1906), 36, BUA.

73. Alexander Meiklejohn, "Report of the Dean of the University," *Annual Report of the President to the Corporation of Brown University* (1909), 35, BUA.

74. "Amherst's New Leader: Dr. Meiklejohn and What He Has Done."

75. Walter Goodnow Everett, "Brown's Gift to Amherst," *Amherst Graduates' Quarterly* (January 1913), ACL.

76. Meiklejohn, "Report of the Dean of the University" (1907), 33.

77. Meiklejohn, "Report of the Dean of the University" (1910), 39.

78. J. E. Creighton to Alexander Meiklejohn (May 2, 1908), box 10, folder 18, AMP, SHSW.

79. Alexander Meiklejohn to J. E. Creighton (May 8, 1908), box 10, folder 18, AMP, SHSW.

80. Quoted in W. H. P. Faunce to Alexander Meiklejohn (October 21, 1908), box 12, folder 21, AMP, SHSW.

81. *Pawtucket City Death Records, 1763–1900* (Pawtucket, R.I., 1908), book 4: 229. See also "Brown Dean's Mother Dead," *Providence Journal-Bulletin* (March 25, 1908), Brown University Scrapbook, vol. 8, no. 206: "Death was due to a sudden attack of heart troubles. Mrs. Meiklejohn was in apparently good health during the early morning. At nine o'clock, she was suddenly taken ill and survived the seizure only a few hours. She was 76 years of age. . . . She was a member of the Daughters of the Heather, auxiliary to Clan Fraser, No. 11, O. S. C., and was a devout member of the Pawtucket Congregational Church."

82. Ernest M. Whitcomb to Alexander Meiklejohn (February 3, 1915), box X, folder 10, AMP, ACL.

83. Stanley King, *A History of the Endowment of Amherst College* (Amherst, 1951), 128.

84. Charles E. Hughes, Jr., to the Amherst College Board of Trustees (April 22, 1912), box X, folder 9, AMP, ACL.

85. Morris J. Wessel to the Amherst College Board of Trustees (April 22, 1912), box X, folder 9, AMP, ACL.

86. J. Irving Manatt to William B. Greenough (April 15, 1912), box X, folder 9, AMP, ACL.

87. See "The New President of Amherst," *Boston Herald* (May 22, 1912).

88. W. H. P. Faunce to Alexander Meiklejohn (April 29, 1912), box 12, folder 21, AMP, SHSW.

89. John D. Rockefeller, Jr., to Alexander Meiklejohn (May 8, 1912), box X, folder 7, AMP, ACL.

90. John D. Rockefeller, Jr., to Alexander Meiklejohn (May 23, 1912), box X, folder 7, AMP, ACL.

91. "The Militancy of Alexander Meiklejohn," *Brown Alumni Monthly* (March 1965): 12–15, BUA.

92. Mary E. Woolley to Alexander Meiklejohn (May 21, 1912), box X, folder 8, AMP, ACL.

93. James Meiklejohn to Alexander Meiklejohn (June 17, 1912), box X, folder 6, AMP, ACL.

94. "Meiklejohn Makes Farewell Address; Retiring Dean of Brown University Cheered by Students in Chapel; 'What College Stands For'; President-Elect of Amherst College Tells Undergraduates to Be Fair and Think Hard—Advises Them to Get Understanding of the Big Things of Life," *Providence Journal-Bulletin* (May 29, 1912).

CHAPTER 3. "THE COLLEGE AS CRITIC," 1912–1919

1. "Inauguration of President Meiklejohn," *Amherst Graduates' Quarterly* (November 1912): 47, 38, ACL.

2. Scott Buchanan, "Copy for Ann Ginger," unpaginated typescript (n.d.), "Material by, about, or related to Alexander Meiklejohn," MCLI.

3. Talcott Williams, "The President-Elect," *Amherst Graduates' Quarterly* (June 1912): 321–325, ACL.

4. Arthur H. Washburn to Scott Abbott (June 2, 1964), reminiscences solicited by Scott Abbott, Non-Alumnus Biographical File—Alexander Meiklejohn, ACL.

5. Buchanan, "Copy for Ann Ginger."

6. Alexander Meiklejohn, "Inaugural Address" (October 16, 1912), in Norman Foerster, Frederick A. Manchester, and Karl Young, eds., *Essays for College Men: Education, Science, and Art* (New York, 1913), 28–59, quotation from 30.

7. Meiklejohn, "Inaugural Address" (1912), 43. See also the *Amherst Graduates' Quarterly* (November 1912): 35–95, ACL.

8. Meiklejohn, "Inaugural Address" (1912), 46–47.

9. Meiklejohn, "Inaugural Address" (1912), 48, 50, 52.

10. Meiklejohn, "Inaugural Address" (1912).

11. See Christopher T. Greene, "The Academic Philosophy of Alexander Meiklejohn," *Amherst Graduates' Quarterly* (spring 1971): 7–9, ACL.

12. E. Benjamin Andrews to Alexander Meiklejohn (January 22, 1914), box I, folder 1, AMP, ACL.

13. Alexander H. Abbott to Alexander Meiklejohn (July 29, 1913), box I, folder 2, AMP, ACL.

14. Alexander Meiklejohn to James Seth (n.d. [1912]), box V, folder 6, AMP, ACL.

15. Frank L. Babbott to Scott Abbott (May 25, 1964), reminiscences solicited by Scott Abbott, Non-Alumnus Biographical File—Alexander Meiklejohn, ACL.

16. "Reminiscences by A. W. Marsh," notes taken from taped interview by Doris E. Abramoor with A. W. Eli Marsh (July 23, 1975), Non-Alumnus Biographical File—Alexander Meiklejohn, ACL.

17. Responses to student questionnaire regarding the curriculum (n.d. [1913]), box IX, folder 5, AMP, ACL.

18. Lucien Price, *Prophets Unawares: The Romance of an Idea* (New York, 1924), 9.

19. Harold E. Jewett to Scott Abbott (May 3, 1964), reminiscences solicited by Scott Abbott, Non-Alumnus Biographical File—Alexander Meiklejohn, ACL.

20. Frank W. Stearns to Alexander Meiklejohn (March 25, 1913), box X, folder 9, AMP, ACL.

21. "Reminiscences by A. W. Marsh."

22. Quoted in Cynthia Stokes Brown, *Alexander Meiklejohn: Teacher of Freedom* (Berkeley, 1981), 13.

23. George Tramontana to Scott Abbott (June 6, 1964), reminiscences solicited by Scott Abbott, Non-Alumnus Biographical File—Alexander Meiklejohn, ACL.

24. Howard S. Bliss to Alexander Meiklejohn (February 10, 1920), box I, folder 9, AMP, ACL.

25. Alexander Meiklejohn to L. A. Crocker (August 11, 1913), box II, folder 10, AMP, ACL.

26. Alexander Meiklejohn, "Report of the President to the Trustees," Amherst (January 1914), 36, box VI, folder 1, AMP, ACL.

27. "Hundred Thousand Dollars for New Chair in Economics and Social Institutions," *Amherst Student* (January 12, 1914): 1, 5, ACL.

28. "A Tentative Definition of a Course of Study in Social and Economic Institutions," unpaginated typescript (n.d. [1914]), box IX, folder 5, AMP, ACL.

29. "A Tentative Definition of a Course of Study in Social and Economic Institutions."

30. William DeWitt Hyde to Alexander Meiklejohn (March 27, 1914), box VI, folder 10, AMP, ACL.

31. Alexander Meiklejohn to W. Evans Clark (January 16, 1914), box VI, folder 10, AMP, ACL.

32. Walton Hamilton to Alexander Meiklejohn (April 1, 1915), box III, folder 2, AMP, ACL.

33. Francis B. Randall, "The Meiklejohn Tragedy" (March 1957), unpaginated typescript, 28 pp., Non-Alumnus Biographical File—Alexander Meiklejohn, ACL.

34. Untitled notes (n.d.), box IX, folder 5, AMP, ACL.

35. Alexander Meiklejohn to George B. Churchill (July 21, 1913), box VII, folder 9, AMP, ACL.

36. See George Bosworth Churchill, "Is the College Making Good?" (1913), box III, folder 7, George Bosworth Churchill Papers, ACL.

37. John Erskine to Alexander Meiklejohn (April 26, 1915), box VII, folder 9, AMP, ACL.

38. Alexander Meiklejohn to John Erskine (April 30, 1915), box VII, folder 9, AMP, ACL. See also John Erskine to Alexander Meiklejohn (July 8, 1915), box VII, folder 9, AMP, ACL.

39. Chauncey Brewster Tinker to Samuel Henry Cobb (August 26, 1915), box VII, folder 9, AMP, ACL.

40. Alexander Meiklejohn to Robert Palfrey Utter (September 13, 1915), box VII, folder 9, AMP, ACL.

41. Robert Frost to Alfred Harcourt (December 1916), in *Selected Letters of Robert Frost,* ed. Lawrance Thompson (New York, 1964), 207–208.

42. Clarence Ayres to Alexander Meiklejohn (August 2, 1919), box I, folder 6, AMP, ACL.

43. Quoted in Randall, "The Meiklejohn Tragedy."

44. Buchanan, "Copy for Ann Ginger."

45. Frank L. Babbott to Scott Abbott (May 25, 1964), reminiscences solicited by Scott Abbott, Non-Alumnus Biographical File—Alexander Meiklejohn, ACL.

46. "The College Year of 1912–1913," *Amherst Graduates' Quarterly* (October 1913): 34–39, quotation from 35, ACL.

47. Alfred H. Washburn to Scott Abbott (June 1, 1964), reminiscences solicited by Scott Abbott, Non-Alumnus Biographical File—Alexander Meiklejohn, ACL.

48. George A. Gordos to Alexander Meiklejohn (February 2, 1915), box X, folder 10, AMP, ACL.

49. Merrill Anderson to Scott Abbott (January 12, 1965), reminiscences solicited by Scott Abbott, Non-Alumnus Biographical File—Alexander Meiklejohn, ACL.

50. John Erskine to Alexander Meiklejohn (December 22, 1916), box II, folder 9, AMP, ACL.

51. Merrill Anderson to Scott Abbott (January 12, 1965), reminiscences solicited by Scott Abbott, Non-Alumnus Biographical File—Alexander Meiklejohn, ACL.

52. Price, *Prophets Unawares*, 103.

53. Alexander Meiklejohn to Mary Waterman (November 25, 1964), box 30, folder 20, AMP, SHSW.

54. See "President Joins State Military Commission; President Meiklejohn, Though Not a Militarist, Accepts Governor's Appointment," *Amherst Student* (October 4, 1915): 1, 5, ACL.

55. Edward L. Dyer to Alexander Meiklejohn (February 1, 1916), box II, folder 1, AMP, ACL.

56. Alexander Meiklejohn to Edward L. Dyer (February 12, 1916), box II, folder 1, AMP, ACL.

57. Alexander Meiklejohn to George R. Dickinson (May 25, 1916), box II, folder 1, AMP, ACL.

58. Augustus W. Bennett to Scott Abbott (June 5, 1964), reminiscences solicited by Scott Abbott, Non-Alumnus Biographical File—Alexander Meiklejohn, ACL.

59. Alexander Meiklejohn, "A Schoolmaster's View of Compulsory Military Training," *School and Society* (July 1916): 9–14.

60. Meiklejohn, "A Schoolmaster's View of Compulsory Military Training," 10.

61. Meiklejohn, "A Schoolmaster's View of Compulsory Military Training," 14. See also William James, *The Moral Equivalent of War* (New York, 1910).

62. "Culture by Forcible Feeding at Amherst," *Boston Evening Transcript* (June 20, 1914), miscellaneous newspaper clippings, Non-Alumnus Biographical File—Alexander Meiklejohn, ACL.

63. "Speaks to College on National Crisis," *Amherst Student* (12 February 1917): 1, ACL. See also Alexander Meiklejohn, "Keep on in College," *Christian Endeavor World* (July 1918), box 33, folder 6, AMP, SHSW.

64. Robert Lyman Grant to Alexander Meiklejohn (March 29, 1917), box VIII, folder 5, AMP, ACL.

65. "War Extra! Amherst Rises to Meet Nation's Need; Campus to Be Partially Transformed into Training Camp; Course in Military Instruction to Start Monday; President Meiklejohn Makes Inspiring Address," *Amherst Student* (April 6, 1917): 1–4, ACL.

66. "Ames Back from Front Speaks to College Body," *Amherst Student* (16 April 1917): 1, 5, ACL.

67. A. Thomas Atkinson to Alexander Meiklejohn (September 29, 1918), box VIII, folder 6, AMP, ACL.

68. Everett Glass to Alexander Meiklejohn (n.d.), box VIII, folder 6, AMP, ACL.

69. "War Extra!" 2.

70. Eric H. Marks to Scott Abbott (June 2, 1964), reminiscences solicited by Scott Abbott, Non-Alumnus Biographical File—Alexander Meiklejohn, ACL.

71. See Augustus Bennett to Scott Abbott (June 5, 1964), reminiscences solicited by Scott Abbott, Non-Alumnus Biographical File—Alexander Meiklejohn, ACL.

72. Eric H. Marks to Scott Abbott (June 2, 1964), reminiscences solicited by Scott Abbott, Non-Alumnus Biographical File—Alexander Meiklejohn, ACL.

73. Alexander Meiklejohn to Abbott Lawrence Lowell (February 14, 1918), box III, folder 28, AMP, ACL.

74. Alexander Meiklejohn to Albert Parker Fitch (October 8, 1917), box II, folder 14, AMP, ACL.

75. Alexander Meiklejohn to John Erskine (October 15, 1917), box II, folder 9, AMP, ACL.

76. Charles Beard to Alexander Meiklejohn (October 29, 1917), box VIII, folder 4, AMP, ACL.

77. Alexander Meiklejohn to Woodrow Wilson (October 8, 1917), box 32, folder 5, AMP, SHSW.

78. Alexander Meiklejohn to Woodrow Wilson's secretary (October 15, 1917), box 32, folder 5, AMP, SHSW.

79. Randolph Bourne, "Twilight of Idols," *Seven Arts* (October 1917): 688–702, quotation from 697–698.

80. Alexander Meiklejohn, "Fiat Justitia: The College as Critic," *Harvard Graduates' Magazine* (September 1917): 1–14, quotation from 8.

81. Meiklejohn, "Fiat Justitia," 7.

82. Meiklejohn, "Fiat Justitia," 8.

83. Bourne, "Twilight of Idols," 698.

84. Meiklejohn, "Fiat Justitia," 10.

85. Talcott Williams to Alexander Meiklejohn. (September 14, 1918), box V, folder 37, AMP, ACL.

86. "Special War Courses Fill New Curriculum," *Amherst Student* (October 7, 1918): 1, ACL.

87. "The Day's Work," *Amherst Student* (October 7, 1918): 3, ACL.

88. Alexander Meiklejohn, "Chapel Talk" (September 20, 1918), box 33, folder 6, AMP, SHSW.

89. "President Meiklejohn Speaks at First Chapel," *Amherst Student* (September 23, 1918): 1, 2, ACL.

90. Alexander Meiklejohn to Woodrow Wilson (October 23, 1918), box 32, folder 5, AMP, SHSW.

91. Everett Glass to Alexander Meiklejohn (November 19, 1918), box VIII, folder 6, AMP, ACL.

92. Howans Robinson to Alexander Meiklejohn (November 21, 1918), box VIII, folder 6, AMP, ACL.

93. Alexander Meiklejohn to Woodrow Wilson (n.d.), box 32, folder 5, AMP, SHSW.

94. Quoted in "Meiklejohn a Stirring Figure in American College Life," *New York Times* (June 24, 1923).

95. "President Meiklejohn Speaks on Our Social Problems," *Amherst Student* (February 23, 1920): 1, 8, ACL.

CHAPTER 4. "TO WHOM ARE WE RESPONSIBLE?"
1920–1924

1. William Lloyd Garrison, Jr., to Alexander Meiklejohn (January 24, 1920), box VIII, folder 3, AMP, ACL.

2. Grant A. Goebel, "Industrial Relations" (n.d.), box X, folder 11, AMP, ACL.

3. Channing H. Cox to Alexander Meiklejohn (October 27, 1921), box VI, folder 1, AMP, ACL.

4. Alexander Meiklejohn to C. W. Woodward (October 26, 1921), box VI, folder 1, AMP, ACL.

5. Alexander Meiklejohn, "English Impression," *Amherst Graduates' Quarterly* (November 1919), 8–9, ACL. See also Alexander Meiklejohn, "Chapel Speech" (September 18, 1919), box 33, folder 6, AMP, SHSW.

6. John Gaus to Alexander Meiklejohn (n.d. [1920]), box 14, folder 1, AMP, SHSW.

7. Alexander Meiklejohn to John Gaus (June 19, 1920), box 14, folder 1, AMP, SHSW.

8. See "Classes for Workers," *Amherst Graduates' Quarterly* (November 1922): 30–31, ACL.

9. "The Amherst-Holyoke Classes for Workers" (n.d. [1920s]), "Worker's Classes—Announcements" folder, General Files, ACL.

10. "Classes for Workers," *Amherst Graduates' Quarterly* (August 1925): 286, ACL. See also "Holyoke Courses for Workers," *Amherst Graduates' Quarterly* (February 1926): 128, ACL.

11. "Classes for Workers" (August 1925), 286.

12. "Classes for Workers" (October 1920), "Worker's Classes—Announcements" folder, General Files, ACL.

13. Paul H. Douglas and William A. Orton, "Outline of Labor Problems in Modern Society" (n.d. [1924]), "Worker's Classes—Announcements" folder, General Files, ACL. See also "Courses Announced for New Industrial Classes," *Amherst Student* (October 4, 1920): 1, ACL.

14. Douglas and Orton, "Outline of Labor Problems in Modern Society."

15. Lucien Price, *Prophets Unawares: The Romance of an Idea* (New York, 1924), 97–98.

16. Alexander Meiklejohn to J. H. Tufts (April 2, 1914), box VI, folder 10, AMP, ACL.

17. "Meiklejohn Case in Amherst Recalled," newspaper unidentified (January 8, 1937), Meiklejohn newspaper clippings, AMP, BUA.

18. Thorstein Veblen, *The Higher Learning in America: A Memorandum on the Conduct of Universities by Businessmen* (New York, 1918; reprinted 1957), 143–144.

19. Samuel H. Jameson to Scott Abbott (n.d. [1964]), reminiscences solicited by Scott Abbott, Non-Alumnus Biographical File—Alexander Meiklejohn, ACL.

20. Alexander Meiklejohn to H. Nelson Gay (May 28, 1920), box II, folder 17, AMP, ACL.

21. See Stanley King, *A History of the Endowment of Amherst College* (Amherst, 1951), 141.

22. Randall, "The Meiklejohn Tragedy."

23. Trustees' Finance Committee minutes, 1911–1934, Amherst College Financial Records, ACL.

24. "Dr. Meiklejohn's Plans Uncertain, Causes of Ouster Still Obscure," *New York World* (June 22, 1923), Meiklejohn newspaper clippings, AMP, BUA.

25. Randall, "The Meiklejohn Tragedy."

26. Randall, "The Meiklejohn Tragedy." See also King, *A History of the Endowment of Amherst College,* 137–138.

27. King, *A History of the Endowment of Amherst College,* 129.

28. Stanley King, "President Meiklejohn's Resignation" (1948), unpaginated typescript, 16 pp., box II, folder 7, Trustee Materials Concerning Alexander Meiklejohn, ACL.

29. Clarence Ayres reported a story from the Amherst postmistress that, "when Harvey, the butcher, had gone into bankruptcy his largest asset had been a claim against the president." Quoted in "Report by the Special Committee of the Board of Trustees of Amherst College" (October 20, 1923), box I, folder 4, Trustee Materials Concerning Alexander Meiklejohn, ACL.

30. F. Stetson Clark to Scott Abbott (June 6, 1964), reminiscences solicited by Scott Abbott, Non-Alumnus Biographical File—Alexander Meiklejohn, ACL.

31. William L. Brunt to Scott Abbott (June 10, 1965), reminiscences solicited by Scott Abbott, Non-Alumnus Biographical File—Alexander Meiklejohn, ACL.

32. See Merrill Anderson to Scott Abbott (January 12, 1965), reminiscences solicited by Scott Abbott, Non-Alumnus Biographical File—Alexander Meiklejohn, ACL. "I am quite sure that if I had been a trustee of Amherst and had found that Dr. Meiklejohn was not paying his bills and had a redheaded mistress (rumored), I should have been disturbed. . . ."

33. Ralph W. Westcott to Scott Abbott (June 24, 1964), reminiscences solicited by Scott Abbott, Non-Alumnus Biographical File—Alexander Meiklejohn, ACL.

353

34. "Dr. Meiklejohn's Plans Uncertain, Causes of Ouster Still Obscure."

35. Clark to Abbott (June 6, 1964).

36. See "Report by the Special Committee of the Board of Trustees of Amherst College" (October 20, 1923).

37. Randall, "The Meiklejohn Tragedy."

38. See transcriptions of interviews with members of the faculty for the Special Committee of the Board of Trustees (June 9, 1923), box II, folder 9, Trustee Material Concerning Alexander Meiklejohn, ACL.

39. Randall, "The Meiklejohn Tragedy."

40. Brunt to Abbott (June 10, 1965).

41. Price, *Prophets Unawares*, 158. See also John M. Gaus, "The Issues at Amherst," *Nation* (July 4, 1923): 12.

42. Randall, "The Meiklejohn Tragedy."

43. Alexander Meiklejohn, "Address at the Inauguration of Herman C. Bumpus" (1915), box 33, folder 3, AMP, SHSW.

44. King, "President Meiklejohn's Resignation."

45. Randall, "The Meiklejohn Tragedy."

46. "Report of the Special Committee Appointed June 3rd, 1922, Pursuant to Vote of the Executive Committee of the Trustees" (May 25, 1923), box I, folder 2, Trustees Materials Concerning Alexander Meiklejohn, ACL.

47. Brunt to Abbott (June 10, 1965).

48. See "Statement of Professor Churchill," *Schedules A, B, C, D, & E* (Amherst, May 1923), box I, folder 3, Trustee Materials Concerning Alexander Meiklejohn, ACL. See also Alexander Meiklejohn, "The College Teacher: Tenure of Office and Academic Freedom," *Proceedings of the Association of American Colleges* (April 1916), box 33, folder 4, AMP, SHSW.

49. Alfred S. Romer to Scott Abbott (June 19, 1964), reminiscences solicited by Scott Abbott, Non-Alumnus Biographical File—Alexander Meiklejohn, ACL.

50. Meiklejohn claimed to seek faculty approval for his actions. "I am quite certain," he wrote to Arthur Lovejoy in 1919, "that, both with respect to appointments and to promotions or dismissals of men of lower grade, the advice of the teaching force is essential." Alexander Meiklejohn to Arthur O. Lovejoy (May 23, 1919), box VI, folder 2, AMP, ACL.

51. Robert Frost to Louis Untermeyer (August 12, 1924) in *Selected Letters of Robert Frost*, ed. Lawrance Thompson (New York, 1964), 301–304, quotation from 303.

52. Morris A. Copeland to Scott Abbott (June 8, 1964), reminiscences solicited by Scott Abbott, Non-Alumnus Biographical File—Alexander Meiklejohn, ACL.

53. Randall, "The Meiklejohn Tragedy."

54. Frank R. Otte to Scott Abbott (August 10, 1964), reminiscences solicited by Scott Abbott, Non-Alumnus Biographical File—Alexander Meiklejohn, ACL.

55. Craig P. Cochrane to Scott Abbott (June 14, 1964), reminiscences so-

licited by Scott Abbott, Non-Alumnus Biographical File—Alexander Meiklejohn, ACL.

56. Lee B. Wood to Scott Abbott (June 3, 1964), reminiscences solicited by Scott Abbott, Non-Alumnus Biographical File—Alexander Meiklejohn, ACL.

57. Harold M. Bixby to Scott Abbott (May 22, 1964), reminiscences solicited by Scott Abbott, Non-Alumnus Biographical File—Alexander Meiklejohn, ACL.

58. Bixby to Abbott (May 22, 1964).

59. Rolfe Humphries to Scott Abbott (June 5, 1964), reminiscences solicited by Scott Abbott, Non-Alumnus Biographical File—Alexander Meiklejohn, ACL.

60. King, "President Meiklejohn's Resignation."

61. "Brint" to the class of 1910 (April 14, 1922), miscellaneous newspaper clippings, Non-Alumnus Biographical File—Alexander Meiklejohn, ACL.

62. Clarence Ayres to Alexander Meiklejohn (April 7, 1920), box I, folder 8, AMP, ACL.

63. Quoted in Price, *Prophets Unawares*, 114. See also: Alexander Meiklejohn, "What Are College Games For?" *Atlantic Monthly* (November 1922); "For Athletic Disarmament," *Amherst Graduates' Quarterly* (May 1922); "Meiklejohn Answers Moore and Mendell; Declares Students Should Play and Run Own Sports, in Speech at New Haven; Deplores Extensive Coaching Systems," *Boston Globe* (March 28, 1922); and "College Faculties to Rule Athletics; Coaches to Be Members of Board with Status and Duties as Professors," *New York Times* (April 11, 1922); all in box 34, folder 1, AMP, SHSW.

64. See Alexander Meiklejohn to Harold Bailty (September 1, 1921), box VIII, folder 7, AMP, ACL.

65. "Meiklejohn Seeks More Democracy; Amherst President Says Good Things in Life Belong to All the People" (March 8, 1922), Brown University Scrapbook, volume 17 (December 13, 1921—June 29, 1923), BUA.

66. See Alexander Meiklejohn, "Democracy and Excellence," unpaginated typescript (n.d. [1922]), box 34, folder 2, AMP, SHSW. See also "Education the Salvation of Democracy," *Portland Spectator* (n.d. [1923]), box 34, folder 2, AMP, SHSW.

67. "Meiklejohn Seeks More Democracy."

68. "Education Is Basis of True Democracy, Says Meiklejohn," newspaper unidentified (n.d.), miscellaneous newspaper clippings, Non-Alumnus Biographical File—Alexander Meiklejohn, ACL.

69. "Meiklejohn Seeks More Democracy."

70. Alexander Meiklejohn to J. S. Douglas (January 13, 1922), box II, folder 1, AMP, ACL.

71. Alexander Meiklejohn, *Freedom and the College* (New York, 1924), 135. See also "Remarks of Meiklejohn at Amherst Commencement" (n.d.), box 59, folder 13, AMP, SHSW.

72. See Harold Wade, Jr., *Black Men of Amherst* (Amherst, 1976), 111–112;

De Witt C. Morrell to Alexander Meiklejohn (June 30, 1922), box VII, folder 12, AMP, ACL.

73. Morrell to Meiklejohn (June 30, 1922).

74. "Reminiscences by A. W. Marsh."

75. "The Militancy of Alexander Meiklejohn," *Brown Alumni Monthly* (March 1965): 12–15, BUA, quotation from 14.

76. See copy of article and editorial in the *Springfield Daily Republican* (June 14, 1923), box I, folder 4, Trustee Material Concerning Alexander Meiklejohn, ACL. See also Price, *Prophets Unawares,* 130–131.

77. "Amherst Seniors Delay Report on Meiklejohn Case," *New York Times* (June 16, 1923).

78. King, "President Meiklejohn's Resignation."

79. Randall, "The Meiklejohn Tragedy."

80. Babbott to Abbott (May 25, 1964). See also Alexander Meiklejohn, "Welcome to Returning Alumni Delivered from the Chapel Steps," *Some Addresses Delivered at Amherst College, Commencement Time, 1923* (Amherst, 1923), 16–17, box 34, folder 2, AMP, SHSW.

81. King, "President Meiklejohn's Resignation."

82. Randall, "The Meiklejohn Tragedy."

83. Price, *Prophets Unawares,* 108–110.

84. Alexander Meiklejohn, "Baccalaureate Address," *Amherst Graduates' Quarterly* (August 1923), 225, ACL.

85. "Amherst and Beyond," *Brooklyn Standard Union* (June 24, 1923), miscellaneous newspaper clippings, Non-Alumnus Biographical File—Alexander Meiklejohn, ACL.

86. "Coolidge Shows Disfavor," *New York World* (June 21, 1923).

87. Price, *Prophets Unawares,* 163.

88. Frank A. Meyers to Scott Abbott (June 14, 1964), reminiscences solicited by Scott Abbott, Non-Alumnus Biographical File—Alexander Meiklejohn, ACL.

89. "Meiklejohn Charges Trustees with Failure to Support Their Ideas; 13 Reject Degrees; Two Faculty Members Resign and Two Instructors May Also Quit; President Challenges Entire Fabric of U.S. College Education and Says When Americans Find Out How to Run Universities They Will Not Have Trustees—Fears Colleges' Standards Will Be Lowered," *Springfield Daily Republican* (June 21, 1923). See also "An Open Letter to Dwight Morrow," *New Republic* (July 25, 1923), 221–222.

90. "Meiklejohn Charges Trustees."

91. Price, *Prophets Unawares,* 170.

92. "Meiklejohn Charges Trustees."

93. H. Harry Giles to Scott Abbott (June 8, 1964), reminiscences solicited by Scott Abbott, Non-Alumnus Biographical File—Alexander Meiklejohn, ACL.

94. Albert Parker Fitch to George Plimpton (May 28, 1923), box II, folder 9, Trustee Material Concerning Alexander Meiklejohn, ACL.

95. Felix Frankfurter to Alexander Meiklejohn (June 20, 1923), box XI, folder 5, AMP, ACL.

96. Zechariah Chafee, Jr., to Alexander Meiklejohn (June 19, 1923), box XI, folder 4, AMP, ACL.

97. "The Meiklejohn Type of Democracy," newspaper unidentified (n.d.), miscellaneous newspaper clippings, Non-Alumnus Biographical File—Alexander Meiklejohn, ACL.

98. Walter Lippmann, "The Fall of President Meiklejohn," *New York World* (July 24, 1923). See also John M. Gaus, "The Issues at Amherst," *Nation* (July 4, 1923).

99. Alexander Meiklejohn, "To Whom Are We Responsible?" *Century* (September 1923): 643–650. Meiklejohn originally gave this article as a speech at the Cosmopolitan Club in New York more than a year earlier on March 23, 1922.

100. Arthur Upham Pope, "Meiklejohn," American Scholar (autumn 1965): 641–645.

101. Babbott to Abbott (May 25, 1964).

102. King, "President Meiklejohn's Resignation."

103. Alvin Johnson to Alexander Meiklejohn (June 21, 1923), box XI, folder 7, AMP, ACL. Johnson served as the Henry Ward Beecher Lecturer at Amherst during the 1914–1915 academic year.

104. Philip Burnet to Alexander Meiklejohn (June 21, 1923), box XI, folder 4, AMP, ACL.

105. "Dr. Meiklejohn's Plans Uncertain, Causes of Ouster Still Obscure."

106. Lyman B. Sturgis to Alexander Meiklejohn (July 13, 1923), box 8, folder 14, AMP, SHSW.

107. Frank C. Davison to Alexander Meiklejohn (September 1923), box VI, folder 13, AMP, ACL.

108. Glenn Frank to Alexander Meiklejohn (June 2, 1923), box 8, folder 14, AMP, SHSW.

109. Glenn Frank to Alexander Meiklejohn (July 11, 1923), box 8, folder 14, AMP, SHSW.

110. Alexander Meiklejohn, *Freedom and the College* (New York, 1923). See also Glenn Frank to Alexander Meiklejohn (June 18, July 3, 11, and 14, 1923); and Alexander Meiklejohn to Glenn Frank (July 2, 5, 9, 13, and 25, 1923); all in box 8, folders 14 and 15, AMP, SHSW.

111. W. H. P. Faunce to Alexander Meiklejohn (September 17, 1923), box II, folder 11, AMP, ACL.

112. "Want Meiklejohn as President of Knox," newspaper unidentified (December 17, 1924) and "Meiklejohn May Get Bid to University of Oklahoma," newspaper unidentified (June 21, 1923), miscellaneous newspaper clippings, AMP, BUA.

113. "Meiklejohn Calls America Land of Dull Mob," *Providence Journal-Bulletin* (October 22, 1923).

114. See "Statement on the Need for a New Liberal College, Prepared for a New York Committee" (n.d.), box 34, folder 2, AMP, SHSW.

115. "Meiklejohn May Found College Here," *New York Tribune* (September 12, 1924). See also "A Meiklejohn College," *New York Herald* (September 13, 1924). Both in miscellaneous newspaper clippings, Non-Alumnus Biographical File—Alexander Meiklejohn, ACL.

116. "Meiklejohn Calls America Land of Dull Mob."

117. Abraham Flexner to Alexander Meiklejohn (November 14, 1924), box 8, folder 15, AMP, SHSW.

118. Alexander Meiklejohn to Bernard Baruch, draft (n.d.), box 8, folder 15, AMP, SHSW.

119. See Alexander Meiklejohn, "Statement Prepared for a Committee Formed in New York to Consider a New College" (1923), box 34, folder 2, AMP, SHSW.

120. Glenn Frank to Alexander Meiklejohn (December 17, 1924), box 8, folder 15, AMP, SHSW.

121. "A Meiklejohn College," *New York Herald* (September 13, 1924).

122. W. H. P. Faunce to Alexander Meiklejohn (October 30, 1923), box 12, folder, 71, AMP, SHSW.

123. Alexander Meiklejohn to W. H. P. Faunce (November 5, 1923), box 12, folder 21, AMP, SHSW.

124. Meiklejohn to Faunce (November 5, 1923).

125. Memorandum from Douglas Wilson (December 1982), Non-Alumnus Biographical File—Alexander Meiklejohn, ACL. "When Mrs. Alexander Meiklejohn was dying of cancer in Baltimore a year or two after Meiklejohn left Amherst," Wilson wrote, "her husband—who was traveling and lecturing—asked their old friend from Brown University days, Professor George Boas, who was then teaching at Johns Hopkins, to look in on her from time to time. Trustee Emeritus Seelye Bixler of Amherst told me in the Fall of 1982 that Boas once told him that when he called on Mrs. Meiklejohn during that period, 'she broke down when he saw her and said, "I am responsible for the whole Amherst debacle."' Bixler concluded: 'I'm sure that his going into debt was mismanagement of his wife's, dear lady that she was.'"

126. "Mrs. Alexander Meiklejohn," *New York Times* (February 13, 1925). See also "Mrs. N. L. Meiklejohn Dies in Baltimore," *New York Herald Tribune* (February 14, 1925); and "Mrs. Meiklejohn Dies in Hospital," newspaper unidentified (n.d.), Meiklejohn newspaper clippings, AMP, BUA.

127. Alexander Meiklejohn to John Gaus (February 18, 1925), box 14, folder 1, AMP, SHSW.

128. Felix Frankfurter to Alexander Meiklejohn (February 14, 1925), box 13, folder 20, AMP, SHSW.

129. Alexander Meiklejohn, "Philosophers and Others," *Philosophical Review* (December 29, 1924), box 34, folder 4, AMP, SHSW.

CHAPTER 5. "A NEW COLLEGE WITH A NEW IDEA,"
1925–1928

1. Alexander Meiklejohn, "A New College: Notes on a Next Step in Higher Education," *Century* (January 1925): 312–320. For more information on the publication of this article in *Century*, see box 8, folders 14 and 15, AMP, SHSW. The content of this article matched almost exactly the plan Meiklejohn drew up for Glenn Frank's group in New York. See Alexander Meiklejohn, "Statement Prepared for a Committee Formed in New York to Consider a New College" (1923); and "What American Education Lacks," *Columbia* (May 1923); both in box 34, folder 2, AMP, SHSW.

2. For a list of contemporary experiments in higher education, see the American Association of University Women, "Current Changes in Liberal Arts Education," a supplement to the National Society for the Study of Education, ed., *Yearbook, 1930–1931* (New York, 1932).

3. Meiklejohn, "A New College," 312.

4. Meiklejohn, "A New College," 312–314.

5. Meiklejohn, "A New College," 314.

6. Herbert Croly to Alexander Meiklejohn (February 17, 1925), box 8, folder 15, AMP, SHSW.

7. Glenn Frank to Alexander Meiklejohn (August 27, 1925), box 32, folder 4, AMP, SHSW. See also Alexander Meiklejohn to Glenn Frank (August 30, 1925), box 10, Alexander Meiklejohn folder, 4/13/1, Frank Presidential Papers, UWA.

8. Glenn Frank to Alexander Meiklejohn (December 26, 1925), box 32, folder 4, AMP, SHSW.

9. Alexander Meiklejohn to Glenn Frank (n.d.), box 10, Alexander Meiklejohn folder, 4/13/1, Frank Presidential Papers, UWA. See also an untitled newspaper article (September 1, 1925), Meiklejohn newspaper clippings, AMP, BUA. "Dr. Alexander Meiklejohn, president of Amherst College for the twelve years preceding 1924, has been added to the faculty of St. John's College, this city, though his connection with the local institution, it is announced, is temporary."

10. Glenn Frank to Alexander Meiklejohn (December 6, 1925), Western Union telegram, box 10, Alexander Meiklejohn folder, 4/13/1, Frank Presidential Papers, UWA. Frank's initial draft of this telegram specified "special salaries from $8,000 to $10,000." See also E. B. McGilvary to Alexander Meiklejohn (December 2, 1925), box 10, Alexander Meiklejohn folder, 4/13/1, Frank Presidential Papers, UWA.

11. Alexander Meiklejohn to Glenn Frank (December 8, 1925), box 10, Alexander Meiklejohn folder, 4/13/1, Frank Presidential Papers, UWA.

12. Glenn Frank to Alexander Meiklejohn (December 10, 1925), Western Union telegram, box 10, Alexander Meiklejohn folder, 4/13/1, Frank Presidential Papers, UWA.

13. For more information on Glenn Frank, see Lawrence H. Larsen, *The President Wore Spats: A Biography of Glenn Frank* (Madison, 1965). For more information on Edward A. Birge, see George C. Sellery, *E. A. Birge: A Memoir* (Madison, 1956).

14. See "Dean Pound Won't Go to Wisconsin," *New York Times* (February 3, 1925).

15. Glenn Frank to Alexander Meiklejohn (January 16, 1926), reprinted in Alexander Meiklejohn, *The Experimental College* (New York, 1932), 336–337.

16. Quoted in Meiklejohn, *The Experimental College*, 333, 332.

17. Before Meiklejohn arrived, the University of Wisconsin had already begun a new program in the arts and humanities which closely resembled his plan for the Experimental College. According to the university catalogue, students in this program "will come into vital contact with at least one of the great civilizations of the ancient world. They will acquire the power to acquaint themselves with at least one of the great foreign civilizations of the modern world." See E. David Cronon and John W. Jenkins, *The University of Wisconsin: A History*, vol. 3 (Madison, 1994), 163–164. See also University of Wisconsin catalogue, 1925–1926, *Bulletin of the University of Wisconsin*, Serial No. 1354, General Series No. 1130 (August 1926), 85.

18. See Alexander Meiklejohn, "The Experimental College," *Bulletin of the University of Wisconsin* (Madison) (June 1927): 1, Experimental College Departmental Folder, 7/37, UWA.

19. "Statement by Glenn Frank on the Creation of the All-University Study Commission" (n.d.), box 113, Experimental College Departmental Folder, 4/13/1, Frank Presidential Papers, UWA. See also Glenn Frank, "An Experiment in Education," *Wisconsin Alumni Monthly* (December 1926): 51–53, 55, 87–91.

20. Frank and Meiklejohn first discussed this plan in November 1925, but at that time the plan seemed premature. "I gather from your telegram," Meiklejohn wrote, "that the immediate appointment of a commission *with me in charge* seems to you inadvisable" (emphasis in original). See Meiklejohn to Frank (December 8, 1925).

21. See Cronon and Jenkins, *The University of Wisconsin: A History*, 3: 155, 236–244.

22. *Capital Times* (Madison) (February 12, 1926). See also Cronon and Jenkins, *The University of Wisconsin: A History*, 3: 156.

23. See "Meiklejohn in New Post," *New York Times* (January 23, 1926), Meiklejohn newspaper clippings, AMP, BUA. See also "Dr. Meiklejohn Accepts Faculty Post," *Daily Cardinal* (Madison) (January 7 and 23, 1926).

24. *Capital Times* (December 31, 1925).

25. Glenn Frank to Alexander Meiklejohn (January 16, 1926), excerpts reprinted in Alexander Meiklejohn, *The Experimental College* (New York, 1932), 336–337.

26. See Alexander Meiklejohn, "Report on Experimental College of Liberal Studies" (April 1926), box 55, folder 5, AMP, SHSW.

27. For articles outlining the Experimental College program, see: "A New College," *New Republic* (April 1926); "A New College with a New Idea," *New York Times Magazine* (May 1927); "Wisconsin's Experimental College," *Survey Graphic* (June 1927); "The Experimental College," *University of Wisconsin Bulletin* (May 1928); all in box 34, folder 4, AMP, SHSW.

28. In the beginning, the Experimental College curriculum avoided the natural sciences, but, in the fall of 1928, Meiklejohn hired physicist Robert J. Havighurst to offer a unit centered on the study of evolutionary biology, including opportunities for lab work. See Robert Havighurst, "Report on the Physics Period" (November 12, 1931), box 55, folder 8, AMP, SHSW. See also Meiklejohn, *The Experimental College,* 394–397.

29. Paul Knapland to Dorothy King (May 4, 1926), 8/25, Paul Knaplund Papers, UWA. See Cronon and Jenkins, *The University of Wisconsin: A History,* 3: 160.

30. "Statement by Glenn Frank on the Creation of the All-University Study Commission" (n.d.), box 113, Experimental College Departmental Folder, 4/13/1, Frank Presidential Papers, UWA.

31. "An Experimental College," *Providence Journal-Bulletin* (February 15, 1927), Meiklejohn newspaper clippings, AMP, BUA.

32. See, for example, "Think, or Get Out," *Houston Post-Dispatch* (July 26, 1927); "Meiklejohn Begins the College of His Dreams," *Boston Transcript* (June 26, 1927); "Meiklejohn Heads New Type College," *New York Evening Post* (February 12, 1927); and "The Meiklejohn Idea," *Brooklyn Daily Eagle* (11 June 1927); all in Meiklejohn newspaper clippings, AMP, BUA.

33. Editorial, *Ashland Daily Press,* quoted in Madison's *Capital Times* (June 7, 1927). See Cronon and Jenkins, *The University of Wisconsin: A History,* 3: 168.

34. "Dr. Meiklejohn's Engagement Culmination of True Romance," *Springfield Daily Republican* (May 20, 1926), miscellaneous newspaper clippings, Non-Alumnus Biographical File—Alexander Meiklejohn, ACL.

35. Statement of Roger Baldwin, "Tribute to Alexander Meiklejohn," *Rights* (February 1965), box 58, folder 6, AMP, SHSW.

36. See applications for teaching positions and dormitory fellowships, 1926–1932, box 1, 7/37/1-4, Experimental College Papers, UWA.

37. Alexander Meiklejohn to John Gaus (April 24, 1926), box 14, folder 1, AMP, SHSW.

38. Alexander Meiklejohn to John Gaus (April 28, 1926), box 14, folder 1, AMP, SHSW.

39. Eventually, Meiklejohn added Paul M. Herzog and Carl Russell Fish in history, Douglas Orr in philosophy, and H. H. Giles in literature. Carl Russell Fish later withdrew. See "Press Release on the Experimental College" (n.d.), Experimental College Departmental Folder, 7/37, UWA.

40. Meiklejohn, "A New College," 313–314.

41. Transcript of interview with Walter Agard, Oral History #1 (Madison, 1972), 3–4, Oral History Collection, UWA.

42. Transcript of interview with Carl Bögholt, Oral History #7 (Madison, 1975), Oral History Collection, UWA. Quoted in Cronon and Jenkins, *The University of Wisconsin: A History,* 3: 168.

43. See "Meiklejohn Tells Education's Ills," *Providence Journal-Bulletin* (January 15, 1929), Meiklejohn newspaper clippings, AMP, BUA.

44. For Experimental College registration statistics, see "The Report of the Bureau of Guidance and Records on the Experimental College" (February 1932), 1–8, boxes 1 and 2, 7/37/5-1 through 7/37/5-3, Experimental College Papers, UWA. See also "Class Data," boxes 1 through 10, 7/37/3-3, Experimental College Papers, UWA. In addition, consult Russell Francis Lewis, "A Personnel Study of the Experimental College Student Body" (unpublished M.A. thesis, University of Wisconsin, 1928); Gertrude Margaret Schmidt, "A Personnel Study of the Experimental College Freshman Class of 1928–29" (unpublished M.A. thesis, University of Wisconsin, 1929); and Mary Dean Scott, "A Personnel Study of the Experimental College Freshman Class of 1929–30" (unpublished B.A. thesis, University of Wisconsin, 1930); all in box 2, 7/37/00-6 through 7/37/00-7, Experimental College Papers, UWA.

45. See "Data on Residence of Students," in "The Report of the Bureau of Guidance and Records on the Experimental College," 1. See also "Population of Home Cities" in Scott, "A Personnel Study of the Experimental College Freshman Class of 1929–30."

46. "Home Location Analysis of the Experimental College Student Body, 1927–28" in Scott, "A Personnel Study of the Experimental College Freshman Class of 1929–1930," 2–8.

47. Nathan Berman, "A New Kind of College," *Forward* (July 16, 1928), box 1, "Articles and Statements by Experimental College Students and Advisers" folder, 7/37/1-9, Experimental College Papers, UWA.

48. Transcript of interview with David Parsons (n.d.), Experimental College Departmental Folder, 7/37, UWA.

49. "Scholastic Aptitude Tests," *Report of the Bureau of Guidance and Records on the Experimental College* (February 1932), 9, Experimental College Departmental Folder, 7/37, UWA.

50. "Wisconsin Language (English Usage) Test," *Report of the Bureau of Guidance and Records on the Experimental College* (February 1932), 11–12, Experimental College Departmental Folder, 7/37, UWA.

51. "Preparatory School Grades of Experimental College Students," *Report of the Bureau of Guidance and Records of the Experimental College* (February 1932), 4, Experimental College Departmental Folder, 7/37, UWA.

52. See Allan Loeb Cohn, "A Personnel Study of the Experimental College

Freshman Class of 1930–31, Including a Comparison of the Experimental College Freshman Classes of 1927, 1928, 1929, and 1930" (unpublished B.A. thesis, University of Wisconsin, 1931).

53. Alexander Meiklejohn, "Annual Report of the Experimental College," *Document 46* (June 1930): 8, box 11, "Letters and Science Faculty Documents" folder, 7/37/00-4, Experimental College Papers, UWA.

54. Meiklejohn, "The Experimental College," 12.

55. Zona Gale to Alexander Meiklejohn (May 16, 1928), box 2, "Discussion by Outsiders" folder, 7/37/1-9, Experimental College Papers, UWA. See also Edith Abbott, "Meiklejohn at Wisconsin," *New Republic* (August 15, 1928): 334.

56. Alexander Meiklejohn to Zona Gale (May 25, 1928), box 2, "Discussion by Outsiders" folder, 7/37/1-9, Experimental College Papers, UWA.

57. Meiklejohn, "The Experimental College," 14.

58. Benjamin B. Goldman, ed., "The First Year of the Experimental College: An Informative Resumé Published by the Pioneer Class of the Experimental College" (1928), 17, Experimental College Departmental Folder, 7/37, UWA.

59. Goldman, ed., "The First Year of the Experimental College," 18.

60. See Meiklejohn, "The Experimental College," 7–8.

61. Meiklejohn, *The Experimental College,* 226–228.

62. Transcript of interview with David Parsons.

63. Meiklejohn, *The Experimental College,* 34, 107.

64. Meiklejohn, *The Experimental College,* 40.

65. Meiklejohn, *The Experimental College,* 368–371, 107, 73, 57–58. Meiklejohn made a similar point at Amherst in 1919; see Alexander Meiklejohn, "The Future of Our Liberal Colleges after the War," *New York Sun* (October 19, 1919), box 33, folder 6, AMP, SHSW.

66. Wilber Cohen, "Alexander Meiklejohn and the Experimental College: Reflections 50 Years Later" (May 20, 1982), box 1, folder 17, 94/34/1, "Alexander Meiklejohn, Experimental College and post-College, Meetings, Organizations, and Projects," UWA.

67. J. A. Munro to Mervyn Cadwallader (May 30, 1982), box 1, folder 17, 94/34/1, "Alexander Meiklejohn, Experimental College and post-College, Meetings, Organizations, and Projects," UWA.

68. John W. Powell, Jr., "Philosophy Period," quoted in Meiklejohn, *The Experimental College,* 391.

69. Goldman, ed., "The First Year of the Experimental College," 14. See also Sidney Hertzberg, "Where Freshmen Follow Socrates," *New Student* (October 5, 1927): 5–6.

70. Meiklejohn, *The Experimental College,* 386.

71. Walker H. Hill, ed., *Learning and Living: Proceedings of an Anniversary Celebration in Honor of Alexander Meiklejohn, Chicago, May 8–10, 1942* (Chicago, 1942): 107–108.

72. Robert Lynd and Helen Lynd, *Middletown: A Study in American Culture* (New York, 1929).

73. Meiklejohn, *The Experimental College,* 90–93. See also "Regional Studies," box 1, "Assignments, Reading Lists, Notices, etc. from Class I, 1927–1929" folder, 7/37/2-3, Experimental College Papers, UWA.

74. See "Meiklejohn College Was Major Influence" (n.d.), box 1, folder 5A, 94/34/1, "Alexander Meiklejohn, Experimental College and post-College, Meetings, Organizations, and Projects," UWA.

75. See John C. Schmidtmann to Carl Russell Fish (December 16, 1929), box 8, folder 3, Carl Russell Fish Papers, SHSW. See also box 1, "Assignments, Reading Lists, Notices, etc. Class I: 1927–1929" folder, 7/37/2-3, Experimental College Papers, UWA.

76. Meiklejohn, "The Experimental College," 7.

77. Meiklejohn, *The Experimental College,* 74, 144.

78. "Reunion of the X-College of Late 20's Brings Meiklejohn and Students Together Again—His Views Unchanged," *Providence Journal-Bulletin* (May 19, 1957), Meiklejohn newspaper clippings, AMP, BUA.

79. Meiklejohn, *The Experimental College,* 87.

80. Transcript of interview with David Parsons.

81. Frank Donner, "Notes on Henry Adams and His 'Education' " in James S. Slotkin, ed., *An Experimental College Miscellany* (Madison, 1932), 11–14, box 1, "Student Publications" folder, 7/37/00-5, Experimental College Papers, UWA.

82. Meiklejohn, *The Experimental College,* 109.

83. Goldman, ed., "The First Year of the Experimental College," 31, 27. See Clarence Ayres, *Science: The False Messiah* (New York, 1927). John Dewey reviewed Ayres's book for the *New Republic.* See John Dewey, *The Later Works, 1925–1953,* ed. Jo Ann Boydston, 17 vols. (Carbondale, 1981–1990), 3: 306–310.

84. Goldman, ed., "The First Year of the Experimental College," 32.

85. Goldman, ed., "The First Year of the Experimental College," 28.

86. Lewis Mumford to Alexander Meiklejohn (May 2, 1929), box 1, folder K–R, 7/37/1-2, Experimental College Papers, UWA.

87. Goldman, ed., "The First Year of the Experimental College," 33–34.

88. F. Louise Nardin to Julia M. Wilkinson (July 26, 1929), box 56, 4/13/1, Frank Presidential Papers, UWA.

89. Meiklejohn, "The Experimental College," 7.

90. Meiklejohn, "The Experimental College," 3.

91. Meiklejohn, *The Experimental College,* 135, 134.

92. Goldman, ed., "The First Year of the Experimental College," 17.

93. Transcript of interview with David Parsons.

94. University registrar to Alexander Meiklejohn (n.d. [1929]), box 1, "Administration: General" folder, 7/37/1-2, Experimental College Papers, UWA.

CHAPTER 6. "A MOST LAMENTABLE COMEDY," 1929–1932

1. Howard Jay Graham, "College as It Might Be," *New Republic* (May 22, 1929): 13–15.

2. See Walter Lippmann, *A Preface to Morals* (New York, 1929).

3. Justin A. Silverstein, "Oration" (n.d.), box 1, "Articles and Statements by Experimental College Students and Advisers" folder, 7/37/1-9, Experimental College Papers, UWA.

4. "Meiklejohn Declares War on Influence of Money; Educator Believes Nation Is in Peril; Says All Enlightening Agencies Are Failing Because of U. S. Wealth," *Providence Journal-Bulletin* (October 15, 1929), Meiklejohn newspaper clippings, AMP, BUA.

5. Ralph Crowley to Alexander Meiklejohn (January 15, 1930), box 1, "College Loan Fund, 1930–31" folder, 7/37/4-1, Experimental College Papers, UWA.

6. Alexander Meiklejohn to Ralph Crowley (January 17, 1930), box 1, "College Loan Fund, 1930–31" folder, 7/37/4-1, Experimental College Papers, UWA.

7. "Experimental College Loan Fund" (n.d.), box 1, "College Loan Fund, 1930–31" folder, 7/37/4-1, Experimental College Papers, UWA.

8. Meiklejohn, "College Bulletin" (December 17, 1931), box 1, "College Council Loan Fund" folder, 7/37/4-1, Experimental College Papers, UWA. See also box 1, "Koplick Loan Fund" folder, 7/37/4-1, Experimental College Papers, UWA.

9. Transcript of interview with David Parsons (n.d.), 36, Experimental College Departmental Folder, 7/37, UWA.

10. Carroll Blair to Alexander Meiklejohn (March 8, 1944), box 5, folder 4, AMP, SHSW.

11. Carroll Blair to Alexander Meiklejohn (April 5, 1948), box 5, folder 4, AMP, SHSW.

12. See Carroll Blair to Alexander Meiklejohn (March 23, 1962), box 5, folder 4, AMP, SHSW. See also E. David Cronon and John W. Jenkins, *The University of Wisconsin: A History,* Vol. 3 (Madison, 1994), 867.

13. David Gordon, "America," *Daily Worker,* New Magazine Section (March 12, 1927): 2.

14. Lawrence H. Larsen, *The President Wore Spats: A Biography of Glenn Frank* (Madison, 1965), 101.

15. Quoted in Cronon and Jenkins, *The University of Wisconsin: A History,* 3:179–180.

16. Richard Lloyd Jones to Alexander Meiklejohn (October 3, 1928), box 2, "Discussion by Outsiders" folder, 7/37/1-9, Experimental College Papers, UWA. See also "Alexander's Ragtime Radicalism," *Daily Cardinal* (fall orientation issue 1973): 4.

17. Alexander Meiklejohn to Frederick P. Keppel (December 12, 1932), box 1, "Correspondence Relating to Financing of Proposed Study, 1932–33" folder, 7/37/1-6, Experimental College Papers, UWA.

18. Alexander Meiklejohn, *The Experimental College* (New York, 1932), 70–71.

19. John Walker Powell, "Discussion of the Sophomore Curriculum" (1930), box 1, "Minutes of the Meetings of the Faculty of the Experimental College of the University of Wisconsin, 1927–1932," "Faculty Minutes, 1929–30" folder, 7/37/2-1, Experimental College Papers, UWA.

20. Meiklejohn, *The Experimental College,* 112, 72.

21. Minutes from faculty meeting (March 19, 1930), box 1, "Minutes of the Meetings of the Faculty of the Experimental College of the University of Wisconsin, 1927–1932," "Faculty Minutes, 1929–30" folder, 7/37/2-1, Experimental College Papers, UWA.

22. "Dr. Meiklejohn Insists Schools Are Ineffectual," *New York Herald Tribune* (March 2, 1930), Meiklejohn newspaper clippings, AMP, BUA.

23. Cronon and Jenkins, *The University of Wisconsin: A History,* 3:155.

24. Grant Showerman, "A Most Lamentable Comedy," *School and Society* (April 11, 1931): 481–488. See also Ole Man Ribber, "Why the Wisconsin Experiment Was Bound to Fail," *School and Society* (August 1, 1931): 150–153.

25. Robert N. Cool, "X-College and Its Guinea Pigs; Individualism Had Field Day" and "Reunion of the X-College of Late 20's Brings Meiklejohn and Students Together Again—His Views Unchanged," *Providence Journal-Bulletin* (May 19, 1957), Meiklejohn newspaper clippings, AMP, BUA.

26. Harold C. Bradley to Glenn Frank, draft (March 5, 1928), box 4, "A Most Lamentable Comedy" folder, clippings and related correspondence, 6/1/2, Graduate School Papers, UWA.

27. "Report of the Student Committee" (January 20, 1930), box 1, "Correspondence, Memoranda, etc. Relating to Student Activities" folder, 7/37/6-1, Experimental College Papers, UWA.

28. Lawrence B. Kerstetter, "Response to the 'Report of the Student Committee'" (January 20, 1930), box 1, "Correspondence, Memoranda, etc. Relating to Student Activities" folder, 7/37/6-1, Experimental College Papers, UWA.

29. Benjamin B. Goldman, ed., "The First Year of the Experimental College: An Informative Resumé Published by The Pioneer Class of the Experimental College" (1928), 38, Experimental College Departmental Folder, 7/37, UWA. See also Meiklejohn, *The Experimental College,* 222.

30. Alexander Meiklejohn, "From the Chairman to the Students" (May 28, 1928), reprinted in Goldman, ed., "The First Year of the Experimental College," 47.

31. John Newcomb Reddin, "Guinea Pigs vs. Bohemia," unpaginated typescript (1940), box 56, folder 6, AMP, SHSW.

32. Goldman, ed., "The First Year of the Experimental College," 44.

33. "Facts, Figures Disprove Ex-College Queerness," *Daily Cardinal* (March 9, 1930), box 1, "Statements by University Students and Alumni, Parents, and Faculty, 1929–1933" folder, 7/37/1-9, Experimental College Papers, UWA.

34. Alexander Meiklejohn to Glenn Frank (December 11, 1930), box 100, Alexander Meiklejohn folder, 4/13/1, Frank Presidential Papers, UWA.

35. Minutes of faculty meeting (March 12, 1931), box 1, "Psychiatric Material, 1931–1932" folder, 7/37/2-1, Experimental College Papers, UWA. See also Meiklejohn, *The Experimental College*, 350–361.

36. Minutes of faculty meeting (March 12, 1931).

37. Minutes of faculty meeting (March 12, 1931). See also transcript of interview between advisers and Frankwood Williams (n.d.), box 1, "Psychiatric Material, 1931–1932" folder, 7/37/2-1, Experimental College Papers, UWA.

38. See Meiklejohn, *The Experimental College*, 236–238.

39. A. C. Kinsford to Alexander Meiklejohn (June 7, 1929), box 1, "High School Relations" folder, 7/37/1-2, Experimental College Papers, UWA.

40. Evan A. Evans to John L. Bergstresser (emphasis in original) (August 25, 1930), box 1, "Statements by University Students and Alumni, Parents, and Faculty, 1929–1933" folder, 7/37/1-9, Experimental College Papers, UWA.

41. Glenn Frank to Alexander Meiklejohn (August 11, 1928), box 47, folder "McG–My," 4/13/1, Frank Presidential Papers, UWA. See also Glenn Frank, untitled press release (December 9, 1929), box 74, folder "Ea–Fi," 4/13/1, Frank Presidential Papers, UWA. See also Glenn Frank, "The Experimental College" *Journal of Higher Education* (June 1930): 305–307.

42. George Clarke Sellery, *Some Ferments at Wisconsin, 1901–1947: Memories and Reflections* (Madison, 1960), 28.

43. Alexander Meiklejohn, "Letter to High School Principles" (n.d.), box 1, "High School Relations" folder, 7/37/1-2, Experimental College Papers, UWA.

44. Experimental College Graduate Committee (Nathan Berman, C. David Connolly, and Neal Gordon Kuehn) to Alexander Meiklejohn (December 18, 1929), box 74, folder "Ea–Fi," 4/13/1, Frank Presidential Papers, UWA.

45. See the report of a trip taken through north and central Wisconsin by John Bergstresser and Campbell Dickson as informal representatives of the Experimental College (May 1929), box 1, "Trips to High Schools of State" folder, 7/37/1-2, Experimental College Papers, UWA. See also "Experimental College Enrollment Program" (n.d.), box 74, folder "Ea–Fi," 4/13/1, Frank Presidential Papers, UWA. See also "Public Schools" (June 7, 1929), box 1, "High School Relations" folder, Experimental College Papers, UWA.

46. Bergstresser's report of a trip (May 1929).

47. John L. Bergstresser to Glenn Frank (June 24, 1929), box 55, folder "Be," 4/13/1, Frank Presidential Papers, UWA.

48. "Comments by Parents in Letters Replying to the Request for Impressions of Their Sons' Development during Two Years at the College" (n.d.), box 1,

"Statements by University Students and Alumni, Parents, and Faculty, 1929–1933" folder, 7/37/1-9, Experimental College Papers, UWA.

49. Alfred Harcourt to Alexander Meiklejohn (November 30, 1927), box 2, "Discussion by Outsiders" folder, 7/37/1-9, Experimental College Papers, UWA.

50. Quoted in Meiklejohn, *The Experimental College,* 208.

51. Katherine Newborg to Alexander Meiklejohn (September 10, 1939), box 1, "Articles Requested" folder, 7/37/1-6, Experimental College Papers, UWA.

52. Eugene S. Duffield, "Memorandum" (1931), box 56, folder 3, AMP, SHSW.

53. Grant Showerman, "A Most Lamentable Comedy," *School and Society* (April 11, 1931): 485.

54. See Alice Shoemaker to Helen Meiklejohn (June 20, 1930), box 81, folder "McG–My," 4/13/1, Frank Presidential Papers, UWA.

55. Cronon and Jenkins, *The University of Wisconsin: A History,* 3:139.

56. See the *Capital Times* and the *Daily Cardinal* (March 9, 1929). See also Cronon and Jenkins, *The University of Wisconsin: A History,* 3:186.

57. Larsen, *The President Wore Spats,* 102.

58. See Alexander Meiklejohn to George Sellery and George Sellery to Alexander Meiklejohn (May 1929), box 1, "Advanced Standing Cases" folder, 7/37/1-2, Experimental College Papers, UWA. See also Alexander Meiklejohn to Julia M. Wilkinson (March 19, 1930), box 81, folder "Me–Mi," 4/13/1, Frank Presidential Papers, UWA.

59. Jane M. Shlaes, "The Experimental College" (unpublished undergraduate essay, University of Wisconsin, December 11, 1984), 16, Experimental College Papers, UWA.

60. Larsen, *The President Wore Spats,* 77.

61. Rumors of the attempt to depose Sellery surfaced before Frank could act. "Sellery soon heard ominous reports of Frank's undercover maneuvering, and at least one friend urged him to resign the deanship before he was fired. . . . Subsequently, Frank told intimates he should have gotten rid of Sellery when he first arrived in Madison, but explained that after the dean's public criticism [of the Experimental College in 1929], it was impossible to fire him." See Cronon and Jenkins, *The University of Wisconsin: A History,* 3:188–189.

62. Alexander Meiklejohn to Glenn Frank (March 30, 1931), box 100, Alexander Meiklejohn folder, 4/13/1, Frank Presidential Papers, UWA.

63. Steven D. Zink, "Glenn Frank of the University of Wisconsin: A Reinterpretation," *Wisconsin Magazine of History* (winter 1978–1979): 90–127.

64. For mention of this trip, see Ernest Peterffy to Alexander Meiklejohn (January 27, 1950), box 23, folder 4, AMP, SHSW.

65. Meiklejohn, *The Experimental College,* 292–293.

66. F. A. Gutheim, "The Experimental College Ends," *Midwestern* (April 1931): 17, 60–62, quotation from 60.

67. H. H. Giles, "Outside Looking In" (November 1930), Experimental College Departmental Folder, 7/37, UWA.

68. J. H. Goodnight to George Sellery (n.d.), box 21, folder "Mad–Mel," 7/1/13-1, G. C. Sellery Correspondence Files, UWA.

69. J. H. Goodnight to George Sellery (n.d.); and Donald Meiklejohn to George Sellery (February 15, 1931), box 21, folder "Mad–Mel," 7/1/13-1, George C. Sellery Correspondence Files, UWA.

70. Donald Meiklejohn to George Sellery (February 15, 1931), box 21, folder "Mad–Mel," 7/1/13-1, George C. Sellery Correspondence Files, UWA.

71. George Sellery to Donald Meiklejohn (February 20, 1931), box 21, folder "Mad–Mel," 7/1/13-1, George C. Sellery Correspondence Files, UWA. See also Meiklejohn to Sellery (15 February 1931).

72. Maurice Neufeld to Mark Levenson (March 3, 1978), box 3, Maurice F. Neufeld folder, 94/34/1, "Alexander Meiklejohn, Experimental College and Post-College, Meetings, Organizations, and Projects," Experimental College Papers, UWA. See also Maurice Neufeld to Alexander Meiklejohn (June 15, 1962), box 22, folder 16, AMP, SHSW.

73. Alexander Meiklejohn, "Annual Report of the Experimental College," Document 48 (February 1931), box 100, Alexander Meiklejohn folder, 4/13/1, Frank Presidential Papers, UWA.

74. Eliseo Vivas, "Wisconsin's Experimental College," *Nation* (March 25, 1931): 322–325. For Meiklejohn's response to Vivas, see "Rejoinder," *New Republic* (March 1931). "What," Meiklejohn asked, "shall one do in the face of a story which seems essentially inaccurate as to facts and superficial in its analysis of problems? The situation is a very awkward one."

75. Showerman, "A Most Lamentable Comedy," 481–488.

76. Phillip L. Garman, "Reflections—A Half Century Later," *Alexander Meiklejohn Experimental College Foundation Quarterly* (December 1982): 16, quoted in Cronon and Jenkins, *The University of Wisconsin: A History,* 3:870–871.

77. Arthur Justin to Alexander Meiklejohn (February 10, 1934), box 17, folder 20, AMP, SHSW.

78. Ernest L. Meyer, "Making Light of the Times" (n.d.), Experimental College Departmental Folder, 7/37, UWA.

79. "Enlightenment, or What?" *New Orleans Tribune* (March 21, 1932), Meiklejohn newspaper clippings, AMP, BUA.

80. Quoted in "Enlightenment, or What?" See also "The Experiment Ends," *New Haven Journal Courier* (July 5, 1932), Meiklejohn newspaper clippings, AMP, BUA.

81. Alexander Meiklejohn, "Report of the Committee on the Experimental College," Document 56 (April 1932), Experimental College Departmental Folder, 7/37, UWA.

82. All quotation in this paragraph come from Reddin, "Guinea Pigs vs. Bohemia."

83. Transcript of interview with David Parsons (n.d.), 35.

84. Phillip F. La Follette to Isen La Follette (February 2, 1930), box 134, folder 6, P. F. La Follette Papers, SHSW. Quoted in Cronon and Jenkins, *The University of Wisconsin: A History,* 3:201.

85. *Capital Times* (June 6, 1932).

86. John Dewey, "The Meiklejohn Experiment," *New Republic* (August 17, 1932): 23–24.

87. Dewey, "The Meiklejohn Experiment," 24.

88. Meiklejohn to Keppel (December 12, 1932).

89. Alexander Meiklejohn to John Warbeke (May 10, 1923), box 30, folder 16, AMP, SHSW.

90. Goldman, ed., "The First Year of the Experimental College," 8.

91. Alexander Meiklejohn, Experimental College memorandum (May 6, 1931), box 32, folder 4, AMP, SHSW.

92. Cronon and Jenkins, *The University of Wisconsin: A History,* 3:226–229.

93. Alexander Meiklejohn to Glenn Frank (June 27, 1932), box 118, folder "Me," 4/13/1, Frank Presidential Papers, UWA. See also Alexander Meiklejohn to Glenn Frank (August 21, October 24, and November 25, 1932); Glenn Frank to Alexander Meiklejohn (December 5, 1932); and M. E. McCaffrey to Alexander Meiklejohn (June 30, 1932); all in box 32, folders 2 and 3, AMP, SHSW. See also Cronon and Jenkins, *The University of Wisconsin: A History,* 3:862.

94. See "Hart Says Attack on 'Ex' College Like One Made on Socrates School," newspaper unidentified (n.d.), box 1, "A Most Lamentable Comedy" folder, 7/7/12, clippings and related correspondence, Experimental College Papers, UWA.

95. David Gordon to Alexander Meiklejohn (February 4, 1933), box 15, folder 2, AMP, SHSW. See also David Gordon to Alexander Meiklejohn (March 21, 1933), box 15, folder 2, AMP, SHSW.

96. Quoted in Charlotte Serber, "Adult Study Unit to 'Educate' a City," newspaper unidentified (n.d.), Meiklejohn newspaper clippings, AMP, BUA. For the original source of this quotation, see Alvin Johnson to Alexander Meiklejohn (April 15, 1933), box 17, folder 26, AMP, SHSW.

97. Alexander Meiklejohn, "Baccalaureate Address," *Amherst Graduates' Quarterly* (August 1923), ACL.

CHAPTER 7. "ADULT EDUCATION: A FRESH START," 1933–1940

1. Alexander Meiklejohn to Glenn Frank (April 12, 1933), box 134, folder "Me," 4/13/1, Frank Presidential Papers, UWA.

2. Alexander Meiklejohn to Glenn Frank (June 2, 1933), box 134, folder "Me," 4/13/1, Frank Presidential Papers, UWA.

3. "Meiklejohn: Educator to Head Adult Research Center," *Newsweek* (August 1933). See also "Guide of Adult Social Study," *Brown Alumni Monthly* (October 1933): 58, BUA; and "Meiklejohn, Ousted Once by Amherst, Continues Liberalism on Coast," *New York Evening Post* (October 6, 1933), box 58, folder 1, AMP, SHSW.

4. "Guide of Adult Social Study," 58. See also "Roost for Meiklejohn," *Time* (June 26, 1933): 56, Meiklejohn newspaper clippings, AMP, BUA

5. See miscellaneous materials regarding San Francisco School of Social Studies administration, box 57, folder 8, AMP, SHSW.

6. See John Walker Powell, Jr., *School for Americans: An Essay in Adult Education, Based on the Work of the School of Social Studies, San Francisco, 1933–1940* (San Francisco, 1942), 98.

7. Alexander Meiklejohn to Andrew Welch (May 23, 1933), box 26, folder 18, AMP, SHSW.

8. Alexander Meiklejohn to Morse Cartwright (August 22, 1933), box 26, folder 18, AMP, SHSW.

9. See John Walker Powell, Jr., *Preliminary Survey of Adult Education Opportunities in San Francisco* (San Francisco, 1938).

10. Statement from brochure reprinted in Alexander Meiklejohn, "Adult Education: A Fresh Start: Progress Report on the San Francisco School of Social Studies," *New Republic* (August 15, 1934): 14–17.

11. Alexander Meiklejohn, "Tentative Prospectus for an Adult Educational Organization in San Francisco" (n.d.), box 57, folder 6, AMP, SHSW.

12. Powell, *School for Americans*, 26.

13. Alexander Meiklejohn, "Tentative Prospectus for an Adult Educational Organization in San Francisco."

14. See Helen Meiklejohn, "The San Francisco School of Social Studies" (December 1940), box 57, folder 6, AMP, SHSW.

15. Powell, *School for Americans*, 32.

16. Powell, *School for Americans*, 91–92, 85–88.

17. H. Meiklejohn, "The San Francisco School of Social Studies."

18. Powell, *School for Americans*, 88, 89, 202.

19. Powell, *School for Americans*, 93, 91–92.

20. Meiklejohn, "Adult Education," 14.

21. Memorandum quoted in Powell, *School for Americans*, 55–56.

22. Powell, *School for Americans*, 109, 106–107.

23. "Plan for the San Francisco School of Social Studies" (n.d.), box 57, folder 8, AMP, SHSW.

24. See "$4000 Granted Social School," newspaper unidentified (n.d.), Meiklejohn newspaper clippings, AMP, BUA. See also Powell, *School for Americans*, 114–115.

25. Powell, *School for Americans,* 200–201, 111.

26. Powell, *School for Americans,* 109–110. See also Alexander Meiklejohn to Glenn Frank (August 1 and November 13, 1934); and Glenn Frank to Alexander Meiklejohn (November 8, 1934); both in box 32, folder 4, AMP, SHSW.

27. See Walter Ricks to Alexander Meiklejohn (September 10 and October 15, 1934), box 32, folder 16, AMP, SHSW.

28. "My sympathies are all with Harry Bridges," Meiklejohn wrote to a friend in 1950. "He seems to me to have done valuable service during these past seventeen years." See Alexander Meiklejohn to Benjamin Dreyfuss (April 23, 1950), box 11, folder 25, AMP, SHSW.

29. Powell, *School for Americans,* 101. See also "Adult Education Urged as Mediator of Future Strikes," *Christian Science Monitor* (July 18, 1934), box 58, folder 1, AMP, SHSW.

30. Alexander Meiklejohn to John Gaus (July 30, 1934), box 14, folder 2, AMP, SHSW.

31. Alexander Meiklejohn to John Gaus (December 8, 1934), box 14, folder 2, AMP, SHSW.

32. Alexander Meiklejohn to Robert Sproul (November 7, 1934), box 7, folder 25, AMP, SHSW.

33. See Roger Baldwin to Alexander Meiklejohn (May 22, 1935), box 4, folder 4, AMP, SHSW.

34. Myer Cohen to Alexander Meiklejohn (April 14, 1939), box 9, folder 24, AMP, SHSW.

35. "Savant Makes Plea for Aid to Education: Dr. Meiklejohn Speaks at State Conference for Social Workers in San Francisco Session," newspaper unidentified (May 6, 1935), Meiklejohn newspaper clippings, AMP, BUA.

36. "New Mental Coinage," newspaper unidentified (n.d.), Meiklejohn newspaper clippings, AMP, BUA.

37. Alexander Meiklejohn, "Liberty—For What?" *Harper's Monthly* (August 1935): 364–372, quotations from 364 and 369, respectively.

38. See Alexander Meiklejohn, "The Crisis in American Institutions" (1934), box 35, folder 1, AMP, SHSW.

39. Alexander Meiklejohn, *What Does America Mean?* (New York, 1935): viii, vii, 22–23.

40. Mciklejohn, *What Does America Mean?* 104, 154.

41. Meiklejohn, *What Does America Mean?* 246–247, 193, 194–195.

42. Meiklejohn, *What Does America Mean?* 234, 235, 236.

43. Florence Kelly, "Review of *What Does America Mean?*" *New York Times Review of Books* (January 5, 1936): 3, 17.

44. Joseph M. Smith, *New York Herald Tribune Books* (February 2, 1936), Meiklejohn newspaper clippings, AMP, BUA.

45. Raymond Fosdick to Alexander Meiklejohn (May 11, 1936), box 13, folder 11, AMP, SHSW.

46. Louis D. Brandeis to Alexander Meiklejohn (November 14, 1935), box 5, folder 28, AMP, SHSW.

47. David Riesman to Alexander Meiklejohn (February 10, 1936), box 25, folder 34, AMP, SHSW.

48. Henry Wallace to Alexander Meiklejohn (March 7, 1938), box 30, folder 15, AMP, SHSW.

49. Meiklejohn, *What Does America Mean?* 79. See also Chard Powers Smith, "Static on the Red Network: The Menace of Reaction in America," *Scribner's Magazine* (May 1936): 257–265.

50. "Excerpts from a Complaint Filed in the Office of the San Francisco County Clerk in the Case of Ivan Francis Cox against the Thirteenth District of the Communist Party, et al." (n.d.), box 58, folder 1, AMP, SHSW.

51. Harper L. Knowles to Alexander Meiklejohn (August 1, 1936), box 58, folder 1, AMP, SHSW.

52. "Dr. Meiklejohn Urges Freedom For Teachers," *San Francisco Chronicle* (May 1, 1936), Meiklejohn newspaper clippings, AMP, BUA.

53. Alexander Meiklejohn, "Speech to Teachers Union" (May 11, 1936), box 58, folder 1, AMP, SHSW.

54. "Dr. Meiklejohn Urges Freedom for Teachers," newspaper unidentified (May 1, 1936), Meiklejohn newspaper clippings, AMP, BUA. See also Alexander Meiklejohn, "Shall Our Teachers Be Allowed to Teach Controversial Questions?" *Pacific Coast Weekly* (June 1936), box 35, folder 2, AMP, SHSW.

55. Alexander Meiklejohn, letter to the editor, *Pacific Coast Weekly* (May 26, 1936), box 23, folder 6, AMP, SHSW

56. Part of the confusion regarding Meiklejohn's views stemmed from the ambiguity between "communism" as an abstract political ideology and "Communism" as an organized political party. Meiklejohn did not clearly distinguish between the two because, for him, such a distinction was irrelevant to his position on the freedom of speech. Meiklejohn consistently defended the right of *all* speakers—even those belonging to the most undemocratic groups—to participate in public deliberation. Therefore, unless the context of a passage clearly indicates that communist ideology instead of Communist Party affiliation is at issue, the term has been capitalized. As a result, the boldness of Meiklejohn's absolutist interpretation of the First Amendment, rather than his (more ambiguous) sympathies for potentially radical social and economic reform, receives the primary emphasis.

57. David Gordon to Alexander Meiklejohn (August 12, 1937), box 15, folder 2, AMP, SHSW. See also James Lerner and Frederick Silber, "Experimental Collegers Who Fought in Spain's Revolution," *University of Wisconsin Alumni Quarterly* (September 1985).

58. Irving F. Reichert to Alexander Meiklejohn (February 26, 1936), box 25, folder 27, AMP, SHSW.

59. "Dr. W. G. Everett Dies in California," *Providence Journal-Bulletin* (July 29, 1937), Meiklejohn newspaper clipping, AMP, BUA.

60. See Alexander Meiklejohn to "Jasha" (November 29, 1955), box 26, folder 12, AMP, SHSW.

61. George Sellery to Alexander Meiklejohn (May 13, 1938), box 32, folder 2, AMP, SHSW.

62. Alexander Meiklejohn to George Sellery (May 17 and 25, 1938), box 32, folder 2, AMP, SHSW.

63. Alexander Meiklejohn to Max Otto (May 25, 1938), box 23, folder 2, AMP, SHSW.

64. Maurice Picard to Alexander Meiklejohn (May 25, 1938), box 10, folder 35, AMP, SHSW. See also E. Gordon Bill to Alexander Meiklejohn (June 17 and November 16, 1938), box 10, folder 35, AMP, SHSW.

65. Theda A. Carter to Alexander Meiklejohn (August 29, 1938), box 31, folder 8, AMP, SHSW. See also Mark H. Ingraham to Alexander Meiklejohn (July 28 and August 11, 1938), box 31, folder 8, AMP, SHSW. See also M. E. McCaffrey to Alexander Meiklejohn (June 6, 1938), box 32, folders 2 and 3, AMP, SHSW.

66. Anonymous to Henry Pritchett (July 7, 1924), box 8, folder 7, AMP, SHSW.

67. Alexander Meiklejohn to O. C. Carmichael. (September 20, 1948), box 8, folder 6, AMP, SHSW.

68. Carnegie Foundation secretary to Alexander Meiklejohn (June 8, 1926), box 8, folder 6, AMP, SHSW.

69. See Mary Jane Keeney to Alexander Meiklejohn (November 26, 1955), box 18, folder 9, AMP, SHSW.

70. "Gordon Meiklejohn, U.S. Born Star on McGill Hockey Team," *New York Herald Tribune* (December 31, year unknown), Meiklejohn newspaper clippings, AMP, BUA.

71. See Alexander Meiklejohn to Ralph M. Crowley (September 5, 1934), box 10, folder 21, AMP, SHSW.

72. See quotation in John W. Nason, "Tribute to Alexander Meiklejohn," *Rights* (February 1965), box 58, folder 6, AMP, SHSW.

73. Walter Ricks to Alexander Meiklejohn (March 18 and 20, 1935), box 32, folder 16, AMP, SHSW.

74. Alexander Meiklejohn, "The Adult Study Association of Sonoma County" (n.d.), box 57, folder 7, AMP, SHSW.

75. See "The School of Social Studies" (n.d.), box 57, folder 7, AMP, SHSW. See also Myer Cohen to Alexander Meiklejohn (April 29, 1939, and April 20, 1940), box 9, folder 24, AMP, SHSW.

76. Powell, *School for Americans,* 201, 203.

77. Powell, *School for Americans,* 95–96, 34.

78. Powell, *School for Americans,* 168–169. See also H. Meiklejohn, "The San Francisco School of Social Studies."

79. Powell, *School for Americans,* 65–66. See also Myer Cohen to Alexander Meiklejohn (April 14, 1939), box 9, folder 24, AMP, SHSW.

80. Alexander Meiklejohn, "Teachers and Controversial Questions," *Harper's Monthly* (June 1938): 15–22.

81. Meiklejohn, "Teachers and Controversial Questions," 18–19, 22. See also Cohen to Meiklejohn (April 14, 1939).

82. Horace Kallen to Alexander Meiklejohn (May 24, 1938), box 17, folder 39, AMP, SHSW.

83. Walter Agard to Alexander Meiklejohn (March 25, 1939), box 1, folder 11, AMP, SHSW.

84. Walter Agard to Alexander Meiklejohn (October 3, 1939), box 1, folder 11, AMP, SHSW.

85. "Mrs. Meiklejohn Hurt in Wreck," *Providence Journal-Bulletin* (August 15, 1939), Meiklejohn newspaper clippings, AMP, BUA.

86. Hugh Greeley to Alexander Meiklejohn (February 1, 1939), box 15, folder 7, AMP, SHSW.

87. See Cohen to Meiklejohn (April 14, 1939).

88. See H. Meiklejohn, "The San Francisco School of Social Studies." See also Powell, *School for Americans,* 116.

89. Powell, *School for Americans,* 101–103.

90. Edward Lamb Parsons to Alexander Meiklejohn (November 29, 1940), box 23, folder 10, AMP, SHSW.

91. Walter Agard to Alexander Meiklejohn (February 9, 1941), box 1, folder 11, AMP, SHSW.

92. "Statement to the Press by the ACLU to Accompany Announcement of Resolution Adopted on February 5, 1940" (February 5, 1940), box 47, folder 3, AMP, SHSW.

93. Alexander Meiklejohn, "Suggested Revision for 'Why We Defend Civil Liberty Even for the Enemies of Civil Liberty'" (September 18, 1942), box 47, folder 8, AMP, SHSW.

94. Roger Baldwin to Alexander Meiklejohn (February 27 and March 5, 1940), box 4, folder 4, AMP, SHSW.

95. Ernest Besig to Alexander Meiklejohn (February 20, 1940), box 4, folder 22, AMP, SHSW.

96. See Verne A. Stadtman, *The University of California, 1868–1968* (New York, 1970), 320.

97. Alexander Meiklejohn to George Adams (n.d.), box 1, folder 5, AMP, SHSW.

98. James Conant to Alexander Meiklejohn (April 24 and May 6, 1940), box 9, folder 38, AMP, SHSW.

99. James Conant to Alexander Meiklejohn (June 14, 1940), box 9, folder 38, AMP, SHSW.

CHAPTER 8. "A REPLY TO JOHN DEWEY," 1941–1947

1. Alexander Meiklejohn, "Higher Education in a Democracy," *North Central Association Quarterly* (October 1941): 149–154. See also "In Seclusion Here to Write on Pet Subject, The State and Education; Here are Some of His Beliefs" *Vineyard Gazette* (n.d. [1941]), box 59, folder 5, AMP, SHSW.

2. Meiklejohn, "Higher Education in a Democracy," 151.

3. Meiklejohn, "Higher Education in a Democracy," 152.

4. Meiklejohn, "Higher Education in a Democracy," 149–150.

5. Meiklejohn, "Higher Education in a Democracy," 154.

6. Alexander Meiklejohn to John McCloy (September 30, 1942), box 19, folder 32, AMP, SHSW.

7. Alexander Meiklejohn to Roger Baldwin (March 17, 1942), box 4, folder 4, AMP, SHSW.

8. Meiklejohn to McCloy (September 30, 1942).

9. Felix Frankfurter, "Concurring Opinion," *Korematsu v. United States*, 323 U.S. 214 (1944).

10. See Felix Frankfurter to Alexander Meiklejohn (January 8, 1945), box 13, folder 20, AMP, SHSW.

11. Alexander Meiklejohn to John Gaus (March 27, 1942), box 14, folder 2, AMP, SHSW.

12. See Alexander Meiklejohn to John Gill (May 21, 1942), box 14, folder 11, AMP, SHSW.

13. Alexander Meiklejohn, *Education Between Two Worlds* (New York, 1942), ix.

14. Meiklejohn became interested in a comparison of Comenius and Locke as early as the spring of 1940. See Karel Cervenka to Alexander Meiklejohn (May 14, 1940), box 7, folder 9, AMP, SHSW.

15. See "Education Called 'One-Sided' Today," *Providence Journal-Bulletin* (May 6, 1939), Meiklejohn newspaper clippings, AMP, BUA.

16. Meiklejohn, *Education Between Two Worlds*, 33–34.

17. Meiklejohn, *Education Between Two Worlds*, 72–73.

18. Meiklejohn, *Education Between Two Worlds*, 81.

19. Meiklejohn, *Education Between Two Worlds*, 81. "To paraphrase Comenius," Meiklejohn concluded, "we may say that 'only by becoming a citizen does one become a man.'"

20. Meiklejohn, *Education Between Two Worlds*, 91.

21. "Rousseau and Dictatorships Linked by Meiklejohn," *Brown Daily Herald* (April 24, 1941): 4, BUA.

22. Meiklejohn, *Education Between Two Worlds*, 92.

23. Meiklejohn, *Education Between Two Worlds*, 180.

24. Meiklejohn, *Education Between Two Worlds*, 102–103.

25. See Alexander Meiklejohn to John Gaus (March 27, 1942).

26. Meiklejohn, *Education Between Two Worlds*, 200, 207, 204.

27. See Ralph C. Preston, "Reason as a Guide for Education," *Christian Century* (December 1, 1943): 1404–1405. "Meiklejohn is one of those moderns who reject the concept of God yet whose aspirations for the human race challenge the most devout believer," Preston wrote.

28. Meiklejohn, *Education Between Two Worlds*, 258, 264, 265, 266–267, 276.

29. Max Lerner to Ordway Tead (August 18, 1942), box 19, folder 13, AMP, SHSW.

30. Preston, "Reason as a Guide for Education," 1404.

31. Walter Agard to Alexander Meiklejohn (October 16, 1942), box 1, folder 11, AMP, SHSW.

32. See Carol Thigpen, "Meiklejohn and Maritain: Two Views on the End of Progressive Education," *Teachers College Record* 96, no. 1 (1994): 89–101.

33. John Dewey to Alexander Meiklejohn (September 25, 1942), box 11, folder 11, AMP, SHSW.

34. Quoted in Robert Westbrook, *John Dewey and American Democracy* (Ithaca, N.Y., 1991), 246.

35. Quoted in Westbrook, *John Dewey and American Democracy*, 247.

36. Meiklejohn, *Education Between Two Worlds*, 258.

37. Alexander Meiklejohn to Lewis Mumford (October 20, 1942), box 21, folder 33, AMP, SHSW.

38. Alexander Meiklejohn to Stringfellow Barr (October 22, 1942), box 4, folder 6, AMP, SHSW.

39. Sidney Hook "Education for the New Order," *Nation* (February 27, 1943): 308–312.

40. See Eugene Perry, "Alexander Meiklejohn and the Organic Theory of Democracy" (unpublished M.A. thesis, Syracuse University, 1969).

41. Edward W. Strong to Alexander Meiklejohn (June 22 through July 15, 1943), box 28, folder 5, AMP, SHSW.

42. Morse Erskine to Alexander Meiklejohn (December 26, 1943), box 12, folder 9, AMP, SHSW.

43. Meiklejohn, *Education Between Two Worlds*, 223.

44. John Gaus to Alexander Meiklejohn (June 4, 1944), box 14, folder 2, AMP, SHSW.

45. Alexander Meiklejohn to John Gaus (June 16, 1944), box 14, folder 2, AMP, SHSW.

46. See Alexander Meiklejohn to Anson Morse (November 24, 1914), box IV, folder 6, Non-Alumnus Biographical File—Alexander Meiklejohn, ACL.

47. Clarence Ayres to Alexander Meiklejohn (June 24, 1943), box 3, folder 26, AMP, SHSW. See also Clarence Ayres to Alexander Meiklejohn (December 13, 1943), box 3, folder 26, AMP, SHSW.

48. Alexander Meiklejohn to Horace Fries (April 20, 1944), box 2, folder 10, AMP, SHSW.

49. Quoted in Horace Fries to Alexander Meiklejohn (April 20, 1944), box 2, folder 10, AMP, SHSW.

50. Meiklejohn reviewed Robert Hutchins's book, *Education for Freedom,* in the *New Republic.* See Alexander Meiklejohn, "Mr. Hutchins' Dogma," *New Republic* (August 2, 1943): 147–148.

51. John Dewey, "Challenge to Liberal Thought," *Fortune* (August 1944): 155–157, 180.

52. Alexander Meiklejohn to Stringfellow Barr (August 1, 1944), box 4, folder 6, AMP, SHSW.

53. Alexander Meiklejohn to Stringfellow Barr (September 9, 1944), box 4, folder 6, AMP, SHSW.

54. Alexander Meiklejohn, "A Reply to John Dewey," *Fortune* (January 1945): 207–208, 210, 212, 214, 217, 219, discussion and quotation from 210 and 212.

55. Meiklejohn, "A Reply to John Dewey," 217.

56. Meiklejohn, "A Reply to John Dewey," 219.

57. Meiklejohn, "A Reply to John Dewey," 219.

58. Sidney Hook, "The Apologists for St. John's College," *New Leader* (November 25, 1944); see also Sidney Hook, "Ballyhoo at St. John's College," *New Leader* (May 27 and June 3, 1944).

59. Alexander Meiklejohn to Sidney Hook (January 4, 1945), box 16, folder 40, AMP, SHSW.

60. Sidney Hook to Alexander Meiklejohn (January 6, 1945), box 16, folder 40, AMP, SHSW.

61. Hook to Meiklejohn (January 6, 1945).

62. Alexander Meiklejohn to Sidney Hook (n.d. [January 1945]), box 16, folder 40, AMP, SHSW.

63. Sidney Hook to Alexander Meiklejohn (January 13, 1945), box 16, folder 40, AMP, SHSW.

64. Alexander Meiklejohn to Sidney Hook (January 15, 1945), box 16, folder 40, AMP, SHSW.

65. John Dewey, "Letter to the Editor: Dewey vs. Meiklejohn," *Fortune* (March 1945): 10, 14.

66. Ralph D. Paine to Alexander Meiklejohn (October 2, 1944), box 13, folder 7, AMP, SHSW.

67. Alice van Arsdale to Alexander Meiklejohn (March 9, 1945), box 30, folder 4, AMP, SHSW.

68. Clarence Ayres to Alexander Meiklejohn (April 24, 1945), box 3, folder 26, AMP, SHSW. See also Clarence Ayres to Alexander Meiklejohn (May 7, 1945), box 3, folder 26, AMP, SHSW.

69. "Meiklejohn's Philosophy of Kant," *St. John's Collegian* (February 2, 1945), box 57, folder 4, AMP, SHSW.

70. Alexander Meiklejohn, "Education as a Factor in Postwar Reconstruction," *Free World* (January 1943): 27–31.

71. See Alexander Meiklejohn, untitled speech (July 25, 1946), box 36, folder 1, AMP, SHSW. See also Alexander Meiklejohn, "Memorandum" (n.d.), box 50, folder 7, AMP, SHSW.

72. Charles Bunn to Alexander Meiklejohn (February 25, 1943), box 7, folder 2, AMP, SHSW.

73. William Benton to Alexander Meiklejohn (October 17, 1945), box 29, folder 13, AMP, SHSW.

74. See Esther Brunauer to Alexander Meiklejohn (April 17, 1950), box 3, folder 27, AMP, SHSW. "I, too, remember our walks on the *Queen Mary* back in 1945."

75. Alexander Meiklejohn, "To Teach the World How to Be Free," *New York Times Magazine* (August 11, 1946): 5, 48–50, quotation from 5.

76. Meiklejohn, "To Teach the World How to Be Free," 48.

77. Alexander Meiklejohn, "Fiat Justicia: The College as Critic," *Harvard Graduates' Magazine* (September 1917): 14.

78. Meiklejohn had begun to back away from his strict idealism as early as 1942. See Alexander Meiklejohn, "What the Liberal College Is" in Cynthia Stokes Brown, ed., *Alexander Meiklejohn: Teacher of Freedom* (Berkeley, 1981), 80–81.

79. Alexander Meiklejohn, "Inclinations and Obligations," *University of California Publications in Philosophy* (Berkeley, 1948), 203–204, quotation from 203.

80. Hugh Greeley to Alexander Meiklejohn (August 21, 1946), box 15, folder 7, AMP, SHSW.

CHAPTER 9. "WHAT DOES THE FIRST AMENDMENT MEAN?" 1948–1954

1. Alexander Meiklejohn, "Free Speech and Justice Holmes," quoted in Philip Glick to Alexander Meiklejohn (February 14, 1946), box 14, folder 15, AMP, SHSW.

2. Glick to Meiklejohn (February 14, 1946). Meiklejohn received extensive comments from Glick on the substance of his argument. He also received comments from Roger Baldwin. See Roger Baldwin to Alexander Meiklejohn (January 22, 1946), box 4, folder 4, AMP, SHSW.

3. Ordway Tead to Alexander Meiklejohn (April 12, 1946), box 15, folder 34, AMP, SHSW. In his letter rejecting Meiklejohn's manuscript, Tead attributed his decision to a paper shortage and a "terrific congestion in publication."

4. Robert M. Brown to the editor, *Brown Alumni Monthly* (December 23, 1947), BUA. See also Thomas W. Braden, "The Great Issues Course: Dartmouth's Educational Experiment, Launched This Fall For All Seniors, Attracts Wide In-

terest and the Support of National Leaders Who Are to Lecture in the Course," *Dartmouth Alumni Magazine* (October 1947): 15–16.

5. Ordway Tead to Alexander Meiklejohn (January 5, 1948), box 15, folder 34, AMP, SHSW. "This is to corroborate my day letter of December 29 indicating our delight in publishing the Holmes volume."

6. Alexander Meiklejohn, *Free Speech and Its Relation to Self-Government* (New York, 1948), x.

7. Meiklejohn, *Free Speech and Its Relation to Self-Government*, 17, xii, 27.

8. Meiklejohn, *Free Speech and Its Relation to Self-Government*, 23–25.

9. See also Alexander Meiklejohn, "Everything Worth Saying Should Be Said," *New York Times Magazine* (June 18, 1948): 8, 32.

10. Meiklejohn, *Free Speech and Its Relation to Self-Government*, 38–39.

11. Harry Kalven to Alexander Meiklejohn (March 11, 1953), box 17, folder 40, AMP, SHSW.

12. *Schenck v. United States*, 249 U.S. 47 (1919). See also Meiklejohn, *Free Speech and Its Relation to Self-Government*, 29.

13. *Schenck v. United States*, 47.

14. Meiklejohn, *Free Speech and Its Relation to Self-Government*, 34, 71–72.

15. See *Jacob Abrams v. United States*, 250 U.S. 616, 624 (1919).

16. Meiklejohn, *Free Speech and Its Relation to Self-Government*, 86–87.

17. Meiklejohn, *Free Speech and Its Relation to Self-Government*, 77.

18. Meiklejohn, *Free Speech and Its Relation to Self-Government*, 105, 65–66.

19. Max Lerner to Ordway Tead (June 23, 1948), box 19, folder 13, AMP, SHSW.

20. Max Lerner, "Review of *Free Speech and Its Relation to Self-Government*," *New Republic* (September 13, 1948): 21.

21. Lerner, "Review of *Free Speech and Its Relation to Self-Government*," 21.

22. See Zechariah Chafee, *Freedom of Speech* (New York, 1920) and *Free Speech in the United States* (New York, 1946).

23. Zechariah Chafee, "Review of *Free Speech and Its Relation to Self-Government*," *Harvard Law Review* (1948): 891–901, quotations from 891 and 892, respectively.

24. Chafee, "Review of *Free Speech and Its Relation to Self-Government*," 894.

25. Alexander Meiklejohn to Zechariah Chafee (November 29, 1948), box 8, folder 17, AMP, SHSW.

26. Chafee, "Review of *Free Speech and Its Relation to Self-Government*," 896.

27. Zechariah Chafee to Alexander Meiklejohn (November 23, 1948), box 8, folder 17, AMP, SHSW.

28. See Milton Mayer, "Alec Meiklejohn's Maytime," *Progressive* (August 1965): 18.

29. Robert Kenny to Alexander Meiklejohn (October 31, 1948), box 18, folder 17, AMP, SHSW.

30. Alexander Meiklejohn, "Brief of Alexander Meiklejohn on Behalf of Cultural Workers in Motion Pictures and Other Arts, and of Members of the Professions, as Amici Curiae, in the Supreme Court of the United States" (October term, 1949), 13, box 36, folder 5, AMP, SHSW.

31. Meiklejohn, "Brief on Behalf of Cultural Workers in Motion Pictures," 19–24, quotation from 22.

32. See *Communism and Academic Freedom: The Record of the Tenure Cases at the University of Washington, Including the Findings of the Committee on Tenure and Academic Freedom and the President's Recommendations* (Seattle, 1949).

33. Alexander Meiklejohn, "Should Communists Be Allowed to Teach?" or "Professors on Probation," *New York Times Magazine* (March 27, 1949): 10, 64–66. This article was a response to Sidney Hook, "Should Communists Be Allowed to Teach?" *New York Times Magazine* (February 27, 1949): 7, 22–29.

34. J. B. Harrison to Alexander Meiklejohn (April 4, 1949), box 15, folder 27, AMP, SHSW.

35. Sidney Hook, "Academic Integrity and Academic Freedom, How to Deal with the Fellow-Travelling Professor," *Commentary* (October 1949): 329–339. See also letters to the editor, *Commentary* (December 1949): 593–601.

36. George Stone to Alexander Meiklejohn (March 28, 1949), box 26, folder 6, AMP, SHSW.

37. Helen E. McNulty to Alexander Meiklejohn (March 30, 1949), box 19, folder 30, AMP, SHSW.

38. Alexander Meiklejohn to Robert G. Hooker (April 21, 1949), box 17, folder 1, AMP, SHSW.

39. American Civil Liberties Union of Northern California, "Crisis at the University of California: A Further Statement to the People of California" (December 15, 1951), box 1, folder 20, AMP, SHSW. This statement was first written in December of 1950. See also Alexander Meiklejohn, "The Teaching of Intellectual Freedom," *Bulletin of the American Association of University Professors* (spring 1952): 10–25.

40. See David Caute, *The Great Fear: The Anti-Communist Purge under Truman and Eisenhower* (New York, 1978): 403–427, quotation from 424.

41. Alexander Meiklejohn, *Crisis at the University of California* (December 1950), pamphlet, box 1, folder 20, AMP, SHSW.

42. Clarence Ayres to Alexander Meiklejohn (November 27, 1949), box 3, folder 26, AMP, SHSW.

43. Meiklejohn drafted a letter to President Truman asking for clemency on behalf of Julius and Ethel Rosenberg. See Alexander Meiklejohn to Harry Truman (December 1, 1952), box 25, folder 41, AMP, SHSW.

44. See the materials of the National Committee to Repeal the McCarran Act (1951), box 22, folder 4, AMP, SHSW.

45. C. Douglas Mercer to Alexander Meiklejohn (April 29, 1951), box 21, folder 3, AMP, SHSW.

46. See "Dr. Meiklejohn at 79 Still Battling for Free Speech," *Providence Journal-Bulletin* (October 4, 1951), box 1, folder 3, Meiklejohn newspaper clippings, AMP, BUA.

47. See Stringfellow Barr to Alexander Meiklejohn (November 8, 1948), box 4, folder 6, AMP, SHSW. "Like you," Barr wrote, "I cast my ballot for Wallace. Like you, I was rejoiced by the Truman victory. Like you, I had been made dizzy by these two facts."

48. Royal W. France to Alexander Meiklejohn (October 18, 1952), box 13, folder 15, AMP, SHSW.

49. Stringfellow Barr to Alexander Meiklejohn (November 6, 1952), box 4, folder 6, AMP, SHSW.

50. American Civil Liberties Union, "Statement on the Nature of the Communist Party" (May 8, 1953), box 48, folder 9, AMP, SHSW.

51. Alexander Meiklejohn, "Comment on the 'Three Statements of Policy' Regarding the Communist Party" (September 10, 1953), 3, box 48, folder 9, AMP, SHSW.

52. Roger Baldwin to Alexander Meiklejohn (September 11, 1953), box 4, folder 4, AMP, SHSW.

53. Alexander Meiklejohn, "The Crisis in Freedom," *Progressive* (June 1952): 15–18.

54. Alexander Meiklejohn, "What Is the Meaning of the First Amendment?" *University of Chicago Law Review* 20, no. 3 (1953): 467. Originally, this article bore the title "The Right to Advocate Revolution." See Alexander Meiklejohn to Corliss Lamont (October 24, 1952), box 18, folder 33, AMP, SHSW. "I'm just finishing a paper on 'The Right to Advocate Revolution,' a comment on Frankfurter's opinion in the *Dennis* case. It's promised to the *Chicago Law Review*." Eight years later, Meiklejohn elaborated on this paper in "The Balancing of Self-Preservation against Political Freedom," *California Law Review* (March 1961): 1–11. See *Eugene Dennis v. United States*, 339 U.S. 162 (1950).

55. Meiklejohn, "What Is the Meaning of the First Amendment?" 467.

56. Meiklejohn made the same point five years earlier. See Alexander Meiklejohn, "There They Stand, Face to Face . . ." (August 4, 1948), box 36, folder 2, AMP, SHSW.

57. Meiklejohn, "What Is the Meaning of the First Amendment?" 468.

58. Meiklejohn, "What Is the Meaning of the First Amendment?" 468.

59. Meiklejohn, *Free Speech and Its Relation to Self-Government,* 16.

60. Philip Glick to Alexander Meiklejohn (June 15, 1953), box 14, folder 15, AMP, SHSW.

61. William O. Douglas to Alexander Meiklejohn (October 6, 1954), box 11, folder 21, AMP, SHSW.

62. Clarence Ayres to Alexander Meiklejohn (October 1, 1953), box 3, folder 26, AMP, SHSW.

63. See "Lecture Tour, 1951," box 60, folder 3, AMP, SHSW.

64. Scott Buchanan to Ernest Brooks (November 7, 1952), box 6, folder 16, AMP, SHSW.

65. Alexander Meiklejohn to Scott Buchanan (November 27, 1952), box 6, folder 16, AMP, SHSW.

66. Alexander Meiklejohn to Scott Buchanan (June 19, 1953), box 6, folder 16, AMP, SHSW.

67. Alexander Meiklejohn to Scott Buchanan (August 13, 1953), box 6, folder 16, AMP, SHSW.

68. Meiklejohn to Buchanan (August 13, 1953).

69. Alexander Meiklejohn, "Notebook from European Tour," unpaginated script (1953–1954), box 60, folder 1, AMP, SHSW.

70. Meiklejohn to Buchanan (August 13, 1953).

71. See Meiklejohn, "Notebook from European Tour."

72. Scott Buchanan to Alexander Meiklejohn (September 30, 1953), box 6, folder 16, AMP, SHSW.

73. Alexander Meiklejohn to Scott Buchanan (September 28, 1953), box 6, folder 16, AMP, SHSW.

74. "I have not taken a trip by air yet," Meiklejohn wrote in 1949. See Alexander Meiklejohn to Major General Anderson (July 15, 1949), box 29, folder 16, AMP, SHSW.

75. See Jacques Maritain to Alexander Meiklejohn (December 15, 1953), box 20, folder 10, AMP, SHSW.

76. Meiklejohn, "Notebook from European Tour."

77. Helen Meiklejohn to Miriam Buchanan (February 15, 1954), box 6, folder 16, AMP, SHSW.

78. H. Meiklejohn to M. Buchanan (February 15, 1954).

79. H. Meiklejohn to M. Buchanan (February 15, 1954).

80. Meiklejohn, "Notebook on European Tour."

81. Alexander Meiklejohn to Corliss Lamont (February 13, 1954), box 18, folder 33, AMP, SHSW.

82. Alexander Meiklejohn to Corliss Lamont (February 28, 1954), box 18, folder 33, AMP, SHSW.

83. See Myer Cohen to Alexander Meiklejohn (November 23, 1957), box 9, folder 24, AMP, SHSW.

84. H. Meiklejohn to M. Buchanan (February 15, 1954).

85. Meiklejohn, "Notebook from European Tour."

86. Alexander Meiklejohn to Clark Foreman (April 21, 1954), box 12, folder 2, AMP, SHSW.

87. Alexander Meiklejohn to Scott Buchanan (June 14, 1954), box 6, folder 16, AMP, SHSW.

88. Helen Meiklejohn to Miriam Buchanan (July 2, 1954), box 6, folder 16, AMP, SHSW.

89. H. Meiklejohn to M. Buchanan (July 2, 1954).

90. Alexander Meiklejohn to Scott Buchanan (July 16, 1954), box 6, folder 16, AMP, SHSW.

91. Meiklejohn, untitled draft (1954), box 37, folder 2, AMP, SHSW.

CHAPTER 10. "THE FAITH OF A FREE MAN," 1955–1964

1. Meiklejohn first learned of the Hennings Committee hearings shortly after his return from Europe, more than a year before his testimony. See Clark Foreman to Alexander Meiklejohn (June 29, 1954), box 12, folder 2, AMP, SHSW.

2. Testimony of Alexander Meiklejohn before Hennings Committee (November 14, 1955), box 29, folder 18, AMP, SHSW.

3. Harry Kalven to Alexander Meiklejohn (December 1, 1952), box 17, folder 40, AMP, SHSW.

4. John Frank to Alexander Meiklejohn (March 7, 1949), box 13, folder 19, AMP, SHSW. See also John Frank to Alexander Meiklejohn (February 22 and December 8, 1949), box 13, folder 19, AMP, SHSW.

5. See John Frank to Alexander Meiklejohn (November 17, 1949), box 13, folder 19, AMP, SHSW.

6. See *Yates v. United States*, 354 U.S. 298 (1957); and *Watkins v. United States*, 354 U.S. 178 (1957).

7. *Watkins v. United States,* 178.

8. John Frank to Helen and Alexander Meiklejohn (June 21, 1957), box 13, folder 19, AMP, SHSW.

9. Frank Wilkinson to Alexander Meiklejohn (June 17, 1957), box 30, folder 39, AMP, SHSW.

10. David Caute, *The Great Fear: The Anti-Communist Purge under Truman and Eisenhower* (New York, 1978), 102.

11. See Alexander Meiklejohn to Clark Foreman (July 7, 1957), box 12, folder 2, AMP, SHSW.

12. Alexander Meiklejohn to Clark Foreman (July 17, 1957), box 12, folder 2, AMP, SHSW.

13. Alexander Meiklejohn to Clark Foreman (July 22, 1957), box 12, folder 2, AMP, SHSW.

14. Alexander Meiklejohn, "Petition for Redress of Grievance" (December 13, 1957), box 29, folder 14, AMP, SHSW. See also the *New York Times* (January 1, 1958) and the acknowledgement of the receipt of Meiklejohn's petition, *Congressional Record,* 85th Cong., 2d session, 1958, 104, pt. 1: 40.

15. Meiklejohn, "Petition for Redress of Grievance."

16. Frank Wilkinson to Alexander Meiklejohn (August 31, 1957), box 30,

folder 39, AMP, SHSW. "In each instance," Wilkinson explained in a long letter to Meiklejohn, "I sat down within five minutes after the interview to write up as accurately as possible exactly what was said."

17. In 1950, Judge Learned Hand upheld the conviction of eleven Communist leaders under the Smith Act, interpreting Holmes's clear and present danger test to mean that the courts must ascertain "whether the gravity of the 'evil,' discounted by its improbability, justifies such invasion of free speech as is necessary to avoid the danger." See Caute, *The Great Fear,* 148.

18. Howard W. Smith to Alexander Meiklejohn (April 16, 1958), box 29, folder 17, AMP, SHSW.

19. Raymond Fosdick to Alexander Meiklejohn (October 9, 1957), box 29, folder 17, AMP, SHSW.

20. Alexander Meiklejohn to Scott Buchanan (December 7, 1957), box 6, folder 17, AMP, SHSW.

21. "Reunion of the X-College of Late 20's Brings Meiklejohn and Students Together Again—His Views Unchanged," *Providence Journal-Bulletin* (May 19, 1957).

22. A. W. Marsh to Helen and Alexander Meiklejohn (May 18, 1964), reminiscences solicited by Scott Abbott, Non-Alumnus Biographical File—Alexander Meiklejohn, ACL.

23. Alexander Meiklejohn to Ernest Angell (July 17, 1957), box 1, folder 21, AMP, SHSW.

24. *Barenblatt v. United States,* 360 U.S. 109 (1959).

25. Hugo Black, dissenting opinion in *Barenblatt v. United States,* 109, 134.

26. *Barenblatt v. United States,* 109, 134.

27. See Alexander Meiklejohn to Hugo Black (July 28, 1957), box 5, folder 2, AMP, SHSW. "It gave me great pleasure to see your reference to me in your concurring-dissenting opinion in the *Yates* case," Meiklejohn wrote. "P.S. I'm glad you brought Chafee in too. I wish it were not too late to get you to arbitrate between him and me."

28. Hugo Black to Alexander Meiklejohn (January 30, 1952), box 5, folder 2, AMP, SHSW.

29. *Barenblatt v. United States.* See also Hugo L. Black, "The Assault on Liberty," *Progressive* (January 1961): 26–28.

30. Alexander Meiklejohn to Thomas Emerson (November 23, 1959), box 12, folder 5, AMP, SHSW. See also Hugo Black to Alexander Meiklejohn (July 25, 1962), box 5, folder 2, AMP, SHSW.

31. Alexander Meiklejohn to Seelye Bixler (October 12, 1960), box 5, folder 1, AMP, SHSW.

32. Alexander Meiklejohn, "The Barenblatt Opinion," *University of Chicago Law Review* (winter 1960): 329–340, quotations from 331 and 332.

33. Roger Traynor to Alexander Meiklejohn (January 13, 1960), box 29, folder 1, AMP, SHSW.

34. Joseph Rauh to Alexander Meiklejohn (May 20, 1960), box 25, folder 21, AMP, SHSW.

35. See *Uphaus v. Wyman*, 360 U.S. 72 (1959); *Uphaus v. Wyman*, 364 U.S. 388, 389 (1960); *Braden v. United States*, 365 U.S. 431, 438 (1961); and *Wilkinson v. United States*, 365 U.S. 399, 415 (1961).

36. *Wilkinson v. United States*, 399, 415.

37. *Wilkinson v. United States*, 399, 415. See also Alexander Meiklejohn, "The Balancing of Self-Preservation against Political Freedom," *California Law Review* (March 1961): 1–11.

38. See Alexander Meiklejohn to John Gill (March 2, 1961), box 14, folder 11, AMP, SHSW.

39. Harry Kalven to Alexander Meiklejohn (March 7, 1961), box 17, folder 40, AMP, SHSW.

40. Alexander Meiklejohn to Rowland Watts (July 11, 1959), box 30, folder 22, AMP, SHSW.

41. Alexander Meiklejohn to Harris Wofford (November 30, 1961), box 32, folder 8, AMP, SHSW.

42. Frank Wilkinson to Alexander Meiklejohn (February 5, 1961), box 30, folder 39, AMP, SHSW.

43. Alexander Meiklejohn to Frank Wilkinson (January 27, 1962), box 30, folder 39, AMP, SHSW.

44. Meiklejohn, "Notebook from European Tour" (1953–1954), box 60, folder 1, AMP, SHSW.

45. Alexander Meiklejohn to Lawrence Speiser (January 2, 1961), box 27, folder 32, AMP, SHSW.

46. Alexander Meiklejohn to Lawrence Speiser (January 18, 1961), box 27, folder 32, AMP, SHSW.

47. See Helen Meiklejohn to Martin Popper (April 16, 1966), box 24, folder 10, AMP, SHSW.

48. Alexander Meiklejohn to Scott Buchanan (February 1, 1963), box 6, folder 17, AMP, SHSW.

49. Alexander Meiklejohn to Corliss Lamont (January 28, 1956), box 18, folder 34, AMP, SHSW.

50. Alexander Meiklejohn to W. H. Ferry (August 14, 1961), box 12, folder 27, AMP, SHSW.

51. Alexander Meiklejohn to Scott Buchanan (August 16, 1961), box 6, folder 17, AMP, SHSW.

52. See Clarence Ayres to Helen and Alexander Meiklejohn (September 3, 1962), box 3, folder 26, AMP, SHSW.

53. See Alexander Meiklejohn to Glenn Burch (September 5, 1961), box 7, folder 3, AMP, SHSW.

54. W. H. Ferry to Alexander Meiklejohn (August 25, 1961), box 12, folder 27, AMP, SHSW.

55. Alexander Meiklejohn to Otto Nathan (March 19, 1964), box 21, folder 42, AMP, SHSW.

56. Alexander Meiklejohn to Otto Nathan (August 29, 1964), box 21, folder 42, AMP, SHSW.

57. Corliss Lamont to Alexander Meiklejohn (February 19, 1963), box 18, folder 34, AMP, SHSW.

58. A year earlier, President Kennedy sent Meiklejohn a birthday greeting. "I learned too late of your ninetieth birthday, which I understand you celebrated in Madison, Wisconsin. Please accept my belated wish for a very happy birthday and my congratulations for so many years of work for the freedom of our institutions." See John F. Kennedy to Alexander Meiklejohn (n.d. [1962]), box 29, folder 28, AMP, SHSW. See also Alexander Meiklejohn to John F. Kennedy (July 26, 1962), box 29, folder 28, AMP, SHSW.

59. John W. Macy, Jr., to Alexander Meiklejohn (November 19, 1963), box 29, folder 28, AMP, SHSW.

60. Alexander Meiklejohn to Robert F. Kennedy (December 20, 1963), box 18, folder 14, AMP, SHSW.

61. Alexander Meiklejohn to W. H. Ferry (December 25, 1963), box 12, folder 27, AMP, SHSW. See also Alexander Meiklejohn to William O. Douglas (January 28, 1964), box 11, folder 21, AMP, SHSW. Meiklejohn noted how delighted he had been to see the Supreme Court sitting by when the president gave him a medal he hardly felt he deserved. "My doubts were considerably relieved," he wrote to Douglas, "when you and Hugo and the Chief Justice and Goldberg, whom I knew fairly well, came up to congratulate me. Somehow the attitude seemed a lot more authoritative, and it was certainly more pleasant. Many, many thanks to all of you from me and, even more, from Helen!"

62. Lewis Mumford to Alexander Meiklejohn (December 31, 1963), box 21, folder 33, AMP, SHSW.

63. Lewis Mumford to Alexander Meiklejohn (August 29, 1963), box 21, folder 33, AMP, SHSW.

64. Alexander Meiklejohn to John Gill (September 10, 1963), box 14, folder 11, AMP, SHSW.

65. See Grace Lee Boggs and James Boggs, *Revolution and Evolution in the Twentieth Century* (New York, 1974).

66. Alexander Meiklejohn to Grace Lee Boggs (September 9, 1963), box 5, folder 12, AMP, SHSW.

67. Alexander Meiklejohn to W. H. Ferry (August 28, 1962), box 12, folder 27, AMP, SHSW.

68. Alexander Meiklejohn to Scott Buchanan (February 3, 1963), box 6, folder 17, AMP, SHSW. In these later years, Meiklejohn appreciated the unfailing companionship of Buchanan. "I can say that, in the fifty years . . . which have passed since 1912, no one else outside of my immediate family has brought me so much of significance or happiness as you have done."

69. See Alexander Meiklejohn to John Frank (March 9, 1963), box 13, folder 19, AMP, SHSW.

70. Alexander Meiklejohn to W. H. Ferry (July 20, 1963), box 12, folder 27, AMP, SHSW.

71. Alexander Meiklejohn to W. H. Ferry (August 15, 1963), box 12, folder 27, AMP, SHSW.

72. See Alexander Meiklejohn to John Gaus (July 3, 1964), box 14, folder 3, AMP, SHSW. "I'm trying these days to write about what, more or less blindly, we were driving at in the Experimental College," he added.

73. See Clark Kerr to Alexander Meiklejohn (July 8, 1963), box 7, folder 24, AMP, SHSW. "Enclosed is a copy of the Godkin lectures you requested in your letter of June 26. They will be changed considerably before publication by Harvard this fall."

74. Alexander Meiklejohn to Clark Kerr (September 19, 1963), box 7, folder 24, AMP, SHSW.

75. Alexander Meiklejohn to Frank Wilkinson (June 18, 1963), box 30, folder 39, AMP, SHSW.

76. Arthur Upham Pope, "Alexander Meiklejohn," *American Scholar* (autumn 1965): 641–645.

77. Alexander Meiklejohn to Scott Buchanan (May 5, 1961), box 6, folder 17, AMP, SHSW.

78. See Alexander Meiklejohn to Seelye Bixler (January 23, 1959), box 5, folder 1, AMP, SHSW.

79. Alexander Meiklejohn to Seelye Bixler (September 6, 1963), box 5, folder 1, AMP, SHSW.

80. Alexander Meiklejohn to Seelye Bixler (September 10, 1959), box 5, folder 1, AMP, SHSW.

81. Seelye Bixler to Alexander Meiklejohn (September 23, 1963), box 5, folder 1, AMP, SHSW.

82. Bixler to Meiklejohn (September 23, 1963).

83. Alexander Meiklejohn, "Heidegger—Reply to Vera Maslow" (n.d.), box 20, folder 14, AMP, SHSW.

84. Alexander Meiklejohn to Seelye Bixler (October 27, 1963), box 5, folder 1, AMP, SHSW.

85. Meiklejohn to Bixler (October 27, 1963). "I fear that all this is very blind," Meiklejohn confessed. "As you suggest, I do find myself in practical sympathy with such a Stoic as Epictetus, but I am not quite sure that he understood what he was doing, as, for example, Kant did. The *Critiques* are my homeland. At multitudes of points I cannot agree. And yet they give me the sense of what seems worth trying as our way of life."

86. Meiklejohn's relationship with Hutchins was never very close. "I have never known him," he wrote to Scott Buchanan in 1952, "and have always felt that for some unexplained reason, he hasn't wanted to know me." See Alexander

Meiklejohn to Scott Buchanan (November 27, 1952), box 6, folder 16, AMP, SHSW.

87. Alexander Meiklejohn to Robert Hutchins (August 10, 1964), box 17, folder 11, AMP, SHSW. Hutchins responded in kind. "You have been a bright and guiding star for so long," he wrote to Meiklejohn, "that I am afraid you may sometimes forget how important you are to all of us." See Robert Hutchins to Alexander Meiklejohn (August 20, 1964), box 17, folder 11, AMP, SHSW.

88. Scott Buchanan, address at Memorial Meeting, Berkeley, California (January 31, 1965), Experimental College Department Folder, 7/37/6-1, UWA.

89. Buchanan, address at Memorial Meeting.

90. Joseph Popper to Alexander Meiklejohn (August 30, 1964), box 24, folder 6, AMP, SHSW.

91. Alexander Meiklejohn to Joseph Popper (September 2, 1964), box 24, folder 6, AMP, SHSW.

92. Milton Mayer, "Alec Meiklejohn's Maytime," *Progressive* (August 1965): 17–19. "In an abstract discussion," Mayer added, "he once tried to persuade Roger Baldwin that gaiety of spirit was the most desirable of all personal attributes."

93. See Mary Jane Keeney to Alexander Meiklejohn (October 16, 1962), box 25, folder 15, AMP, SHSW.

94. Alexander Meiklejohn to W. H. Ferry (August 28, 1962), box 12, folder 27, AMP, SHSW.

95. Alexander Meiklejohn to David Winslow (November 12, 1964), miscellaneous newspaper clippings, Non-Alumnus Biographical File—Alexander Meiklejohn, ACL.

96. See Corliss Lamont, "Philosopher of Freedom," *Humanist* (March/April 1965): 54–55. "He died while he was talking with friends. One of them, President Barnabee [*sic*] Keeney of Brown University, said: 'The way he went was the way he lived, doing gaily difficult and dangerous things.' Also with him at the end was his best friend of all, Helen Everett Meiklejohn."

AFTERWORD: EDUCATION AND THE DEMOCRATIC
IDEAL—THE MEANING OF ALEXANDER MEIKLEJOHN

1. See "World-Famed Dr. Meiklejohn Succumbs Here," *Berkeley Daily Gazette* (December 17, 1964).

2. See *Washington Post* (December 18, 1964). See also "Milestones," *Time* (December 25, 1964): 64. "Died . . . of pneumonia in Berkeley, California."

3. "Alexander Meiklejohn, 1872–1964," unpaginated typescript, Memorial Meeting, Berkeley, California (January 31, 1965), Experimental College Departmental Folder, 7/37/6-1, UWA.

4. "The Militancy of Alexander Meiklejohn," *Brown Alumni Monthly* (March 1965): 12–15, BUA.

5. Peter Weiss, remarks in "Alexander Meiklejohn, 1872–1964."

6. "Ex-Meiklejohn Students above Average in Income," *Capital Times* (May 14, 1957). See also "Experimental College Takes 50th-Anniversary Spotlight," *Wisconsin State Journal* (June 10, 1982). See also Robert J. Havighurst, Margaret M. Holmes, and John W. Powell, Jr., "The Meiklejohn Experimental College: Learning and Living: A Fifty-Year Record, Based on a Questionnaire Study of Alumni" (October 14–16, 1977), Experimental College Departmental Folder, 7/37, UWA.

7. Saul Brahms to Alexander Meiklejohn (February 25, 1949), box 5, folder 26, AMP, SHSW.

8. Harry Kalven, remarks in "Alexander Meiklejohn, 1872–1964." As Arthur Upham Pope wrote, "[E]ven the sharpest controversy he kept impersonal, perhaps hating the intellectual sin, but not the sinner." Once, after a sharp exchange between Meiklejohn and Felix Frankfurter, Pope asked Meiklejohn if either combatant had any scars. "Of course not," Meiklejohn gently replied. "We are still, and always will be, the best of friends.'" See Arthur Upham Pope to Theodore R. Crane (March 9, 1966), box 24, folder 7, AMP, SHSW.

9. Alexander Meiklejohn quoted in Arthur Upham Pope, "Alexander Meiklejohn," *American Scholar* (autumn 1965): 641–645.

10. Alexander Meiklejohn, "The Future of Our Liberal Colleges after the War," *New York Sun* (October 19, 1919), box 33, folder 6, AMP, SHSW.

11. Alexander Meiklejohn, *Education Between Two Worlds* (New York, 1942), 114.

12. Plato, *The Republic*, trans. Benjamin Jowett (New York, 1944), 369.

13. Plato, *The Republic*, trans. Allan Bloom (New York, 1968), 199.

14. Alexander Meiklejohn, "The First Amendment Is an Absolute," *Supreme Court Review* (1961): 245–266.

15. Meiklejohn, *Education Between Two Worlds*, 282–283.

16. Alexander Meiklejohn, "Teachers and Controversial Questions," *Harper's Monthly* (June 1938): 22.

Bibliography and Suggestions for Further Reading

A number of unpublished theses have been written on Meiklejohn or Meiklejohn-related topics. They include Robert Baldwin, "A Quest for Unity: An Analysis of the Educational Theories of Alexander Meiklejohn" (unpublished Ph.D. dissertation, University of Pittsburgh, 1967); Charles Cooper, "Alexander Meiklejohn: Absolutes of Intelligence in Political and Constitutional Theory" (unpublished Ph.D. dissertation, Bryn Mawr College, 1967); Scott Abbott, "Philosopher and Dean: Alexander Meiklejohn at Brown, 1901–1912" (unpublished Ph.D. dissertation, University of Denver, 1967); E. Hugh Overfield, "The First Amendment, Mr. Meiklejohn, and Justice White" (unpublished M.A. thesis, St. Mary's University, San Antonio, Texas, 1968); Hermione Shantz, "The Social and Educational Theory of Alexander Meiklejohn" (unpublished Ph.D. dissertation, Michigan State University, 1969); Eugene Perry, "Alexander Meiklejohn and the Organic Theory of Democracy" (unpublished M.A. thesis, Syracuse University, 1969); Carol Ann Smetts, "Mr. Justice Black and Dr. Alexander Meiklejohn: Two Theories of Absolutism and Freedom of Speech and Press" (unpublished M.A. thesis, Kent State University, 1970); James Milburn Green, "Alexander Meiklejohn: Innovator in Undergraduate Education" (unpublished M.A. thesis, University of Michigan, 1970); Ernest Racz, "Meiklejohn" (unpublished Ed.D. dissertation, Teachers College, Columbia University, 1979); Mack Palmer, "The Qualified Absolute: Alexander Meiklejohn and Freedom of Speech" (unpublished Ph.D. dissertation, University of Wisconsin, 1979); Gari Cheever, "An Alternative Look at the First Amendment: Professor Meiklejohn and the U.S. Supreme Court" (unpublished B.A. honors thesis, Arizona State University, 1980); Margaret G. Frantz, "Radical Visions: Alexander Meiklejohn on Education, Culture, Democracy, and the First Amendment" (unpublished Ph.D. dissertation, University of California, Santa Cruz, 1984); Robert Brennan, "The Making of the Liberal College: Alexander Meiklejohn at Amherst" (unpublished qualifying paper, Harvard Graduate School of Education, 1986); LaVerne Elizabeth Thomas Thompson, "A

391

Study of Influence in Liberal Education and Liberal Educational Thought: Presidents Alexander Meiklejohn and Charles W. Cole of Amherst College" (unpublished Ph.D. dissertation, University of Toledo, 1991); and Paul Gates, "The Professor, Freedom, and the Court: Alexander Meiklejohn and the First Amendment" (unpublished Ph.D. dissertation, University of Florida, 1996). The only published book on Alexander Meiklejohn is Cynthia Stokes Brown, *Alexander Meiklejohn: Teacher of Freedom* (Berkeley, Calif., 1981).

Many other secondary sources informed this work as well. Following is a list of the most relevant, arranged by chapter and topic.

PREFACE: MEIKLEJOHN, SOCRATES, AND THE PARADOX OF DEMOCRATIC EDUCATION

For more information on higher education and postmodernism with specific reference to the philosophy of John Dewey, see Wilfred Carr, "Education and Democracy: Confronting the Postmodernist Challenge," *Journal of Philosophy of Education* (March 1995): 75–91. For a reply to Carr's article, see Nigel Blake, "The Democracy We Need: Situation, Post-Foundationalism, and Enlightenment," *Journal of the Philosophy of Education* (July 1996): 215–238. See also Wilfred Carr, "Professing Education in a Postmodern Age," *Journal of the Philosophy of Education* (July 1997): 309–328; Nigel Blake, "Ideal Speech Conditions: Modern Discourse and Education," *Journal of Philosophy of Education* (November 1995): 355–368; Michael Peters, "Education and the Postmodern Condition," *Journal of Philosophy of Education* (November 1995): 387–400; Paul Smeyers, "Education and the Educational Project I: The Atmosphere of Postmodernism," *Journal of Philosophy of Education* (March 1995): 109–120; William B. Stanley, *Curriculum for Utopia: Social Reconstructivism and Critical Pedagogy in the Postmodern Era* (Albany, 1992); Jurgen Habermas, *Moral Consciousness and Communicative Action* (Cambridge, Mass., 1990); Jean-Francois Lyotard, *The Postmodern Condition: A Report on Knowledge* (Minneapolis, 1984; originally published in French, 1979); and Joseph Margolis, *Pragmatism without Foundations: Reconciling Realism with Relativism* (Oxford, 1986).

CHAPTER 1. "A VOYAGE ACROSS THE ATLANTIC" AND "KANT'S ETHICS"

For centennial celebrations of the Rochdale Society of Equitable Pioneers, see William Brown, *The Rochdale Pioneers: A Century of Cooperation in Rochdale* (Manchester, England, 1944); Joseph Reeves, *A Century of Rochdale Cooperation, 1844–1944: A Critical but Sympathetic Survey of a Significant Movement of the Workers for Economic Emancipation* (London, 1944); and George Cole, *A Century of Cooperation* (Manchester, England, 1945). Useful studies of working-class immigrant experiences in the late nineteenth century include John Bodnar, *The Transplanted: A History of Immigrants in Urban America* (Bloomington,

Ind., 1985) and *Immigration and Industrialization: Ethnicity in an American Mill Town, 1870–1940* (Pittsburgh, 1977); and Leonard Dinnerstein, *Ethnic Americans: A History of Immigration and Assimilation* (New York, 1982). For information on the history of Pawtucket, see Susan Marie Boucher, *The History of Pawtucket, 1635–1986* (Pawtucket, R.I., 1986), 96–100; and Paul Buhle, Scott Molloy, and Gail Sansbury, *A History of Rhode Island Working People* (Providence, R.I., 1983), 15–21. For more information on labor history in Rhode Island, see Gary Kulik, "Pawtucket Village and the Strike of 1824: The Origins of Class Conflict in Rhode Island"; Paul Buhle, "The Knights of Labor in Rhode Island"; and Scott Molloy, "Rhode Island Communities and the 1902 Carmen's Strike"; all in *Radical History Review* (spring 1978): 5–98.

For more on Kantian idealism, see Henry E. Allison, *Idealism and Freedom: Essays on Kant's Theoretical and Practical Philosophy* (Cambridge, England, 1996) and *Kant's Transcendental Idealism: An Interpretation and Defense* (New Haven, 1987); Moltke S. Gram, *The Transcendental Turn: The Foundation of Kant's Idealism* (Gainesville, Fla., 1984); and Klaus Christian Kohnke, *The Rise of Neo-Kantianism: German Academic Philosophy between Idealism and Positivism* (Cambridge, England, 1991). For treatments of Hume, particularly as he relates to Kant, see Allan Goldman, *Moral Knowledge* (London, 1990); and Lewis White Beck, *Essays on Kant and Hume* (New Haven, 1978). See also Andrew Seth, *Scottish Philosophy: A Comparison of the Scottish and German Answers to Hume* (Edinburgh, 1890). For more information on the link between Scottish commonsense realism and American higher education, see Douglas Sloan, *The Scottish Enlightenment and the American College Ideal* (New York, 1971).

The literature on John Dewey is vast. See especially Robert Westbrook, *John Dewey and American Democracy* (Ithaca, N.Y., 1991); Steven C. Rockefeller, *John Dewey: Religious Faith and Democratic Humanism* (New York, 1991); Neil Coughan, *Young John Dewey: An Essay in American Intellectual History* (Chicago, 1975); George Dykhuizen, *The Life and Mind of John Dewey* (Carbondale, Ill., 1973); Morton G. White, *The Origin of Dewey's Instrumentalism* (New York, 1943); Cornel West, *The American Evasion of Philosophy: A Genealogy of Pragmatism* (Madison, 1989); Alan Ryan, *John Dewey and the High Tide of American Liberalism* (New York, 1995); John Patrick Diggins, *The Promise of Pragmatism: Modernism and the Crisis of Knowledge and Authority* (Chicago, 1994); James T. Kloppenberg, "Pragmatism: An Old Name for Some New Ways of Thinking," *Journal of American History* (June 1996): 100–138; and James Campbell, *Understanding John Dewey: Nature and Cooperative Intelligence* (Chicago, 1995).

CHAPTER 2. "COLLEGE EDUCATION AND THE MORAL IDEAL"

For biographies of such legendary university presidents as Charles William Eliot, William Rainey Harper, and Woodrow Wilson, see Hugh Hawkins, *Between Harvard and America: The Educational Leadership of Charles William Eliot* (New

York, 1972); James P. Wind, *The Bible and the University: The Messianic Vision of William Rainey Harper* (Atlanta, 1987); Richard J. Storr, *Harper's University: The Beginnings: A History of the University of Chicago* (Chicago, 1966); and Hardin Craig, *Woodrow Wilson at Princeton* (Norman, Okla., 1960). For more information on the College Entrance Examination Board, see Harold S. Wechsler, *The Qualified Student: A History of Selective College Admission in America* (New York, 1977); College Entrance Examination Board, *The Work of the College Entrance Examination Board, 1901–1925* (Boston, 1926); and Claude M. Fuess, *The College Board: Its First Fifty Years* (New York, 1950). On education and progressive liberal thought, see Lawrence Cremin, *The Transformation of the School: Progressivism in American Education, 1876–1957* (New York, 1964); David Tyack, *The One Best System: A History of American Urban Education* (Cambridge, Mass., 1974); and Raymond Callahan, *Education and the Cult of Efficiency: A Study of the Social Forces That Have Shaped the Administration of the Public Schools* (Chicago, 1962).

For more information on football in the late nineteenth and early twentieth centuries, see Michael Pearlman, "To Make the University Safe for Morality: Higher Education, Football, and Military Training from the 1890s through the 1920s," *Canadian Review of American Studies* (spring 1981): 37–56. For information on the rise of intercollegiate athletics, see Ronald A. Smith, *Sports and Freedom: The Rise of Big-Time College Athletics* (New York, 1988); and Edwin H. Cady, *The Big Game: College Sports in American Life* (New York, 1978). See also Alan Sack, "The Commercialization and Rationalization of Intercollegiate Football: A Comparative Analysis of the Development of Football at Yale and Harvard in the Latter Nineteenth Century (unpublished Ph.D. dissertation, Pennsylvania State University, 1974); David Riesman and Reuel Denney, "Football in America: A Study in Cultural Diffusion," *American Quarterly* (winter 1951): 309–325; and Guy M. Lewis, "The Beginning of Organized Collegiate Sport," *American Quarterly* (summer 1970): 220–229. For consideration of the amateur question in intercollegiate baseball, see Ronald A. Smith, "The Rise of College Baseball," *Baseball History* (winter 1986): 23–41; and Richard Stone, "The Graham Plan of 1935: An Aborted Crusade to De-emphasize College Athletics," *North Carolina History Review* (summer 1987): 274–293.

CHAPTER 3. "THE COLLEGE AS CRITIC"

For the history of Amherst College, see Claude Fuess, *Amherst: The Story of a New England College* (Boston, 1935); Harold Wade, *Black Men of Amherst* (Amherst, Mass., 1976); and Thomas Le Duc, *Piety and Intellect at Amherst College, 1865–1912* (New York, 1946). For more information on the professionalization of higher education during the Progressive Era, see Burton Bledstein, *The Culture of Professionalism: The Middle Class and the Development of Higher Education in America* (New York, 1976).

Bibliography

For a critical appraisal of pragmatism during World War I, see John Patrick Diggins, "John Dewey in Peace and War," *American Scholar* (February 1981): 213–230. For information on the fate of academic freedom during the war, see Carol S. Gruber, *Mars and Minerva: World War I and the Uses of the Higher Learning in America* (New York, 1975); and Charles F. Thwing, *The American Colleges and Universities in the Great War, 1914–1919: A History* (New York, 1920); Paul L. Murphy, *World War I and the Origin of Civil Liberties* (New York, 1979); Bruce Tap, "Suppression of Dissent: Academic Freedom at the University of Illinois during the World War I Era," *Illinois History Journal* (winter 1992): 2–22; Clifford Wilcox, "World War I and the Attack on Professors of German at the University of Michigan," *History of Education Quarterly* (spring 1993): 59–84; and Charles F. Howlett, "Academic Freedom versus Loyalty at Columbia University during World War I: A Case Study," *War and Society* (January 1984): 43–53.

CHAPTER 4. "TO WHOM ARE WE RESPONSIBLE?"

For the story of Brookwood and the workers education movement of the 1920s and 1930s, see Richard J. Altenbaugh, " 'The Children and the Instruments of a Militant Labor Progressivism': Brookwood Labor College and the American Labor College Movement of the 1920s and 1930s," *History of Education Quarterly* (winter 1983): 395–411; Richard J. Altenbaugh, *Education for Struggle: The American Labor Colleges in the 1920s and 1930s* (Philadelphia, 1990); Jonathan D. Bloom, "Brookwood Labor College and the Progressive Labor Network of the Interwar United States, 1921–1937" (unpublished Ph.D. dissertation, New York University, 1992); Jerry Lembke, "Labor and Education: Portland Labor College, 1921–1929," *Oregon History Quarterly* (summer 1984): 117–134; and Rita Rubinstein Heller, "The Women of Summer: The Bryn Mawr Summer School for Women Workers: 1921–1938" (unpublished Ph.D. dissertation, Rutgers University, 1986). For more information on student strikebreakers, see Stephen H. Norwood, "The Student as Strikebreaker: College Youth and the Crisis of Masculinity in the Early Twentieth Century," *Journal of Social History* (summer 1994): 331–349. For more on R. H. Tawney, see Ross Terrill, *R. H. Tawney and His Times: Socialism as Fellowship* (Cambridge, Mass., 1973); and Anthony Wright, *R. H. Tawney* (New York, 1987).

CHAPTER 5. "A NEW COLLEGE WITH A NEW IDEA"

For the definitive history of the University of Wisconsin, see E. David Cronon and John W. Jenkins, *The University of Wisconsin: A History*, vol. 3 (Madison, 1994); and Merle Curti and Verne Carstensen, *The University of Wisconsin: A History*, vols. 1 and 2 (Madison, 1949). For more information on the La Follette family leadership during the Progressive Era, see Robert S. Maxwell, *La Follette and the*

Rise of the Progressives in Wisconsin (Madison, 1956); Edward Newell Doan, *The La Follettes and the Wisconsin Idea* (New York, 1947); and Stephen D. Zink, "Glenn Frank of the University of Wisconsin: A Reinterpretation," *Wisconsin Magazine of History* 62, no. 2 (1978–1979): 90–127. For a biography of Charles Van Hise, consult Maurice M. Vance, *Charles Van Hise: Scientist Progressive* (Madison, 1960); and Charles McCarthy, *The Wisconsin Idea* (New York, 1912).

For the record of anti-Semitism in college admissions in the 1920s, see David O. Levine: *American Colleges and the Culture of Aspiration, 1915–1940* (Ithaca, N.Y., 1986); and *Jewish Learning in American Universities: The First Century* (Bloomington, Ind., 1994). For more information on women's higher education in the 1920s, see Lynn D. Gordon, *Gender and Higher Education in the Progressive Era* (New Haven, 1990); Barbara Miller Solomon, *In the Company of Educated Women: A History of Women and Higher Education in America* (New Haven, Conn., 1985); Patricia Albjerg Graham, *Women in Higher Education* (Washington, D.C., 1974); and Mabel Newcomer, *A Century of Higher Education for American Women* (New York, 1959).

For critical interpretations of Henry Adams, see Robert Davidoff, *The Genteel Tradition and the Sacred Rage: High Culture Versus Democracy in Adams, James, and Santayana* (Chapel Hill, 1992); T. J. Jackson Lears, "In Defense of Henry Adams," *Wilson Quarterly* (1983): 82–93; David Partenheimer, "The Education of Henry Adams in German Philosophy," *Journal of the History of Ideas* (1988): 339–345; George Monteiro, "Henry Adams's Jamesian Education," *Massachusetts Review* (1988): 371–384; Joseph G. Kronick, "The Limits of Contradiction: Irony and History in Hegel and Henry Adams," *Clio* (summer 1981): 391–410; James M. Mellard, "The Problem of Knowledge and the Education of Henry Adams," *South Central Review* (summer 1986): 55–68; and Earl Klee, "Henry Adams and the Patrician Response to the Liberal Polity," *Humanities in Society* (summer 1980): 243–263.

CHAPTER 6. "A MOST LAMENTABLE COMEDY"

Regarding student culture in the 1920s, see Paula Fass, *The Bold and the Beautiful: American Youth in the 1920s* (New York, 1973). For more general studies of American culture in the 1920s, see William E. Leuchtenberg, *The Perils of Prosperity* (Chicago, 1958); and Roderick Nash, *The Nervous Generation, 1917–1930* (Chicago, 1969). For more information on American culture during the depression, see Richard H. Pells, *Radical Visions and American Dreams: Culture and Social Thought in the Depression Years* (New York, 1973); Warren I. Susman, "The Culture of the Thirties," in his *Culture as History: The Transformation of American Society in the Twentieth Century* (New York, 1984): 150–183; Alan Brinkley, *Voices of Protest: Huey Long, Father Coughlin, and the Great Depression* (New York, 1982); and Robert S. McElwaine, *The Great Depression: America, 1929–1941* (New York, 1984). For an interpretation of Alexander Meiklejohn as an educational conservative, see Michael R. Harris, *Five Counterrevolutionists in Higher Education: Irving Babbitt, Albert Jay Nock, Abraham Flexner, Robert Maynard Hutchins, and Alexander Meiklejohn* (Ann Arbor, Mich., 1980).

CHAPTER 7. "ADULT EDUCATION: A FRESH START"

For more information on the American Association of Adult Education, see Alan Lawrence Jones, "Gaining Self-Consciousness While Losing the Movement: The American Association of Adult Education, 1926–1941" (unpublished Ph.D. dissertation, University of Wisconsin, Madison, 1991). See also Morse A. Cartwright, *Ten Years of Adult Education: A Report on a Decade of Progress in the American Movement* (New York, 1935). For more information on adult education during the 1930s, see Dorothy Hewitt, Adult *Education: A Dynamic for Democracy* (New York, 1937); Ruth Kotinsky, *Adult Education in the Social Scene* (New York, 1933); John Ward Studebaker, *The American Way: Democracy at Work in the Des Moines Forums* (New York, 1935); Thomas Fansler, *Discussion Methods for Adult Groups: Case Studies of the Forum, the Discussion Group, and the Panel* (New York, 1936); Frank Ernest Hill, *Listen and Learn: Fifteen Years of Adult Education on the Air* (New York, 1937); and the Brooklyn Conference on Adult Education, *The Making of Adult Minds in a Metropolitan Area* (New York, 1931). For more information on adult education in rural areas, see Benson Y. Landis, *Rural Adult Education* (New York, 1933); and Edwin de Schweinitz, *Rural Adult Education: Rural Trends in Depression Years* (New York, 1937).

For more on the longshoremen's strike of 1934, see Howard Kimeldorf, *Reds of Rackets? The Making of Radical and Conservative Unions on the Waterfront* (Berkeley, Calif., 1988); Bruce Nelson, *Workers on the Waterfront: Seamen, Longshoremen, and Unionism in the 1930s* (Urbana, Ill., 1988); and Richard White, *"It's Your Misfortune and None of Ours": A History of the American West* (Norman, Okla., 1991): 490–491. See also John Kagel, "The Day the City Stopped," *California History* 63, no. 3 (1984): 212–225; Lawrence M. Kahn, "Unions and Internal Labor Markets: The Case of the San Francisco Longshoremen," *Labor History* 21, no. 3 (1980): 369–391; and Robert W. Cherny, "The Making of a Labor Radical: Harry Bridges, 1901–1934," *Pacific Historical Review* 64, no. 3 (1995): 363–388.

For work on the history of the Communist Party in the 1930s, see Fraser M. Ottanelli, *The Communist Party of the United States from the Depression to World War II* (New Brunswick, N.J., 1991); Guenter Lewy, *The Cause That Failed: Communism in American Political Life* (New York, 1990); James G. Ryan, *Earl Browder: The Failure of American Communism* (Tuscaloosa, Ala., 1997); and Michael E. Brown, ed., *New Studies in the Politics and Culture of U.S. Communism* (New York, 1993). See also Judy Kutulas, " 'Becoming More Liberal': The League of American Writers, the Communist Party, and the Literary People's Front," *Journal of American Culture* 13, no. 1 (1990): 71–80; and Van Gosse,

" 'To Organize in Every Neighborhood, in Every Home': The Gender Politics of American Communists between the Wars," *Radical History Review* 50 (1991): 108–141. For the activities of the American Legion in the 1930s, see William Pencak, *For God and Country: The American Legion, 1919–1941* (Boston, 1989). For work on the Dies Committee, see Walter Goodman, *The Committee: The Extraordinary Career of the House Committee on Un-American Activities* (New York, 1968).

CHAPTER 8. "A REPLY TO JOHN DEWEY"

For more information on Japanese internment, read Roger Daniels, *Concentration Camps USA: Japanese Americans and World War II* (New York, 1981); and Thomas James, *Exile Within: The Schooling of Japanese Americans, 1942–1945* (Cambridge, Mass., 1987). See also Paul M. Nagano, "United States Concentration Camps," *American Baptist Quarterly* 13, no. 1 (1994): 48–78; Donald H. and Matthew T. Estes, "Further and Further Away: The Relocation of San Diego's Nikkei Community, 1942," *Journal of San Diego History* 34, nos. 1–2 (1993): 1–31; Eric Bittner, " 'Loyalty . . . Is a Covenant': Japanese-American Internees and the Selective Service Act," *Prologue* 23, no. 3 (1991): 248–252; and Lloyd Chiasson, "Japanese-American Relocation during World War II: A Study of California Editorial Reactions," *Journalism Quarterly* 68, nos. 1–2 (1991): 263–268.

For interpretations of John Amos Comenius and John Locke on education, consult W. S. Monroe, *Comenius and the Beginnings of Educational Reform* (New York, 1912); Robert Fitzgibbon Young, ed., *Comenius in England* (London, 1932); Nathan Tarcov, *Locke's Education for Liberty* (Chicago, 1984); and Peter A. Schouls, *Reason and Freedom: John Locke and Enlightenment* (Ithaca, N.Y., 1992). See also Diane Elizabeth Willard, "Natural Order in the Works of Comenius and Dewey" (unpublished Ph.D. dissertation, Boston College, 1982). For the link between Rousseau and totalitarianism, see Thomas Davidson, *Rousseau and Education According to Nature* (New York, 1971); Alessandro Ferrera, *Modernity and Authenticity: A Study of the Social and Ethical Thought of Jean-Jacques Rousseau* (Albany, N.Y., 1993); and Mira Morgenstern, *Rousseau and the Politics of Ambiguity: Self, Culture, and Society* (University Park, Pa., 1996). See also Edward A. Purcell, *The Crisis of Democratic Theory: Scientific Naturalism and the Problem of Value* (Lexington, Ky., 1973); David Milton Steiner, "The Possibility of Paideia: Democratic Education in Jean Jacques Rousseau and John Dewey" (unpublished Ph.D. dissertation, Harvard University, 1985); and Fred David Kierstead, Jr., "Education for a Transitional Democracy: A Comparison of Jean Jacques Rousseau's Concept of General Will to John Dewey's Concept of Cultivated Intelligence" (unpublished Ph.D. dissertation, University of Oklahoma, 1974). For a study of William James as a religious thinker, see Paul Croce, *Science and Religion in the Era of William James* (Chapel Hill, N.C., 1995); Ellen Kappy Suckeil, *Heaven's Champion: William James's Philosophy of Religion*

(Notre Dame, 1996); Mark Andrew Hadley, "Religious Thinking in an Age of Disillusionment: William James and Ernest Troeltsch on the Possibilities of a Science of Religion" (unpublished Ph.D. dissertation, Brown University, 1987); Bennett Ramsey, *Submitting to Freedom: The Religious Vision of William James* (New York, 1993); and William Joseph Gavin, *William James and the Reinstatement of the Vague* (Philadelphia, 1992). See also Paul F. Boller, Jr., "William James as an Educator: Individualism and Democracy," *Teachers College Record* 80, no. 3 (1979): 587–601.

For an examination of Clarence Ayres, consult Donald R. Pickens, "Clarence Ayres and the Legacy of German Idealism," *American Journal of Economics and Sociology* 46 no. 3 (1987): 287–298; Charles Camic, "Reputation and Predecessor Selection: Parsons and the Institutionalists," *American Sociological Review* 57, no. 4 (1992): 421–445; Floyd B. McFarland, "Clarence Ayres and His Gospel of Technology," *History of Political Economy* 18, no. 4 (1986): 617–637; and David Hamilton, "Ayres's Theory of Economic Progress: An Evaluation of Its Place in Economics Literature," *American Journal of Economics and Sociology* 40, no. 4 (1981): 427–438.

For the history of UNESCO, see Fernando Valderrama Martinez, *A History of UNESCO* (Paris, 1995); William Preston, *Hope and Folly: The United States and UNESCO, 1945–1985* (Minneapolis, 1989); and Michel Conil-Lacoste, *The Story of a Grand Design: UNESCO, 1946–1993* (Paris, 1994). For more information on Hans Kohn, see H. Vincent Moses, "Nationalism and the Kingdom of God According to Hans Kohn and Carlton J. H. Hayes," *Journal of Church and State* 17, no. 2 (1975): 259–274.

CHAPTER 9. "WHAT DOES THE FIRST AMENDMENT MEAN?"

For work on the history of the American Civil Liberties Union, see Cletus E. Daniel, *The A.C.L.U. and the Wagner Act: An Inquiry into the Depression-Era Crisis of American Liberalism* (Ithaca, N.Y., 1990); Samuel Walker, *In Defense of American Liberties: A History of the ACLU* (New York, 1990); and Donald Oscar Johnson, *The Challenge to American Freedoms: World War I and the Rise of the American Civil Liberties Union* (Lexington, Ky., 1963). For a biography of Roger Baldwin, see Peggy Lamson, *Roger Baldwin, Founder of the American Civil Liberties Union: A Portrait* (Boston, 1976). For information on the Smith Act, see Michael R. Belknap, *Cold War Political Justice: The Smith Act, the Communist Party, and American Civil Liberties* (Westport, Conn., 1977). See also Mark A. Sheft, "The End of the Smith Act Era: A Legal and Historical Analysis of *Scalen v. United States*," *American Journal of Legal History* 36, no. 2 (1992): 164–202.

For an interpretation of Zechariah Chafee and the clear and present danger test, see Donald L. Smith, *Zechariah Chafee, Jr.: Defender of Liberty and Law* (Cambridge, Mass., 1986); Jonathan Prude, "Portrait of a Civil Libertarian: The

Faith and Fear of Zechariah Chafee, Jr.," *Journal of American History* 60, no. 3 (1973): 633–650; Jerold S. Auerbach, "The Patrician as Libertarian: Zechariah Chafee, Jr. and Freedom of Speech," *New England Quarterly* 42, no. 4 (1969): 511–531; Fred D. Regan, "Justice Oliver Wendell Holmes, Jr., Zechariah Chafee, Jr., and the Clear and Present Danger Test for Free Speech: The First Year, 1919," *Journal of American History* 58, no. 1 (1971): 211–245; John Wertheimer, "Freedom of Speech: Zechariah Chafee and Free Speech History," *Reviews in American History* 22, no. 2 (1994): 365–377; and Richard Polenberg, *Fighting Faiths: The Abrams Case, the Supreme Court, and Free Speech* (New York, 1987). See also Marc Charisse, "Milton, Mill, Meiklejohn, and the Marketplace: Mixing the Metaphors of the First Amendment" (Worldcat Accession No. 25863100, 1990).

For more information on McCarthyism and the House Un-American Activities Committee, see David Caute, *The Great Fear: The Anti-Communist Purge under Truman and Eisenhower* (New York, 1978); Melvyn P. Leffler, *The Specter of Communism: The United States and the Origins of the Cold War, 1917–1953* (New York, 1994). For the legal philosophy of Oliver Wendell Holmes, Jr., see Jeremy Cohen, *"Congress Shall Make No Law": Oliver Wendell Holmes, the First Amendment, and Judicial Decision Making* (Ames, Iowa, 1989); Frederick Rogers Kellogg, ed., *The Formative Essays of Justice Holmes: The Making of an American Legal Philosophy* (Westport, Conn., 1984); and H. L. Pohlmann, *Justice Oliver Wendell Holmes: Free Speech and the Living Constitution* (New York, 1991).

For more on Sidney Hook during the Cold War, see John P. Rossi, "Farewell to Fellow-Travelling: The Waldorf Peace Conference of March 1949," *Continuity* 10 (1985): 1–31; Edward S. Shapiro, ed., *Letters of Sidney Hook: Democracy, Communism, and the Cold War* (Armonk, N.Y., 1995); Edward S. Shapiro, "The Sidney Hook–Corliss Lamont Letters," *Continuity* 12 (1988): 59–95; Paul Kuntz, ed., *Sidney Hook: Philosopher of Democracy and Humanism* (Buffalo, N.Y., 1983); Paul Gottfried, "Critics of Hegel in America," *Modern Age* 28, no. 1 (1984): 44–54; Stephen J. Whitfield, "The Imagination of Disaster: The Response of American Jewish Intellectuals to Totalitarianism," *Jewish Social Studies* 42 , no. 1 (1988): 1–20; Neil Jumonville, "The New York Intellectuals' Defence of the Intellect," *Queens' Quarterly* 97, no. 2 (1990): 290–304; Neil Jumonville, "The New York Intellectuals and the Mass Cultural Criticism," *Journal of American Culture* 12, no. 1 (1989): 89–95; and Sidney Hook, "Breaking with the Communists: A Memoir," *Commentary* 77, no. 2 (1984): 47–53.

For more information on the California loyalty oath crisis, read David P. Gardner, *The California Oath Controversy* (Berkeley, Calif., 1967); Edward R. Long, "Earl Warren and the Politics of Anti-Communism," *Pacific Historical Review* 51, no. 1 (1982): 51–70; and John W. Caughey, "Farewell to California's 'Loyalty' Oath," *Pacific Historical Review* 38, no. 2 (1969): 123–128. For the history of academic freedom, particularly in the twentieth century, see Richard Hofstadter and Walter E. Metzger, *The Development of Academic Freedom in the United States* (New York, 1955); Sigmund Diamond, *Compromised Campus: The*

Collaboration of the Universities and the Intelligence Community, 1945–1955 (New York, 1992); Jane Sanders, *Cold War on the Campus: Academic Freedom at the University of Washington, 1946–1964* (Seattle, 1979); and Ellen W. Schrecker, *No Ivory Tower: McCarthyism in the Universities* (New York, 1986).

For more on the First Amendment theory of Harry Kalven, see Kenneth L. Karst, "The First Amendment and Harry Kalven: An Appreciative Comment on the Advantages of Thinking Small," *U.C.L.A. Law Review* (November 1965). See also two articles by Harry Kalven, Jr.: "The Metaphysics of the Law of Obscenity," *Supreme Court Review* (1960); and "The Concept of the Public Forum: *Cox v. Louisiana,*" *Supreme Court Review* (1965). For more information on the Bollingen Foundation, read William McGuire, *Bollingen: An Adventure in Collecting the Past* (Princeton, N.J., 1982); and William McGuire, "The Bollingen Foundation, Mary Mellon's 'Shining Beacon,'" *Quarterly Journal of the Library of Congress* (1982): 200–211.

CHAPTER 10. "THE FAITH OF A FREE MAN"

For more details on the Campaign to Abolish the House Un-American Activities Committee, see Jerold Simmons, "The Origins of the Campaign to Abolish HUAC, 1956–1961: The California Connection," *Southern California Quarterly* 64, no. 2 (1982): 141–157. For more on Justice Hugo Black, consult James F. Simon, *The Antagonists: Hugo Black, Felix Franfurter, and Civil Liberties in Modern America* (New York, 1989); Mark Silverstein, *Constitutional Faiths: Felix Frankfurter, Hugo Black, and the Process of Judicial Decision Making* (Ithaca, N.Y., 1984); Gerald T. Dunne, *Hugo Black and the Judicial Revolution* (New York, 1977); Roger K. Newman, *Hugo Black: A Biography* (New York, 1994); James T. Magee, *Mr. Justice Black: Absolutist on the Court* (Charlottesville, Va., 1980); Tinsley E. Yarbrough, *Mr. Justice Black and His Critics* (Durham, N.C., 1988); Howard Ball, *Of Power and Right: Hugo Black, William O. Douglas, and America's Constitutional Revolution* (New York, 1992); Tony Freyer, ed., *Justice Hugo Black and Modern America* (Tuscaloosa, Ala., 1990); David M. O'Brien, "Justice Hugo L. Black, Liberal Legalism, and Constitutional Politics," *Reviews in American History* 19, no. 4 (1991): 561–567; and Loren P. Beth, "Mr. Justice Black and the First Amendment: Comments on the Dilemma of Constitutional Interpretation," *Journal of Politics* 41, no. 4 (1979): 1105–1124.

For treatment of the free speech movement, see David Lance Goines, *The Free Speech Movement: Coming of Age in the 1960s* (Berkeley, Calif., 1993); W. J. Rorabaugh, *Berkeley at War* (New York, 1989); Nancy Zarolis and Gerald Sullivan, *Who Spoke Up? American Protest against the War in Vietnam, 1963–1975* (Garden City, N.Y., 1984); and William L. O'Neill, *Coming Apart: An Informal History of America in the 1960s* (Chicago, 1971).

For more information on the work of Martin Heidegger, see Richard Wolin, *The Political Thought of Martin Heidegger* (New York, 1990); Hans Sluga, *Hei-*

degger's Crisis: Philosophy and Politics in Nazi Germany (Cambridge, Mass., 1993); Mark Okrent, *Heidegger's Pragmatism: Understanding, Being, and the Critique of Metaphysics* (Ithaca, N.Y., 1988); Mark Blitz, *Heidegger's* Being and Time *and the Possibility of Political Philosophy* (Ithaca, N.Y., 1981); Hubert L. Dreyfus, *Being-in-the-World: A Commentary on Heidegger's* Being and Time (Cambridge, Mass., 1991); Stanley Rosen, *The Question of Being: A Reversal of Heidegger* (New Haven, 1993). And, finally, for more information on midcentury existentialism, see Ann Fulton, "Apostles of Sartre: Advocates of Early Sartreanism in American Philosophy," *Journal of the History of Ideas* 55, no. 1 (1994): 113–127; and Walter Kaufmann, "The Reception of Existentialism in the United States," *Midway* 9, no. 1 (1968): 97–126.

Index